O\S Ordnance Survey
WOODLAND
WALKS

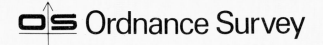

WOODLAND WALKS

Gerald Wilkinson

Guild Publishing
London

WOODLAND WALKS B.C A. EDITION

This edition published 1985 by
Book Club Associates
by arrangement with
Webb & Bower (Publishers) Limited,
and Ordnance Survey

First published 1985

Designed by Peter Wrigley

Production by Nick Facer

Typeset in Great Britain by Keyspools Limited, Golborne, Lancashire
Printed and bound in Great Britain by Hazell Watson and Viney Limited,
a member of the BPCC Group.

TITLE PAGES: The Trent Valley side of Cannock Chase.
Redesigned by twentieth-century expediency and neatly
framed by tractor-managed fields, the forest still dominates a
noble landscape. Only the oaks in the fields are anything like
natural.

Contents

Introduction

Woodland, now only eight per cent of the land, is the natural habitat of Britain below 1500 feet. Nothing remains of the original forest which followed the last Ice Ages except possibly some parts of the Scottish pine forest. But many small woods in the south and east can be dated back to mediaeval times and consist of native trees. Modified as they are by the centuries of management and by changes in climate and surroundings, these woods are a direct link with the past and are part of our social and economic history.

Woodland remains the largest part of our inland countryside which is close to being a natural habitat – for wild creatures and perhaps for ourselves.

We define a wood, simplistically, as any collection of trees. The Saxon *wudu* could be anything of wood, or a tract of country. Woods are very varied, and are described usually by the most common – 'dominant' – tree in the wood. This leads to many different mixtures being described, for instance, as oakwoods.

Trees in a wood form a community and react together to outside influences. Because they are large, living and semi-permanent they are able to alter their own environment. In particular the dominant tree will tend to shade out other vegetation and thus perpetuate its dominance, forming high forest, until some stronger force intervenes. It is the interplay of human and natural forces which makes woods interesting – more interesting if one can recognize the different species and understand their behaviour.

Many trees will put out several new shoots if the stem is cut to the ground. A wood of trees treated in this way is a coppice. The shoots are harvested at regular intervals – annually, or every four or seven or twenty years, for

Hembury Woods

example. The shoots which remain rooted in the ground live longer than the virgin tree, may become very large, and may sometimes have been there for over a thousand years. A coppice produces more wood of volume than the same acreage under the same trees for timber. But coppice poles are no longer much needed, and

Tuetoes Hills, Laughton Forest

coppices are cleared to plant fast-growing American or European conifers producing softwood, which is in demand. The regular cutting and, usually, temporary enclosure of the coppices in rotation allow many wild flowers, birds and insects to survive continuously, leaving no room for weeds and aliens to invade. Close-grown conifers permanently shade out the natural vegetation and reduce the habitat.

A more laborious form of coppicing high above the ground, so that animals cannot reach the shoots, produces pollards. A collection of pollards is likely to be an old wood-pasture, exemplified by large parts of Epping Forest, now neglected. Both coppicing and pollarding can occur naturally because of storms, and both can prolong the life of the tree. Ancient oaks have usually been lopped by storms many times, and even hollowed out by fire.

Besides reproducing by seed, many trees regenerate in the same place by producing sucker shoots from the roots or by the natural

Ashridge, January: red leaves on the beechwood floor; green algae on the trunks

layering of branches which take root in the surrounding soil.

A Forest, with a capital F, is a region, or a large wood or plantation so named. The ancient Forests were large, usually royal, and often included whole towns as well as the woodlands which sometimes now bear their names. All the people living within the Forest were subject to Forest law.

A Forest may be a collection of woods, as the Forestry Commission has revived the term. Micheldever Forest in Hampshire consists of Micheldever Wood with the nearby Black Wood and the distant Chawton Park, and any other bits that the Commission may acquire in the area.

A thicket is a group of young trees growing too close together for their, or our, comfort: a place where a ram might be caught by the horns. In forestry terms a thicket is all of one species and will be thinned artificially. In nature, thinning will be effected by the stronger individual shading out the weaker. Woods still called thickets or thicks give no impression of ever having been of one species only. Birches colonizing newly exposed ground will form a thicket. Otherwise underwood and bushes without standard trees are called scrub unless controlled by coppicing.

Scrub sounds derogatory, and we often hear of its being cleared. In natural history terms it is a perfectly recognizable habitat, and is a transitional stage between grassland and woodland: the shrubs will shelter the seedlings of forest trees and later will be shaded out by them. A shrub is defined as a woody plant which does not grow large enough to be called a tree. Hazel, sallow, alder, buckthorn and hawthorn can be defined as either, but since surveys of trees and woods are done by foresters they are usually not counted as trees. Hawthorns and hazels, if counted, would surely far outnumber the oak, our dominant native tree. Hazel woods once covered much of England and most of Ireland. Hawthorn woods do survive, and such a wood is properly called a spinney ('spiney'). A hanger is a beechwood, usually, on the side of a hill, from Hampshire to Devonshire.

A plantation is an artificial wood. No plantation appears to have been made before the time of Henry VIII, when some attempts were made to enclose and plant parts of the Royal Forests of Alice Holt, Bere, and the Dean and New Forests. Most plantations have been made since the late eighteenth century. Often they are on the sites of old woods, particularly so in south-east England, where land use is most intensive.

Some Victorian plantations were for recreation and shooting, with forestry a secondary consideration. Modern ones are usually only for timber production. Here the trees are all of the same age or in patches (stands) of the same age.

Native trees are those which were here or got here after the last Ice Age, which denuded most of the land, and before men colonized the islands, then a peninsula attached to Europe.

Trees can be naturalized, that is, imported but behaving like natives in that they regenerate naturally. They can be exotic – a vague term usually applied to a specimen grown for its interest and/or beauty. An exotic may or may not be capable of naturalization – it will usually be outside its natural range (the climatic limits within which it can reproduce). Alien is the term applied to trees which are not necessarily outside their natural range but have been imported for one reason or another.

Any wood will consist of a community not only of trees but at least a shrub layer and two levels of ground flora. Underwood may consist of shrubs, or of trees naturally or artificially smaller than the standard trees. Some woods are entirely of underwood: this was the rule rather than the exception in mediaeval woods, for large timber was only rarely needed. A wood may consist of standard trees encouraged to grow up from old coppice shoots. Mature woodland and close-grown plantations shade out all other plants so that the field layer is absent altogether, except for saprophytes (plants without chlorophyll). But natural gaps in the canopy are frequent as old trees die, and the spaces are filled with new life.

Natural forests, especially on rocky or marshy ground, make a formidable countryside, where walking may be almost impossible in thick undergrowth and fallen

Scots pines, Loch Maree

trunks. Yet whenever I have come across natural woods I have always been amazed at the order and beauty of the scene, whatever the chaos about one's knees. I cannot explain this.

Woods traditionally managed achieve various sorts of compromise with naturalness. They are not dark or melancholy, but airy and full of variety. Only neglected, secondary woodland is unkempt, malevolent, forgotten and overgrown. Things get dumped, and the drainage goes wrong. Such forbidding woods do exist, but they are not typical of true wildness.

Somewhere between neglect (which may be the result of over-protectiveness and the falling into disuse of old rights of exploitation) and over-use, which results in erosion and scares away wildlife, is a broad level of human access and enjoyment compatible with the conservation of woodland habitat. Conservation must always attempt to preserve the local character which is often the result of centuries of careful husbandry. Tree protection and replanting are suspect and certainly not sufficient or even desirable on their own. Of course, protecting woods against actual destruction is a first essential.

This book is not, as some may believe, an attempt to exploit a territory best left alone, or to blow wide open the security of the woods. People must go back to the woods, not just to the famous beauty-spots, to know and understand them. Where there are no woods, tracts of land should now be set apart, fenced and left alone for nature to take its course. We cannot put the clock back to 5000 BC, but we can have decent secondary woodland and maintain a fair proportion of our ancient woods. We need more 'access woodland' near where we all live, or most of us. The London Wildlife Trust and the Councils of Greater London, Essex and the West Midlands have taken the initiative, as have many other local authorities. The Forestry Commission has destroyed and converted many old woods, but has given us access to an enormous amount of wooded countryside – maybe more dialogue is needed, not just angry letters to the press about ugly conifers.

Many textbooks describe the trees and to some extent their behaviour in woodland. The commonest deciduous trees are summarized on pages 10–11. Native evergreens are few and easily recognized: the Scots pine by its orange-coloured upper bark and its usually rounded crown, the yew by its heavy form and colour, the juniper by its distinctive shapes, bushy or columnar, and its blue berries. Holly and ivy are known to all, and so are gorse and broom.

Naturalized evergreens are the common *Rhododendron ponticum* and two cherries with dark largish leaves: cherry laurel and Portugal

Common deciduous trees in Britain

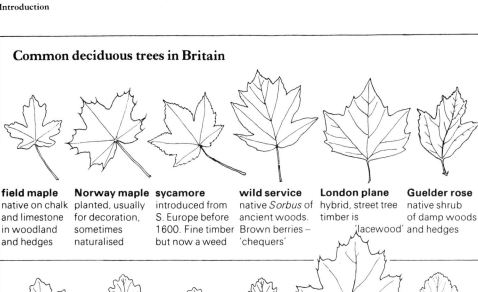

field maple
native on chalk
and limestone
in woodland
and hedges

Norway maple
planted, usually
for decoration,
sometimes
naturalised

sycamore
introduced from
S. Europe before
1600. Fine timber
but now a weed

wild service
native *Sorbus* of
ancient woods.
Brown berries –
'chequers'

London plane
hybrid, street tree
timber is
'lacewood'

Guelder rose
native shrub
of damp woods
and hedges

white poplar
young leaves
5-lobed, all are
white beneath.
'Abele' tree

sessile oak
acorns without
stalks. Native
and rarely
planted

pedunculate oak
acorns on stalks
Native English
oak, often
planted for timber

Turkey oak
long planted,
naturalised in S.
Red oak (right)
amenity tree from
N. America

Swedish whitebeam
imported hybrid
Sorbus, true to
seed, a neat tree
for parks, roads

hawthorn
hedge, left, and
woodland or
Midland, right:
may blossom

whitebeam
commonest native
whitebeam, *Sorbus*
aria. All love
limey soils

Wych elm
native to
all Britain

**Smooth-leafed
elm** one of several
natives such as
Cornish elm,
Plot's elm

English elm
or field elm, tall,
now almost extinct
but sucker shoots
still grow

hazel
common small
tree of hedges
and oakwoods,
often coppiced

hornbeam
native to S.E.
woods, once
valuable as
firewood

beech
tallest native of
best-loved woods,
also used in
shelterbelts

cherries
bird cherry and gean
or wild cherry,
plums, crab apple
and sloe

alder buckthorn
now uncommon
native of damp
woods in the
south

buckthorn
native shrub.
Flowers (green)
& berries stalked
from axils

dogwood
native reddish
shrub. Flowers
(white) & berries
in round clusters

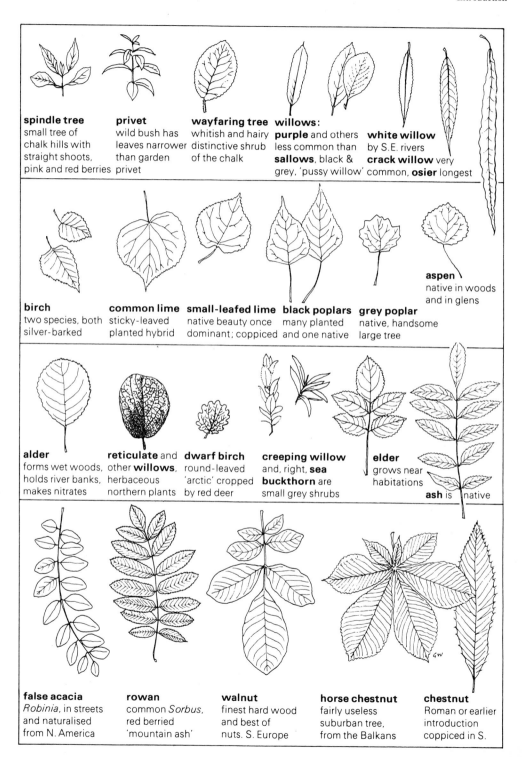

spindle tree
small tree of
chalk hills with
straight shoots,
pink and red berries

privet
wild bush has
leaves narrower
than garden
privet

wayfaring tree
whitish and hairy
distinctive shrub
of the chalk

willows:
purple and others
less common than
sallows, black &
grey, 'pussy willow'

white willow
by S.E. rivers
crack willow very
common, **osier** longest

birch
two species, both
silver-barked

common lime
sticky-leaved
planted hybrid

small-leafed lime
native beauty once
dominant; coppiced

black poplars
many planted
and one native

grey poplar
native, handsome
large tree

aspen
native in woods
and in glens

alder
forms wet woods,
holds river banks,
makes nitrates

reticulate and
other **willows**,
herbaceous
northern plants

dwarf birch
round-leaved
'arctic' cropped
by red deer

creeping willow
and, right, **sea
buckthorn** are
small grey shrubs

elder
grows near
habitations

ash is native

false acacia
Robinia, in streets
and naturalised
from N. America

rowan
common *Sorbus*,
red berried
'mountain ash'

walnut
finest hard wood
and best of
nuts. S. Europe

horse chestnut
fairly useless
suburban tree,
from the Balkans

chestnut
Roman or earlier
introduction
coppiced in S.

laurel, the latter with definitely serrated leaves and crimson leaf stalks.

Three alien conifers have become part of the landscape, planted for decoration. Cedar of Lebanon has been familiar for three centuries, and the Atlantic cedar, usually in its silver or blue form, was introduced in the last century shortly before the Big Tree, called Wellingtonia – *Sequoiadendron* – now the tallest tree in many an English view. The more purely functional conifers are summarized briefly below. Conifers, like Chinese to westerners, tend to look more or less the same to those famillar with the more broadly characterized native trees, but comparatively few are actually used in forestry.

Sitka spruces occupy 1.3 million acres out of 3 million under conifers. They occupy three times as much ground as the native dominant, the oak – but not much of it is ground upon which oaks or any other tree would grow well. Of thirty-odd spruces all over the northern hemisphere, perhaps twenty are planted for their beauty and only three are used for softwood production in this country.

The Sitka spruce has bluish needles, very sharp to the touch, and its cones are rather small and squashy. The Norway spruce, our Christmas tree, has long cylindrical cones and softer, greener foliage. The bark is reddish and relatively finely scaled as compared with the purplish-grey of the Sitka, which soon forms rounded, loose-looking plates. A third spruce, the Serbian, will grow on chalky soil. It has pointed cones and makes a more rigidly conical shape than the other two: all have the familiar, curving zig-zag outline that any competent child-artist can draw. All may vary in form according to their region of origin. All spruces have cones becoming pendulous. A dozen other spruces are common in ornamental plantations. Easily recognized is the Brewer's or weeping spruce from Central North America. The oriental spruce, with decidedly the shortest needles, is also found in old plantations.

The native Scots pine accounts for half a million acres of our forests, where it looks a good deal straighter than it does in the wild – partly because the varieties have been selected.

The orange bark on the upper trunk and branches usually shows. The Corsican pine seems to be everywhere, with longish leaves and fairly distinctive grey, flaking, sometimes pinkish, bark divided by often whitish fissures. It is in fact less planted than the lodgepole pine, which covers 300,000 acres, mostly in north-east England. The bark of this tree is warm-toned and finely scaled. It is a variety of *Pinus contorta*, which is named for its twisted leaves. The cones are prickly and face backwards down the shoot.

There are ninety-six species of pine in the northern hemisphere and only about twenty are planted here at all frequently. Monterey pines are common on southern coasts, with rugged bark and often wandering branches bearing persistent, lopsided cones. The beautiful Bhutan pine has long, graceful leaves in bundles of five and cones up to twelve inches long: it may be found in many parks and gardens.

The three larches, European, Japanese and their hybrid, Dunkeld larch, are much used, with a preference for the last. There is little point in distinguishing between them. Larches are deciduous and so stand out in plantations by their different colours.

The Douglas fir, with soft foliage, sharp buds and cones with prominent three-pointed bracts, is a fairly important forestry tree. Old trees survive in Scottish policies particularly, the ragged, flat tops sticking out above the other trees. The bark is extremely rugged in older trees.

Western hemlock, *Tsuga heterophylla*, is a dark tree with varied leaves and small, oval cones. The leading shoot is always bent over.

The western red cedar, *Thuja plicata*, has scented scale leaves and soft reddish bark in wavy strips. The rather similar Lawson's cypress is much varied horticulturally, but usually narrow and well-clothed to the base, where an older tree's heavy branches sweep upwards. Leading shoots droop. The cones of *Thuja* are very individual in style, like short unrolling cigars. Those of Lawson's cypress are spherical, splitting later into segments. The flowers also are distinctive: small and terminal, the males black, later red, and the females an unearthly dark blue. Thuja and cypress are only rarely grown for timber, but are frequent as shelter trees.

Nootka and Leyland cypresses, both of good conical – or inverted exclamation-mark – form, are commonly planted for decoration. The Monterey cypress, with strong bole and ascending branches is a frequent seaside tree in south-west England. It is *Cupressus macrocarpa*, the specific name referring to the knobby, heavy cone.

Silver firs, grand fir, *Abies grandis*, and noble fir, *A. procera*, have a small place in forestry, perhaps increasing in the case of *grandis*. Low's fir, a variety of *A. concolor*, also promises rapid growth. Low's fir has longish, lax leaves, well spaced on each side of the shoot. Grand fir has leaves of two different lengths, rather straight. Noble fir leaves curve away from the shoot as if combed in a parting. All the leaves are smooth, long ovals, more or less white below. All fir cones are large and held erect. All firs are beautiful. There are about fifty species scattered about the northern hemisphere, sometimes in quite small populations which have retreated to the cooler slopes of mountains. The Spanish fir is one such. It will tolerate chalk. The Korean fir is sometimes sold as a small garden tree with abundant cones. Delavay's fir, or a variety, is fairly often planted in large gardens. Otherwise, few firs of any sort are planted for fun, perhaps because they nearly all grow very tall. The commonest in old plantations is *A. grandis*.

One more conifer is planted occasionally for timber, but is much more often seen as an old specimen tree: the redwood, *Sequoia sempervirens*, tallest of all trees and easily recognized by its fibrous red bark.

Broad leaves used in forestry are mostly well known. The hybrid black poplars are familiar, geometrical in appearance, usually in smallish triangular plots of damp ground. There are still 400,000 acres of English oak, nearly 200,000 acres of beech and similar amounts of birch and sycamore. Ash covers 120,000 acres, but we still import tool handles. The fast-growing southern beeches, *Nothofagus obliqua* and *procera* are increasingly

Picnic place, Fedw Woods

planted, especially by private owners reluctant to coniferize.

Norway maple and red oak are much used as decorative trees by the Forestry Commission. Anything may turn up as an 'amenity tree'.

This short summary of forest trees is offered as a sort of reading list. There have been many textbooks published in the last ten years with excellent illustrations, but they rarely stress behaviour, use or distribution, and may tell you a good deal more than you need to know at first. H. L. Edlin's *Trees, Woods and Men* (Collins New Naturalist) remains a classic. Edlin was for many years the chief information officer of the Forestry Commission and his work has provided much of my background information, for he had a hand in many of the forest guides published by the HMSO. Oliver Rackham's *Trees and Woodland in the British Landscape*, 1976, and his other works, explain the history of our woodland in terms of modern scholarship and sensitive natural history. Alan Mitchell is the perfect tree-spotter, ripely observant and encyclopaedic – see his *Field Guide to the Trees of Britain and Northern Europe*, 1974 etc., the first best-seller on trees since Loudon's eight volumes of 1838 and John Evelyn's *Sylva* of 1664.

Key

The book is divided into sections which follow on numerically from west to east and south to north of the region. At the beginning of each section the relevant Ordnance Survey Landranger sheet numbers are listed. Each entry is headed with factual information in the form below:

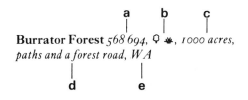

Burrator Forest *568 694,* ♀ ♨, *1000 acres, paths and a forest road, WA*

a Ordnance Survey Landranger map reference – usually of the nearest car park
b Type of woodland: ♀ deciduous
                 ♠ coniferous
                 ♨ marsh
c Size of wooded area
d Type of walk
e Owner of site

The following abbreviations are used:
AONB   Area of outstanding natural beauty
CNT   County Naturalists' Trust
CP   Country Park
FC   Forestry Commission
FNR   Forest Nature Reserve
fp   footpath
LNR   Local Nature Reserve
MAFF Ministry of Agriculture Fisheries and
           Food
NC   Nature Conservancy
NCR   Nature Conservancy Reserve
NNR   National Nature Reserve
NT   National Trust
NTS   National Trust for Scotland
pf   private forestry
pos   public open space
SSSI   Site of Special Scientific Interest
SWT   Scottish Wildlife Trust
WA   Water Authority

Map of the Sections

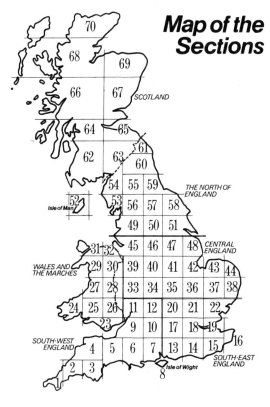

1:625,000 maps

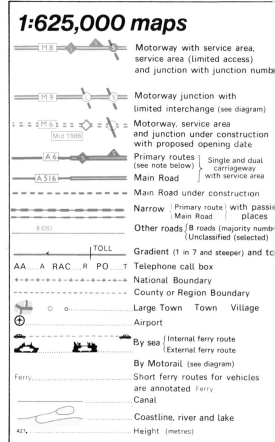

Motorway with service area, service area (limited access) and junction with junction numb

Motorway junction with limited interchange (see diagram)

Motorway, service area and junction under construction with proposed opening date
Mid 1986

Primary routes (see note below) } Single and dual carriageway with service area
Main Road }

Main Road under construction

Narrow { Primary route } with passi { Main Road } places

Other roads { B roads (majority numb { Unclassified (selected)
B 6357

Gradient (1 in 7 and steeper) and to
TOLL

AA.....A RAC....R PO....T Telephone call box

National Boundary

County or Region Boundary

Large Town   Town   Village

Airport

By sea { Internal ferry route { External ferry route

By Motorail (see diagram)

Short ferry routes for vehicles are annotated Ferry
Ferry.........

Canal

Coastline, river and lake

Height (metres)
427.

1:316,800 maps

RELIEF

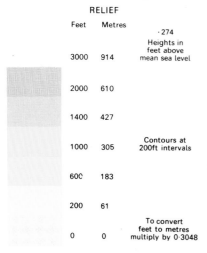

Feet	Metres	
		· 274
		Heights in feet above mean sea level
3000	914	
2000	610	
1400	427	
1000	305	Contours at 200ft intervals
600	183	
200	61	
0	0	To convert feet to metres multiply by 0·3048

TOURIST INFORMATION

 Abbey, Cathedral, Priory

 Ancient monument

Aquarium

Camp site

Caravan site

Castle

Cave

Country park

Craft centre

Garden

Golf course or links

Historic house

 Information centre

Motor racing

Museum

Nature or forest trail

Nature reserve

Other tourist feature

Picnic site

Preserved railway

Racecourse

Skiing

Viewpoint

Wildlife park

Youth hostel

Zoo

ROADS Not necessarily rights of way

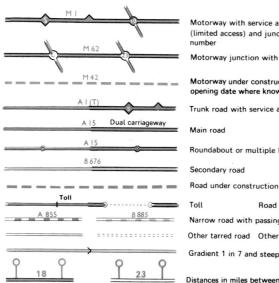

Motorway with service area, service area (limited access) and junction with junction number

Motorway junction with limited interchange

Motorway under construction with proposed opening date where known

Trunk road with service area

A 15 Dual carriageway — Main road

A 15 — Roundabout or multiple level junction

B 676 — Secondary road

Road under construction

Toll   Road tunnel

Narrow road with passing places

A 855   B 885   Other tarred road   Other minor road

Gradient 1 in 7 and steeper

18   23   Distances in miles between markers

The representation on this map of a road is no evidence of the existence of a right of way

GENERAL FEATURES

  Buildings

Wood

Lighthouse (in use)   Lighthouse (disused)

Windmill   Radio or TV mast

Youth hostel

Civil aerodrome { with Customs facilities / without Customs facilities

Heliport

Public telephone

Motoring organisation telephone

ANTIQUITIES

※ Native fortress   Castle · Other antiquities

Site of battle (with date)   Roman road (course of)

CANOVIUM ·   Roman antiquity

Ancient Monuments and Historic Buildings in the care of the Secretaries of State for the Environment, for Scotland and for Wales and that are open to the public.

WATER FEATURES

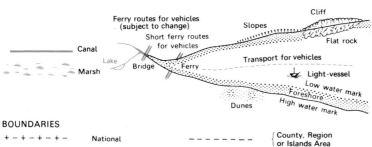

Canal

Lake

Marsh

Ferry routes for vehicles (subject to change)

Short ferry routes for vehicles

Bridge   Ferry

Cliff

Slopes

Flat rock

Transport for vehicles

Light-vessel

Low water mark

Foreshore

Dunes

High water mark

RAILWAYS

Standard gauge track

Narrow gauge track

Tunnel

Road crossing under or over

Level crossing

Station

BOUNDARIES

+ − + − + − + −   National

− − − − − − −   { County, Region or Islands Area

1:50,000 maps

ROADS AND PATHS Not necessarily rights of way

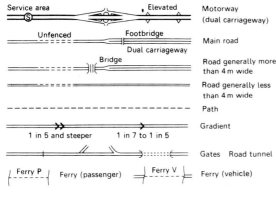

Service area

Elevated

Motorway (dual carriageway)

Unfenced

Footbridge

Main road

Dual carriageway

Bridge

Road generally more than 4 m wide

Road generally less than 4 m wide

Path

Gradient

1 in 5 and steeper   1 in 7 to 1 in 5

Gates   Road tunnel

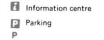

Ferry P   Ferry (passenger)   Ferry V   Ferry (vehicle)

PUBLIC RIGHTS OF WAY (Not applicable to Scotland)

— — — — — — — —

Public rights of way indicated by these symbols have been
derived from Definitive Maps as amended by later enactments
or instruments held by Ordnance Survey on and are shown subject
to the limitations imposed by the scale of mapping

**The representation on this map of any other road, track or
path is no evidence of the existence of a right of way**

TOURIST INFORMATION

🄸 Information centre   📞 Telephone, public/motoring organisation

🅿 Parking   Golf course or links

P   Public convenience (in rural areas)
    PC

✕ Picnic site   Viewpoint

GENERAL FEATURES

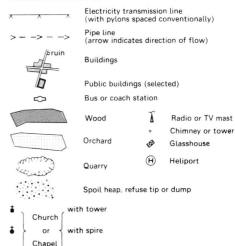

Electricity transmission line
(with pylons spaced conventionally)

Pipe line
(arrow indicates direction of flow)

Buildings

Public buildings (selected)

Bus or coach station

Wood   Radio or TV mast

Chimney or tower

Orchard   Glasshouse

Quarry   Ⓗ Heliport

Spoil heap, refuse tip or dump

with tower

Church

or   with spire

Chapel

without tower or spire

Graticule intersection at 5' intervals

△ Triangulation pillar

Windmill with or without sails   Windpump

HEIGHTS

•144   Heights are to the nearest
    metre above mean sea level

Heights shown close to a triangulation pillar refer to tne station
height at ground level and not necessarily to the summit.

WATER FEATURES

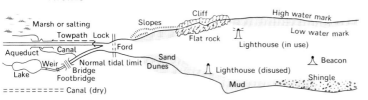

Marsh or salting   Slopes   Cliff   High water mark

Towpath Lock   Low water mark

Aqueduct   Canal   Ford   Flat rock   Lighthouse (in use)

Weir   Normal tidal limit   Sand   Beacon

Lake   Bridge   Dunes   Lighthouse (disused)

Footbridge   Mud   Shingle

═══════ Canal (dry)

ABBREVIATIONS

P   Post office
PH   Public house
MS   Milestone
MP   Milepost
CH   Clubhouse
PC   Public convenience (in rural areas)
TH   Town Hall, Guildhall or equivalent
CG   Coastguard

BOUNDARIES

— + — + — National   — · — · — · County, Region
    or Islands Area

–o– –o– –o– London Borough   + + + + District

ANTIQUITIES

VILLA Roman   ⚔ Battlefield (with date)   ✝ Position of antiquity which
Castle Non-Roman   ☆ Tumulus   cannot be drawn to scale

The revision date of archaeological information varies over the sheet

RAILWAYS

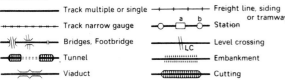

Track multiple or single   Freight line, siding
    or tramway
Track narrow gauge   Station

Bridges, Footbridge   Level crossing

Tunnel   Embankment

Viaduct   Cutting

HOW TO GIVE A GRID REFERENCE (BRITISH NATIONAL GRID)

100 000 Metre GRID SQUARE IDENTIFICATION	TO GIVE A GRID REFERENCE TO NEAREST 100 ME	
	SAMPLE POINT: The Talbots	
SN SO 200	1. Read letters identifying 100 000 metre square in which the point lies.	ST
SS ST	2. FIRST QUOTE EASTINGS Locate first VERTICAL grid line to LEFT of point and read LARGE figures labelling the line either in the top or bottom margin or on the line itself. Estimate tenths from grid line to point.	05
300	3. AND THEN QUOTE NORTHINGS Locate first HORIZONTAL grid line BELOW point and read LARGE figures labelling the line either in the left or right margin or on the line itself. Estimate tenths from grid line to point.	
IGNORE the SMALLER figures of any grid number: these are for finding the full coordinates. Use ONLY the LARGER figure of the grid number.	SAMPLE REFERENCE	ST 05
EXAMPLE: ²69 ⁰⁰⁰m	For local referencing grid letters may be omitted.	

South-West England

Larch and wild cherry in Ditchley Woods

St Clement Woods, Truro *825 477,* ⚲ ♣, *500 acres, 1⅓m, muddy, FC*

The car park is well into the trees down a lane from the village of Idless, to the north of Truro.

This is the first of many Forestry Commission woodlands in this book. The Commission is under a statutory obligation to provide access to its woods and forests, where this will not interfere unduly with young plantations or conflict with other responsibilities – local shooting rights for instance. Capacious and secluded car parks are provided, with picnic areas; 450 of them in Britain. Forest walks and trails are usually waymarked from these places. Leaflet guides are often available. At the more important sites there are toilet facilities. Disabled people's trails are provided here and there.

It may be objected that providing WCs institutionalizes the atmosphere, and this is true. But much worse is the waste paper and plastic left about by us, the visitors. The

Commission does not usually undertake to clear litter, and notices pleading 'Please take your litter home' are irritating: either unnecessary or not complied with.

St Clement Woods has none of these facilities and irritants beyond a decently surfaced car park. But this wood does show the Commission at its best in integrating softwood production with the broadleaf character of British woodland.

The wood is old, as appears from its shape on the map: irregular with many concave bays where in the past ploughland has eaten into the wood. Much gorse on the lower levels of the forest road suggests former heathland, not unexpected on higher ground in Cornwall. The prevailing hardwood tree in the wood is hazel. Many acres, in total, of hazel coppice have been left by the foresters, both in and out of the plantations, where *Tsuga heterophylla*, the western hemlock, is the main timber tree.

The hazel stools obviously offer protection and provide the light shade which this conifer

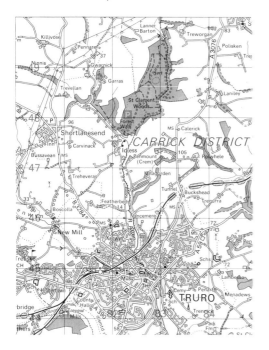

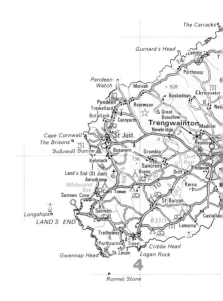

Stitchwort and bluebells in St Clement Woods

19

demands in the early years of growth.

Beech and hybrid poplars are also planted. The beech stands are full of bluebells, obviously the original ground cover: under the conifers are only dead needles and dry twigs.

The glory of the place for me is a section of wet oak and sallow woodland which remains by the stream at the east side of the wood. Here the native trees, once coppiced regularly, now sprawl grotesquely, green with moss, holly and honeysuckle amongst them, cowslips and bluebells wherever they can take root beneath. It is a scene of decay, perhaps, but fascinating and decorative. This furthest south-west of the Forestry Commission's woods is well worth visiting.

Carleon Cove *727 157, ♀, 10 minutes' walk, NT*

Of many wooded coves Carleon is car-less, and once contained, uniquely I believe, a wood of pure Cornish elm, *Ulmus angustifolia* var. *stricta*, a most distinctive tree and beautiful in every way. The cove now contains the corpses and to me is a very sad place. However, a man walking there was clearly deeply satisfied with the quiet beauty of the place and had not

Beeches by the Fal estuary, Trelissick

noticed that the trees were dead or that they were elms.

Cadgwith, nearby, has a wood of scrub elm – a hybrid sort, and scrubby because it climbs down a fairly exposed cliff, protected to some extent by a vast natural rock formation called the Devil's Frying-pan.

Inland is Goonhilly Down, bleak but lovable, with a dark, dramatic patch of Sitka spruce in the middle, contrasting beautifully with the clean shells of the several satellite-tracking aerials. This lonely forest, Croft Pascoe, is a Forestry Commission experiment which seems to be succeeding.

North of Goonhilly are the wooded shores of the Helford River, from Gweek to Durgan. Glendurgan, with famous subtropical gardens belonging to the National Trust, is probably magnificent, but unfortunately I always arrive on a Tuesday or a Thursday or at a weekend, none of these times being suitable.

Trengwainton, Penzance *445 313, ♀ ♣, easy, ⅔m total, NT*

Penzance is a plant experience in itself; the town park, though not a woodland, is full of palms, tree ferns, myrtle and gorgeous rhododendrons. See the fine row of cabbage trees in the Memorial Garden.

Trengwainton is a great garden and its walled compartments contain many rare and extremely beautiful plants: among trees are very fine magnolias; *Davidia*, perhaps not so rare but splendid here; a line of real tree ferns, *Dicksonia antarctica*; the rare *Nothofagus moorei*; several *Eucalyptus* species, and at the top a fine old *Cephalotaxus* (horribly named the Chinese cow's tail pine) with purple, peeling bark.

Trelissick *836 396, ♀ ♣, 3m or shorter options, NT*

Another famous garden, Trelissick, has a perimeter Woodland Walk, so described, which is always open. You can start near the King Harry Ferry where the notice invites you, or from the house, where parking is free. Actually, it is dull, except for the ships in the Fal and some more open, less overgrown, parts of the footpath.

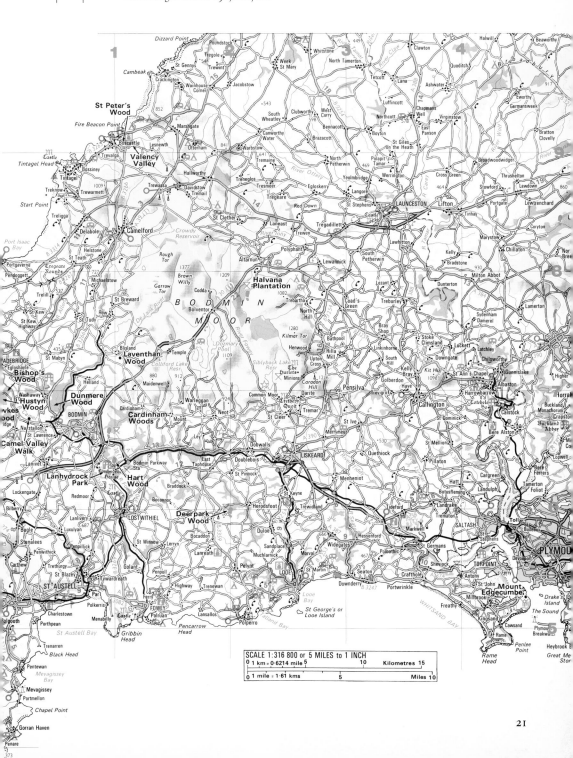

SCALE 1:316 800 or 5 MILES to 1 INCH

0 1 km = 0·6214 mile 5   10   Kilometres 15

0 1 mile = 1·61 kms   5   Miles 10

Between Bodmin and Wadebridge is a quiet countryside of narrow lanes, banked with flowers, in and out of deep valleys. Some very fine woods are here all coniferized but not less dramatic for that, and retain some old features and boundaries. There are no Forestry Commission car parks but access is perfectly easy.

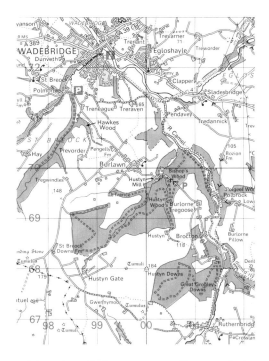

Hawkes Wood ♀, *9 acres, NNR*, Treneague Woods *985 715*, ♠, *1½m, FC*

From the centre of Wadebridge turn down by the Bridge on Wool pub, and go ¾ mile to the crossroads where a signpost points to St Breock. Take the small road opposite to this, up and then down into the valley of the stream – a few yards only. Here you may well admire the patch of beech and sycamore over the stream, the banks snowed under with wild garlic, more than the rather grim-looking Forestry Commission entrance opposite. But tramp up the forest road at least for ¼ mile in order to see the fine oaks of the small nature reserve.

Hustyn Wood and Bishop's Wood

005 697, ♠, *500 acres, forest roads, FC*

This plantation is just magnificent. Forest roads are open, and, since everyone makes for the coast, there are few visitors.

A Camel Valley Walk *015 681*, ♀ ♠, *metalled road or footpath, 1¾m, FC*

You can walk in the Forestry Commission woods, but it is uphill and not very promising. My walk is along the lane towards Ruthernbridge, conifers on one side, native streamside vegetation on the other. It is a very quiet lane. Walking back, you see everything the other way round. I know it sounds vague for a walk, but on a fine summer's morning it is perfect.

Dunmere Wood *043 688*, ♀ ♠, *at least 750 acres, FC*

This great wood, on a hill and down to the Camel Valley just north of Bodmin, is an old oakwood now converted into slabs of alternate beech and spruce by the Forestry Commission. There ought to be proper access so that one

might at least find some traces of its past, for it is well known; but there is nowhere to park and I am told there is no plan for a car park in the foreseeable future.

Lavethan Wood, Blisland *104 729*, ♀, *25 acres, easy, ½m, WT*

From the ugly Bodmin Moor of the A30(T), Blisland is like heaven (Helland is the next village). Blisland has a wood, in a valley bottom to the south: beech and oak with yew, invaded by sycamore and rhododendron. Great work is being done in coppicing the rhododendron and there is much natural regeneration of the native trees – not that this will get rid of the rhododendron. This is a faultless woodland walk; but take your wellies – it is a bridleway too.

Hart Wood *098 642, FC*, Lanhydrock Park *NT*

Take the second by-road right after the roundabout on the Bodmin to Liskeard road, A38, for Hart Wood, *103 639*, which has a small woodland walk through oaks and flowers, then larches and spruces. Across the road (at

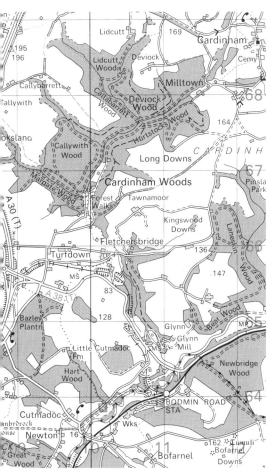

Lanhydrock shelter-belt

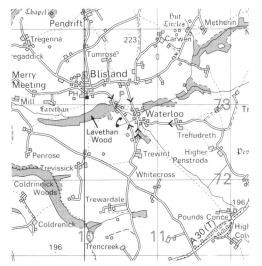

the map reference), through a red gate, is a driveway by the riverside to Bodmin Road Station. Here are fine old oaks and yews by the river, while along the drive are mighty specimens of Victorian conifer favourites, notably a well-shaped Lawson cypress, and many others. This is part of a $1\frac{3}{4}$-mile carriage drive from Lanhydrock House to the station, seemingly rather an expensive addition to the owner's first-class season ticket; but when you see the size of the estate you realize it must have been a relatively small item.

The drive, interrupted by a short stretch of roadway, continues to the house over parkland. Car parking, *085 636*, for the house and park is at the north-west side. The great lines of Lanhydrock's beeches are landscape features, visible from the trunk road, grander and more impressive as you come closer. Functionally essential shelter-belts for this hilltop estate, they have great architectural quality – beautifully massed and balanced. Even the parking place is like the nave of a great cathedral. You can walk all round the park under the beech trees. Who would have thought that prosaic-sounding Bodmin Road Station could lead to all this? The best approach is surely by that forgotten, sequestered driveway with its avenue of Victorian conifers.

Cardinham Woods *099 667*, (♀) ♣, *1000 acres, 4 walks and trails, FC*
The steep-sided, deep valleys of streams, particularly the Glynn, which drain the southern slopes of Bodmin Moor were almost

Cardinham Woods: a Glynn valley viewpoint

Mount Edgecumbe *453 533 and 446 521,*
♀ ♠, *96 acres, 3m or much less, CP*
The Mount was named by the Edgecumbe
family who moved in the seventeenth century
to the grand mansion here from Cotehele, their
ancestral home on the Tamar. In 1816 a local
journalist described Edgecumbe as 'that other
Eden', referring presumably only to its
landscape. It has a very good view of
Devonshire and retains a dense belt of
woodland round the deer park – as well as
numerous follies, a Grand Avenue etc. The
parking place at Cremyll is a bit towny; the
other, by the lonely church on the hill, is
attractive. The important tree at Edgecumbe is
the beech, but there are natural-looking oaks as
well, mostly over a hundred years old.

The great attraction is the coastal path,
through woodland, which I failed to explore.
This is a very successful Country Park, the
only one in Cornwall. It is fine parkland – the
woodland is incidental – and it is worth a day's
outing.

Boscastle: St Peter's Wood *119 905,* ♀,
(Minster Church), fp, wooded valley,
50 acres, NNR
Valency Valley *300 acres, NT*
St Peter's Wood, with sessile oak, is on the
north side of the valley, all of which belongs to
the National Trust. You can also park near the
main road opposite the Cobweb Inn, and walk
up the heavily wooded valley.

certainly oak-covered before human settlement
and then coppiced until cleared and planted by
the Forestry Commission. But admiration of
this now Canadian landscape leaves little room
for regret at the loss of native heritage. Alders,
willows, oaks and beeches can, anyway, still
keep a foothold by the streams and margins,
and there is an impressive group of oaks as you
drive in: be thankful! (The turning off the A38
to Liskeard from Bodmin is just after the
roundabout, signposted Fletchersbridge.)

You could spend days in this romantic place,
where Douglas fir and Sitka spruce grow 100
feet in thirty years. At the least you can drive
through the Glynn Valley, pausing to look
back where a small stopping place has been
made, and then nosing out through tiny lanes
to a fine gorse common on Long Downs.

Northwards, on Bodmin Moor, is the
enormous 1000-acre plantation of
Smallacombe Downs, as yet mysterious and
inaccessible. The only slightly smaller
Halvana Plantation, more mature, is close to
the A30 and has a picnic place at *215 788* and a
waymarked walk of 1½ miles of spruce and
pine, with moorland mining relics and views.

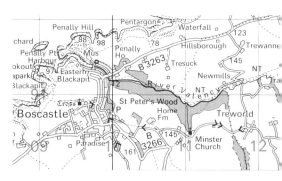

Dartmoor

Landranger sheets 191, 192, 201, 202

Looking across the tree-filled Bovey Valley

DARTMOOR FOREST

The moors (poor grass, heather, bracken, gorse and peat) occupy the western half of the compact 365-square-mile blob-shaped National Park. In the middle are three great conifer forests. The eastern side of the blob (which is a block of granite) is largely hill-farming country, broken by the wooded valleys of the Teign, the Bovey and the Dart (and its tributaries). The Lyd Gorge is to the west.

Three very small oakwoods remain in the high moors. Perhaps they are fragments of greater woods long ago; but their origins are mysterious. Much of the moorland is common land and as such must have been grazed for centuries unrecorded – before it ever came to be called a forest. Deer and the commoners' animals – sheep and ponies – have seen to it that very few trees indeed in the 120,000 acres

of moorland have ever had a chance of natural reproduction.

Wistman's Wood, Two Bridges
609 750, ♀, 63 acres, 2m, FNR
You have to walk for a mile northwards from the hotel at Two Bridges, near Princetown. The wood is signposted at the cottage ¼ mile from the gate. The origins of Wistman's Wood, long famous for its weirdly contorted, moss-hung trees, are obscure, and it consists entirely of pedunculate oak, some trees very old, where sessile oak would be expected.

Piles Copse, Torr *625 612, ♀, about 40 acres, 2½m, FNR*
The map reference is a parking place just on the moorland. The wood is 1¼ miles north-east. A permit is required from the Water Authority if you cross their land, but you can

Dartmoor oaks in Wistman's Wood

follow the waymarked path around it. This route, from Cornwood and Torr, brings you to the west bank of the River Erme, opposite the wood; the river may be impossible to cross after rain. But you get a very good view of the wood, and can examine the natural growth on the near side.

Black Tor Copse, Meldon *562 918*, ⚲, *about 50 acres, 4m, FNR, Army Danger Area*

The only access is from the excellent parking place (the map reference) at the dam of Meldon Reservoir, clearly signposted from the village. The wood is 2 miles south-south-west. Take the bridleway signposted 'To the Moors and Sourton', but follow an old contour path which branches off before the line of beeches. At the head of the reservoir cross the arched bridge and the wet plain: continue up the West Okement River. A notice gives clear instructions about warning flags, but only after you have covered $1\frac{1}{2}$ miles of rough country.

Each of these woods requires a non-woodland walk in well-soled gumboots: each is well worth the effort. The walk to Wistman's is dull, but the other two are not just walks; they are experiences: of water, rocks and space, as well as of trees.

These oakwood curiosities are minute compared with the Forestry Commission's transformations of the moorland scenery.

Fernworthy Forest *669 839*, (⚲) ⚹, *1600 acres, forest trails, FC*

The superb stands of forestry conifers are spread in a vast arc over the several moorland valleys which drain into the Fernworthy Reservoir. In the wide, wet margins of the water, sheltered on all sides by the plantations, a rich sallow woodland has developed. Amongst the pines and the spruces are many ancient standing stones, hut circles and cairns. The setting is superlative and the approach road (west from Chagford) climbs dramatically to moorland from beautiful wooded farmland, between massive stone hedges crowned with beeches.

North of the forest is **Gidleigh Common**, a Site of Special Scientific Interest, with scattered trees amongst hut circles and beautiful views over the lowlands.

Bellever Forest *652 771*, ⚹, *1300 acres, waymarked trail with options, FC*

The forest looks complicated on the map, not quite filling the spaces between the road, the B3212, the East Dart River, and Bellever village and Bellever Tor (1453 feet) but it looks very well shaped from the surrounding high moors – a lesson in landscaping to answer the critics of conifer plantations. The car park is a bit dark and forbidding. A map identifies the areas occupied by various species: Douglas fir, silver fir, Japanese larch and Sitka spruce. Sitka and Japanese larches are the oldest trees here, planted in 1921: they look very big. *Pinus contorta*, the lodgepole pine, is also used.

The old Lych Way through the forest was used by church-goers to Lydford.

Burrator Forest *568 694*, ⚲ ⚹, *1000 acres, paths and a forest road, WA*

The gleaming water with its tree-clad slopes, close to Yelverton, is an attractive focus for sightseers. Statistics of the Dartmoor National Park Authority show that of all visitors to Dartmoor, 29 per cent never leave their car, 35 per cent stray only 100 yards and 34 per cent go about a mile. Walking only 200 yards from the main car park here brings you to a typical Dartmoor oakwood on boulders, by a loud stream, and all covered in vivid green moss. A mile takes you into pleasantly varied conifer country, much of it mature woodland, and out on to the moors.

The Dartmoor Valley woods are numerous and complex and would require a whole guidebook of their own. Taking the main wooded valleys in clockwise order, starting at 1 o'clock:

Teign Valley Woods *743 899*, ♀ ♣, *1500 acres, fp, 8m, pf, NT*

The map reference gives an awkward, steep access point for a car, Fingle Bridge, but which at least takes you into the middle of the dark, conifer-clad valleys, via photogenic Drewsteignton and close to the fast A30(T). At the upper end of the valley are National Trust woodlands dominated by the grandiose Castle Drogo. A footpath to Fingle Bridge begins on the Drewsteignton to Sandy Park road, just to the north-west of Castle Drogo's hill. At the lower end **Dunsford Wood, Cod Wood** and the National Trust **Bridford Wood**, well known for daffodils, lie across the Moreton-hampstead road from Exeter. There is a nature trail here at *804 883*.

Becka Falls and Houndtor Wood, Manaton *757 800*, ♀ ♣, *300yds or 3m, pf*

This is a beauty spot, and it *is* beautiful. Parking is free and there is a café. There are steps down to the view of the falls.

The path goes on by hemlock and western red cedar plantations, but with primroses, and you soon reach a fourways signpost where you must choose your route, long or short.

Yarner Wood *785 793*, ♀, *450 acres, walk 3½m or shorter, nature trail, NR*

This is a good example of a valley oakwood and is carefully managed to provide the maximum range of habitat and to produce wood for fencing etc. Some years ago the pied flycatchers left the wood because of a shortage, not of food, but of suitable holes to nest in. As with other oakwoods around Dartmoor there are few old trees. Nest-boxes were provided and the pied flycatchers returned.

The nature trail delights everyone. What I would have thought impossible is here achieved with style: the provision of museum showcases, waterproofed with felt, amongst the trees. One case describes and illustrates with

models the habits of the wood ant. Very good; but what rivets the visitor is a real, active community of wood ants opposite the showcase. No wonder there are entries like TERRIFIC in the visitors' book at the car park.

The oldest trees here are a row of beeches, their silver trunks beautifully marked with lichen. The walks are carefully signposted and not difficult.

A mile north-west of Bovey Tracey off the Manaton road is **Parke**, *805 785*, the local headquarters of the National Trust and the Dartmoor National Park Authority. Here are an Interpretation Centre – posh name for a bookstall – and a Bovey Valley Walk under beeches, a mile or so if you just cross the bridge into Parke Wood, or nearly 3 miles if you go up through Ledge Wood, by the Rare Breeds Farm, and cross the river by the road.

Holne Woods and Cleve Wood *705 695*, *Holne, 711 709, New Bridge*, ♀ ♣, *riverside walks of optional length, NT (Holne Woods)*

The New Bridge car park is busy and you may prefer to park in Holne village and walk by the signed footpath over two fields down into the woods; this route will show you from above what you are about to plunge into – and will fill your lungs with air. Gumboots are essential.

Turn left at the river path for the exquisite beeches of Holne Woods. Words will not describe their perfection. On the way there are lots of sycamore and rhododendron escaped from jealously guarded estates above. The rhododendrons are, mercifully, being cut, but of course *Rhododendron ponticum* coppices like the devil and is extremely difficult to uproot.

The whole of the Dart Valley woodlands, over 900 acres, are 'dedicated', either belonging to the Devon Trust for Nature Conservation or the National Trust, from *672 731* north, to *708 704* south, and there are several access points, from the (most-visited) car park at Dartmeet downwards.

At Ashburton, a cramped little town which seems to catch many holidaymakers, the **River Dart Country Park** is signposted. In its 23 acres, *734 701*, it accommodates a quiet

In the Dart Valley in early summer

woodland walk by the river. Parking was fairly costly.

Hembury Woods *728 680, ♀, 374 acres, steep in places, NT*
By contrast the National Trust Hembury, to the south, is peaceful and asks only for a ten-pence donation. It is a very beautiful oakwood and there is a walk down to the river with beeches (15 minutes) or up to Hembury Castle among birches – a stiff climb. The parking and picnic place, *728 680*, struck me as one of the most lovely places I had ever visited, the fairly young (sixty years) oaks decorated with lichen and ivy and the whole place dotted with the blue of bluebells and the yellow of broom which grow between the oaks. There is a lot of bramble away from this pleasant grassy patch.

To reach Hembury, go out of Buckfast in the direction of Scorriton but fork right, not signposted, instead of left to Scorriton and Holne.

SOUTH AND EAST OF DARTMOOR

Lady's Wood, Ugborough *685 594, ♀, 8 acres, easy but damp, NR*
Park by the charming bridge on a minor road from South Brent to Cheston, signposted Owley. This is a depressing little wood of oak and ash over hazel and holly, much overgrown in spite of supposedly being coppiced on a

seven-compartment cycle. But I suppose on a fine morning it could be heavenly. Trains rush over a viaduct.

It is incredible to think that Ivybridge was once a well-known beauty-spot around 1800, painted by Turner as the essence of perfect peace. Woods north of Cornwood are Sites of Special Scientific Interest including **Dendles Wood**, but Dendles Waste is a heavy block of conifers.

Shaugh Prior Wood on the River Meavy, *534 636*, is also a Site of Special Scientific Interest. **Hardwick Wood**, *530 555*, belonging to the Woodland Trust, is practically in Plymouth. There is a forest walk in **Cann Wood**, *545 595*, which is coniferous – the Forestry Commission's Plym Beat, so called. This is rather difficult to find because of poor signposting in Plympton: take the Shaugh Prior road. The forest walk was closed when I eventually found it.

The National Trust **Lydford Gorge** is well known with great trees in nearly subtropical mist from the waterfall. There is a charge for parking. **Lydford Forest**, *489 845*, Forestry Commission, has a forest trail.

Ancient oak trees at Meavy, just in the Park at the west, and at Teigngrace just outside at the south-east, have been preserved for sentiment, otherwise old trees and old coppice stools are nowhere to be seen on or near Dartmoor. The oldest trees in the Dartmoor

Forest are in Wistman's Wood, hardly more than 10 feet high. Was the Dartmoor Forest once a great oakwood? I do not know, but I am quite sure that the pathetically small remains on the moors should be allowed to increase naturally by the simple erection of fences. Surely there is enough room.

But as you emerge from the woods once more to the bare, brown moor you breathe deeply and exclaim again what a very beautiful place it is. No wonder 8 million people come to see it every year.

Avon Valley Woods *736 509 to 732 483, ♀, 2m, easy, wet, WT*

Avon is pronouced here with a short 'a'. Finding the south end of the walk at Loddiswell's old railway station is not easy. You should be on the east bank of the river on the road to Woodleigh. The wood is not all that marvellous, but its wet carpet of flowers is; here wild garlic or ramsons predominates, and there is yellow archangel, lugubriously named *Galeobdolon*, a sort of yellow deadnettle, amongst the anemones, bluebells and primroses. The disused railway is an alternative and parallel path. What a railway

this must have been, deep in the valley woods!

At the north or upstream end there is nowhere to park near Topsham Bridge and you have to squeeze in to the roadside where a gate leads to a private driveway. The Woodland Trust obviously intends one to use this drive. Head downhill at the first opportunity. The bluebells at this end of the wood are magnificent. There is a lot of sycamore but soon you come to some fine beeches. It is very quiet except for the laughing of the Avon.

Great Haldon *897 840* and **Mamhead** *922 805, (♀) ♠*

Familiar to drivers from Exeter to Plymouth on the A38(T) is the noble shape of the forested Great Haldon, 3 miles from the end of the motorway, M5. Views are enormous through the dignified ranks of fine Scots pines, while the road is bordered by a great beech hedge grown up into an avenue. Great Haldon is impressive, almost overwhelming, and needs plenty of time to be explored.

From the A380 Torquay road, you can get to the Obelisk at the Forestry Commission's Mamhead picnic place, *921 808*, again with magnificent views, here taking in the Exe Estuary and the Blackdown Hills.

Very close to Exeter, **Stoke Woods** has a Forestry Commission picnic place on the A396 to Tiverton. The walk here is in mature oakwoods and younger forestry plantation.

Close to the motorway and north-east of Exeter are **Killerton House and Park** and **Ashclyst Forest**. Killerton, National Trust, is famous and much visited for its garden. All its trees are fine specimens (well-formed as trees commonly are in Devonshire vales) and the park woods are open when the house and garden are not.

Exeter University grounds are in 300 acres once belonging to the famous seedsmen Veitch & Co, and are full of interesting trees.

Ashclyst Forest *000 995, ♀ ♠, 1250 acres, 3 waymarked walks, muddy, NT, FC*

Clyst is a river name, common in this enviably mild and long-settled Devonshire countryside. Ashclyst is a very attractive forest, a landscape of great variety, interest and charm.

North Cornwall, North Devon and Exmoor

Landranger sheets 180, 181, 190

Kilkhampton: Coombe Valley Woods

208 116, ♀, 1½m, wooded valley, NT
The woods arise ¼ mile inland: oaks at first
child-high, then rapidly building up in lovely
wind-cut curves which fill the fold of the quiet
valley. Above on the hill some parabolic dish
aerials have a similar perfection of form,
arrived at less empirically. In the empty lower
valley where the small trees begin, a boy sat on
a gate, alone and motionless in the wind and
sun – a poetic moment.

The Forestry Commission has a picnic place
here, and has probably cleared a few thousand
beautiful oaks, but has been discreet. A nature
trail is run in conjunction with the County
Naturalists' Trust.

The Hobby Drive, Clovelly: Hobby Lodge

336 234, ♀, 1¼m, wooded cliff, pf
You have to pay to take a car, but not too
much. The drive finishes just north-west of
Clovelly, where the paved footpath descends to
the village. The trees are fascinating,
particularly beeches, twisted but large and
with richly patterned trunks. There are places
to stop along the drive.

Buck's Mills Wood

357 234, ♀, 23 acres, inaccessible, WT
Towards Bideford from Clovelly it is the slight
shelter of the north-facing bay which means
that woods can clothe the cliffs. The Woodland
Trust has done a great service by preserving
this section of oakwood with its ferns and
bluebells, but it is too early to talk of access.
There is a Forestry Commission car park on
the opposite side of the valley with a short
woodland walk, and this is our map reference.
Once on the cliff top – via steps past the
cottages of the coastguard lookout – the view of
Barnstaple Bay and Lundy Island is splendid.

Melbury Woods

364 191, ♣, 1000 acres plus, forest trail, FC
The land south-east of Woolsery (sometimes
spelt Woolfardisworthy) is low and marshy,

and the plantations of spruce and pine are
richly embroidered with sallows – all doing
much, one feels, to improve the ground. The
place seemed very remote and silent on a fine
Sunday in May.

Hartland Forest: Welsford and Summerwell Woods

278 211, ♣, 350 acres plus, 1½m trail and others, FC
Here the slowly undulating brown moorland is
cut by marshy streams feeding the Upper
Torridge, and lined with grey willows – a
painter's colours: the broad strokes of dark
green conifers complete the colour scheme be
the sky grey or blue. This is a forest for
striding through, or even driving through (very
slowly): a fine visual experience not added to
by a tatty 'scientific' display at the Information
Centre. Avoid it, avoid the trail, wander and
enjoy the clean, scented air, the distances, the
dark, rich colours.

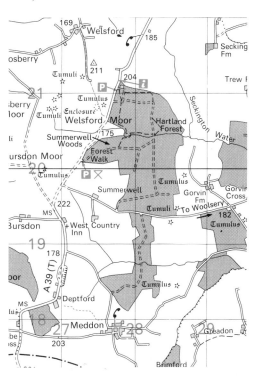

Holsworthy Woods *353 018*, ♣, *450 acres, trail, FC*

A cramped parking place and a sad forest of spruces which fall over because the roots cannot strike deep enough in the clay.

Arlington Court *614 408*, ♀ ♣, *3500 acres (not all woodland)*, *1½m or more, NT*

It must have looked just the same a hundred years ago, except that the monkey puzzles would be much smaller. The walk round the park takes in an avenue of these mighty trees and then descends to the lake where older oaks and beeches are reflected. Determined walkers can then add a couple of miles or so to Loxhore Cott, by a stream which laps the feet of coppiced oaks, or, less energetic, may climb up again through the shady Wilderness of much rhododendron, redwoods, and a Japanese cedar.

EXMOOR AND THE BRENDON HILLS

Rising dark to the east of the Torr and the Yeo, Exmoor Forest is as bald as the Forest of Rossendale in Lancashire, and it can be bleaker in winter. Simonsbath Farm, the first to be made on Exmoor, contained in 1814 four ash trees, three large beeches, twenty-three sycamores and seven lime pollards, in all thirty-seven trees. Forestation of the moors was considered, then given up, and the forest was enclosed, small lots being given to commoners – no substitute for their ancient roving grazing rights. The warden got 3000 acres and the Crown 10,000 , which it sold for £60,000. Heroic attempts were made by the buyers, the Knight family of ironmasters, to create farmland, but the old rump remains, bare, and, to many, beautiful in its barrenness.

In a forest so forbidding to trees we can make no pretence here to study the moorland. I have also missed the coastal valleys of **Lynton** and **Lynmouth**, and, less forgivably, the **Heddon Valley**, *655 482*, and **Woody Bay, Martinhoe**, *675 487*, a total together of over 1000 acres of National Trust land: woodland, moorland and cliffs.

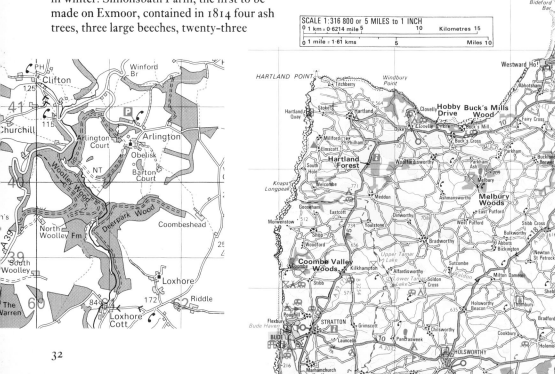

SCALE 1:316 800 or 5 MILES to 1 INCH

Horner Wood and Webber's Post

899 455, ♀, ♣ (Horner Village), 903 437
(Webber's Post), many routes, 2–4m,
NT etc

Dunkery Hill belongs to the National Trust, and the Beacon, 1705 feet, is the highest point on Exmoor. Horner Water flows out northwards to Porlock Bay through the deepest of shadowy coombes, filled with native oaks. The road over the moors to Exford at first follows the tributary of the Horner, East Water. There is a large parking place in this valley at Cloutsham, among fine woods of durmast oak. At Webber's Post and on Horner Hill are pinewoods diversified with birch and holly; gorse and bracken on the slopes. You can start a walk from Porlock or from Horner, either following the stream on the west bank or climbing Horner Hill. A short section along the road links the footbridge over East Water with Webber's Post.

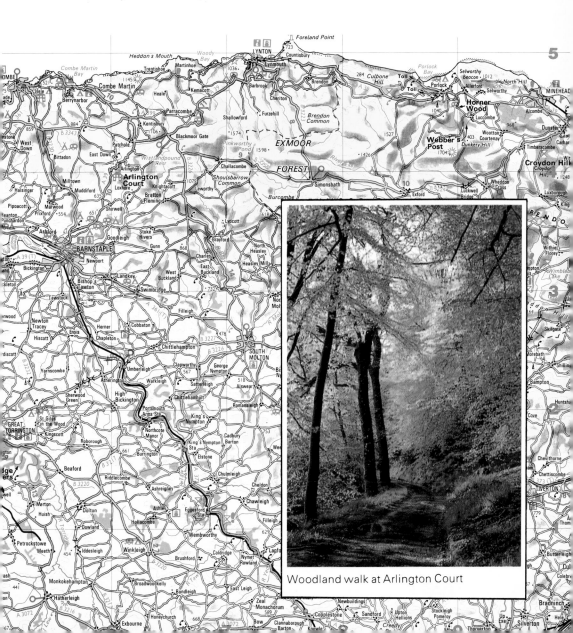

Woodland walk at Arlington Court

Horner Hill and Porlock Bay

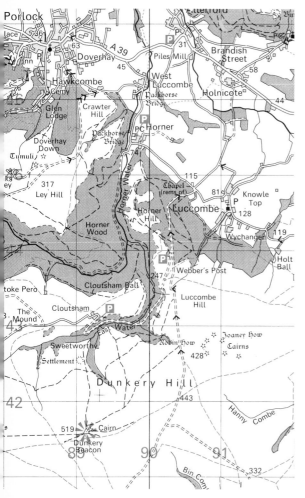

Croydon Hill (Brendon Forest)

973 420, picnic place, forest roads, FC
This pleasant acre, a clearing in the pines, is reached via Dunster village (touristy but tasteful). Turn left towards Luxborough from the A396 Tiverton road about a mile south-west of Dunster. There are no Forestry Commission walks arranged – indeed there were preparations for a motor rally when I visited – but it is not difficult to keep your bearings in the hilly country. A waymarked walk surfaces here – 'D2' to Timberscombe; yellow markers.

Two other Forestry Commission picnic places are on the unclassified road from Wheddon Cross to Raleigh's Cross – at Kennisham, *963 359*, and Chargot, *965 355*.

Wootton Courtenay is a centre for walks in the coniferized commons which lie to the north and east.

Winsford Hill and South Hill, north of Dulverton, are National Trust lands preserving 1100 acres of moorland here heavily invaded by thorns. The Exmoor foothills about **Withypool Common** are remarkable for many fine beech hedges, maintained, as essential windbreaks. The distinctive, graceful yet grotesque patterns of old beech hedges are typical of Somerset hill farms. They seem to grow very vigorously, exposed on the tops of ancient hedge banks. There is no machine to keep the hedges in shape; only human skill can do it. The effect is worth our attention.

South-East Devon and the Quantocks Landranger sheets 181, 193

Lyme Regis to Axmouth Undercliff

327 915 to 254 902, ♀, *5½m hard going each way*, *NNR*

This famous nature reserve was discovered by Professor Tansley. The Dowlands Landslip in 1839 opened a chasm, which has been filled by natural ashwood and native jungle.

Landslips reveal new ground, so the woodland could be described as uniquely primary, or at least 'natural secondary'. The growth of ivy is staggering. Usually this plant has no place in native woodland – this is the exception to the rule, a result of the frost-free air, the shelter and the strong light from the sea. Ivy makes most of its growth before the late-leafing ash. Madder and stinking iris grow here, and no doubt many other plants I did not notice in primrose time. There are large hart's tongue ferns everywhere, and cuckoo pint.

There is another landslip at the **Spittles**, below Timber Hill, Lyme Regis, with a tiny parking place at *344 932*. This area is largely meadow with old hedges: 130 acres National Trust, leased to the Royal Society for Nature Conservancy. The woodland is scrub in the dangerous unstable part. Timber Hill has fine tall beeches with unsuitable *Tsuga* under-storey: perhaps young beeches will be planted or encouraged: the *Tsugas* will shelter them.

The Forestry Commission woodlands inland are of little interest. St **Mary's Forest**, Trinity Hill, *305 955*, has a filthy parking place but a pleasant perimeter bridleway with ancient hedge trees including Scots pine. The forest itself is not open. Wootton Hill, called **Charmouth Forest**, is open. You can drive in

Chalk cliffs in the Lyme Regis landslip

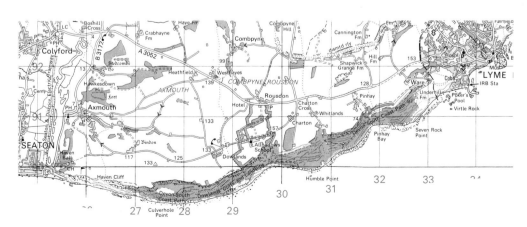

Tree-clad ramparts of Neroche Castle

at various points: *355 975* is one. The plantation is mature. It is quiet and dark, most of the available light being efficiently absorbed into production of softwood timber.

Neroche Forest *274 157, ♀, 2200 acres, forest trail, 2½m or 1½m, mud, FC*

The eleventh-century castle ramparts are set with 150-year-old oaks, beeches, chestnuts and larches. Castle Farm, in the ramparts, is 200 years old and has a respectably foul midden. The trail includes several important forestry species, including Lawson cypress, and the attractively produced leaflet, available on site, identifies the trees as you go.

There is another access point at *229 164*, a picnic place in the old Prior's Park, 6 miles south of Taunton.

An outer rampart of the Forestry Commission's Neroche Forest is at the interesting long-ridge woodland of **East Hill**, with ample parking space at *117 930* and elsewhere provided by Devon County Council. East Hill Strips are parallel wood banks forty paces apart with extremely picturesque old polled and hedged beeches. There is a longish walk here – the ridge is 3 miles long – but the

motor road runs alongside. Could this ridge really have been an old boundary of the Neroche Forest, centred over 12 miles away?

A more complex escarpment carries a small wood on **Sheldon Hill**, *114 093*, above South Farm. This belongs to the Woodland Trust. Like many other Woodland Trust properties it does not offer much of a walk, and it is at present rather messily coniferized, though much of the ancient character of the margins remains – the ridge lanes provide the walking. It must be said that the Woodland Trust is the only organization working against the enormous loss of native woodland which has occurred in the last forty years. In time this pioneering work will be gratefully appreciated.

Leaving the motorway (M5) at junction 24 between Bridgwater and Taunton avoids traffic delays and brings you at once into the steep, hedged lanes where perspective seems to be on holiday. The hedges are all sheared mechanically, which contours them smoothly to the roads and of course is death to any aspiring hedgerow tree, but vigorous growth here keeps the hedges thick.

Fyne Court, *223 321*, in the tiny village of Broomfield, west of North Petherton, has a Visitors' Centre from which several woodland walks and a nature trail start. The beautiful parkland is full of scraps of old woodland, some 'promoted' from old coppices.

Quantock Forest *190 363 (Cockercombe Camp ♀♣), 168 377 (Rams Combe ♣), various walks, FC*

The main Forestry Commission parking ground takes you to tall, alien conifers which are very impressive, but are, I believe, an outrage on the curvaceous intimacies of the Quantock coombes.

By contrast the Cockercombe viewpoint is very quiet. Spruce, hemlock and larch fill the valley, but the carefully arranged Disabled Viewpoint could make someone's day, and the approaches, with fine boundary beeches, are superb. The bridleway along the south side of the forest offers a recommendable walk with Aisholt Common open on your left. Then, striking right into the forest, it is not difficult to follow the larch-filled coombe downwards and back to the Camp (it is a prehistoric one). A road through the trees runs parallel to Cockercombe on its north side.

Two National Trust woodland-and-heath sites are reached from the A39. **Shervage Wood**, 136 acres of oak, with coppice, has a parking place at *161 404*. Don't leave valuables in the car. Longstone Hill, 61 acres, is reached via **Hodder's Combe** and the village of Holford, a short detour from the main road. The land is heath, but the way lies through ragged old beeches; silver-grey bark with the blue greys of sea and sky, the dark pink of the rock, and paintbox-green moss. Park by the ancient dogpen, *153 412*.

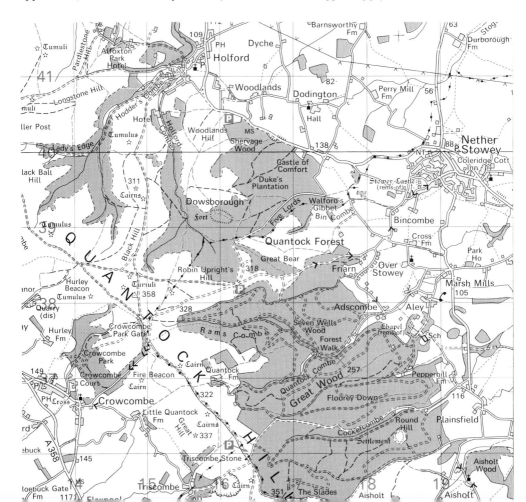

The Somerset, Dorset and Wiltshire Borders
Landranger sheets 183, 184, 194, 195

Alfred's Tower

A clear landmark to be seen from the north and west is Alfred's Tower, *745 351*, a sturdy folly on a rather logical triangular plan, erected by Henry Hoare the 2nd, of Stourhead, to commemorate Alfred's victory over the Danes eleven centuries before – as good a reason as any for building a folly. The hill on which it stands is 770 feet high. Lines of beeches, very picturesque and sprawling by the narrow approach road almost constitute a wood, and provide a long glade to park in, apart from the National Trust car park for the tower itself. Bridleways into the ridge-top woodland do not seem to lead very far before dipping to the plain, but it is easy enough to find a roughly oval or a floppy orbital route around the tower, through spruce woods planted amongst old beeches. Old or new, all the trunks are vividly modelled by lichen in green and black. You can also walk through to the Stourhead Estate, about 2 miles south-eastwards.

Downhill and westwards is the little town of Bruton, heavy with charm, which gives its name to the Bruton Forest. Only scattered woods remain of this forest, which has no particular history; 1000 acres belong to the Forestry Commission. Many elms survive by the B3092 south from Frome. The elm is a farmland tree, but something of the forest atmosphere survives around Gare Hill – and many forest names.

Great Bradley Wood and Gare Hill
797 404, ♀ ♣, 2½m *walk, pf*

Between the great houses and parks of Longleat and Stourhead lies a broad sheaf of fine woodland mostly on greensand ridges. At the map reference you can just park one car in the farm road, and follow a clearly signed footpath under elms with a rhododendron understorey into a splendid plantation, a wonderful blend of forestry and landscape design. Large areas are being cleared of underwood, revealing the trunks of excellent oaks, and well-grown conifers line the route:

grand fir, Douglas fir, Sawara cypress, Sitka spruce. You are warned not to leave the pathway, but there really is no need. Bear left to reach an exit at a picturesque corner with old beeches, or right to Gare Hill village.

Stourhead
779 349, ♀ ♣, *2507 acres, 1½m lakeside walk, NT*

The pleasure gardens, begun in 1741, surround an artificial lake below the tastefully preserved village of Stourton. There is a hotel, with parking for patrons, but definitely nowhere to park in the village. The National Trust car park is above on the hilltop. You must choose, and turn aside from the gateway of the house (except for a look at the mighty sweet chestnuts by the drive) if you want to spend your time with the trees: or allow time for the house and its treasures as well.

Magic is a word which enters all but the barest description of Stourhead, and it is a sort of double enchantment. First was the idea (of Henry Hoare, the banker's son) to build classical temples in a landscape designed to be 'natural' – rejecting the then traditional formality of gardens. Second is the enchantment that has settled over the beautiful valley, which is now filled with well-grown conifers planted by the Victorian Hoares: conservation has waved a wand and the whole thing looks perfect.

Snail-creep Hanging
955 365, ♀, *fps, pf*

Take the No Through Road from the railway bridge east of Sherrington and drive as far as possible. The Snail-creep glistens ahead, a chalk track, at first through bleached grass, elders and hawthorns. Continuing uphill there are wayfaring trees and sloes, buckthorn, bramble, privet, rose, then scrubby birch, beech and oak. The path divides into several, roughly parallel ones, in the manner of the old chalk pathways – avoiding obstacles long since vanished. Juniper and whitebeam appear, holly and hazel hint at real woodland, but the gleaming trunks of ashes, with some planted

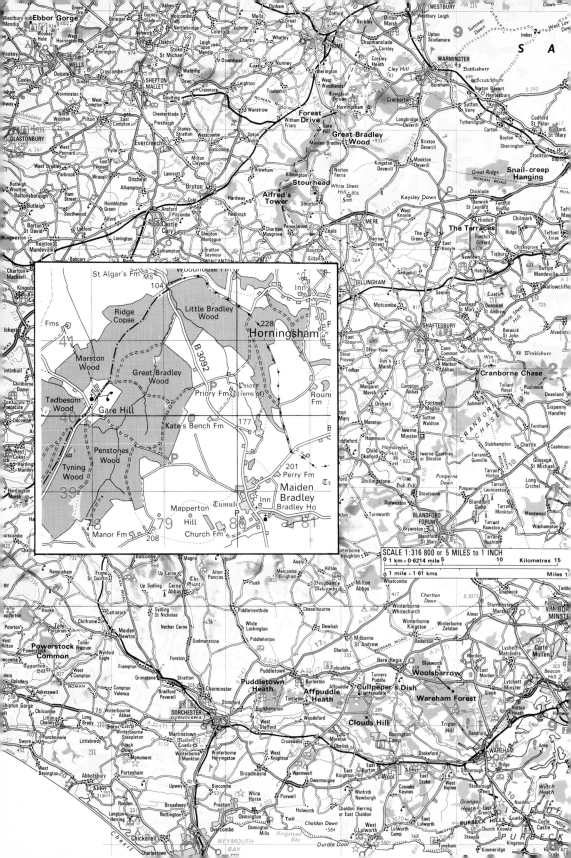

spruce beyond, suggest that this was once grassland. Beech and fine, tall whitebeams fill grassy spaces where burdock thrives. Near the top of the down the chalk disappears below sand. Snail-creep Hanging is not a beech hanger but an old hazel and oak coppice, now well organized for shooting. A straight ride, in fact an old Roman road, goes right and west along the ridge, spruce forestry on the left, oak woodland on the right. You can continue or turn north and back to rejoin one of the downward valley trackways which converge eastwards on to Sherrington Down.

South of this main road is Fonthill Bishop. At the mighty beeches of **The Terraces**, *917 322*, there is a ridgeway track. But Fonthill itself, the colossal abbey built for £300,000 in 1799 by the dilettante Beckford – the site now marked by very tall conifers – is private. Not long ago all was open and you could thread your way by a fallen *Araucaria* and a mighty redwood to mouldering garden nymphs and the weedy steps of the misbegotten structure – it was felled by the wrath of a storm almost before it was finished. There is a footpath through some of the very tall beech and spruce woods from Beacon Hill; *912 217*.

Sixpenny Handley, *990 180*, and Tollard Royal are centres for Cranborne Chase, which contains a long strip of woodland. Chases were subject to forest laws but privately owned – this one since James I. Owners and their keepers were often at war with poachers and others asserting what they believed to be their rights. Weapons are preserved at Farnham Museum. The woods of Cranborne Chase remain well guarded old coppices, now mainly coniferized, though chase laws were abolished in the early nineteenth century.

Large forests occupy the Dorset heathlands east of Dorchester, an area rich in tree interest though one may deeply regret the loss of heathland habitat. The large **Wareham Forest** is traversed by a long straight road north-west from Wareham to Bere Regis. Here, 1½ miles from Wareham, one may park and follow a forest trail which passes a bog nature reserve and a small arboretum. The

The path to Snail-creep Hanging, looking towards Salisbury Plain

pines are as dull as can be, on ground deeply ridged by the plough, and pylons litter the skylines. The ancient fortified hilltop of **Woolsbarrow**, *892 925*, is a 19-acre heathland reserve reached by forest rides from the A35 or from the road through the forest.

Isolated fragments of preserved heathland are, I feel, a poor substitute for the real thing, vast and various, and most interesting where wetlands or woodlands merge. At **Clouds Hill**, *824 909* just south of Lawrence of Arabia's Cottage (National Trust and smothered in rhododendron), you may see what the Army tanks do to the heath. There is even a small car park provided. Considering that the Army also preserves large patches from its own infernal machines one may conclude that the Forestry Commission is the more destructive, ploughing and then blanketing the ground with dense conifer crops, so that the native gorse, heather and grasses and their attendant fauna are lost for ever. Driving towards Dorchester by minor roads from Clouds Hill you can divert north-west to Tolpuddle and cheer yourself up with the Martyrs' Tree, an ancient, propped-up sycamore preserved by the T.U.C. There are useful parking places which allow access to remnants of heathland vegetation: at **Cull-pepers Dish**, *815 925*, and **Affpuddle Heath**, *804 925*. **Puddletown Heath**, with Hardy's birthplace at *728 924*, is heavily coniferized, with rhododendron and cherry laurel to boot,

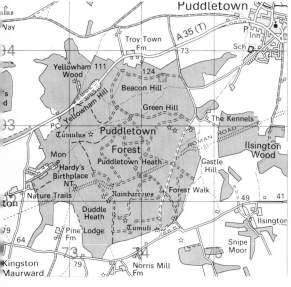

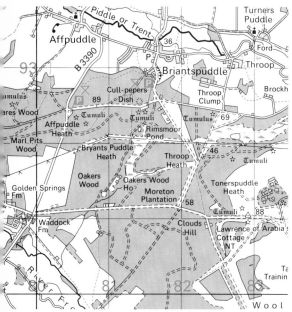

but a (rather dirty) parking place at *743 936* is approached via handsome beeches on a south-facing outcrop of chalk, where even the fastidious may be tempted to stop. There is no need yet to join the A35: the minor road runs on via Stinsford, where Hardy's heart is buried and sheltered by nice trees.

West of Dorchester, fork right 4½ miles out of the town on to a ridge (Roman) road, the A35(T), over the vivid scenery of tumuli-studded downs to Powerstock Common.

Powerstock Common *547 974*, ♀, *4m or less, easy, 100 acres, NR (and FC)*
You can no longer book a railway ticket to Toller Porcorum, but you can walk along the suture of the railway which is stitched with a pretty vegetation inadequately described as scrub. Blackthorn, field rose and wayfaring tree grow on the chalky embankment above a placid stream. Healthy young oak trees invade, and lovely old goat willows remember the days of steam.

A mile west of Toller the railway crossed a lane by a bridge, which remains, and its line continues as the north-west boundary of the nature reserve. Here, at the map reference, is a small parking place. The bridleway leads you to a wood-bank with a line of bent oaks where ash and hazel are coppiced to make a grove to delight the eye. What appears to have been a line of ancient fishponds leads to a patch of heather, gorse and rushes, and more old oak-crowned banks ten paces apart provide a corridor of natural vegetation to the south-east part of the reserve, where bracken heath declines to woodland of oak and willow. Lines of conifers accentuate the curving skyline of sculptured hills.

Ebbor Gorge *525 485*, *2m, steep, 142 acres, NT (NR)*
Park at the Churchill Memorial 1½ miles from Wells, 2 miles south of Wookey Hole. The limestone gorge contains a rich ash-oak wood. A fine polished axe found in a cave at the head of the gorge is now in Wells Museum. There are good views from the tops and from the cliffs of the gorge.

SOUTH-WEST ENGLAND
Salisbury and the New Forest

Landranger sheets 183, 184, 195, 196

Wilton Park, in the old town of Wilton, has fine cedars, hemlocks, planes and flowering cherries, and a selection of exotic specimen broadleaves; but there are many better and larger arboreta. A beech-lined road south-west (signposted Broad Chalke) leads to the coniferized woods of **Hare Warren**, *081 288* with well-surfaced paths.

Great Yews, *120 230*, and **Little Yews** are woods south of Homington, which is east of Coombe Bissett, across the A354.

Grovely Wood West *015 349*, ✦, *about 2000 acres, easy, FC*

Grovely Wood was once an oakwood in the more acid soils held on top of a limestone ridge. Access is from the minor road between Dinton and Wylye. Near the crest of the downs, turn eastwards down a track for about a mile. The eastern end is controlled by the Wilton Park Estate; fine, large beeches on the slopes with ash thrusting in at clearings. In the Forestry Commission's western part the old character has gone, and a great crop of larch nursed by beech is now perhaps ten years old. There being nothing much to see, I read the Forestry Commission bylaws: you can take a pushchair provided there is an infant in it, but no other vehicle.

Birch, ash, oak, and sallow are springing at the margins; depressed wood spurge and wan-flowered primroses remain under some Douglas firs – not for long. But, as I waited for a shower or two to pass, the place began to grow on me: it is silent, high, lonely and, after all, full of trees. Watching the clouds and their shadows form a wooden 'high seat', I decided it was beautiful.

Harewood Forest *404 441*, ♀ (✦), *1900 acres, about 1 hour or all day, many easy paths and rides, pf*

Secretive and from outside plain-looking, with no special parking places and no notices, welcoming or otherwise, Harewood lies on its hill above the Test, breathing gently like a dragon unslain. His old fangs are mossy oaks and birches with double and treble stems; his rotting molars ancient stubs of oak – acres of them. Clouds of real, not imaginary smoke emerge from his belly, for charcoal is made here. The burners are cauldron-shaped with pipes at odd angles, set amongst the sessile oak standards in a space the size of a football ground. Already the ground cleared last year is planted with new oaks. There are large stands of larch fenced from the deer, which are many. I did not see any hares, and birds other than pheasants and woodpigeons seemed to be absent. The map reference gives a parking place on the A303(T), a noisome and noisy spot. Cleared underwood and probably, still, charcoal burning, are towards Cow Down at the west side. There are several points of entry.

The New Forest ♀ ✦ ☙, *105 sq miles, FC*

Nearly half of these 67,082 acres, administered by the Forestry Commission, is woodland, with one-third of this unenclosed, 'natural' woodland, often the remains of old inclosures. The rest is open heath, bog and grassland with scattered trees and small woods. The National Forest Park is 40 square miles larger than the forest, and includes some, though not all, of a series of contiguous commons totalling 6299 acres to the north and west, and some farmland towards the coast at the south. Some of the commons belong to the National Trust, and join imperceptibly to the forest heaths, beasts being allowed to wander indiscriminately. In fact the forest itself is a large common, or a mosaic of common land with the inclosures for timber belonging to the Crown. Within the forest are large areas of private land, as well as towns, villages, roads, farms, riding schools and many hotels. The Forestry Commission maintains 130 parking grounds, most with picnic places, and several camping grounds. Of 129 wooded 'inclosures', thirty are ancient woods now unenclosed.

The Forestry Commission has to work alongside the Court of Verderers (which looks

after the needs of the commoners who graze 5000 animals in the forest) and its duty is to conserve the 'Ancient and Ornamental' woodlands, to keep the balance between conifer and broadleaf with a minimum of disturbance to the latter, and to maintain the two Ornamental Drives of exotic trees. The Nature Conservancy is consulted, and drainage of bogs is allowed only where it is necessary to preserve the woodlands. The commoners' horses and cattle conserve the heathland naturally apart from some 'rehabilitation' (burning). Where new trees do spring up they remain unenclosed.

The Hampshire Basin, facing south and for many centuries of the post-glacial period connected by land to the continent of Europe, was a sort of natural tree nursery in prehistoric time. Species now native to Scotland here survived the last of the Ice Ages, and as the ice retreated northwards, but before the sea rose to form the English Channel, oaks, elms, beeches and limes took root here as the European forest spread back to the British peninsula.

Near the middle of the Basin a segment of impermeable rock covered by sand, gravel and clay forms a series of plateaux intersected by shallow stream valleys. Because of the hard rock below, the lower ground, and some of the higher, is ill-drained, and heath turns to bog. But, partly because of the benign climate, native trees regenerate freely, particularly the Scots pine. Before it was called a New Forest (in 1079 by William I) it was partly the waste of 45 manors named in Domesday, partly the property of the Saxon Kings, and partly common land since time immemorial. In fact ever since the Bronze Age when Jutish settlers on the coast and rivers grazed their animals on the heath, it can have changed comparatively little.

Before Neolithic times it was woodland of oak, beech, pine and perhaps lime. The first farmers cleared or killed the trees, grew crops for a few years, built burial mounds, then left the infertile soil once the woodland humus was exhausted. The land became heathy and the animals kept it so. It has miraculously survived for 1500 years, the largest area of unenclosed land in England.

Canada Common, National Trust, *287 172*, adjoins Furzley and Cadnam at the north of the forest. Beyond the heath are trees on every horizon, while houses, beasts – and people collecting wood or just walking – give a domestic atmosphere.

The miracle has occurred because of the subtle balance between the rights of the commoners and the demands of the Crown, at first for the products of the chase, later for timber. Inclosures for whatever purpose could only be made provided sufficient land was left free for pasture and for a variety of other rights including commons of mast (pigs to eat nuts and acorns for 60 days), turbary ($\frac{1}{3}$ of turf cut for domestic fuel), estovers, or fuel wood, also domestic only, and marl, from twenty-three pits, for manure. Only the right of pasture is now largely used.

While this beautiful balance of opposing demands has kept the forest intact, both demands have of course modified the

Little Witch and Great Witch, small hills near Hasley Inclosure. Pine regenerates easily over heathland remote from traffic and only lightly grazed. Footpath eastwards from ford at Ogdens, *182 124*, over Latchmore Brook— blackthorn and bog myrtle.

OPPOSITE: ageing beech in Tantany Wood, home of Sika deer, where oaks, beeches and thorns flourish and die untouched. Westwards, interrupted only by the railway, is the largest area of continuous woodland in the forest. Park at Culverley, *367 047*, among pines.

vegetation very considerably. Deer and ponies, cattle and donkeys, all will eat hazel before they bother with gorse, while the Navy, from the seventeenth century to the nineteenth, demanded open-grown pedunculate oaks with copiously spreading branches to provide the crucks and knees for the ribs of ships. This is often pointed out, but did they not also need planks from straight-grown trees? Scots pines were first planted in 1776, at Ocknell Clump, and have since become the dominant tree of the forest, that is if you disregard gorse as being a bush.

The New Forest Act of 1870 largely perpetuated the nature, shape and picturesque character of the area. From the point of view of natural history its main interest is in its bogs, in its long-untended woodland, and in its relative size, which enables the survival of true heathland habitat.

But many new threats have occurred in the last hundred years: some, like a couple of

airfields, have been absorbed, even turned to recreational use. Only forty years ago there was much argument over whether the main roads should be fenced, thus destroying the continuity of heaths and woods. Now the forest is neatly sliced in three by the A31(T) and A35, and further fragmented by the A337 running north to south. The skyline is everywhere sawn and pierced by the outline of alien conifers – and by shining industrial smoke stacks to the east. The fame of the forest, its ponies and its posh pubs, brings 7 million visitors a year, who deposit 2000 tons of litter, not all of it successfully removed by the patient foresters. Tons of yellow gravel are deposited to make car parks and forest roads. A thick ring of new houses surrounds the perimeter. Planes and helicopters cross the northern half every few minutes. In spite of all this the forest remains at peace, enwrapped in its own unique atmosphere.

The forest is divided into 'walks', old

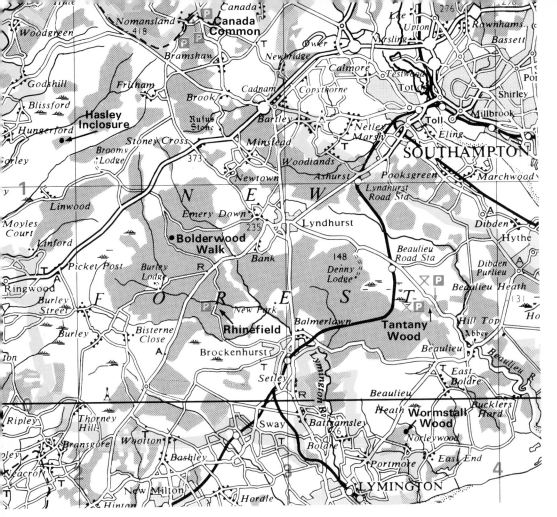

administrative areas like parishes in a town, and these fifteen regions make a good basis for exploring the forest; they are used in the official guidebook. With 129 large woods to choose from I cannot be any sort of guide. Trying to be systematic, I have investigated the six or so different types of countryside in the forest. In such a forest park I think one must regard all the different types of country as potentially interesting – perhaps potentially woodland.

The official guide, *Explore the New Forest*, is excellent, with detailed walkers' maps, interesting articles illustrated in colour, useful addresses, book list, etc. HMSO.

Major Forestry Commission walks with leaflets are Bolderwood Walk, Ornamental Drive (Rhinefield), Oberwater Walk. The Rhinefield Ornamental Drive leaflet is essential.

Ringwood Forest, to the west of the New Forest, is heavily coniferized and not generally open to walkers. It provides a pleasant drive. In the larger context of the Forestry Commission's Ringwood Forest are picnic places, with walks, at **Broom Hill**, *050 035*, (turn south from the Three Legged Cross to Holt road), and, close to Bournemouth – $\frac{1}{2}$ mile east of Hurn – the Rams Down car park by the Avon. Near Ringwood itself, 2 miles south-west, is the **Avon Forest Country Park**, with heath and pines, run by the Dorset County Council.

Osborne *around 525 952,* ♀ ♣, *1m, muddy, Crown property*
The woods begin only a mile from the East Cowes Ferry, or you can start the walk from the Swiss Cottage in the grounds of Osborne House. Parking is available here between April and September. Queen Victoria's Swiss Cottage was designed to have a view of the sea, and the view is still there between the trees. A dark green gate to your right leads to a fairy-tale woodland by the shore. Turn left downhill for *Cupressus macrocarpa* and *Pinus radiata*, the latter truly magnificent and threatening to burst a circular iron seat built long ago round its base. There are also some very old and characterful oaks which, though less in stature than the largest of the *macrocarpa*, must date back to before 1844, when Albert designed the great house for his Queen. In fact there are many suggestions of old woodland amongst the exotic trees: durmast oak, wood sage beneath the redwoods, butcher's broom under the *Ilex* on the shore; and primroses in the mud of the paths. In spite of the great size and vigour of the pines, evergreen oaks and cypresses, it is the redwoods which give these woods their

strange atmosphere. They are quite naturalized and, over bright green moss, form a true wilderness, with the rotting trunks of other trees including many silver birches. The coast redwood, *Sequoia sempervirens*, the only species of the genus remaining from the family Taxodiacea, formed a worldwide forest in the Cretaceous: fossils of the trees a hundred million years old are found in the rocks of the Isle of Wight, as they are in the American Yellowstone.

Brighstone Forest *419 846,* ♀ ♣, *at least 2 walks of up to 4m total, rough in places, NT, FC*
Following part of the Tennyson Trail along the ridge eastwards from the car park takes you uphill for $\frac{3}{4}$ mile along the edge of the forest, then, on the level, follow the signposted Worsley Trail for a few yards past a covered reservoir, where turkey oaks and Monterey pines are planted. Then turn into the forest by the bridleway. Downhill and bearing right you will soon see a wooden gate which leads to a hedge along the forest margin. The hedge is worth seeing: oak, hazel and hawthorn weirdly

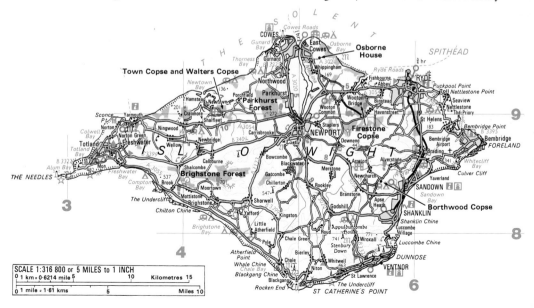

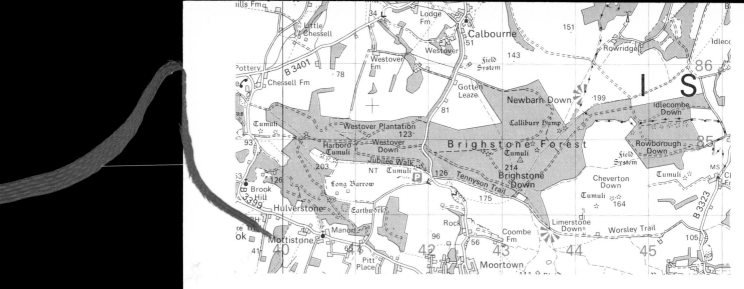

shaped and intermingled. The true nature of the forest reveals itself – not regimented pines but a loose mixture of beech and hemlock with many ferns. The walk may be any length: strike up through the trees to find a forest road and you can be sure that it will lead you back to base.

Brighstone Down is part of the chalk outcrop which divides the island east to west, though cut by the Medina River. The southern part contains the multifarious strata for which the Isle of Wight is famous; the northern part is clay, uninteresting for geologists but fine for oaks.

Newtown: Town Copse and Walters Copse *424 905*, ♀ ♠, *100 acres, easy paths, NT*
Fortunately some oakwood is preserved, and in the context of a beautiful, unspoilt corner of countryside at Newtown. The woods continue to the edge of the marshes – which are also a nature reserve. Coppices are little more than thickets, but perhaps there are plans for regular coppicing.

Parkhurst Forest *480 900*, ♀ ♠, *easy waymarked walks, 3½m or less, FC*
I was expecting gloomy ranks of conifers surrounding the prison walls, but the place is cheerful enough, and well patronized. Some oakwood survives from planting after the Napoleonic Wars; the rest is fairly young coniferous plantation in the familiar Forestry Commission pattern with good gravelled roadways and a decent picnic place. Parkhurst

is the largest wooded area in the island and is on the site of an old forest or chase.

There is another Forestry Commission picnic place in a beechwood at **Firestone Copse**, *559 911*, 2 miles west of Ryde, with a waymarked walk of 1½ miles including the Blackbridge Brook and two shorter walks. A National Trust wood of 57 acres near Sandown is **Borthwood Copse**, *573 846*.

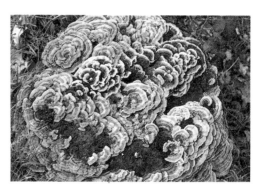

Richly embroidered stump of oak, Newtown

Avon, Mendips and Westonbirt

Landranger sheets 172, 173, 182

Leigh Woods *553 740 and 564 731,* ♀ ♣,
600 acres, various paths, FC, NT, NNR
The first map reference is for the Forestry
Commission's car park, reached by turning off
the A369, which runs roughly parallel to the
Avon Gorge. The second identifies the west
bank of the gorge at the Clifton Suspension
Bridge. From Bristol city centre simply make
for Clifton, cross the bridge on foot and turn
right, and you are on the Avon Walkway in the
National Trust-nature reserve part of the
woods. This is much the better part, with older
trees than at the Forestry Commission's
Stokeleigh Forest, to the west and north.

The Avon woods are of oak, ash, beech and
yew, and also contain small-leaved lime. Three
very rare whitebeams grow on the cliffs of the
Gorge, two of them found nowhere else,
Sorbus bristoliensis and *S. wilmottiana*, while
the third, *S. anglica,* is more or less local to the
River Avon and the Mendips.

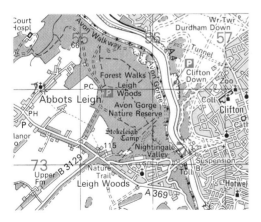

Brockley Wood *484 664,* ♀ ♣, *nature trail,*
1m plus return, pf
Turn off the Bristol to Weston-super-Mare
road (A370) on to the minor road up Brockley
Combe (signposted Bristol Airport). The
nature trail is just a nice walk, marked with
posts carrying the initials NT, from a car park
near the top of the Combe. Yews among tall
oaks and beeches give an air of poetry and

mystery in spite of the rather rubbishy roadside and the spruces crowded beyond the fence.

Another footpath, from Cleeve, a mile
south-west, traverses Goblin Combe. Turning
right in Congresbury, which is another mile
down towards Weston, brings you to a small
road marked 'No right turn onto A370'. At this
junction is a driveway marked as a footpath to
Cadbury Hill (National Trust, 39½ acres
including the Iron Age hill fort, *442 650*).

Clevedon

For a look at the Levels, the wind-curved
thorns and willows (some attractively
pollarded) continue on the road past Cadbury
to Yatton and turn right after the railway
bridge; continue thus over Kenn Moor to
Clevedon Court (a National Trust manor
house, with a chapel and terraced gardens,
closed in winter) which has a magnificent plane
tree and backs on to wooded hills familiar to
travellers on the M5. These woods, described
on the map as **The Warren,** *421 717,* are of
very secondary character, but there are
bridleways up the north slope.

Rowberrow Woods *456 575 (Shipham),*
♣, *650 acres, fp only, FC*
The well-marked lines of the hill fort remind
us once again of the ancient history of the hills.
Just the place for a few Austrian pines, thought
the Forestry Commission. You can walk
through, but must stick to public rights-of-
way; also, there is nowhere to park. You have
to stop in School Lane, Shipham, and walk
down to Rowberrow Bottom. Here you can
join the Mendip Way going east.

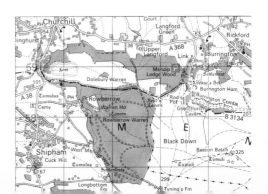

Burrington Combe *476 587*, ♀ *(and yew)*, *fps*

The Combe is wooded, with almost pure ash/hazel on one side and quite large yews clinging to the rock slope on the other. There are several access points, all of which soon bring you out onto the Downs – but this is a better place than Cheddar Gorge for walkers interested in trees.

Cheddar Gorge *482 545*, ♀, *318 acres, NT and nature trail, limited access, CNT*

The incredible commercialization of the caves stops suddenly, and wondering admiration takes over: one's driving becomes inaccurate. The National Trust part is around Black Rock, reached by a green gate where the road straightens out. On the dark, wet, December day of my visit I couldn't see very much, but the impression of golden ash trunks and black triangles of yews among the amazing rocks is distinct: a simple but satisfying pattern. It is also satisfying to realize that one of the more remarkable and famous parts of England can be preserved unspoilt.

The best preserved ashwood in the Mendips is at **Rodney Stoke**, a nature reserve, *490 503*.

Weston Woods *310 to 332 626*, ♀, *open woodland*

With all its charms Weston-super-Mare has also a fine wood. Beech is common, though not, I think, native, amongst oak and chestnut, with yew, and the wood is nearly as original looking as those in the Mendips, the sea and sands below adding quietly to its charm. The bramble layer is almost absent, and you can enter anywhere along the mile or so of toll road which begins near the Victoria Pier.

Colerne Park and Monks Wood

837 727, ♀, *111 acres, fp, WT*
Access is from the village of Thickwood, west of the woodlands. This is an important tract of oak and ash (wych elm now dead) in an area not notable for woods. As with many Woodland Trust properties, there is much work to be done.

Blackmore Copse, *928 648*, is a nature reserve of Wiltshire County Naturalists' Trust.

Westonbirt Arboretum *849 897*, ♀ ♣, *160 acres (plus 'reserve' ground)*, *FC*

In Gloucestershire, but almost in Wiltshire, on the A433, 3 miles south-west of Tetbury, is the most comprehensive tree collection in Britain with 5000 species of trees and shrubs. Since 1956 the Forestry Commission has been in charge, but planting has continued systematically since 1829. A Centre caters for every reasonable need, rather seasonally. The grounds are open every day until sunset, dogs are allowed, riding is by arrangement. Parking is costly, but you can walk in for nothing. The bus, Cirencester to Bristol, stops at the gate.

Westonbirt is comprehensive and it is difficult to pick out any single item of interest – you are almost certainly going to be seduced by some exotic beauty on the way to see it. The task of getting to know it all is formidable but richly rewarding. Planted, planned and maintained with loving care over a century and a half, this arboretum is a great deal more than a collection of trees. Trees and shrubs from many scattered and varied habitats combine

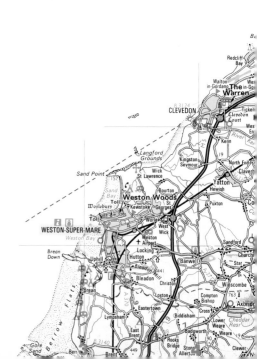

together to give a unified effect of grandeur yet with many small glades and islands of intimate quality. Nowhere is one conscious of the skills and efforts that have been applied. Each tree, whether it is the giant Nikko fir (north of Loop Walk) or the tiny white-berried *Sorbus discolor* (Whitmoor Bottom, south-east) looks happy.

On balance, for a woodland walk, I would recommend the Silk Wood path; it is worth it just for the sudden revelation of the Brewer's spruce, foliage spread like a majestic stage curtain, or for the poetic style of a Japanese larch in a clearing (Concord Glade). Corsican pines here look quite different from their commercial forestry brothers. There are plenty of larger shrubs: at the parking place, and on the Circular Drive.

Bowood, Calne *970 703*, ♀ ♠, *82 acres, woodland and woodland walks, pf*

This is a mature collection of fine trees, nicely spaced on assiduously mown lawns and no obtrusive shrubbery: you won't need your wellingtons here. Bowood does not quite fit our

BELOW: a Brewer's spruce, Westonbirt

conditions of availability (not open on Mondays, then only afternoons from April to September), but it makes up for this by the extreme thoroughness and clarity of the booklet, which lists every specimen under genera with a key to its position in the grounds, and, vice versa, summarizes each section of the grounds identifying the trees. You really cannot go wrong. An ancient oriental plane and numerous interesting shrubs – including an inky purple hazel – are close to the house.

Phillips' Woodland Park 839 525, ♀ ♠, 80 acres, easy, named paths, pf

Signposted from the Westbury outskirts, this pleasant working wood also works for visitors, who pay to park or camp but may then roam at will, with tree and bird leaflets to guide them.

A feature of the wood is that the paths are named like streets and identified in a leaflet map so that children can find their own way. There is a tea-room and a museum. It is pleasant to find a private Country Park.

Savernake and the Downs

Landranger sheets 173, 174, 184

Savernake Forest *195 682*, ♀ *(♣)*,
28,000 acres, FC

Savernake (with two short 'a's) means 'Severn oak' – Severn being a common river name. The forest rises steeply from the eastern streets of Marlborough – a curiously beautiful place. There is still the atmosphere of a coaching town, and the High Street still has an unbroken line of shops with verandas over the pavement. The journey to London took three days and nights in the seventeenth century, shortened in about 1800 to one day – in the summer. In the early nineteenth century the railway was successfully resisted by the Ailesbury family, whose head is the hereditary warden and owner of the forest, by descent through the Seymours from the Esturmeys, who had it from King John. The railway was never allowed through the forest, so in the years of urban expansion Marlborough stayed small, under the protection of the forest at its side.

In King John's time it was 98 square miles, but this was not allowed in Magna Carta, and land was eventually disafforested to reduce the area to 13 square miles in the reign of Edward I. The bounds of the central bailiwick in about 1300 place the centre near Bedwyn Common. It was not a heavily wooded forest, perhaps more a productive and, usually, well-managed piece of land. For instance, warrens, let in the sixteenth century, had to pay rent of 1520 rabbits to the warden at Tottenham Lodge.

A large part of the forest was enclosed in the seventeenth century, 2200 acres being left unpaled. The forest decayed somewhat. In

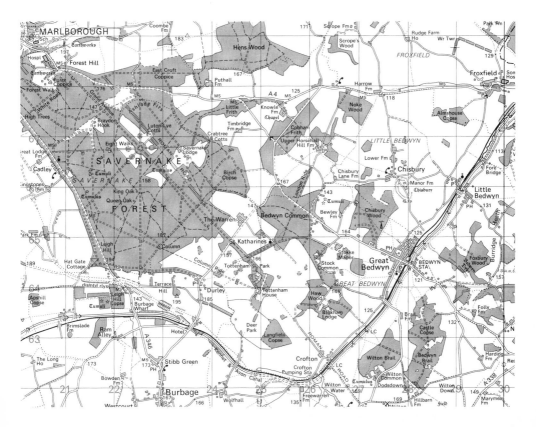

1814 the then warden, Charles Brudenell, married money and was able to join up scattered coppices in a great planting programme, using oak and chestnut and starting nurseries to stock the forest with 'oak, beech, elm and fir'. Grassy walks were planned, with advice from landscape gardeners. Brudenell's father Thomas had already established the Eight Walks in a star shape typical of early eighteenth-century landscape planning. But Charles also spent £250,000 on the house and gardens at Tottenham: it has never been out of debt since, they say.

Mighty beech trunks in Savernake Forest

Nowadays Savernake is a large, old beech plantation bearing little relation to the ancient forest, except in the many ancient pollard oaks which remain. Both the beeches and the oaks are remarkable specimens and occur in great quantity. This is a forest for today, accessible, large and extremely beautiful. For tomorrow it will be a different story. The beeches are already too old – they are amazingly tall – and the many old pollard oaks, superb in decay, are gradually succumbing, many shaded by the massive beeches, others hollow and infirm. Everywhere the progeny of these trees begins to threaten change, and the Forestry Commission, which now manages the forest, is not likely to allow a jungle to develop. The greatest trees are in the area called High Trees; among the intervening thickets of junior trees are picturesque old thorns. The King Oak and the Queen Oak, marked on Ordnance maps, are gone. There are good timber oaks in this area. The Grand Avenue is lined with enormous beeches, once very regularly, now beautifully grouped in fantastic perspectives. You can drive down this and other avenues.

Collingbourne Forest: Stert Copse
272 515, ♀ copse, 50 acres, easy, fp, pf
Not many people in Ludgershall are interested in woods it seems, but they have a beauty on their doorstep. Not quite on the doorstep: turn down Central Street, east out of the town's tiny middle, for Crawlboys Farm. Ten minutes' struggle in the mud of the bridleway brings you to a corner of the forest, an old wood-bank with weirdly contorted hornbeams. The forest

Primroses in Collingbourne Forest

interior here is dull. Continue by the footpath across the field to the gate in the fence of the copse. Here among hazel coppice with oak standards are arrayed in profusion the spring flowers which we look for in English woodland, anemones, primroses and bluebells all together, with strongly formed wood spurge as well. The hazel wands are shiny, the oaks mossy, lichenous and blurred: blackthorn and sallow at the edges.

Botley Down Wood *298 600, ♀, 50 acres, 1 hour, easy, fps*
This lovely little wood looks over downland and, beyond the Wilton windmill, to Savernake Forest. Paths and trackways pass on two sides. At its south corner hazel coppice with oaks gives way to scrub and grass; at the west is a beechwood over ancient mounds and a long barrow. These are protected by a bank with more beech, contorted by wind and use and in extreme contrast with their tall brothers in the forest below.

Catmore Wood *458 804, ♀, 50 acres, easy fps, pf*
This is a fine and lonely place, up in the sky, the wind blowing through dry grasses and a long line of conifers only adding to its mystery. Take the ride between the oaks and the evergreens, then turn into the wood for a classic hazel coppice with oak standards, bluebells all over the ground. It is picturesque and still looks practical, but it is not without its sinister side – mind you don't step into a trap.

Great Park Wood *345 756, ♀ (♣), easy or very rough, fps*
Turn south out of Eastbury for Woodlands St Mary, or turn there north-east from the pleasant B4000, and you will find yourself at what seems the silent centre of our Emerald Isle. In fact the smooth fields are remarkably emerald and weedless, thanks to assiduous spraying with chemicals. Conversely the wood is neglected, a trackless overgrown wilderness, once a thriving hazel coppice with ash standards, some oak, some beech. Drifts and heaps of *Clematis* cover the margins, which are full of elderberries.

The wood divides into north-west and south-east halves; access to the latter is easier. Each half contains a bracken glade with oaks on a little plateau of less limy soil. There are bluebells and primroses and there would be much more if only this old wood could be taken in hand. The spruces marked on the map make a small, well-grown stand and are ready for felling.

Newbury Southwards

Over the flat riverside meadows Greenham Common looms dark: again heath vegetation begins, then stops short at a great fence. Fences are illegal on common land, but most of this common was taken over under emergency powers during the last war, as were many others for airfields, now returned to public use. 'Some hundreds of acres' – I quote Newbury District Council – remain as common land. Everyone knows the rest of the story.

Beyond some curiously symbolic burnt gorse and clean new grass stretches **Sydmonton Common** to the south-west. You could walk across it and into the Forestry Commission's plantation, or drive round it to join a road, unnumbered and without fame, which traverses a nearly perfect landscape south towards Watership Down. The Sydmonton Court Estate has many footpaths in and out of the woodland to right or left, and, when you reach the end, a revealing corner. Here cleaned-up hedges and banks, new-planted cherries, old beech, yew and cherry left to grow, in a tidy, clean, arable environment, are in remarkable contrast to the miserable, dark, overgrown commons and woodland that we see so much of in the south. This corner, *489 593*, is worth seeing. It is not a woodland walk but it is a piece of good thinking and decisive action.

Great Pen Wood, *452 622*, is a Forestry Commission parking place and picnic spot hard to recommend, completely surrounded by suburban housing, or on the south side, the forbidding *strictly private* Highclere Park. The wood is gloomy and dank, with a lot of birch and every sort of forestry conifer except fir and Sitka all doing well, and creating a thoroughly funereal environment.

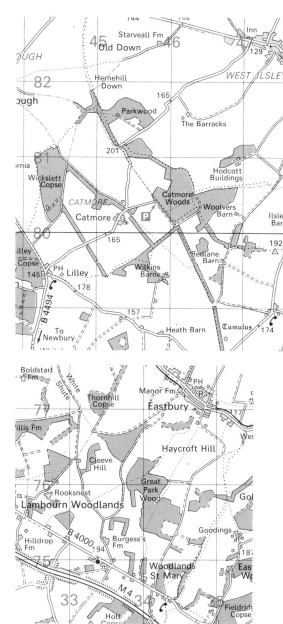

Shelsmore Common Country Park, *464 709*, is a popular stopping place with a well-laid-out picnic area including some sheltered tables. Wide birch heath gives way to oak.

The West Cotswolds and the Forest of Dean
Landranger sheets 149, 150, 162, 163

Cirencester Park: Oakley Wood

970 045, ♀(♠), 1500 acres, 3m or less, easy, muddy, pf

If you are going to walk in woodland it is nice to park in woodland and although it would be feasible to leave your car in Cirencester we suggest the parking place at the map reference. There is some hard surface for winter and wet weather, and some grass (also some rubbish, but, at least, no notices telling you how good the foresters are for preserving the wildlife).

The great beeches here are black and shiny, or clad in moss, or sometimes silver-grey as they are supposed to be. Some are patterned with islands of white lichen. The oaks are black and green on the weather or western side and a lovely pastel grey on the east: ashes likewise. All are fine timber trees and you will find one large area clear-felled. This is a working timber woodland with a healthy buzz of activity, as well as deer and plenty of birds.

Beeches in Cirencester

Western Cotswold Ridges

The beech is a native tree here and the western folds of the Cotswolds are clothed in some of the finest beech: many woods are open to walkers but the banks are steep, and also private residences tend to intervene. Villages like Edgeworth, *947 060*, are impressive, not just charming; and both these adjectives apply to many a corner of the lanes which wander in and out of the escarpments. Again if you explore by car it really is better in winter: less traffic and more to see. **Painswick**, *867 097*, has, it is said, 99 yew trees in the churchyard; actually there are more. This is almost a wood, or two woods since they make two groups, but the yews are clipped to architectural form. Painswick also has its beechwood, with a well-worn footpath climbing into pine towards the Beacon. It is a centre for many walks (set out with great thoroughness in a Gloucestershire County Council booklet, *Walking around*

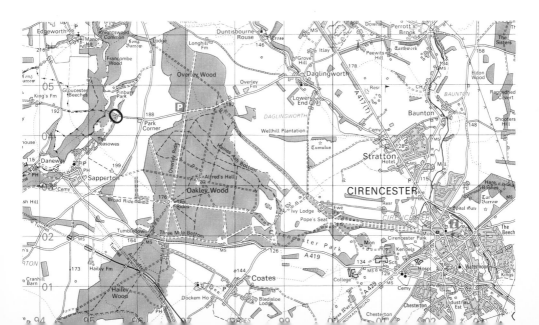

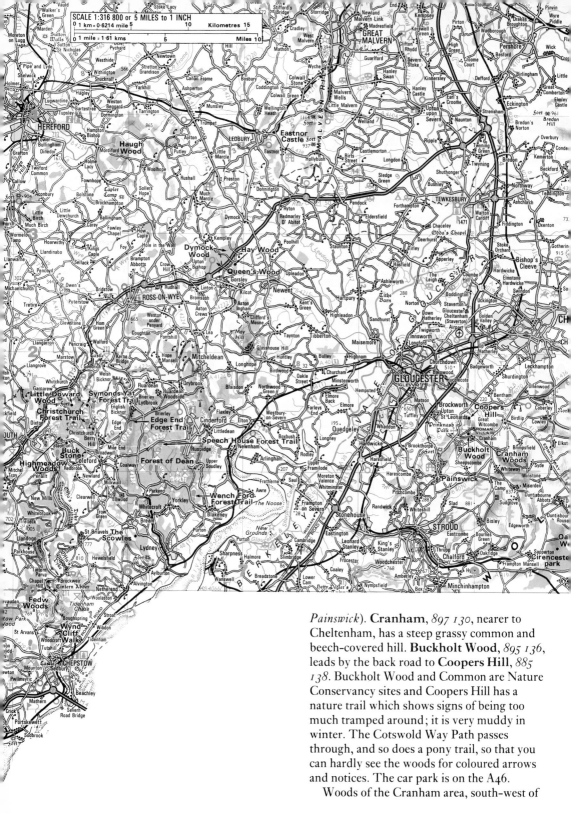

Painswick). **Cranham**, *897 130*, nearer to
Cheltenham, has a steep grassy common and
beech-covered hill. **Buckholt Wood**, *895 136*,
leads by the back road to **Coopers Hill**, *885
138*. Buckholt Wood and Common are Nature
Conservancy sites and Coopers Hill has a
nature trail which shows signs of being too
much tramped around; it is very muddy in
winter. The Cotswold Way Path passes
through, and so does a pony trail, so that you
can hardly see the woods for coloured arrows
and notices. The car park is on the A46.

Woods of the Cranham area, south-west of

Birdlip, are supposed to be the best of our beechwoods; avoid the beaten track, or go the extra mile, to get to know this intimate and intricate escarpment.

The Forest of Dean ♀ ♠, *285,000 acres, countless walks, many picnic sites, FC (National Forest Park)*
Like the New Forest, Dean was a royal forest before Domesday and remained under the Crown until taken over by the Forestry Commission in the 1920s. It is a rough, upland plateau of Old Red Sandstone bearing Carboniferous rocks which outcrop variously; limestone in the deep Wye Valley to the west.

Between the Severn and the Wye the Dean is on the road to nowhere. It is full of coal and iron and the iron has been mined since Roman times or before. With iron below and deep forests of oaks, with deer, above, it continued a mysterious and self-sufficient existence for many centuries. The people were independent and unruly, the country covered with 'irregular tracks and horrid shade so dark and dreary as to render its inhabitants more fierce and audacious in robberies' – William Camden, 1607. Most of the foresters were miners, and to this day any man born in the Forest of Dean who has worked a year and a day in a mine has the privileges of a Freeminer, entitled to dig for iron ore or coal under licence from the Crown. The King's Gaveller once took a third of the profits: now the Deputy Gaveller at Coleford still grants the 'gales', and small two-man drift mines (along the 'drift' of the rocks) are still working for coal, all the major collieries being long since closed.

Between the thirteenth and seventeenth centuries over sixty forges were at work in the forest. Coppices were maintained for charcoal for the fixed forges.

The Dean oaks were needed for the Navy and iron working was stopped for a century after 1650. The Commonwealth Government attempted to replant some 16,000 acres: '400 huts belonging to poor people were thrown down. As a result riots broke out ... fences were broken down, cattle driven into enclosures and wood set on fire' – John Rogers, 1941. This struggle between government and

people is a continuing story of the forest. Why did not the Crown take over the mines as it was often advised to do? The answer must be that 'free' is not an empty word. The miners, like commoners elsewhere in England, had rights extending back to 'Tyme out of Minde', as the miners' ancient charter puts it. They were Freeminers before there were effective kings.

The Miners' Court, where miners took the oath on a stick of holly, was eventually moved to Speech House (*620 122*, finished in 1680) where also a Verderers' Court attempted to preserve the vert and venison. The Court still meets four times a year. The forest was divided into six 'walks', each with a keeper and a lodge – one can be seen at Danby Lodge, *645 083*. Other lodges were destroyed by angry miners. Freeminers could sell their gales and 'foreigners' opened large collieries in the nineteenth century such as Trafalgar, New Fancy, Go On and Prosper, Strip and At It: by the 1920s they produced a million tons a year. Rent and royalties of the Dean mines in 1938 were £17,848. The last large pit closed in 1965. 24,000 acres are under productive forestry.

The forest is very beautiful. The bold shapes of the scenery are further broken by quarries and mine workings and the woodlands are not made any the less interesting by the many trackways, from Roman pavements to disused mineral lines, and other signs and remains of human endeavour. The Forestry Commission's conifer plantations are not allowed to intrude, usually, on a foreground of open oak forest or beechwood, where commoners' sheep graze amongst the trees. The rugged topography tends to abrupt changes in soil and vegetation, and provides constantly changing, views of tree-clad hills.

The native oak is the durmast, but sessile oaks were planted for Navy timber. Only 200 trees were estimated to remain after one Sir John Winter, with a royal grant in the seventeenth century, removed 30,333 trees.

All the waymarked Forestry Commission walks are over 2 miles.

The Scowles *606 046*, ♀ ♠, *200 yds, uneven and muddy, private but open*
There is no parking place to speak of on the

road (B4231, Bream to Lydney), but there is a large lay-by $\frac{1}{4}$ mile south-east. A lane full of blood-red puddles leads to the gloomy caves. Overgrown with beeches and shattered yews, full of ferns, the dark red rock sculptured by

The Scowles

the miners is a great open wound of the landscape, bones exposed, flesh removed. You can walk south through the beeches to recover from this – eventually to Lydney Castle.

Speech House Forest Trail *623 123*
The Court Room is now the dining room of the Speech House Hotel (obtain a trail leaflet here) and can be seen by non-diners at 'reasonable hours'. The trail (3 miles long, shorter route of $1\frac{3}{4}$ miles) includes an old inclosure, coppice chestnut, open oak country on sandstone, a reclaimed tip as a picnic place and even high-tension power cables. An arboretum with a fine shelter-belt of redwoods (not so tall as to be remote), includes many interesting and attractive firs and really lovely 'exotic' birches, with southern beech and most other specimens you would expect among 200 different species; informal in lay-out but scrappily labelled.

Wench Ford Forest Trail *655 080*
Short trail (3 miles) in mature oakwood,

schools trail (3 miles) with mine workings, Forest Lodge of Charles II's time, geology notes in leaflets, 'grand old yew', railway sidings grown over and enormous pipe for stream made of old boilers. Longer trail (4 miles) is described as energetic with views.

Blackpool Bridge, $\frac{1}{3}$ mile north of the picnic site, is a former railway bridge over a minor road to Cinderford beside which, a few yards along, can be seen a section of an ancient paved roadway, the Dean Road, possibly Roman.

Edge End Forest Trail *597 142*
The large picnic site is set back from the main road, A4136, but unfortunately you have to cross the road to the trail. The leaflet, good on topography of views, is informative on trees and birds, and notes a mine is only 200 yards from the picnic site and well worth looking at. Trail $3\frac{1}{4}$ miles, or 2 miles.

There are trails also at **New Fancy** viewpoint, *628 096* (parking for coaches), **Abbotswood**, *658 109*, and **The Wilderness**, *659 169*. This last has three loops and is largely concerned with non-woodland features, hot on geology and herbs: it even includes massive waterworks, more pylons, and boggy ground 'once the home of sundew'.

Symonds Yat Forest Trail *565 160*
Everyone wants to see the rock and there is a charge for the coach and car park. Leaflet from a superb log cabin. Viewpoint over the Wye. Durmast oaks of all ages.

Buck Stone *542 122*
The Buck Stone is at 915 feet with distant views of the Black Mountains. It can be reached by a short walk from the end of a lane out of Staunton. From the post office turn right then left and fork right on to a dirt road leading west. After the gate walk 500 yards then turn left through the older, open woodland to the rock.

LITERATURE
Baty, F. W. (1952) *Forest of Dean*, Hale, London
Edlin, H.L. (ed) (1963) *Dean Forest and Wye Valley Forest Park Guide*, HMSO, London
And many others: put in a 'subject request'.

From the Forest Bookshop, Coleford:
Jones (1981) *Walks in the Wye Valley and the Forest of Dean*, published by the author.
Marfell, A. (1981) *Forest Miner*, published by the Forest Bookshop.
From the FC Office:
Leaflets for Forest Trails.
Visitors' Guide and map: refers more to the Wye Valley, lists addresses etc and summarizes the Forestry Commission trails.
Ramblers' Association leaflets: *Forest of Dean* and *Highmeadow Woods*.
An Ordnance Survey Outdoor Leisure Map (1:25,000) of the Wye Valley and the Forest of Dean is published in addition to the normal Landranger series.

Highmeadow Woods seems to be the name used for several woods in a separate but joined western area of the Forest Park which was not administered by the Crown until 1817. The area includes Symonds Yat Rock and a great bight of the Wye in an 'incised' meander begun 600 feet higher than today. **The Christchurch Forest Trail**, *567 127*, $3\frac{1}{2}$ miles, is described by the Forestry Commission as exceptionally interesting and varied.

Little Doward Wood *547 157*, ♣,
1m (seems like 3), rough, steep, dangerous in places, partly outside Forest Park
The rough-and-ready parking place indicated by the map reference is reached from Great Doward or the hotel at Little Doward and is close to King Arthur's Cave, and Lord's Wood and Doward Woods which are known for wild flowers. Some of the contents of this and other caves include extinct mammal bones, now in Monmouth Museum. Going downhill from the cave (to the right off the Biblins forest road), you can turn off right at a great beech root, full of lumps of native limestone, and pick your way by a little-used path through an ash and chestnut coppice up into beechwood. Soon you reach a massive limestone wall, which you may as well climb over where you can. Continue steeply upwards by the great, grey trunks of beeches, past their prime, and by bushes of spurge laurel to the limestone ledge above the Wye. Here grows a small-leaved subspecies of

Rocks and whitebeam at Little Doward

the whitebeam *Sorbus latifolia*.

An easier way to get here might be from the Doward Hotel, but you might miss, in spring, dog violets, wood sorrel, celandine, cowslips, spurge laurel, wood sage, stinking hellebore and green hellebore.

Tintern, the Cistercian Abbey, is generally agreed to be best seen from between trees, being a little gaunt close to. The Forestry Commission has it between redwoods, which does not sound appropriate even if the first trans-Atlantic cable *was* made at Tintern.

The road is lovely but obviously can be extremely congested in the summer time. The several walks from Tintern are easy to find. Another, the **Wynd Cliff and 365 Steps Walk**, starts from a small Forestry Commission car park, *524 973,* a waymarked nature trail somewhat confused with part of the Gwent County Council Wye Valley Walk.

Fedw Woods *505 985,* ♀ ♣, *easy but rocky and ankle-twisting away from the forest road, FC*
The picnic site is high with glimpses of the Monmouth hills but sheltered by conifers and with a nicely crafted children's play area. There are nice big Douglas firs, areas of larch with small oaks, gorse and mossy limestone.

Dymock Wood *677 285,* ♀ ♣, *about 1150 acres, 2 walks, easy, FC*
For wild daffodils, oaks, larches, beeches, ferns – especially daffodils – turn off the M50 at junction 3. Choose your wood up-wind for less noise. **Hay Wood**, east of the road, is more charming, but nearer the road. **Queen's Wood**, to the west, is of maturing oak with yews under, the trail leading to Douglas firs and to wetland by a stream. It is an old forest but bears little sign of it.

Haugh Wood *593 365,* ♀ ♣, *1000 acres plus, 2 walks, 1m and 2m, easy, NT, FC*
A silent hill with an old wood, once belonging to Hereford Cathedral, now partly coniferized. A good parking and picnic place, this is Hereford's local wood (take the B4224 east from Hereford, then the second left turning in Mordiford) and there are many footpaths and bridleways.

At **Eastnor Castle,** *735 369,* near Ledbury, is an arboretum, open seasonally, where Atlas cedars date from 1847. North from here the Malvern Hills are a 40-square-mile Area of Outstanding Natural Beauty.

The Cotswolds
and West of Oxford Landranger sheets 151, 163, 164

Withington Woods *037 142, rough, 1m or 4m, pf*

The road out of Withington village to Chedworth climbs through the woods, and there are several stopping places. To the left, you plunge at once into the deepening shade of mature larch and spruce, strangely alternating with old oak stubs, many of which have been successfully 'promoted' to produce single stems. With many others, something has gone wrong, and they are dead. You will soon, if you go quietly, see why. There are more deer than oaks. The wood is on uneven ground and includes ancient earthworks.

The taller woods east of the road are cut by a smaller, little-used road which is probably the boundary of the private Chedworth Woods which surround the Roman villa of Chedworth or Yanworth.

Guiting Wood *083 258, 450 acres, 1½m easy then 1½m rough, pf*

Woods generally are scarce in the Cotswolds, away from the western ramparts; the land was of course mostly used for wool-producing sheep, the profits, or some of them, invested in richly appointed late mediaeval churches like Chipping Campden, Northleach and Burford. Woods remain only near grand houses and tend to be Victorian plantations even when they look wild. Trees there are in plenty, but mostly in the form of shelter-belts, darkly emphasizing and punctuating the wide curves of the hills. Steeper slopes often retain patches of scrub, worth exploring, and there are deep

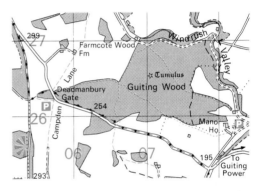

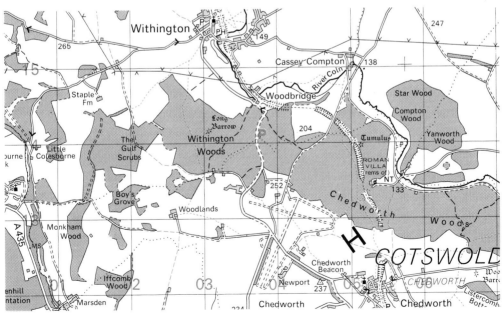

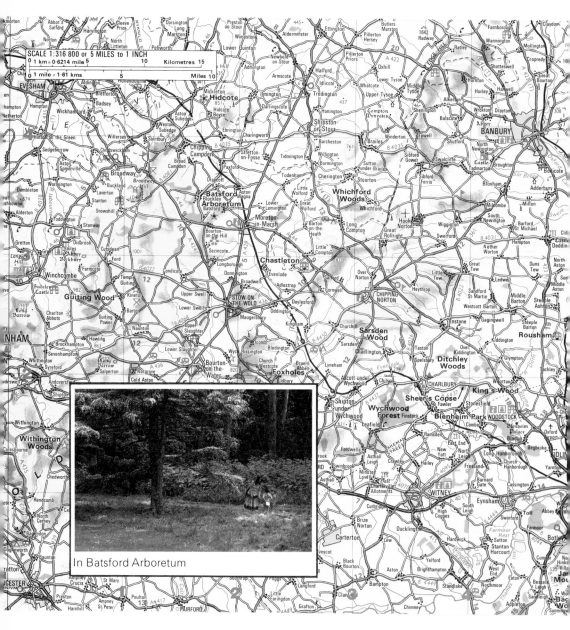

In Batsford Arboretum

valleys here and there containing tall beeches.

Guiting Power and Temple Guiting, by the infant Windrush, are richly wooded.

Near Guiting Power, a parking place, *083 258*, is specially provided for walkers. From here you can continue on foot, through a gate, on to a metalled road in the valley bottom, and through the wood – about $1\frac{1}{2}$ miles. It is a great mixture, with tall larches, poplars and spruces amongst lesser-statured natives including ash, oak, beech and wych elm. The road emerges nowhere in particular, leaving you the choice of returning the way you came, or striking off into the woods.

Beyond the ancient Port Meadow in north Oxford is the tree-covered hill of **Wytham**, an oakwood. It is not available to the ordinary walker because it is a University mouse-catching, owl-observing and caterpillar-counting preserve. Here a great tit, making 700 visits a day to its nest-box, was persuaded to take 700 self-portraits with 700 different tit-bits in its beak – by T. Royama in 1966. Winter moths, whose larvae descend from the oak branches on threads to pupate below, were studied by spreading sheets beneath the trees. Obviously such experiments are not compatible with woodland walkers. However, a footpath from Wytham to Farmoor skirts the woodlands.

Bagley Wood, *507 022,* quite large, and just south-west of Oxford, is also University property. It is dedicated to commercial forestry and casual visitors are excluded. You *can* walk in the woods, if you first apply to the Bursar of St John's College for a permit. The forestry here is all of the first class, and varied too.

Jarn Mound *486 024,* ♀, *a few acres, very easy, private trust*
By the north side of Bagley Wood, at Old Boars Hill, is a bit of 'access countryside' belonging to the Oxford Preservation Trust. Jarn Mound is only the centrepiece, which consists of a spinney, Jarn Heath, a glade of cherry trees and some meadows: all very easy walking (except for the Mound), very domesticated, yet charming – and very close to the far-from-peaceful environs of the Dreaming Spires. In fact, Jarn Mound is one of the few places where you can view the said spires without also viewing half-a-dozen large electricity pylons. 'Arthur John Evans, died 1941, created this viewpoint. . . .' We are grateful. (Sir Arthur also discovered Ancient Crete.)

At one corner is a gate into a meadow, which, a notice informs us, was the 'principal foreground' of the poet Matthew Arnold's vision, in *Thyrsus* and *The Scholar Gypsy*. It is not every field you can say that sort of thing about. The venerable cherry trees form a 'wild garden' through which the very young and the very old can potter, safely.

Blenheim Park *442 168, easy, various walks, pf*
Blenheim Park is at Woodstock, on the A34, 8 miles north-west of Oxford. The famous large park (Winston Churchill is buried at Bladon, the village on its southern border) is an attractive place to walk, but expensive to park a car within, naturally. You can park easily in Bladon, or fairly easily in Woodstock's High Street, and walk in for a few pence.

This is parkland, not woodland, but there are ageing Capability Brown beech clumps and clusters of cedars of quite unusual size and naturalness of disposition. The 'most remarkable' cedar of Lebanon in Britain, according to Mitchell, who literally knows them all, is here. It is slightly bigger than a known original at Childrey Rectory, near Wantage. This mighty Blenheim cedar is near the cascade. There is a fine group west of the Grand bridge – you can't miss the bridge – and a scattered stand of blue Atlantic cedars on the east bank of the lake, towards the Woodstock Gate. Beeches are best seen in the hilly, Old Woodstock corner of the park. Some old oaks survive from the former royal Woodstock Park, it is said, but I have only seen ancient elms, now prostrate or removed.

Ditchley Woods *397 214, easy, marginal fp and road, pf*
Still no real woodland for Oxford escapers. But beyond Woodstock is Ditchley Park: turn south-west off the A34 at Kiddington. The park is not open to the public and it is heavily coniferized. However, the house is only used for conferences, and the foresters are not much in evidence at the present growing stage. You can park at the point marked on the map, walk to the gate down an avenue of cherries, and then turn left under trees along the perimeter wall. You then reach a single-track unfenced road which follows the eastern boundary of the park woods; if you then go through the gates of Lodge Farm and out to the Woodstock-Charlbury road, you are amongst woodland.

The rides of Ditchley Park's larches, cautiously explored, will reveal a pair of quite enormous wild cherries, no doubt the parents of several groups hereabouts, and at least four

wild service trees. The foresters are to be praised for preserving the trees.

Wychwood Forest is claimed locally to have stretched from Burford to the so-called Oxford Heights east of the city. Domesday Book had it at about 80,000 acres. There are remains of many Roman settlements in the area, villas usually occupying 1000 acres, which with their associated native settlements would suggest that much of the forest was cleared of trees

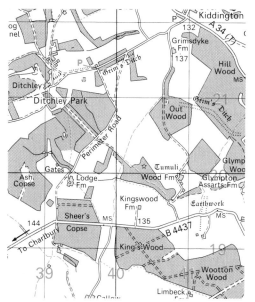

early in its history. By Queen Elizabeth's time Wychwood was a mere 3000 acres somewhere between Woodstock and Burford. Charles I tried to extend it, imposing heavy fines for transgressions of forest law. Throughout the eighteenth century the Oxford gaol held usually three or four Wychwood poachers. There were rights of common only for grazing horses and sheep, and you could be fined for picking up dead wood. An Inclosure Act of 1857 finally destroyed the forest, and the name is now attached to about 1250 acres at Cornbury Park, a hunting lodge of kings past.

This woodland is private so that we cannot recommend a walk; still, the road does run through. Residents of Leafield, to the south-west, are allowed to collect firewood on Tuesday afternoons. Researchers can get a permit from the Nature Conservancy. Dotted with old horse-chestnuts and with a dead patch of invading elms, it is not particularly inspiring woodland, even where not coniferized, but there are oddments like a large maple to remind you of the real thing. There is much to be observed in the hedges.

Foxholes *258 208, uneven, CNT*
Wychwood proper is said to survive in a patch of wet birchwood and tangled oak near Bruern Abbey. The wood is partly a nature reserve of the BBONT (Berks, Bucks and Oxon Naturalists' Trust), which has a small parking

place at Foxholes Farm. The map shows the odd shape of the wood at this point, but the outline of the southern part is altered by new plantations. Though small as a representation of the great Wychwood Forest, this wood is old, and its varied character carefully preserved. For a longer walk you can strike off to the south-east on a choice of two bridleways.

Sarsden. Start at the gate, *302 232*, and walk south-west down a newly planted shallow valley, then by the left bank of an ornamental

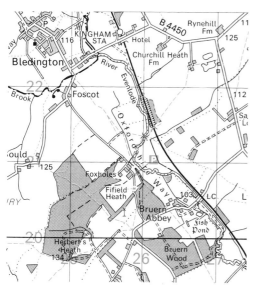

Ashes and other trees on the ramparts of an Iron Age fort at Chastleton, in the Cotswolds.

lake. This is a park plantation, with rhododendron and bamboo: nothing special, but nice on a hot day. Keep to the path. Return by road past a tumulus planted with beech.

Whichford Woods. Beyond Long Compton another overgrown plantation occupies an untillable hollow, *295 343*. A bridleway in the bottom and a footpath around the southern perimeter suggest a possible round route – which may be impeded as felling and replanting (with, you guessed, spruce) are in progress. Native trees are oak, ash and beech; old turkey oak and sweet chestnut, planted.

A much less wooded walk, at **Chastleton**, begins at *264 280*, opposite the by-road to Cornwell on the A436. Ash is the native dominant here.

You may then be diverted by a sea of mud to the minor road at the left, along which runs a pleasant open shelter-belt of beech. Continue north-west to see Chastleton House below; a fine, square block of original Elizabethan design, only faintly resembling a cardboard castle. A small payment entitles you to survey an extraordinary collection of box trees carved into toys and chessmen, round a sundial in the somewhat neglected old garden.

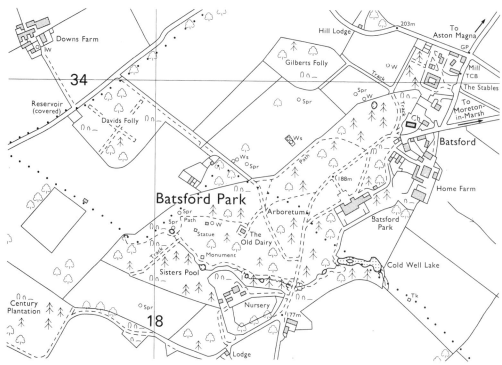

Edge Hill, *378 478*, a surprising steep escarpment, is wooded with beech and other trees and can be walked upon. Upton House here looks out to the Midland Plain. Other great houses with gardens nearby, also belonging to the National Trust, make up for the lack of woodland west of Banbury.

Batsford Arboretum *182 332, 50 acres, good paths but steep*

Batsford Arboretum is near Moreton-in-Marsh. Turn off the A44 opposite Sezincote. There is a nice picnic place under tall hybrid poplars, and a garden centre which also sells ice-cream and tickets for the arboretum. On this unpromising east-facing hillside is a large and impressively wide collection of exotic trees: some rare, as *Cedrus brevifolia* and Wilson's poplar, or very unusual, as the pendulous form of *Picea omorika* and a blue variety of *Abies nobilis* – this very tall.

Only a small part of the garden round the (rather ugly) house is out of bounds for visitors, who are invited to ramble. Like all arboreta of any standing, this collection cannot be fully appreciated in one afternoon. It requires several visits at different seasons. Lord Redesdale, who planted this tree garden, was Ambassador to Tokyo in 1850, hence the rather non-U oriental bronzes dotted about. Not all the trees are Japanese; the western American giants are well represented, and as they have been here since about 1860, they really are giants. In spite of the limy soil (Oolite) and the exposure of the site, there are over forty species and varieties of magnolia at Batsford. The arboretum is closed in winter.

Hidcote, *175 430*, 4 miles north-east of Chipping Campden, is a National Trust property with a very beautiful, dramatically arranged garden, notable for its shrubs – some varieties originating here – and with several good specimen trees.

South-East England

An old Yew in Severells Copse

SCALE 1:316 800 or 5 MILES to 1 INCH

| 0 1 km = 0·6214 mile | 5 | | 10 | Kilometres 15 |

| 0 1 mile = 1·61 kms | | 5 | | Miles 10 |

Queen Elizabeth Forest Park *718 185,*
♀ ♣, 1400 acres, various walks and trails
based on 6 picnic places, FC CC jointly
Some of the trails have WCs and provision for
the disabled. Features include School Trail,
Craft Trail, Wayfaring Course, Pony Trekking
Trails, Ancient Farm; Park Centre with
bookstall and slide theatre, exhibition and
cafeteria. There is a charge for parking.

The park also contains **Butser Hill,** *713 200,*
with a high point of 888 feet, the western end
of the South Downs: a car park with some
marvellous views – not forest but grassland,
with sheep to keep it grazed.

Queen Elizabeth Forest is of beech, mostly
planted since 1930, with old yews and remains
of juniper scrub and thorn. This is not a typical
Forestry Commission forest – it is much more
organized than usual and it costs money – not a
lot, but you cannot get in free. The park is run
as a piece of 'working Hampshire countryside'.

The highest and most remote parking place
in the woods, called Juniper, has a crafts
exhibition and is the start of a tree-recognition
trail – the trees are numbered to agree with a
leaflet with some extra ones which are listed on
a notice at the exhibition site. Craft examples
in the exhibition are fairly downbeat, such as
lapped fencing, ignoring the qualities of the
local timber as one of the finest hardwoods.
There is a reconstructed Victorian sawpit
(for two-handed plank sawing) but there is no
wood-turning. The Tree Trail is fine, but the
leaflet irritatingly condescends with bold line
drawings of, for instance, beech leaves which
you can see millions of on site.

On the Juniper Walk you have fine views of
Butser Down between the beeches (some pine
nurses remaining).

Butser Down, silent, high, inspiring, won
my affections more than the woodlands: but it
could be awful in August. From the Butser
Trail you can look down a deep coombe,

Queen Elizabeth Forest Park from Butser Hill

seagulls turning below as if you were on the Cliffs of Moher. Beyond are beautifully shaped wooded hills, and fields of sheep. A line of pylons spoils the view – there is always something.

The School Trail is good, but again the leaflet, though very informative, adopts an arch manner, with difficult words like 'tree planting' underlined. Can you list ten reasons why we need woods?

The name Forest of Bere is kept by the Forestry Commission for a relatively small area of woodland including what is described as a remnant of the forest in the Meon Valley: West Walk.

West Walk *596 124, ♀ ♣, 900 acres, easy 2 hours, FC*
From the A333 turn north to Hundred Acres, 1 mile east of Wickham. The car park is the quietest of three and is called West Walk – actually it is to the south-east of the woods. The younger trees are on this side, so it is worth combining the walk, waymarked in green, with the Woodend Path, marked in

yellow, which begins on the other side of the wood. The route then includes, besides pine and *Tsuga*, an area of relatively old forest oaks. The whole effect of this fragment of forest is happy, varied and picturesque. Paths are certainly well worn, but there is plenty of natural regeneration of the broadleaves. I met a lady with two dogs who was looking for the lesser spotted woodpecker.

Alice Holt Forest *812 436 (Visitors' Centre), ♀ ♣, 2000 acres, trails, FC*
Alice Holt, the site of large Roman potteries, seems to have been a royal hunting preserve since Saxon times, when, we are told, bears, wolves, foxes, martens, wild cat and red deer were hunted. It was from Aelfsige, Bishop of Winchester, that it got its name, later Axes Holte. *Holt* is Old Saxon for a wood. Much of the hunting forest, then very large since it included Woolmer Forest to the south, would be heathland, but timber was taken for Westminster Great Hall and Windsor Castle. Foresters appointed by the Crown did much as they liked, and the gentry round about poached habitually, simply paying their fines when

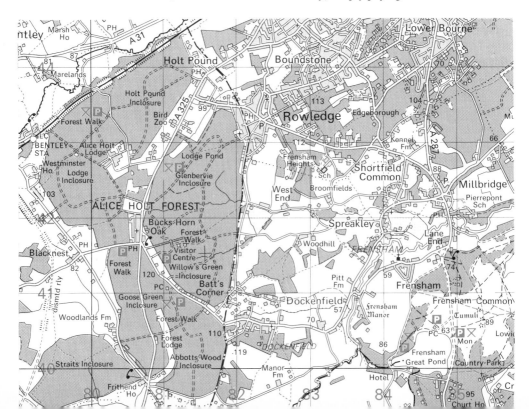

required. By the time of Henry VIII naval dockyards on the Thames were being supplied, presumably via the River Wey, and the tradition of 'cultivating Navy timber' continued until the age of steel. From 1812, some 1600 acres were enclosed and planted with oak. By 1903 there was much surplus oak, the great, large-limbed trees being no longer required, and Alice Holt was transformed by the Commissioners for Crown Lands by the planting of larch, Douglas fir, Scots pine and Corsican pine. In 1924 the forest automatically became the concern of the new Forestry Commission.

New plantations in the southernmost Straits Inclosure ensure that oak will dominate in that area, and many old trees are preserved elsewhere in the forest. Deer, repeatedly removed in the last two centuries as a threat to timber production, returned from about 1960 in the form of a roe deer population, now controlled at about 120 individuals. The Forestry Commission's Research Branch is located at Alice Holt, and there are fields planted with quaintly named poplar cultivars.

The turnpike from Farnham to Petersfield was built in 1826, commendably straight but, short-sightedly, through the middle of the forest. Now, as the A325, it is a hazard; though as you drive south towards the forest all the dark trees do look grand and romantic.

At Bucks Horn Oak on the A325 the Forest Centre is signposted. There are four car parks with picnic sites and forest walks, one suitable for wheelchairs.

The **Willows Green Trail** starts from the Visitors' Centre (open from 11 am to 4 pm on weekdays and holidays) which has leaflets and a historical display as well as hot and cold water.

The **Arboretum Trail**, *802 434*, provides a short, level route for wheelchairs, and a longer trail for walkers.

Abbotts Wood, *812 410*, ½ mile along the Dockenfield road from Bucks Horn Oak, is the 'Habitat Trail'. The leaflet mentions little unusual, but the point is made that Abbotts Wood with its varied terrain, specialized management and varied planting provides maximum diversity of habitat.

Southern beech plantation floor, Alice Holt

For **Goose Green**, *804 416*, turn off the A325 opposite the Halfway House pub. This is the History Trail, including oaks planted around 1820, when deer were removed and steps taken to repair our 'wooden walls' after the Napoleonic threat. As everyone knows, but no one knew then, the ships were soon to be made of iron. There is a reconstructed Roman kiln, this having been the site of a large Roman pottery. Goose Green, and Straits Inclosure to the south, will remain predominantly oakwoods.

Woolmer Forest towards Petersfield is a mess of tidy housing, rifle ranges, air strips and the Ministry-of-Defence-only knows what else. It must be said, however, that the modern Army plays an important part in conservation, if only by imposing zero land use and restricting public access to nil, which means no gathering of wild specimens for gardens or collections. Also, I understand that in this and other areas of long occupation by the Army, more positive conservation is undertaken: I hope it does not take the misguided form of planting trees and clearing scrub.

Selborne Hill *730 330*, ♀, *257 acres, fp, NT*

Sacred to naturalists, the National Trust land includes Selborne Hanger (the beechwood on the northern slope) and the common which occupies the top of the hill. It is a chalk hill but with patches of upper greensand – and what I

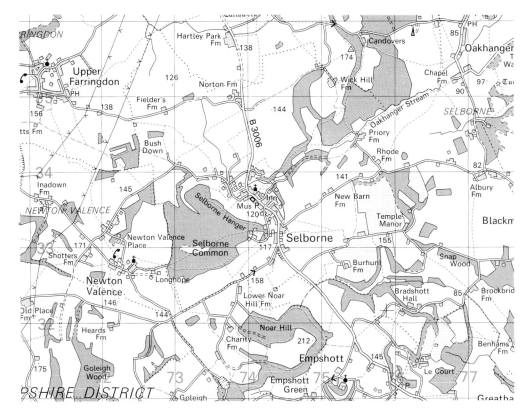

call mud. The common, once presumably
wood-pasture, is neglected to the point of
fantasy, the great, wounded, grey trunks of
beeches now surrounded by thorns which
droop and sway into natural arches covered by
ivy. A wood to dream in, if you are not
searching avidly for some native plant or
creature. There are thickets outside the
shading beech canopy which seem
impenetrable except to the birds which are for
once much in evidence. There are many rides
and footpaths, so that an Ordnance Survey
1:50,000 map is poor guidance: if you try to go
straight across you will probably arrive back
where you started – that is one way of taking a
walk.

The most important, and probably the
oldest, path is from Newton Valence to
Selborne, entering the wood at the west side
near a lovely house called Longhope. This path
runs roughly north-east by east (or south-west
by west) if you use a compass. Another path

follows the contour through the beeches of the
Hanger, and you can descend opposite the
church, where the yew measured in 1789 by
Gilbert White as 23 feet is now 26 feet. To do
the walk in reverse, perhaps more logically,
start at the lane by the museum opposite the
church, and go up the hill by White's zig-zag
path until you meet the transverse path.

Of Woolmer Forest Gilbert White wrote:

> The Royal Forest of Wolmer is a tract of
> land about seven miles in length, two and a
> half in breadth . . . this royalty consists
> entirely of sand covered with heath and
> fern; but is somewhat diversified with hills
> and dales, without having one standing tree
> in the whole extent. In the bottoms, where
> the waters stagnate, are many bogs, which
> formerly abounded with subterraneous
> trees.

Of Alice Holt he wrote:

> Ayles Holt: a strong loam, of a miry nature,

carrying a good turf and abounding with oaks which grow to be large timber; while Wolmer is nothing but a hungry, sandy, barren waste. . . . Fallow deer are never seen in Wolmer, red deer never known to haunt thicket or glade of the Holt.

Durford Heath *790 260, ♀, 62 acres, easy if dry, NT*

The sand road to the woods is like the neck of a flask – bear right or left for a circuit taking about 1½ hours – if you don't linger. Like a flask or a bubble of pure ancient countryside in a great sea of forestry pines, this is a valley and a hill with many odd corners, quiet, and a place to get to know and love. Bearing left down the valley you go by a wood-bank with oaks grown up from old coppice stools. The hillside opposite is patterned with coppice oak and some birch. Deeper into the valley the wood becomes pure oak with large patches of bilberry. There are Scots pines above, apparently seeded from old plantations in Durford Wood to the west, which is private land, and from the gardens of large houses bordering the road. There seem to be no deer to eat the shoots, and oak stubs cut in the autumn already showed new shoots in March. No rabbits were to be seen, and few birds – this part of the country is curiously short of birds. The valley is a suntrap; all is quiet and windless. Nothing disturbs the pattern of warm oak bark, dry leaves and shiny green *Vaccinium*, and the very varied and satisfying shapes of all the trees.

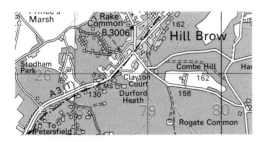

Hindhead and Haslemere Commons

Around Hindhead in Surrey is a record collection of National Trust commons totalling 1076 acres, and heavily wooded in parts. Just to the east is the famous Gibbet Hill, 895 feet

with the Devil's Punchbowl on Hindhead Common below and across the A3(T). There is a parking ground at *891 358*, but the commons are all nearly continuous and accessible on foot from the village. To the north-west are Golden Valley and Whitmore Vale, 155 acres of wood and heath: to the south-east, Inval and Weydown Commons, these latter reaching to Haslemere. Nutcombe Down and Polecat Copse are to the south. Ludshott Common is in Hampshire, to the west beyond Grayshott, and includes Croaker's Patch, Gentle's Copse and Hammer Ponds at Waggoners Wells: in all 645 acres; then Bramshott Common is to the south, and across the A3 the woods of Hammer Bottom.

The best known of Haslemere's surrounding country is Black Down, 918 feet, 1½ miles south-east; there are 600 acres of National Trust land, with Tennyson's Lane and Boarden Door Bottom with a chestnut coppice. Black Down Hill is the highest point in Sussex, and Hindhead is the highest village in Surrey. The hills are sandstone and the vegetation heathland with birch and pine, bracken and heather. Views east and south to the Downs are filled with trees – enough to take your breath away at what seems the expanse of woodland.

Kingley Vale *825 088, ♣ (yew), about 3m, NR*

The map reference is for the parking place at West Stoke, near Mid Lavant just north of Chichester. The road to West Stoke is signposted Funtington from Mid Lavant. This very important site is a Nature Conservancy reserve. There is about a mile to walk – thank goodness you cannot drive into this one. First you come to a patch of chalk scrub with a field museum and leaflet dispenser. There are a lot of unnecessary notices along the very necessary fence. As the ground rises the yews begin. One outlier, perfect in form, is surrounded by a natural bank and shut in by tall grass and brambles. Within its shade you can easily imagine making a temporary home. Some shattered, dead yews become very visible at the edge of the wood. These were killed by war-time rifle practice, which stripped the thin bark.

Twenty very old yews are the parent trees to be found deep in the wood. A conservative guess at their age is 500 years, but they may be much older. There are no other plants in the wood, which is of course very dark and dry, but some clearings occur naturally, and here an occasional robin or chaffinch may be seen or heard. The Tansley Memorial Stone at the head of the vale commemorates the great man who, in the early years of this century, established the study of woodland ecology in Britain.

Kingley Vale can also be reached by Stoughton Down, but this is a long way around if you want to spend time exploring the yews. A Forestry Commission car park at Lambdown Hill, *815 126*, in a field at the edge of the plantation, is strongly recommended in a Commission leaflet as secluded. But even in December about twenty cars occupied the gravel, and the grass was too slippery to drive on. To reach this parking place turn off the B2141 for East Marden, and then take the road to the south in the village.

Micheldever Wood *529 364*, ♣, *easy walk, FC*

$1\frac{1}{2}$ miles north to south, $\frac{3}{4}$ mile wide, this wood is east of the A33(T), 3 miles north of

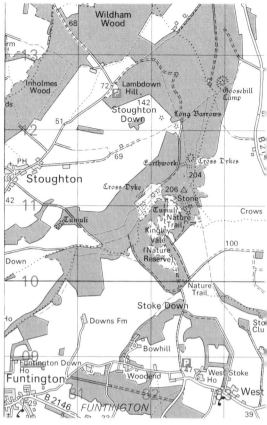

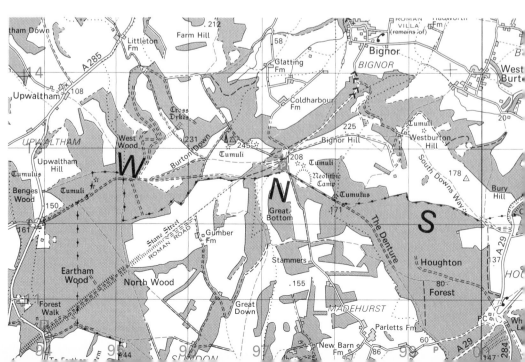

Winchester; turn off at Lunways Inn. The wood retains much beauty because of the various ages and the variety of trees, and the countryside round about has kept its breadth and grandeur.

The M3, as planned, will sweep the east flank of the wood, and this will probably destroy altogether its already threatened silence.

Abbotstone Down 582 362, ♀, *picnic place, CC*

Three or 4 miles east of Micheldever Wood is Abbotstone Down, not primarily a woodland site. There are various parking places and picnic areas among trees and chalk scrub. Here a finger-post beckons walkers with seven-league boots north to Inkpen Beacon, many miles away near Newbury. Less energetically, you can wander on grassland between fine beeches, yews, birches, thorns, and inspect the edges of a fine oak/ash wood, rich in lichens and mosses, and open enough for a very varied field layer, including a good deal of privet – a chalk scrub plant and unusual as an undershrub for oak. Look out for a fine spindle tree, about 200 yards along the bridleway southwards.

Chawton Park Wood 672 362, 2–3m, FC

This wood is off the A31, 3 miles south-west of Alton; turn north out of Four Marks, the first available turning if going south-west.

This wood is a triangle around a dry valley. There are old wood-banks, beeches and a pleasant wide picnic area within the wood, ½ mile from the car park. Conifers are larch and spruce.

Bignor Hill 973 128

You can drive south from Bignor on a very steep road, but for a woodland approach turn towards Madehurst off the A29 immediately after the great roundabout on top of the Downs. Near a bit of a hazel coppice you can park, 994 104, and walk gently uphill by the edge of Houghton Forest on a bridleway amusingly called 'The Denture'. Part of the way is bordered by silver firs, *Abies grandis*, which is agreeable. Try the foliage for its reputed scent of oranges. It is a long plod, with

only an occasional dramatic view, which culminates in a patch of thorns belonging to the National Trust. Do we have to have the Trust preserve a few hawthorns, I asked myself? Then I came upon an open space dominated by a massive signpost pointing to Londinium one way and Noviomagus the other. At first I felt a bit scornful. There are a few yews, more signs; then I noticed Stane Street itself, a dead-straight dyke going off into the woods. As I stood upon this 1950-year-old road, I began to see the point of the self-consciously Roman signpost.

Continuing south-west down Stane Street from Bignor Hill would bring you to **Eartham Wood**, a Forestry Commission conversion of oak into beech with Douglas fir at the centre and spruces round about. A nice enough place to park, 939 107, and a pleasant walk, though far from exciting. The same could be said for **Selhurst Park Woods** just across the A285; there are two parking places on the Goodwood road with great views southwards, and another in the valley on the West Dean road.

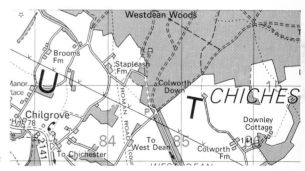

West Dean Estate 872 111

The estate has an arboretum by the Trundle viewpoint; cars can stop but there is no apparent access to the woodlands. Park at the crossways, 846 147, for Westdean Woods: not a grand walk, on the bridleway, by a larchwood with ashes and open fields to the south. Further into the woods is a young plantation of spruce, Douglas fir and western red cedar, with the seductive name of Venus Wood.

Singleton, on the A286, has a National Trust coppice, and West Dean an open-air museum – open in summer.

Ashdown Forest

An area of forest ridges on Wealdon sand, it is
well above the surrounding countryside and
characteristic vegetation is heathland with
birch and pine. 'Deer for six miles', warn
notices on the roads. Ashdown Forest gets a
good press nowadays, probably simply because
it is geographically prominent. It is often cited
as a survivor of Andreadsweald, though it
might well have been a bald patch in that
mighty oakwood. Arthur Young, 1741–1820,
wrote that it was '18,000 acres of nothing
better than the poorest barren sand, the
vegetable covering consisting of ferns, heath
etc' – but he was a horticulturalist. Tradition
has it that the many iron furnaces of Sussex
(32 on record in the sixteenth century) were
responsible for the loss of many trees but this is
unlikely. All the trees would regenerate after
cutting, and we should have been left with
even thicker forest. It was the grazing animals
of the commoners which polished off the trees.

Ashdown Forest, ever since it was first
called a forest in the time of Henry III, has
been the source of much besides mere timber
and firewood: its relatively open glades were a
wood-pasture and its moorland provided
turves; its heather and even its bracken were
valued for litter; the sandy hills were no doubt
full of rabbits from the time of the introduction
of that beast in the twelfth century, and there
would be game for the taking. All these
demands from the ordinary people who lived
there were at variance with those of the owners
of the hunting rights – at first the King, then
the Duchy of Lancaster and later various lords
who competed for the Mastership. Clearly it
was worth having. 7000 acres were enclosed in
the early eighteenth century, and parts were
sold, but commoners asserted their rights until
a Keeper of the Forest in the last century, Lord
de la Warre, attempted to restrain them legally.
He lost his case and the forest of some 6000
acres is now managed by a body representative
of the commoners.

The conservators have provided many car
parks in the Wych Cross area, grouped along
the ridge road (un-numbered) west to east, or
the A22 running south (where in the valley you
may find mature beechwoods).

Grazing is not now a major concern, so birch
and pine are spreading through the heather,
some of which is cut in wide lanes. There are
footpaths everywhere. I have not discovered a
strictly woodland walk here. The heath is to be
enjoyed for its openness, but there are patches
of graceful birchwood, some oaks, and striking
groups of pine.

Gravetye Woods *360 350*, ♀ ♣, *1½m, muddy, FC*

At the north-west edge of Ashdown Forest, the
Forestry Commission has taken over a fine
plantation which is credited to William
Robinson, a great gardener. The parking place
is discreet, not too easy to find: turn off the
B2110, 2 miles south-west of East Grinstead
where the road turns sharply to the right.
Conifers at Gravetye are almost mature but
nicely contrasted; a stand of Serbian spruce is
particularly fine. There are helpful signposts
and a path to a viewpoint above the woods.
There are many native trees.

Forest Way CP *425 356*, ♀, *2½m, easy but wet in places, CC*

From Forest Row to East Grinstead runs the

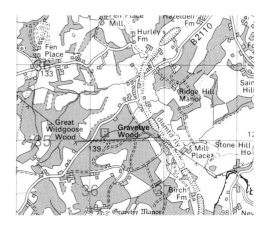

Forest Way Country Park, beginning inauspiciously at the bottom of a hill on a main road, the A22. There is nowhere to park at this end. This Forest Way is an old railway, mostly in a cutting and not too well drained. Its charms are slow to yield on a wet November afternoon: nevertheless they are there. At one point you pass by a particularly charming beech coppice, guarded by a guelder rose. There are many field maples. At another point you find wooden steps to encourage you to walk on the bank, where, from the dignified cover of a row of old thorns, you survey the rolling, wooded landscape to the south.

Sheffield Park *403 237, ♀ ♣, arboretum, NT*

Another dismantled railway through East Grinstead has been for some of its length rebuilt as the Bluebell Line. This is a woodland and arable 'walk' by steam train, from Horsted Keynes, Sussex, to Sheffield Park.

There is no woodland here as such, though the great size and vigour of the many specimen

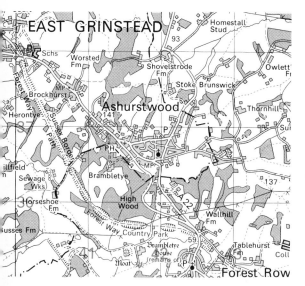

conifers at Sheffield Park make a semblance of woodland. The park is an accumulation of enthusiasms from Capability Brown's planning of lakes, grass and 'clumps', to exotic-tree collecting by A. G. Soames, the owner from 1909, and has been in the care of the National Trust since 1954. There are palms, ornamental bridges, water-lilies and ducks.

Wakehurst Place 340 315, ♀ ♣, arboretum, NT

North of Sheffield Park on the B2028, about 1 mile north of Ardingly, is Wakehurst Place, National Trust but leased to the Royal Botanic Gardens at Kew, which is a branch of the Ministry of Agriculture, Fisheries and Food. Open every day, hot water laid on, invalid chairs available, special policemen to take your money, and well worth every penny.

There is a 'wooded walk' between steep cliffs, a Himalayan valley with, of course, rhododendrons – but you may never reach it because there is so much else to see. If you *can't* get far there is plenty to see, and smell, near the house, where exemplary rock gardens dip down to perfect lawns.

The pinetum, an open woodland in itself, is a mile beyond the house; grand, soberly laid out, well labelled. Most of its specimens are old, and all you see is a piece of trunk, with its

pattern of leaves far overhead. This is often the difficulty with old specimen conifers, but at least the ground is clear. I was delighted to find the not-too-common Spanish or hedgehog fir hiding in a corner near the stables, quite friendly and approachable. You can have tea at the house; the house is lovely too. There is a small museum display of local natural history.

St Leonard's Forest

St Leonard's Forest is more or less between Crawley and Horsham. Cobbett wrote:

> The first two of these miserable miles go through the estate of Lord Erskine. It was a *bare heath* with here and there, in the better parts of it, some scrubby *birch*. It has been in part planted with fir-trees which are as ugly as the heath was; and in short, it is a most villainous tract. After quitting it we went through a *forest*; but a most miserable one; and this is followed by a large common, *now enclosed*, cut up, disfigured, spoiled, and the labourers all driven from its skirts. I have seldom travelled over eight miles so well calculated to fill the mind with painful reflections. The ride has, however, this in it; that the ground is pretty much elevated and enables you to look about you.

Nowadays there are rather more *firs* (Scots pine) and larches but the labourers are as little in evidence. Rides are blocked with warning notices and even pieces of old motor car, an item this part of the world is not short of. St Leonard, you might imagine, was the patron saint of real estate.

Things get a little better to the south, where the plantations thin out among narrow fields. At Lower Grouse you may walk into the woods and even buy an ice-cream at the farm, *234 308*. The chief reason for visiting this part might be to see the great Hammer Pond and Hawkins Pond, where energy was stored to work drop-hammers forging the local iron. Hammer Pond appears to be inaccessible, but Hawkins has the Forestry Commission Old Copse, *218 295*, on its east bank – rather thickly planted but you can park and walk in. There is a scattering of native trees along the waterside, and they look very pretty against the background of dark conifers. Access on the far bank is for the fishermen only, but there is a bridleway – very muddy in winter – a few yards along the road. It fails to afford a view of the pond, but proceeding by beeches in parkland it heads north into the forest for 2 miles, eventually reaching Colgate.

Leonardslee Woods and Furnace Pond
222 259, ♀ (♣), easy, muddy 1–3m
The famous gardens of Leonardslee at Lower Beeding are not open all the year, but a little way south along the A281 is a lane, Mill Lane, labelled as a public bridleway you can walk into the estate woodlands. Here you can see the Furnace Pond, a much better example, if smaller, than the Hammer Pond mentioned above. The original dam has been decorated with a beech hedge, whose contorted branches are reminiscent of the ancient old beeches in the grounds, pollarded many decades ago. The ruined walls of some of the foundry buildings can be seen, and a deeply hollowed cart track winds out of the valley to nowhere in particular. The stream below the dam has been made into another lake at a lower level.

Once beyond the valley of the Furnace Pond and out to the east, you have a choice of footpaths and bridleways.

A car park at *207 298*, off the A281, gives access to 13 acres of nature reserves near Lower Beeding, including the beechwood, Mick's Cross.

To the north of St Leonard's Forest, off the A264 and close to the new estate of Broadfield is a Country Park, **Buchan Park**, *248 336*. Crawley has crept over Pease Pottage Forest and Tilgate Forest, so we must go a little further south on the A23 and turn left onto the B2110 – for Brantridge Forest.

Brantridge Forest *289 316, ♀ ♣ ,*
500 yards, easy, can be wet, fp
A great notice about fire danger marks the start, through a gap in the hedge, of a woodland walk *par excellence* and an experience of deep significance for anyone who can be moved by the dramatic but very, very slow response of beech trees to men's saws and axes. Some will only say, 'grotesque!' Others, like me, will not so much walk as hover, unable to

Ancient pollard beeches, Brantridge Forest

remove their eyes, yet led on to seek out the next revelation. It is the cumulative effect of a double avenue of these strange creatures which is so extraordinary, compared with the more scattered effect of the similar Burnham Beeches. The trees were planted here long before they were lopped, and what we now see is a complete, probably quite unintentional collaboration between the planter, the woodmen, and the trees which have outlived them. This passionate scene gives way soon enough to bracken, birches and pine. Further on northwards into **Worth Forest**, the Paddockhurst Estate has made a parking place, *305 332*, now full of puddles, and invites you, on your best behaviour, to explore the geometrical rides of its conifer plantations.

Box Hill (page 117) is the best known but by no means the most important of Dorking's woodlands. A clockwise survey takes us south to **High Ridge Wood**, *199 470*: nothing special but a nice mixture of conifers, including the bewitchingly scented *Thuja plicata*. A sad pond surrounded by oaks and willows tells the tale of another wood, its heart ripped out and replaced with alien trees – but no doubt it was all felled during the Second World War and would have become arable were it not for the intervention of the Forestry Commission – the usual excuse.

Holmwood Common *184 453*, ♀, *632 acres, various routes, muddy at times, NT*
The indicated parking place is by a pond at the crossroads ¼ mile east of South Holmwood. Half a dozen perpetually hungry Chinese geese live on the pond. The path leads confusingly to

an access road serving some grand houses, notably the Old Croft in Edwardian red brick. The part of the common I explored was very pretty woodland with oak, holly, yew, mature birch, planted larches and invading sycamores.

Abinger Forest, Leith Hill, Abinger and **Wotton Commons** ♀ ♠, *CC, NT*
A very large area of hilly country with a great variety of woodland extremely well preserved. Enchanted Abinger! Barely 30 miles from London, and yet as remote as County Kerry – almost. At a parking place near **Friday Street**, *126 457*, you may plunge at once into a vast community of drunken oaks awash in a sea of bilberry and often covered in green moss. Soon you are aware of very tall, straight pines – good

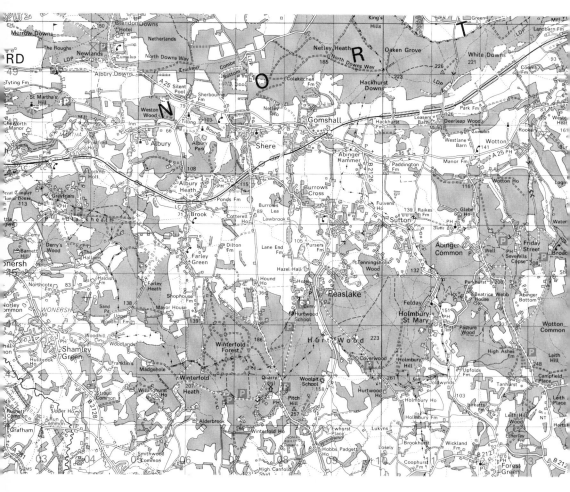

timber trees with a canopy high above the oaks which still writhe in its shade. Let us hope that the oaks will survive the removal, surely imminent, of the pines.

This part, Abinger Common with the adjoining Wotton Common, is administered by Surrey County Council and remains in private ownership. It can only have survived through the care and foresight of the owners, for we all know the type of development which might have occurred.

Beyond Friday Street, which is a sweet little place in a wooded cleft filled by a wide hammer pond, lies another gem, **Severells Copse**. This is a birch coppice with old oaks, National Trust, and seductively beautiful. You can cross it by a well-marked path to another Surrey

Abinger Common oaks

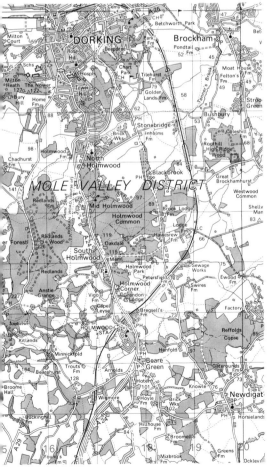

County Council car park on the ridge, *134 454*, beyond which lie Wotton Common and Abinger Forest, south and east respectively. South is Leith Hill, the highest point in south-east England, and below it, Tanners Wood, Ockshott Wood (now cut down), Mosses Wood with its landslip; and all with great views southwards over the Weald. The eastern shoulder of the forest is coniferized.

Hurt Wood

Nearer to Guildford, though still equidistant from Dorking, lies Hurt Wood, a forest or a collection of manorial wastes consisting largely of heathland with pines and birches: tall beechwoods at the southern escarpment edge. As with Abinger and Wotton Commons, which almost adjoin, the greensand dip slope is broken by deep north-to-south valleys, here containing not hammer ponds but seasonal streams, not persistent enough to waterlog the remaining oak trees. Rich homesteads, parks and farmland border the southern slopes, where monkey puzzles, Lawson cypresses and rhododendron are added to the prevailing tall beeches. Coppice trees are less evident here – when the land was abducted or enclosed, there were probably few commoners to stand up for their rights. As long ago as the twelfth century, the Surrey knights paid 200 marks to King Richard, 'to be quit of all things that belong to the Forest from the waters of Wey to Kent, and from the street of Guildford southwards as far as Surrye stretches'. Now the woodland is dedicated to the public and managed by the Lords of the Manors, who have banded

Pine and oak, Hurt Wood

themselves into the sinister-sounding Hurtwood Control.

The impression you get at any of the fourteen or more parking places provided is that you had better be careful. And, so you had. Hurt Wood is a national asset as well as a source of good pine timber. In winter the strong red colour of the bracken contrasts with the full green of the Scots pine. There are birch, oak and beech, with heather on older banks. Pines regenerate naturally. Bilberry persists bright green well into the winter. It is from these berries, once collected and sold, that Hurt Wood gets its name. Hurts – the name whortleberry is only a corruption – were once collected and sold like cherries.

South of the A25 is **Albury Park**, *062 475*, once the home of our first man of the trees, John Evelyn.

Only 2 miles south-east of Guildford is **Blackheath**, *040 462*, with a Surrey County Council parking place and a 20-acre National Trust section of pine and heather. This is just south-east of Chilworth, while to the north of that place is **St Martha's Hill**, the Pilgrims' Way emerging from suburban Guildford onto the chalk hill with its viewpoint, *028 482*. This is not without woodland.

Okewood church was a chapel of ease, a forest chapel in the thirteenth century; it was

rebuilt in the fifteenth. Here we are once again in the grey/brown/green crepuscular mediaeval atmosphere of the forest. A short woodland walk upstream from the churchyard brings you to Walliswood (which has a pub) and back to the twentieth century.

Arundel Park *022 083*
Half a mile out of Arundel under the castle cliff is a large parking place for the Wildfowl Reserve. Here begins Walk No 1 of the Arun Valley Walks designed by West Sussex County Council: leaflet 'usually available'.

Instead of slogging around Offham and South Stoke, if you ascend to the trees via the old quarry you will find yourself in a corner of Arundel Park. Sheltered by tall spruces is a box grove. Some of these box trees are remarkably straight and thick, and it is tragic to see how they have been allowed to fall to the ground.

Emerging from the park wall via a large hole, you can cross a field and pick up a bridleway by Fox's Oven Cottage. A short walk along the road towards South Stoke brings you to a lane leading direct to one of the park gates. Inside, you can return by the sides of mature beech 'clumps', with great views of the castle and the sea, down to Swanbourne Lake. Not entirely a woodland walk, but very invigorating.

Eastern Forest Ridges

Landranger sheets 188, 199

Bedgebury Forest 3500 acres, dominates our map north-east of Flimwell, *716 315*. It is 45 miles from London on the A21, the woodland road. Its mighty folds of green, like a rug thrown over the Garden of England, can be seen from the Flimwell to Hawkhurst road. There are dozens of routes through: you need a compass really, but there are some signposts.

Bedgebury Pinetum *718 337*, ♀ ♦,
80 acres parkland, many routes, FC
Few people with an interest in trees will spend long in the forest itself, for at the north-west corner is the National Pinetum. The **Churchill Wood** walk, close at hand, is short, sheltered, easy and pleasant for the very old and the young. To see the beauties of the pinetum itself, you have to be prepared for a moderately stiff walk downhill and up. There

Scots pine and, beyond, oriental spruce in the Forest Plots at Bedgebury

is a charge, voluntary in winter.

A pinetum is, of course, a collection of what used to be called Pinaceae, now the conifers, yews, *Ginkgo* and *Torreyas* (nutmeg trees) which make up the tree Gymnosperms. These (naked seed plants) are a very ancient class. They evolved about 350 million years ago, give or take a few tens of millions of years. Conifers were at their height of world dominance about 250 million years ago and were nearly equalled 100 million years later by the Ginkgoales, only one species of one genus of one family of the whole order of which survived: *Ginkgo biloba*. There are still over 500 species of conifers and several Taxaceae (yews and nutmeg trees).

Angiosperms, including all the familiar flowering plants and broadleaved trees (hardwoods), have evolved over the past 140 million years, along with the mammals and the declining, but still very strong, Coniferales to which this pinetum is dedicated.

Although it is a sort of living museum, the pinetum strikes one first and foremost as a landscape; not a wild one, but certainly a happy place for any lover of trees. Here the conifers you knew as interesting specimens or all-too-familiar windbreaks can be seen in their true form and vigour. Massed with the skill of a great designer (his name was W. Dallimore, a botanist retired from Kew and no rich lord), the great avenues sweep along shallow valleys or leap across small, rounded hills, with a constantly changing architecture of trees. The soil is said to be poor, but great *Thujas* and *Tsugas*, remarkably rich-looking *Cryptomeria* and *Sciadopitys* flourish, and the cleverly grouped large specimens of Lawson cypress in their two dozen or so different forms and colours are an eye-opener. The juniper section, immediately opposite the entrance, is enlightening; so is the Spruce Valley collection – much wider than elsewhere.

The Forest Plots beyond the pinetum area are of course for instruction, not for beauty. But straight rides do not a prison make, and I for one can muse happily there for hours, re-

87

assured when botany deserts me by the well-placed labels and the diagram – an example of efficient forestry graphics – in the excellent booklet available at the office. Broadleaved trees are in the minority, but those species present are interesting and they gain from their isolation amongst the dark green of the conifers. Not all conifers, of course, remain green through the winter. One of the sights of Bedgebury in the autumn is the dignified, simple group by the lake of swamp cypress and dawn redwood, alternately coloured in two shades of red: the former dark, the latter glowing and light, and by November

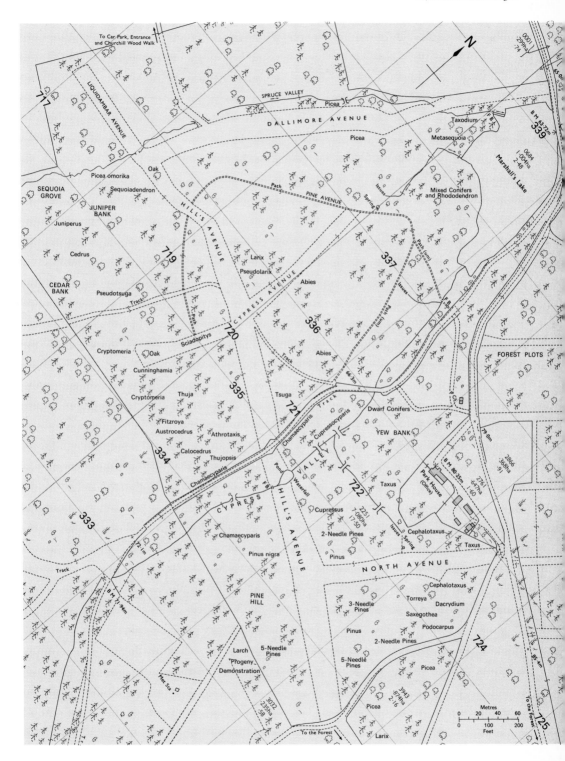

To Car Park, Entrance
and Churchill Wood Walk

717

LIQUIDAMBAR AVENUE

SPRUCE VALLEY

DALLIMORE AVENUE

Picea

Picea

Taxodium

Metasequoia

B M 647m

B M 647m

339

Marshall's Lake

0.694
2.59ha
7-4

1.00ha
2-49

Picea omorika

Oak

Sequoiadendron

Path

PINE AVENUE

Mixed Conifers
and Rhododendron

SEQUOIA
GROVE

JUNIPER
BANK

HILL'S AVENUE

Spring

Ixstus

719

Path (um)

337

Juniperus

Cedrus

Larix

Pseudolarix

CYPRESS AVENUE

Abies

336

Path (um)

Ixstus

F B

CEDAR
BANK

Pseudotsuga

Track

Path

720

Track

Abies

66.3m

FOREST PLOTS

Cryptomeria

Oak

Sciadopitys

Cunninghamia

335

Cryptomeria

Thuja

721

Tsuga

Track

Dwarf Conifers

79.0m

Fitzroya

Austrocedrus

Athrotaxis

Chamaecyparis

Cupressocyparis

YEW BANK

B M 80.25m

2866
368ha
9.1

334

Calocedrus

Thujopsis

VALLEY

722

Taxus

Park
House

B M 80.25m

2761
647ha
60

Chamaecyparis

Pond

Waterfall

F B

CYPRESS

HILL'S AVENUE

Cupressus

2-Needle Pines

2513
7-080ha
17-50

Ixstus

Spring

Cephalotaxus

Taxus

333

Chamaecyparis

Pinus nigra

Pinus

NORTH AVENUE

Cephalotaxus

Track

B M 71.94m

PINE
HILL

3-Needle
Pines

Torreya

Dacrydium

Saxegothea

Podocarpus

724

Pinus

2-Needle Pines

Larch
'Progeny'
Demonstration

5-Needle
Pines

5-Needle
Pines

Picea

Met Sta

3032
2.55ha
58

Picea

3943
8.14ha
2.16

725

To the Forest

Larix

To the Forest

Metres
0 20 40 60

0   100   200
Feet

To the Forest

surrounded by an unbelievable carpet of its strange, feathery leaves.

Chingley Wood 676 338, ♀ ♣ , 2m, easy, WA

On the opposite side of the A21 from Bedgebury is Bewl Bridge Reservoir, with a special turning 1 mile south of Lamberhurst. The woodlands here, notably Chingley Wood, are of native trees, with pines planted in the last century. There is a very tidy car park which demands a fairly high charge in ten-pence pieces; when visited in November it was deserted. The smart Visitors' Centre was open, and empty, except for one lonely trout in a glass tank. He seemed to be quite happy. There is a telephone, of course, and full life-saving equipment all round the water's edge.

Chingley Wood is fenced off, but if you persist you get to a footpath which strikes through, along an ancient bank with old hollies and beeches, birchwood to the right, chestnut coppice with fine native oaks to the left. The coppice is cut, but the wood seems to be left around to rot: rather more than might be necessary for conservation of insect life. You can walk on to Chingley Manor and out to the main road along the Manor drive, which is clearly marked on the map as a footpath.

Pembury Walks 626 426, ♀ ♣ , several hilly fps, LA

Indicated by a finger-post on the A21, Pembury Walk is close to Tunbridge Wells. It sounds like a good place for a woodland walk, and so it proves, but in the plural. Effectively a vast ragged triangle of assorted forestry with a waterworks as the apex and the A21 as the base, it is an easy place to get lost in. The contorted, hilly land and the numerous paths, bridleways and rides not on the map make it confusing. Choose a sunny day or take a compass, because trying to guide yourself by the sound of the main road just does not work.

There is some space to park near the waterworks, 626 426, or near the squat-towered, charming old Pembury church, or, just, at the point marked p on the map.

Two footpaths leave the vicinity of the waterworks. The upper one travels between tall wire fences for all the world as if it were on the border of Russia: fine tall larches reinforce this impression. Soon there appear the old oak stubs, sculptured into complexity by frequent cutting and decay, that are typical of all the miles of wood-banks that surround the Pembury woods. There is a great deal of chestnut, some very old stools 6 feet wide at least, a lot of larch of various ages, and stands of younger Corsican pine.

All these appear as you follow the wire-fenced path as far as the cemetery, then turn right across the grain of the country to emerge near the hospital. Not too promising! And the way back is not clear from here. It is easy to get lost trying to reach the opposite side of the tri-angle. So, take the lower of the two paths at the waterworks and later strike off right to reach the road and return, is my advice, based I must admit on inadequate knowledge of the ground.

It is old woodland, as the oak stubs tell, but full of new life and reflecting a lively management policy that cannot be bad. Pembury Walks only lack a few corners of high forest.

Friston Forest 545 000, ♀ ♣ , 1967 acres, moderately easy trails and walks, FC

The forest is near the Seven Sisters cliffs west of Eastbourne, with three parking places, one at Butchershole Bottom, 557 005. Friston almost certainly means 'furzetun', and furze or gorse is the native vegetation. Unbelievably, gorse, the prickliest of native bushes, was once an important resource as winter fodder, bedding instead of straw, and rapid fuel for firing bread ovens and potteries. This scrub was cleared by the foresters, who also took over some more level agricultural land where the thin soil suffered from erosion. Planting began in 1926, but most of the trees are much younger than this.

The forest walk from Westdean parking place ascends by easy gradients along the ride, where Corsican pine, very bright green here because of the chalky soil, is used to nurse the staple tree, the beech. The nurses are now being removed. The aim is to produce a great beechwood, not a mere catch crop of softwood in this the South Downs Area of Outstanding

Friston Forest

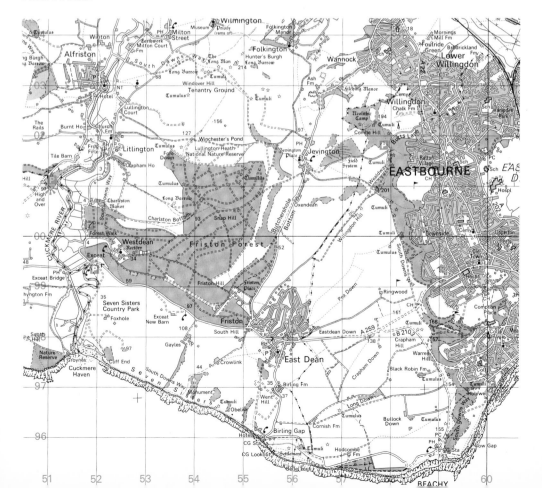

Natural Beauty. Here and there are hints of the grandeur that is to follow in time; now all is clear and simple – a teenage forest, and the smooth haunches of the Downs complete this impression. As the sun reaches into Westdean village an older, richer pattern is revealed, a sheltered richness to contrast with the wind-polished purity of the chalk slopes. Friston Forest does not quite fit in with this theme, but it will in time, and there is plenty of bare grassland still. The trail of $2\frac{3}{4}$ miles marches with a branch of the long-distance path or South Downs Way for some of the way.

A shorter walk starts from the parking place nearest the main road, at Exceat, with views of the gleaming meanders of Cuckmere River. At Butchersole you are more sheltered, and on your own as regards trails: You are free to wander in the forest. The land is a watershed for the Eastbourne waterworks, and afforestation is a sensible use of it.

Lullington Heath, *546 018*, which you can see beyond Jevington and north of the Forest is a National Nature Reserve.

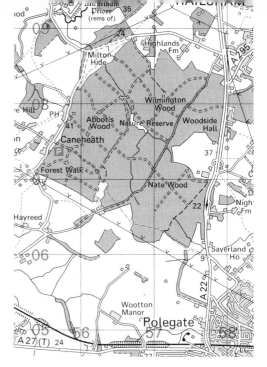

Abbot's Wood *565 077*, ♀ ♣, *forest trail and disabled trail, FC*

A few miles inland at Abbot's Wood the Forestry Commission, with a leaflet, again invites you to examine your heritage. Perhaps it is not the Commission's fault, but most of the interest here seems to be outside or on the edges, where ancient wood-banks still support the fantastic and elegant shapes of many-stemmed coppice trees – hornbeams as well as oak and beech – many covered in ivy. A few oldish oaks still stand in the fields but most were felled during the Second World War. The Abbots were of Battle, until the Dissolution, and their men made the banks, cutting trees every twenty years or so and carting the wood away for fuel. In Victorian times coppice oak was cut and stacked to dry, the bark removed in 'flows' for the tanning industry. In the forest there is still some chestnut, and many old dead oak stools under the pines – I cannot help feeling our heritage lies with them. But the parking place offers all-important space – and more, for a walk has been arranged here for those confined to wheelchairs. Various

organizations have donated trees, planted by the way – and more could be done here for the blind, in the form of bushes to touch and smell.

Footland Wood *763 203*, ♀ ♣, $1\frac{1}{4}$ *miles, easy, FC*

North of Battle, this is a small wood among many in this area. The forest walk is short, the first half coniferous, the second through a beechwood. The older beeches are considered unsatisfactory, having come from poor seed, but if the day is dark you would do well to aim for them, taking the walk in reverse. Much as I admire the western hemlock for its generous, rich green cloak, these crowded stands of equal-age timber strike me as gloomy. They are the battery hens of the woodlands. However, the Forestry Commission has placed a rustic seat for visitors to sit and admire them.

Light at the edges of the wood reveals the ancient character of the wood-banks, the trees once lopped and woven into the hedge. They are mainly beech, though this was originally an oakwood with birch, cut for the iron furnaces once concentrated in the Sussex Weald.

If you come in spring, you may find some flowers of the 140 species of plant mentioned in the leaflet, available for a small fee from a dispenser at the car park.

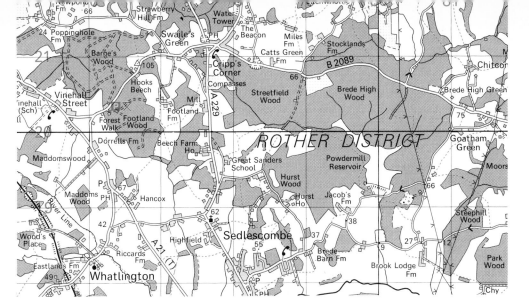

Flatropers Wood *865 233, ♀, several paths, NR*

Flatropers is a nature reserve of the Sussex
Naturalists' Trust – about a square mile, but
adjoining other woods in one of those fascinating, remote country areas one is surprised
to find in this century of sophisticated com-
munications: cottages and farms amongst small
irregular fields seemingly carved out of the
woodland, and reached only by muddy lanes.
Bixley Wood and **Beckley Woods** are
adjacent, the latter devoted to pines and
Douglas fir but with a pleasant curving ride,
littered with fungi in late summer and autumn
– the commonest are Boletus species.

Flatropers is ancient, as its sculptured banks
tell us at once. It contains good standard oaks,
much birch – some trees quite large – and
some chestnut coppice. The wood is kept tidy
by hordes of large black wood ants, which
sweep the litter into heaps of astonishing size
and neatness. There are no formal parking
places for the woods.

Guestling Wood *864, 146, ♀, 26 acres, various easy walks, WT*

Attached to larger woods, privately owned, to
the south, this is high Weald woodland with
views over the River Brede. Guestling Wood is
managed largely by 'non-intervention', while
some chestnut coppice is cut in rotation to
preserve the traditional character. There is no
formal parking place, and access is by the

public footpath marked on the map or by other
paths which cross the wood.

Hemstead Forest is large, 3 miles long,
from north of Benenden to a mile short of
Biddenden. The Forestry Commission car
park, *813 344*, on a sunny Saturday morning
seemed an entirely happy place: the larches
on this high ground fit well enough into a
landscape whose warm, clear colours and clean
contours are familiar from calendar art, but not
the less respectable. Traditional ways of caring
for woods, orchards, hedges, fields and houses
have resulted in a scenery that anyone tired of
haste and urbanization may find restores the
spirit.

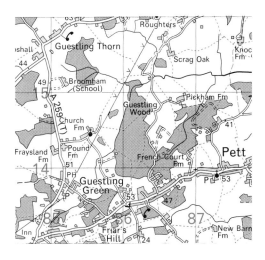

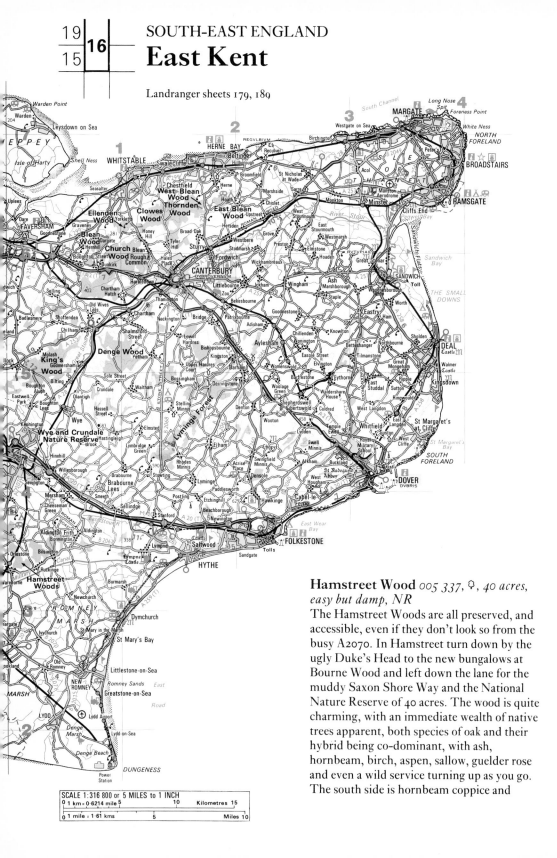

Hamstreet Wood *005 337,* ♀, *40 acres, easy but damp, NR*

The Hamstreet Woods are all preserved, and accessible, even if they don't look so from the busy A2070. In Hamstreet turn down by the ugly Duke's Head to the new bungalows at Bourne Wood and left down the lane for the muddy Saxon Shore Way and the National Nature Reserve of 40 acres. The wood is quite charming, with an immediate wealth of native trees apparent, both species of oak and their hybrid being co-dominant, with ash, hornbeam, birch, aspen, sallow, guelder rose and even a wild service turning up as you go. The south side is hornbeam coppice and chestnut coppice: these are cut and used. It takes a little over an hour to walk all round the wood: take no notice of signs directing you to keep to the muddy bridleway: these are directed at horse riders. This reserve is only a small part of 230 acres of woodland here, which are sensitively managed, using natural regeneration or local seed, and careful selection from old coppice stools, to produce good-quality hardwoods. Perhaps only in Kent, where people seem to be doing very largely what they always have, could such a compromise between nature and commerce be practised in this century. The warden has even found a market for hornbeam pulp wood; the trees are coppiced on a twenty-year cycle. We are told that you have to raise your voice to be heard above the nightingales on May evenings, and that three species of woodpecker have nested in the same tree, a dead oak left standing for that purpose.

Further west, more oakwood can be entered from the by-road parallel to the A2070, at *988 336*. Here you can see south over the marshes and the variety of species is less intense, nature less on its best behaviour. At the north corner of the by-road the Forestry Commission keeps its end up at **Faggs Wood**, *986 348*, with a pretty parking place and a walk through varied woodland around a small stream valley.

Hamstreet Wood: leaves of a wild service tree, with chestnut and hornbeam

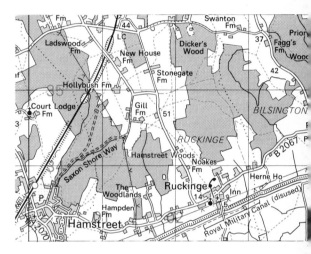

Clowes Wood *136 629*, ♀, ♣, *forest trail, FC and pf*

North and west of Canterbury is a great arc of woodlands known collectively as **Blean Woods**. Blean itself is a village on the Whitstable road with now only an indirect connection with the woodlands. A Forestry Commission picnic site, Clowes Wood, *136 629*, near the centre of the complex, provides a useful stopping place in a region of narrow but busy roads. From Canterbury take an un-numbered road to Tyler Hill. Alternatively, from Whitstable turn off the A299 at Chestfield Industrial Estate – the roundabout is marked by two large garages. Clowes Wood is not the most interesting section, but is welcoming in autumn with the heraldic reds and golds of the Forestry Commission's *Quercus rubra* and *Acer platanoides* which border the blocks of spruce.

A quarter of a mile south of the Clowes Wood car park an even narrower road leads off through **Thornden Wood**, *145 634*, bordered by impenetrable chestnut coppice. Thornden Wood is coniferized towards this, its western side, but there is still original sessile oak with chestnut understorey to the east where it is called, confusingly, West Blean Wood, a National Nature Reserve. It is bisected by a well-worn, decently surfaced public bridleway leading to Herne village.

East Blean Wood, *188 645*, by Herne Common, is 'private' and festooned with threatening yellow notices. The lane to Hoath goes through it and there are footpaths leading off, but absolutely nowhere to park. Enthusiastic walkers could park in Hoath and proceed westwards through East Blean, West

Blean and Thornden Woods, crossing the A291 just north of the so-called Wealden Woodlands Wildlife Park – a commercial set-up – and possibly stopping at the popular Fox and Hounds which is on the route and does food. Emerging onto Thornden Wood Road, the narrow road mentioned above, you have an awkward two sides of a triangle of motor road before you reach the Clowes Wood car park. It is possible to cross the short side of the triangle but there is certainly no right of way at present. Since the alternative is uncomfortable and dangerous, I have written to the local authority to try to get a pathway across. A fine stand of black pine is now being clear-felled and the land replanted, so indiscriminate wandering is bound to be discouraged. It is sad that the tall pines must go.

Blean Wood *075 608*, ♀, *pf*

Woods and commons to the south-west of Blean are quite accessible. Most attractive is Blean Wood – not 'West' or 'East' – near Dargate. Here you can park in Dargate and enter the wood by a path alongside an orchard, or, better, park at Holly Hill, *075 608*, just off a section of the old A2 between Dunkirk and Boughton Street. To enter Blean Wood take the left fork to the so-called Keepers Cottage. Near the house there is a good deal of alien planting – even a silver fir or two. But keeping to the highest ground (a choice of several footpaths) you find yourself in pure oak

coppice with bracken; on lower ground to the north is chestnut; hornbeam towards Dargate. This is an excellent wood, full of interest and not spoiled by containing a few alien specimens. Wild service and aspen are present.

Denge Wood *113 525*, ♀, *64 acres, WT plus adjacent woodland*

Immediately south-west of Canterbury and south of the A28 lies the large Denge Wood – much larger than the 64 acres of it owned by the Woodland Trust; but this section provides access from Garlinge Green where one can park. The woods are old, with pollard hornbeams on ancient banks and some

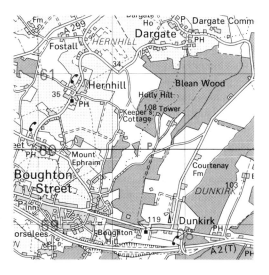

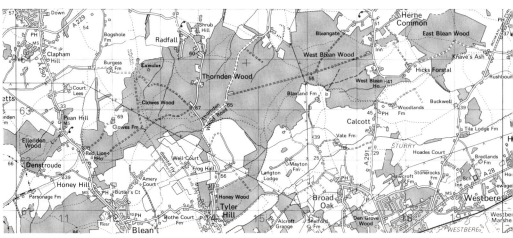

herbaceous plants associated with ancient woodland. The Trust will continue traditional management and will conserve a 14-acre patch of grassland in the middle of the wood.

Between Blean Wood and Canterbury, 2 miles from the city, is a large area of rather tatty oak and chestnut woodland, **Church Wood**, invaded by birch and sycamore towards Rough Common, which is exactly what it says it is. Uneven ground, a breezy place to walk, with too many footpaths at the Rough Common end: more undisturbed where the bridleway reaches Denstroude Farm, *096 611*. Split-chestnut palings or spiles were being made, using froe or dillaxe (side-cutting axe) with break (a vice with three-legged stand) under an awning in a coppice near the Dog and Punchbowl at Rough Common.

At Denstroude, north of these woods, is the smaller, thicker **Ellenden Wood**, *105 625*, a bird sanctuary of the Kent Naturalists' Trust. There is a bridleway from the Honey Hill road: but please don't take the dog. This oak

and hornbeam wood used to contain wild service trees, but they were cut by mistake (for sycamore). Cow wheat grows under the trees, and the heath fritillary is found here. It feeds upon cow wheat and is local to Kent. Wood ants prey upon the caterpillars.

Lyminge Forest West Wood *141 440*, ♣, *FC*

From Canterbury the Roman road called Stane Street leads south straight as a plumb line – use it to reach the Forestry Commission's West Wood, near Mockbeggar. A bright blue-and-white garage marks the turning left: or first turn sharply right to buy untreated double cream at Lymbridge Green. Lyminge Forest West Wood has a most impressive car park used, of course, out of season, by no one except dog owners, at least one of whom does not even leave his car – the dogs know their route. The fine tall trees are mostly Douglas firs with some spruces; more workaday stands of timber lie beyond, including some beautiful young larches; dense, dark hemlock west of the car

Tall Douglas firs at Lyminge Forest West Wood

park. West Wood is quiet: only distant planes to be heard, and the occasional tearing noise as an unwanted native hardwood is uprooted.

King's Wood, Challock *024 500*, ♀ ⚹, *2½m, easy, FC*

Challock is the name of the third Forestry Commission complex in this section, and of the village about 5 miles north of Ashford. King's Wood is spread for 3 miles along the top of the North Downs and is about 2 miles wide. The cark park, *024 500*, is a short distance down the Wye road which forks from the A251 to Ashford less than a mile from Challock. The car park is just that, with no public conveniences. The prescribed walk sets off through chestnut coppice, first some years old, then recently cut with some standard hardwoods. The chestnut stools are, very refreshingly, fairly widely spaced, giving scope for exploration. Some are respectably ancient. I heard a fox bark in the distance, but on this wet, misty morning the visible wildlife was in the lovely forms of numerous spider-webs beaded with moisture, each exploiting exactly the fork of a chestnut twig but conforming to their species plan. After this overture the curtain rises on tall pinewood, very poetic, not dense, much chestnut remaining, and with tall bracken. The solemn arcades, full of mist, were impressive – as they must be in summer.

Wye and Crundale Downs *078 455*, ♀, *about 50 acres open, NNR*

Beyond the old town of Wye, taking the Hastingleigh road, you again climb to the top of the escarpment, this time to 550 feet, which when I went was well into the clouds. The nature reserve in the mist and rain appeared to have little to offer beyond a long row of very individualistic beeches. But, as I walked, the horizon became visible, and with it a strip of creamy light. Soon the sun had altered everything, and the cattle which graze the down began to emerge from a hazel thicket where they had found some slight shelter. Views over Kent and westward along the Downs are inspiring, no less the rich textures of grassland and scrubland below. The whole nature reserve is 250 acres, and the small area

Sheltering in a hazel coppice, on Crundale Downs

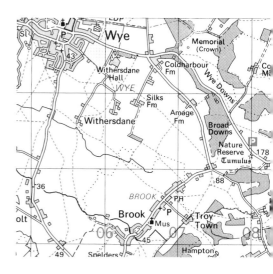

open to the public contains highly characteristic woodland, from hazel coppice with oak standards to pure coppice, and chalk scrub, with spindle, wayfaring tree and hawthorn. One hazel is unbelievably large, bristling with hundreds of shoots. The coppice is cut, but the wood, apparently, is left to rot, the object being really to conserve the coppice and keep dead wood as a habitat; no one needs the fuel. The Visitors' Centre had some graphic panels with facts about geology and wildlife, but I felt it was out of place.

12 20 21 / 10 **17** 18 / 7 13 14 South Chilterns, Thames Downs, Surrey Heath

Landranger sheets 164, 165, 174, 175

Reading is at the centre of this section, but the woodlands are mainly in the Chilterns to the north-west and the commons of the Bagshot Sands to the south-east. From the point of view of Londoners, great roads serve the area: the M40 bypassing High Wycombe; the M4 to Maidenhead; the M3 sweeping over Bagshot.

Cowleaze Wood *726 957*, ♀ ♣, *1m, FC*
Turning off at junction 5, to Stokenchurch, immediately turn left onto the old road, the A40, and left again, signposted Christmas Common. You now cross over the motorway as it plunges over the chalk and, incidentally, through Aston Rowant Nature Reserve – this in spite of fierce opposition in the 1950s. The Forestry Commission car park, large and among the trees, is invaluable, for there are no stopping places on Christmas Common roads. The waymarked walk leads back from the escarpment ridge through a larchwood and into a beechwood, then through spruces and out to a seemingly remote, enclosed countryside, patterned with hanging beechwoods and steep ploughland. The path along the south-east side of the wood is surprisingly well used, as if there were a secret traffic: perhaps lines of pack-horses winding along the wood margins in the dusk. There are maples, whitebeams, oaks; sunlight and shadow, I hope.

On the eastern side of the motorway the A40 to Oxford sweeps in impressive curves down the escarpment through Aston Wood and Juniper Bank, both National Trust properties, not ideal walking country because of the road and the steepness. Woods to the north-east above Chinnor are also of mature beech, probably of natural origin, very beautiful, and somewhat spoiled by over-use and dumping.

South-west, near Christmas Common, is **Watlington Hill**, with two sections totalling 108 acres belonging to the National Trust and a car park at the top of the hill. South-westwards on the high ground are well-shaped yews, like a township of green tents, for which the area is known.

Chiltern beechwood

Maidenhead Thicket *855 812*, ♀ ♣, *364 acres, NT*
Just past the last roundabout of the motorway and miraculously intact is the Thicket, an appropriately triangular patch penetrated only by a muddy road. A popular place to park, but still very much a thicket, this is an old common with grazing long since discontinued. Thorns are old and picturesque; there are some old oaks, some beeches, and a stand of larch. Amongst the thorns a jungle is fast developing, but a wide grassy ride provides an easy walk with many attractive groupings of trees, returning (clockwise) by more open mature beeches and oaks surrounding a monument,

Robin Hood's Arbour, which is an earthwork described in a notice-board on site.

Burnham Beeches *956 852,* ♀, *492 acres, many paths and roads, map on site, LA*
Turn north from the M4 junction 6 through Slough for Farnham, or south from the M40's

junction 2 – a better route. The map reference applies to the large parking ground on East Burnham Common, a piece of open land, but you can drive in the woodland. Walking, the skill is to avoid the roads. I would suggest a circular, anticlockwise route taking in both streams to the north and then striking south to

join the Victoria Drive. This route will take you through the characteristic, grotesque or beautiful to your taste, ancient pollard beeches for which the area is well known. Besides beeches, you will find gorse, broom, ling, rhododendron, oaks (some old pollards), birch, pine, sallow, holly, yew, brambles and bracken. The soil is not the chalk of the Chiltern beechwoods, but gravel of the river terraces.

Burnham Beeches is a sort of public park (since 1879) made out of what was effectively a common used without stint for grazing and firewood until, surrounded by coal-burning houses, it passed simultaneously into disuse and into the affections of Londoners. Stoke Poges, with Thomas Gray's 'sentinel yews', is just to the south-east.

Hodgemoor Woods *960 940 and 968 938, ♀ ♣, 300 acres, 3 walks, easy, sometimes muddy, FC*

Surrounded by lanes as narrow as any in Devonshire – Bottom Lane around the south side and Bottom House Farm Lane leading off the north – this is a rich and highly characteristic patch of old woodland with a very busy birdlife. There are patches of young grand fir and Austrian pine, both looking extremely healthy, amongst oaks and birch coppice, with a few old Scots pines to establish a precedent for this coniferous invasion of a very picturesque wood. A few acres of oak have been cleared to plant beech, such are the mysteries of modern forestry. Though not large this is a wood easy to get lost in, strangely mediaeval and directionless – so follow the markers.

Chesham Bois Wood *960 003, ♀, 40 acres, no particular routes, WT*

Bois is pronounced as Boys. This gloomy patch of close-set beeches is surrounded by houses and cut by a noisy road, and I cannot think why the Woodland Trust bothered. Between the tracks of motorbikes, living dangerously, are scattered plants of woodruff and sanicle, some rather sad bluebells, gooseberry and much *Rubus*, not flowering. A clearing on the east slope has a magnificent display of grasses and rushes, a vigorous birch thicket coming up.

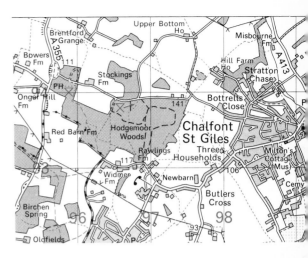

Bix Bottom and Maidensgrove Scrubs
726 871, ♀, 2m or more, steep, muddy in winter, NR

The BBONT Warburg Reserve here is dedicated to conserving the maximum of different habitat. There is a nature trail with a very clear booklet, and an exhibition open every day except Thursdays and Fridays.

For a plain walk with no lectures, follow the Oxfordshire Way path along the side of the

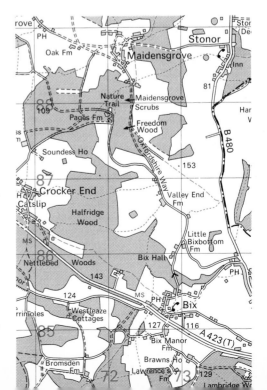

valley, with a hedge of wayfaring trees, and into a wood called Freedom. At once you are in characteristic chalkland scrub with spurge laurel among fiercely armed trailing rose (*Rosa arvensis*) and many other chalk shrubs. At the top of the hill the path joins a rutted cart track and here you are clearly on clay. The Scrubs are on the slope to your left and you will find a path downwards at the corner nearest Maidensgrove. This patch of weird woodland, mainly coppiced beech with hazel, is neither comfortable to walk in nor is it particularly interesting botanically, but I find it fascinating. At the foot of the hill you are at stage 1 of the nature trail: a large Christmas tree and a wide grassy ride, with rabbits and orchids.

The Information Centre is a few yards back down the valley.

Driving in the complicated lanes of the Chilterns between Henley and the escarpment, one is hardly ever out of the cover of beeches. But often what appear to be walkable woods are quite narrow belts of trees, or, as at Nettlebed, so open that you never get away from motor noise. Near Checkendon you can park by a bridleway, *677 828*, which leads between Forestry Commission spruces with a wide and interesting band of native vegetation. You can also walk south-west through the open, mature beeches of the Hook End Estate by bridleways and footpaths marked on our map.

Hambleden Great Wood, on a hogsback of chalk, is easily accessible by footpaths signed at the roadside. But you have to park in Hambleden itself and this can be difficult at holiday times. An official, not so convenient, parking place is provided at *785 856* just north of Mill End.

Ibstone, *756 930*, more easily reached from the Stokenchurch junction (5) of the M40 (turn away from Stokenchurch at the exit lane) has open beechwoods, very beautifully shaped and at the right density, with some oak and holly – **Commonhill Wood** and **Hartmoor Wood**, *750 950*.

Little Wittenham Wood *566 934*, ♀ (♣), *180 acres, bridleway and footpath, muddy, pf*
At Little Wittenham church, tiny and dwarfed

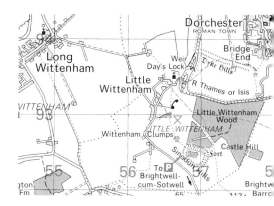

by a great *Sequoiadendron* in a garden, you walk across a field to Little Wittenham Wood. The wood is between the river and on the shade side of the double Sinodun Hills or Wittenham Clumps. Wittenham Dugs, the local name since the mounds were furnished with these clumps, did not get onto the map, nor did Mrs Buntsey's Buttocks (after a local landowner). On the river side are poplars, on the hill side spruces; in between, where the bridleway waits to trap you in mire, is Oxfordshire oak/ash woodland, and very nice too.

You can walk up to the Clumps, which are of beech, and admire the distant Downs, the nearer Didcot Power Station and nearer still Dorchester Meres. From Little Wittenham northwards a line of not very successful, but attractive, fastigiate poplars leads your eye to a forgotten road over the flat land to the site of a lost village – 'lost' little over a century ago.

Ashampstead Common *578 754*, ♀ ♣, *200 acres, bridleway, muddy, common land*
It appears that the common was originally an oak-and-beech wood with holly, yew, hawthorn and some cherry. It is overgrown: Scots and Weymouth pines and Douglas firs are now taller than the oaks and there are weirdly shaped beeches, birches, thorns and hollies grown up from old coppice; moss everywhere, thickets of oak and beech saplings. It is a fairytale wood perhaps; it must have looked a Cinderella wood when all the timber oaks were removed, probably in the 1914–18 war, leaving nothing but misshapen beeches

and frowsty thorns. The Prince, in the person of the Lord of the Manor, came and planted exotic conifers; and Princess Cinderella is now left to decay in her finery. It is a long time obviously since anyone exercised any common rights here; you would think they would at least gather up the dead wood. It is a shame, and nothing like a common, but it is worth seeing and if the sun shines you will be rewarded with an aged smile.

There are other commons like this – Holme Wood near Dorking is one – I suppose no one dares to touch them.

South of the M4 – no barrier but a blessed pipeline bleeding off the noise from this nice countryside – and under it, you come to beautiful Bradfield, Southend, Scotland and

Bucklebury Common, on which last there is a parking place which wins my prize for decency: no rubbish, a sensible litter bin, no sequestering trees, heath of gorse and birch. A shallow screen of sallows is planted. Cars zoom by as if trying to reach take-off speed, but you can't have everything. This is the parking place for Carbins Wood.

Carbins Wood, Bucklebury Common
561 693, ♀ ♣, 600 acres, easy but muddy, ½–3m, FC and common land

The common is lined with houses lurking behind the steep, old wood-bank which separates heath from woodland; the gnarled oaks on the bank are glimpsed beyond the birch and the gorse. Between a house rather confusingly called Carbins Wood and a used car lot of distinctly woodland type, you can progress down to a stream and the pretty edges of the Forestry Commission wood. There are stands of beech and larch, with pines and Douglas firs, all nicely varied. The path along the stream, lined with elegant silver birches, is most attractive, with the plantation shutting off the noise and wind, and a hint or two of old coppice to remind us that the wood is old. Bluebells push vigorously through the dry leaf litter of the beeches.

If you take the direct path southwards on a grassy ride you soon reach the south margins of the wood – another stream and a paddock surrounded by oaks and cherries of some age. Of course, Carbins must have been an oakwood, perhaps with beech on this more fertile side. Perhaps the drama of the place, besides its attractive uneven ground, is the contrast between birch heath and oakwood, in

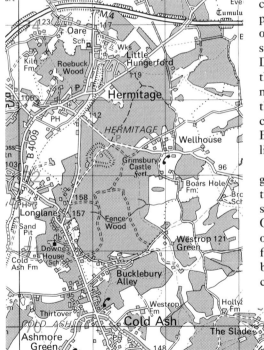

spite of the new planting. Anyway, I thought it was all quite charming.

Bucklebury Common continues to Upper Common, with pines adding a darker note westwards towards Cold Ash. **Basildon Park**, National Trust, is architecturally imposing but boring parkwise, with ugly limes in front and a dull beech plantation marked private. The great arboretum of the area is **Cliveden**, near Taplow, *915 840*, open seasonally, National Trust; the heavily wooded Cliveden reach of the river is often pictured. There are yew hedges, ancient mulberries, great glades of *Ilex*, cypress oaks, butternut trees, and *Rhododendron macabeanum*. Nearby the lamented **Dropmore**, with many great trees, is secured behind tall wire fences, with absentee Arabian owners and resident Alsatian defenders.

Hermitage Woods *513 724*, ♀ ♠ , *400 acres plus, easy, wet, pf*

Hermitage is a suburb, clearly indicated from Newbury's ring road and from the A34(T), and it has some really charming woodland where one can walk at will, only observing the sign-written admonishment of the owners, the Gerald Palmer Trust, to 'behave quietly'. I explored the northern segment of Fence Wood, and was very struck by the intimate and varied quality of mixed woodland clearly exploited for timber yet losing nothing – in fact gaining – in character. Larches were in the pretty fresh green they wear in April, beeches were in leaf already, oaks were impressive in adolescent crowds or decorous in old age. A cuckoo rehearsed its notes and a deer paused in a patch of sunlight. A fine baby owl, fallen from its nest, was spotted by a pair of boxers and hurried off to Newbury by the boxers' owners.

Cow Common, Unhill Wood, Ham Wood *551 813*, ♀ ♠ , *about 500 acres, up to 3m, easy, pf and now a NR*

From the Ridge Way you enter the woods by the Gamekeeper's Cottage to a chorus of loud assorted dog music, and if you have a dog it really must be on a lead.

The shapes of the woods are fascinating around the serpentine, undulating common – not common any more and without cows. In winter the dark branches and green trunks of the beeches contrast vividly with the chalky soil and the bleached grass, and some not-too-oppressive spruces and Douglas firs add their own colours, seemingly a brighter green here on the chalk. The distant Downs are blue. There is a not-very-old wood-bank (say 250 years) alongside the path covered in moss, dog's mercury and bluebells. Many beeches here did not survive the drought a few years back, and there is also a slight plantation effect of even-age and cherry laurel, but these are very beautiful woods, partly coniferized but with much evidence of old use. Large cherries have been allowed to get too old and rotten and little serious forestry is practised: shooting was until recently the *raison d'être* of the woods. You can enter from the other direction by Starveall Farm from the A417, striking up left or south-west from Unhill Bottom.

Silchester Common, Pamber Forest *627 623*, ♀ ♠ ♨, *1½ hours at least, very wet in places, common land and NR*

There is ample parking by the sports ground, prettily surrounded by shining gorse in summer. This gorse common should be treated with respect: its northern segment is peaty and trackless; beware, however innocent it may

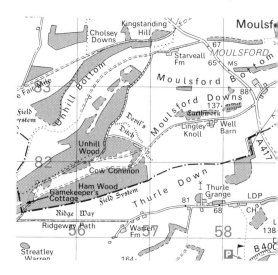

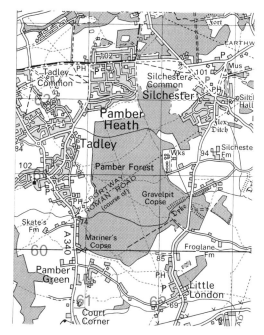

look. Keep on high ground or you may be trapped like a fly in a bottle.

Walk down the road signed to Lords Wood and the Butts, a new housing estate. An old wooden sign points to the footpath, which skirts the backs of the new houses and soon leaves the gorse-and-birch heath for oak woodland. At the bottom, signs lead you left into Pamber Forest and Nature Reserve. This is a fine wood of durmast oak giving way gradually to an equally fine stand of pine, now probably ready for thinning. Turn right at the crossways to descend to a charming stream through oak and hazel coppice, the banks mossy and strewn with common wild flowers – much wood anemone. Continuing, you will meet the prominent double wood-bank at the north side with gnarled oaks of ancient hedges, gorse beyond but all sylvan within. Return to meet the stream again – and this is important – follow it to rejoin the footpath.

Ambarrow Hill

Ambarrow Hill, Finchampstead Ridges, Simons Wood *813 635*,♀♣ *(Scots pine)*, *1¾m one way, easy but uneven, NT*

At Finchampstead, Little Sandhurst, there is a complex of woodland around an avenue of large and impressive *Sequoiadendron giganteum*, the Big Tree of the Sierra Nevada, northern California, and the oldest and biggest tree in the world. Introduced to Britain in 1853 the tree was named after the Duke of Wellington. Wellington College is close by,

Savill Gardens' early specialities: *Narcissus cyclamineus* and *Rhododendron* 'Praecox'

beyond Crowthorne Station, and here are the wellingtonias, unfortunately bordering a motor road and forming an over-dramatic setting for the comings and goings of tradesmen's vans and schoolchildren.

Ambarrow Hill is crowned with tall Scots pines, the ground eroded by many pairs of shoes. The footpath will lead you to Ambarrow Lane, past the gardens of large houses and a field, to Finchampstead Ridges, where a sample of the beautiful Surrey Heath countryside of bracken, heather, birch and pine is preserved, overlooking the Blackwater River. **Simons Wood** contains a large National Trust parking place and here of course this heathland walk might best start: but you can park at the roadside where indicated by a small *p* on the map.

Virginia Water: the Savill Gardens 977 705 and Valley Gardens 984 700, ♀ ✦, easy, Crown Estate

The Savill Gardens, created in 1932, are 35 acres, entrance quite costly, open from March to Christmas Eve, 10–6 (or 7 pm in summer). There is a bookshop and a café. The Valley Gardens, created in 1947, are 300 acres, free and open all the year.

Parking in this part of Windsor Great Park is not free and a supply of ten-pence coins is necessary – unless you pay to walk in the Savill Gardens, when a parking token is issued. From the strict point of view of woodland, the Valley Gardens offer more acreage, obviously, but for the maximum interest in an out-of-season,

short walk the Savill Gardens are hard to beat. The gardens are dominated by a small hill with tall beeches, the floor intriguingly covered with moss, looking like a vast collection of Victorian pincushions. The rhododendron much in bloom in March was 'Praecox', but hidden in the shrubbery 'Golden Oriole' was splendid. Camellias are strong here: *Camellia japonica* 'Gloire de Nantes' was still glorious in early March.

There are some very old English oaks in and around the garden; this is, after all, Windsor Great Park.

At Valley Gardens there is more walking to be done and the effects are broader. Also there is a wide range of pinetum species including *Tsuga* and a grove of *Metasequoia*; amazing great cedars and big Scots pine.

The more typical oak parkland is to be found at the western side of Windsor Great Park.

Crowthorne Wood (Caesar's Camp)
862 661, (♀) ✦, an easy stroll, or a tough hike needing boots and compass
Caesar's Camp, as usual with such names, is not Roman but pre-Roman, the third largest hill fort in Berkshire, with mighty ramparts now clothed in beech. That such a large structure should have been made here is a reflection on the native vegetation, which cannot have been all forest: it may have been grazing land. The site has not been excavated but it has been much trampled over.

Oxford University Arboretum, Nuneham Courtenay 555 987, 45 acres, very easy, pf
The arboretum is 5 miles south of Oxford on the A423, a Victorian collection of conifers, Japanese maples, etc, to which new trees of special botanical or economic interest have been added. A rare patch of Greensand allows the cultivation of calcifuges. (The alluvial terraces of the Thames are mostly limy.) The plantation is informal and resembles woodland, with peacocks as a change from the usual game.

The arboretum is open only between April and September and is closed on Sundays.

20	21	22
17	**18**	19
13	14	15

SOUTH-EAST ENGLAND

London Woodland

Landranger sheets 176, 177, 187, 188

NORTH AND WEST LONDON

Hampstead Heath: Ken Wood *268 874,*
♀, *easy but not flat, 1m, LA*
The nearest wood to the middle of London is
Ken Wood, about 30 acres, 4 miles as the
starling flies from Trafalgar Square. Kenwood
House is an important picture gallery and
museum, the Iveagh Bequest; its gardens and
wood are joined with but distinct from
Hampstead Heath as a whole, like a vital organ
within a living body. The wood is said to be a
remnant of the Middlesex Forest – if so it is
probably the only remnant – and is carefully
fenced off. All the paths are fenced too, for this
is a wood where the visitors annually much
outnumber the trees. Oak, beech and chestnut
are tall, and as classical in character as the
music which on some summer evenings floats,
curiously fragmented, from a concrete shell at

Hampstead Heath Extension in winter – old
hawthorn hedge

the lakeside. There are good specimen trees in
the garden, including a tall swamp cypress by
the water's edge. The car park nearer to
Spaniards Gate best serves the woods.

A Hampstead Heath Walk *about 2½m,*
can be muddy
For the best of Hampstead's woodland, take a
number 24 bus to South End; or there is a
large car park here at *271 859*, sheltered by
fine weeping willows on East Heath Road.
Head towards the ponds, which are
surrounded by large crack willows. Keep to the
lowest ground, following the valley until you
can cross to the far side, where you will find a
wide path which eventually goes by a viaduct
over a small, dark lake. There are many oldish
oaks of characteristic shape, and silver birches,
as well as a great richness of sallows and some
alder. The grey squirrels are tame enough to
eat out of your hand, if you have something
they like. Climbing up towards Spaniards Way
you enter a planted area with maples, Swedish
whitebeam and, left towards the road junction
at the top of Hampstead Heath, a number of
false acacias (*Robinia*) which are naturalized in
the sandy soil. You may now either cross
Spaniards Road for the Hampstead Heath
Extension or go left towards Jack Straw's
Castle for Hill Gardens, West Heath and
Golders Hill Park.
   Option one takes you downhill through
genuine secondary woodland. The land was
quarried for sand and gravel until comparatively recently. Birch has spread over the
broken ground, especially to the south side,
and there are ponds and even mires. Bur-
marigold and Himalayan balsam are common
here. In the steep woodland section to the right
or north are naturally regenerating *Robinia* and
Norway maple among a good mixture of native
species including birch and oak. The short
descent by a tall crab apple brings you to the
Hampstead Heath Extension which
penetrates into the Hampstead Garden
Suburb. This section of the heath is

surrounded by a road with quasi-Georgian houses and plane trees, but you may strike through the centre of the grassland among oaks and overgrown hawthorn hedges (splendid in May) and still think yourself in the country. You may cross the grass to find your way easily through the streets to Golders Green Station.

For option two, cross North End Road with Jack Straw's Castle on your left. The path, between steep banks covered with sycamore suckers and seedlings, leads to West Heath, which is heavily wooded; or, more interestingly, you can climb some iron steps to surface through cherry laurel onto a stone

parapet or walk-way. From this you can look down on a very fine hornbeam, while on your right are the serene lawns and cedars of Inverforth House. A great *Wisteria sinensis* clasps a column and spreads over a timber pergola in a mildly extravagant architectural finish to this agreeable aerial promenade. You descend, almost through the branches of an old, wandering chestnut, to Hill Garden, as peaceful a place as can be found in London. Even here there is an aspect of woodland in a sheltering bank which supports beech trees which have enormous straight trunks. Beyond is **Golders Hill Park**, *258 877*, with deer and other animals in enclosures and many interesting trees. North-west (in springtime) there is a splendid collection of flowering cherries and pears to your right. If it is autumn you will find a few fruits, probably, and easily pick out the dusky pink of *Cercis siliquastrum*, the Judas tree. If you go out by the tennis courts, Golders Green Station is only a street away. If you have children allow at least an hour for looking at the animals.

Big Wood *254 886*, ♀, *18 acres, very easy paths with seats, LA*
Amazingly preserved, almost pickled in ripe suburbia, this is an oak-hazel wood, obviously an old coppice with standards. It is well worth seeking out (make for Temple Fortune Hill). The oaks are carefully looked after, no dead wood being allowed, probably for the safety of those who walk here. The large trees allow enough light for the hazel below to flower and there is a shrub layer of bramble in parts. For Londoners unreasonably missing the country in January, Big Wood is reassuring and delightful. Undoubtedly the isolation and seclusion of this small wood amongst acres of quiet streets and gardens allow it to function as a real wood and as a true bird sanctuary – not just a museum-piece bathed in petrol and diesel fumes. Grey squirrels are many but seem to do no harm.

Big Wood is only big compared with **Little Wood**, 2 acres, 200 yards to the north-west. Beyond are the horrors of the North Circular Road, now without even its Cornish or Wheatley elms. Even so, crossing that road will

bring you to a charming wooded park at Church End, *251 905*, with fine Caucasian wingnut, *Ginkgo*, Bhutan pine, etc, and a rare cut-leaved oak by the pond.

Moat Mount *211 941*, ♀, $\frac{1}{4}m$, *fps, LA*
The entrance, 1 mile north of the junction called Northway Circus on the A1(T) or Barnet Way, is reached by going on to the next roundabout – another mile – and returning on the south-bound carriageway. There is parking only in a lay-by. This wood, which has survived from domestic parkland, is beautiful in spite of institutional trappings, and most remarkable for its hornbeams, once pollarded and now giving just a hint of old London woodland. By the lake (artificial and uphill) are *Ilex* and other park trees.

Whippendell Wood, Watford *073 978*, ♀ (♠), *200 acres, many dry fps, LA*
Watford, 16½ miles from London, and only 15 minutes from London on the M1, could be

described, much to its surprise, as the gateway to the Hertfordshire countryside. At the north end of the High Street is Cassiobury Park, and you can walk through this old and grand, but now sad, parkland, across the Grand Union Canal and the golf links, to Whippendell Wood. By car the more attractive of two car parks is approached by a single-track road from the Clarendon Arms at Chandler's Cross (signpost to the wood).

Though lately circumscribed by the link road A405(T), Whippendell Wood still has an aura of wildness, seeming to absorb the westerly winds and turning its back on industrial Watford. The fields around are very green. Older trees are beeches, their days numbered, and there are many oaks with burred trunks, reassuringly native. The field layer is intermittent bramble and bracken; there are birches of various ages, with holly a frequent shrub. There is a patch of Forestry Commission spruce to the north. Hedge trees are cut as coppice, decorative without being useful, and beech saplings, distinct with red leaves in midwinter, show that, catastrophe avoided, Whippendell Wood will survive.

Bayhurst Wood *070 891*, ♀ , *moderate, many routes, LA*
The car park is in the outermost westerly wood of a group of oakwoods, in total about 700 acres, around Ruislip Common. Across the lane is Mad Bess Wood, while Copse Wood and Park Wood straddle the Common, on the far side of the A4180. Ruislip fields are typically punctuated by kennels, small industries, farmhouses rebuilt in ranch style; but the woods are something like the original vegetation of the London Clay. **Oxhey Woods**, 2 miles north-east of Bayhurst Wood on the A4125, are also of native oak, even more public and accessible, but surprisingly wild in appearance for their suburban status. Many a front garden in the streets round about contains an oak of undoubted native origin, so that Ruislip and Northolt are rich in woodland atmosphere. The woods are Public Open Spaces – a sort of wood-pasture for people. As the trees approach maturity, conservation will have to take more aggressive forms.

Oakwood also survives at **Harrow Weald Common**, *143 926*, with a section of Grim's Dyke, and a viewpoint over Harrow Weald Park.

Black Park *004 833*, ♀ *(♣)*, *about 300 acres, very easy, can be wet, LA*
It really is black, with lovely tall *Pinus nigra* and a lake surrounded by black mud – and very important-looking notices such as 'NO FISHING AFTER 5 P.M.'. There are beeches, silver birches and Scots pines as well, and a patch of pole conifers. Pinewood Studios is to the north. There is a map at the parking place with a suggested walk which takes in the new plantation. Just here and there, and even on the dullest day, there is a hint of a countryside quite unexpected for outer London and even Britain.

NORTH-EAST LONDON

Epping Forest *411 983 (High Beach)*, ♀ , *6000 acres (2000 acres grassland), GLC*
For most of its 6 miles the forest is bisected by the A104, and is like a long, uneven oak leaf veined by roads and streams. There is a close network of paths and rides, but only one formal parking place, at High Beach, and cars are kept strictly to the roads.

Epping Forest occupies a broad ridge of gravel between the Lee and the Roding Valleys and is famous for its hornbeams, lopped for centuries by the commoners of surrounding parishes; there are also grazing rights, for 2000 cattle. Neither lopping nor pasturing occurs now in the woodland, scrub takes over grass (half the acreage since 1920) and the old, gnarled tree trunks send their broad shoots to heaven like gargoyles imitating angels.

In fact there are at least as many beeches as hornbeams, but they nearly always share the same ground and partake of the same character. Oaks, mostly pedunculate, were pollarded with the hornbeam and beech, and are scattered remarkably evenly throughout. Only holly and birch among the commoner trees show any remarkable distribution pattern; in fact the only pure stands in the forest are those of birch – some grown up from

Pollard beeches in Epping Forest

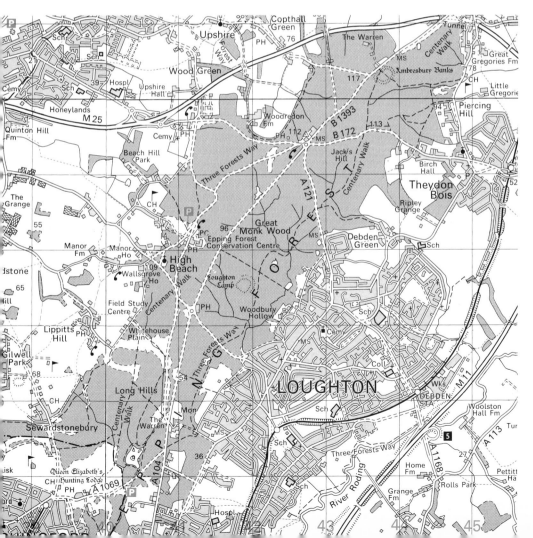

old coppice – and occasionally beech, which has some limited strongholds in the centre and the north-west. Hornbeam comes close to real dominance in the parts closest to Loughton and at Chingford; it tends to occupy the valleys of the turgid forest streams. There are several bogs and ponds, rich in rushes and horsetails.

The forest is unbelievably busy, even now that the M11 takes away most of the traffic. Nevertheless, it is a poetic and lovely woodland, and the poetry begins wherever you step away from a road. In its richness of form and depth of shade it seems to embody all that we expect of a forest. But each picturesque bole with its crown of tall, straight branches is a symbol: centuries of toil and use in the bole, one century of 'conservation' to create the top-heavy crown. There is too much shade. The ground is often bare; the hornbeams decay in the shade of their companion beeches, eventually becoming emaciated corpses amongst the cigarette cartons and beer cans. (Much larger rubbish is also dumped, and no less than 159 stolen cars were abandoned in the forest in 1982, most of them set on fire.) The Corporation of London made a noble gesture in the late nineteenth century when, finding itself the owner of rights of common (because it owned a cemetery), it took the part of less-privileged commoners of Loughton who were fighting against the loss of their rights through inclosures. It has often been praised for the way it has administered this land outside its boundaries. But, for various reasons, no doubt outside its control, it has failed to perpetuate the wood-pasture character of the forest. The Conservation Centre (behind the King's Oak at High Beach) is open every day except Mondays and Tuesdays.

You can walk anywhere at any time: use our map.

Hainault Forest *475 925, ♀, 1000 acres approximately, CP(GLC)*
There are various waymarked woodland walks on this reafforested common. The picnic area is in open parkland by a lake, with various facilities including a café, all indicated by an insignificant symbol on the A1112, 3 miles north-west of Romford. Entrances at the north-west side, from Manor Road, lead directly into the woodland, with more walks.

SOUTH-EAST LONDON

Joyden's Wood *504 720, ♀ ♣, 450 acres, easy walks and Schools' Trail, FC*
This nearest to London (13 miles) of the Forestry Commission's properties is a very attractive wood, almost impossible to get to by road. The main roads are designed to get you away, and the local streets are extremely congested. However, the National Bus 421 from Belvedere to Swanley, via Bexley Post Office, passes an entrance to the wood in Summerhouse Drive on the Joyden's Wood Estate. Or you can walk $\frac{1}{2}$ mile south from Bexley Station, entering via High Street and Vicarage Road. If you must go by car, the best way is to turn off the Maidstone Road, A20(T), just before Swanley (avoiding the bypass) by Birchwood Road through orchards and gooseberry fields, then left and uphill into Summerhouse Drive. There is no official car park. From all these directions you will infer that I think the wood is worth finding. It has indeed the authentic atmosphere of old Kentish woodland, and I was touched by the persistence here amongst the housing estates and flyovers of a quality I find hard to describe. Old chestnut coppice,

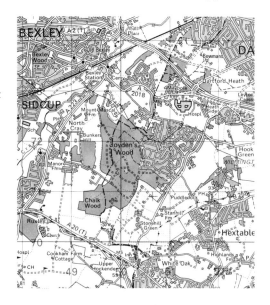

aspens, sallows and very pretty birch trees, with honeysuckle and foxgloves, greet you as you embark on the schools' trail from Summerhouse Avenue, over sandy and uneven ground and before you get to the *raison d'être* of the wood, *Pinus nigra*, larch beyond.

Even closer into the labyrinth of central London are **Bostall Woods**, *466 780*, and **Lesnes Abbey Woods**, *477 787*, dark and overgrown and slightly parkified, but none the less beautiful and the tiny **Maryon Park**, *420 786*, clean and tidy, with lovely specimen trees.

South of Woolwich at Eltham is a largish complex of woods, common and park with **Oxleas Wood**, north and west of Falconwood Station, *446 755*; dense oakwoods looking unbelievably natural on each side of that clogged artery, the A2.

Further south the small **Chislehurst Common**, *440 704*, is well wooded, with enough oak and birch, among some aliens, to convince you that you are in the country only 50 yards from a busy shopping street.

Petts Wood *447 684*, ♀, *88 acres, many easy paths, NT*

The Petts were Elizabethan shipwrights, but most of the wood is called Willet Wood, after the local builder who pioneered Summer Time in the early years of this century. There are a Daylight Inn and a Willet Way – where the inhabitants of gingerbread Tudor houses have made good use of that extra hour in cultivating splendid gardens, many with a very distinctive velvety Lawson cypress cultivar dominating the front garden and giving an unusual unity to the street.

The wood is pretty, with much birch, some mature oak, some chestnut recently coppiced after a fifty-year gap. A very countrified ploughed field of the sandy, pebbly soil intervenes at the north but there is continuous woodland to St Paul's Cray Common – Chislehurst is beyond.

Ide Hill *489 517*, ♀, *easy short walk, NT*
Toy's Hill ♀, *several easy routes, NT*
Ide Hill has only an L-shaped sliver of wood-

Summer time in Petts Wood

land, but very pretty: beech and oak, pines and whitebeams. The path on the steep scarp is easy and provided with handrails and steps, and there is a stone seat. The hilltop view is marvellous, framed by clumps of broom on a green sward, with benches under pines and beeches – a very good place for a picnic.

A mile over the fields westwards is Toy's Hill – it is much further by road. Here is a large National Trust car park (where they charge for parking in the summer), the focal point of a group of National Trust woods rather confusingly intermixed with private estates. Octavia's Wood and Brasted Chart are on the dip slope, old beech and durmast oak coppice with some pollards, and there are some whitebeams – the wood is nice and simple with a bare leaf-litter floor. The twisted and bent shapes of the trunks tell their story of many centuries' exploitation. The more used trees are, the more they seem to assume human shapes. The Chart was a common, a wood pasture. Chert or chart-stone – the local equivalent of flint, is the origin of the peculiar name.

Octavia Hill was a lady whose sister Frances owned the land, which was one of the earliest acquisitions of the National Trust. She was a co-founder of the Trust.

Down House: Sandwalk Wood *432 612, ♀, 20 minutes' easy stroll, Royal College of Surgeons*
The house is open every afternoon except Monday and Friday. You have to be interested to see Darwin's reconstructed study, otherwise the walk works out at two pence per minute. Charles Darwin, author of *The Origin of Species*, lived here for forty-one years and planted the wood with birch, wild cherry and holly. He made a sandy – now grassy – 'thinking path' which offers a choice of shade or sun, according to route. The wood is rather small and linear for a memorial to our greatest naturalist-philosopher, but it is authentic.

From National Trust woodlands at **South Hawke**, *373 540*, the road through the woods continues south and west, bridging the motorway to pretty Godstone and **Tilburstow**

Hill, car park at *350 500*. The point of the place is its view. None of these woods is large; added together as a drive they are impressive and the roads are surprisingly quiet outside commuter times.

SOUTH-WEST LONDON

Gatton Park Wood *264 523, ♀, 150 acres, many easy paths, NT*
Mostly on chalk are beech and ash with, in hollows, rhododendron and sycamore; horses churn the paths in the woods and motorbikes polish the ground of an old quarry. There are nice views, lots of red campion and wood sanicle: but it all needs taking in hand. There are some bluebells and even a bank with a few white helleborines. Turn south from the M25 onto the A217 then immediately left and right for the parking ground.

Margery Wood and **Colley Hill** *246 523, ♀, easy path to the North Downs, NT*
Unfortunately the M25 is to go smack through the middle of Margery Wood. I expect there will be a footbridge, but I would have insisted on a deep cutting with a roof carrying soil, and the trees replaced. Why should a road be more important than a wood? The trees are oaks with birch and aspen, and the path emerges onto a grassy down with masses of hawthorn and a splendid view. From here and from other viewpoints on the North Downs you have the impression that Surrey is about 75 per cent trees: statistically it is 15 per cent woodland, twice the national average, but this takes no account of hedgerow and garden trees.

Kew Gardens *184 775, ♀ ♣, 300 acres, 2m minimum walking, easy but can be exhausting, MAFF*
Properly the Royal Botanic Gardens, Kew, Surrey, and administered by the Ministry of Agriculture, Kew Gardens has been a national botanic garden since 1841, much enlarged by its great first director, Sir William Hooker. It is in a class of its own. For woodland, Kew might seem a tame resort; but it is amongst other things a comprehensive collection of temperate trees, and it breathes a woodland air. Autumn

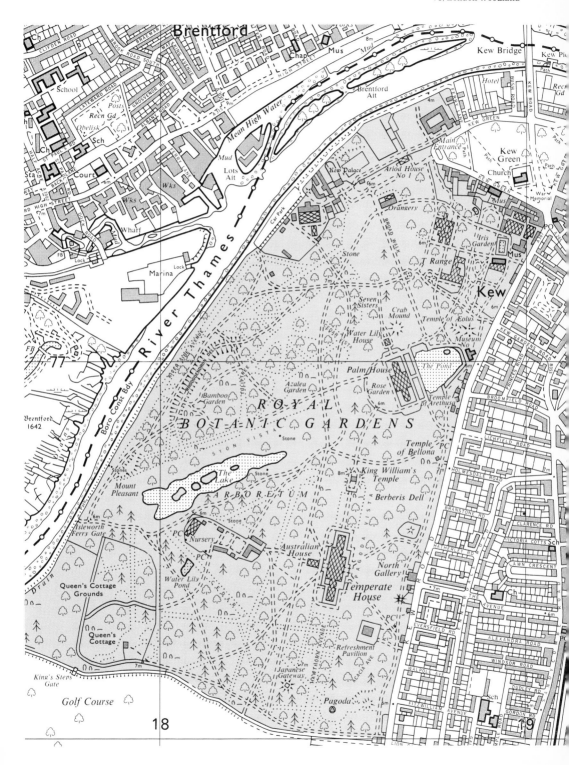

leaves and fruits, winter-flowering trees, in spring the early magnolias, and all the native trees in bud and shoot, fine pines, spruces and oriental conifers generally, even a bluebell wood in spring, and a great collection of flowering cherries; in summer a powerful orchestration of leaf and blossom: and all easily accessible via Kew Gardens Station on the District Line. For drivers out of London the roads can be off-putting. Out of rush-hour times the Hammersmith–Great West Road route will serve. The parking place indicated by the map reference is reached by turning down Ferry Lane from the north side of Kew Green.

Do not leave your visit to the gardens until late in the day; closing time is at sunset. However, the gardens are open every day of the year and only cost ten pence (and probably will do for some time) to enter. One disadvantage of Kew, which does not seem to affect the trees, is the almost continuous roar of jet planes to or from Heathrow. There are some theories that noise and even the tramping of feet stimulate the growth of trees; Kew seems not to disprove these.

> And you shall wander hand in hand
> With love in summer's wonderland:
> Come down to Kew in lilac-time
> (It isn't far from London!)
>
> Alfred Noyes

Syon House, across the river, also has a notable collection of specimen trees. Sadly there is no longer a ferry from the Isleworth Gate of Kew to the London Apprentice, and that gate is now closed.

Chiswick House, *210 775*, Palladian with a now-sprawling *Cedrus libani* avenue, has a bit of woodland (with guelder rose), and **Osterley Park**, *147 774*, house by the Adam brothers, is noted for large Hungarian oaks; there is also a rather tatty woodland fringe. Both parks are easily got to by the Great West Road, A4.

Richmond Park: Isobella Plantation
205 718, ♀ (♣), 50 acres, 1m, very easy, Royal Park
Two or three paths by streams planted with woodland trees provide a charming woodland

December, Isobella Plantation

walk in the middle of the Deer Park: old oaks also in the park to the south. Not all is the result of careful horticulture; there are some old trees and a hint or two that this was once a working coppice. Many picturesque old trees, when I visited, were merely shadows in a gloomy London fog. On a brighter day this woodland garden, so designated, can be strongly recommended. The parking place indicated is large and now planted with trees, the woodland being downhill to the west, across the road. Large trees near the car park are sweet chestnut with good nuts in late autumn. The Robin Hood Gate is the nearest.

Wimbledon Common *230 725, ♀, 1100 acres, up- and downhill paths in all directions, LA*
This extraordinary piece of rough, gravelly hillside, partly covered by birchwood, has had a strong appeal to many Londoners as an accessible wilderness. How did it come to be there? I have skated on Wimbledon's ponds and walked on its varied paths in all seasons without ever asking this question. The earliest name, Winebeald's Dun, tells us little; Dun is a down or lesser mountain, not apparently a dune, which might refer to the sandy nature of the heath. Most of it was the Common of the Manor of Wimbledon when the Lord of the Manor, Lord Spencer, decided to split up the land and with the proceeds of the sale of one part, fence and preserve the other as a public park – with a residence for himself in the

middle. The commoners were thought to be too few to protest, and the justification for Lord Spencer's action was the poor state of the common, full of rubbish, gypsies and tramps, often encroached upon and torn about by excessive gravel digging. But the commoners turned out to be numerous and vociferous and would have none of the Spencer proposal even though he virtually established his legal right to dispose of the land. Influenced by a House of Commons' enquiry into London's open spaces, both parties managed to agree in 1870. His Lordship gave up his rights in return for a perpetual £1200; and eight conservators, five elected by the ratepayers, were to control the common – which they still do.

As for a woodland walk, you will only rarely be out of sight of a bus route, so set a course down the middle and follow your nose into the woodland to the right or left. The reference is for the windmill, where there is a car park.

Surrey is well known for its commons and open spaces and those nearer to London are, like Wimbledon, characteristically sandy heaths with birches and some pines, open rather than wooded. But others are on patches of London clay and are oakwood, with hazel coppice or as wood-pasture, both nowadays overgrown. As with all surviving commons in built-up areas there is unrestricted access, so that many paths are made, some formally by the County Council, many more casually. But there is no grazing to keep the scrub down. The clay commons make for very difficult walking in winter, especially as horse riders do not always keep to the scheduled rides. Surrey wooded commons within 15 miles of Westminster are Esher, Ashstead and Epsom, with Great Bookham a little further out.

Ashstead Common *183 612, ♀, 458 acres, 1 gravel path, many others, usually muddy, LA*
Oaks and bracken are the dominant vegetation, varied by birch, sallows and grey poplars. Bluebells are extinct through over-picking. The main pathway explores the margin between the oakwood of Ashstead and the wet pasture of Epsom Common to the north-east,

where much birch thicket is developing. There are lovely patches of the common rush as well as the (actually more common) other *Juncus* species by two ponds near the parking place on the B280. Fishing is allowed in the pond nearer the road and there is a focus of popular interest here. Few people, even on a fine June Sunday, penetrated as far as the second pond.

Great Bookham Common *134 569, ♀, 300 acres, many paths, NT*
The road on the east side, south from Stoke D'Abernon, is lined with rich houses no doubt occupying the sites of squatters' cottages dating from the seventeenth century, when the practice of the poor or displaced was to build their houses in one day and, having smoke from their chimneys the next morning, establish their right to be there – not in fact legally. One parking place is closed because of persistent rubbish dumping and the other, at the map reference, is not easy to see. There is also a parking place at the north-west. The wood is a solemn timber oakwood with hazel, mostly a wilderness with one or two patches cleared where foxgloves grow. I found it just a little oppressive, but you may find differently.

Box Hill *180 513, many walks, slippery in winter, NT*

> Into a warm electric train
> Which travels sorry Surrey through;
> And crystal-hung the clumps of pine
> Stand deadly still beside the line.

From *Uncollected Poems* by John Betjeman

Sorry Surrey it may seem if we swing from the A24 to the parking ground below Box Hill, where there are actually fruit machines. Back left from the roundabout with its gaudy hotel you will find the National Trust zig-zag road, barely signposted, which leads up to two large parking places on the hilltop. Here you will not be too surprised to find a licensed restaurant attached to the Trust shop. There is a modest charge for parking.

Follow the trail of sweet papers and empty cans to a fine beechwood with many yews and some straggly box trees. The effect of the pale beech trunks against the black-green yews is fine, and perhaps now unique in this part of the country. Box trees are always pretty. You almost never see a straight one, but even from the timber point of view this is all right because boxwood is used only in very short lengths. Supplies for wood engravers are now imported from the Mediterranean – quite unnecessarily if it were not for the fact that we have exterminated or neglected our boxwoods.

Ranmore Common *143 502, ♀⚘, 715 acres, NT*

Abinger and Friday Street are signposted from Dorking, but the nearer Ranmore Common and Denbies Hillside are not. The common stretches back a mile or more from the ridge north of the A25, and can be reached by aiming for Dorking Town Station to the north-west of the town. The common is what is called good walking country and is picturesque; Polesden Lacey adjoins to the north and can be reached from Westhumble.

Norbury Park *166 522, ♀ ♣, 300 acres, open, LA*

For Norbury Park and the heavily wooded ridge facing Box Hill across the ever-noisy A24, go by Crabtree Lane just beyond Westhumble Station. There are no encouraging signposts, but there is in fact a picnic site near the Druids Grove, *156 533* – a once-famous collection of old yews now in some disarray. With the busy road below, thoughts of druids, always anyway an eighteenth-century fiction, are far away. There is a good metalled roadway through Norbury Park, and this can be a relief when the rides are muddy. The park is administered by Surrey County Council and quite open to walkers: the beechwoods are a little sad but there are a couple of healthy wych elms.

This, with the woods described in Section 14, completes the circular perambulation of Dorking, but only hints at the many surprises awaiting walkers. Certainly I completely changed my attitude to 'sorry Surrey'

South of East Horsley is the **Effingham Forest**, which the Forestry Commission calls East Horsley Woodlands. On each side of

Box Hill beeches

Honeysuckle Bottom are the dark woods of Dick Focks Common and Mountain Wood, the roads crossed in places by bridges carrying trees (so the one-time landowner could walk in uninterrupted woodland). The main parking place is in Green Dene, *091 510*, which forks south-west from Honeysuckle Bottom. It all sounds very quaint, but in fact it is dull and dark, and, in spite of everything the Forestry Commission says in leaflets, dedicated 99 per cent to timber production. Honeysuckle Bottom is heavily settled, with all the houses painted whiter than white.

There are many other commons, notably **Wisley Common**, *077 588*, and **Ockham Common**, *078 586*, divided by the A3(T) and with several car parks. Here the Royal Horticultural Society's Gardens, Wisley, *065 584*, are on the infertile Bagshot Sands – and yet this gardening centre of England flourishes, admittedly strong on *Erica* and *Calluna*, but with room for an arboretum in its 300 acres.

North Kent and South Essex

Landranger sheets 175, 177, 187, 188

Knole Park *540 543,* ♀ *(♠), 1000 acres,*
LA (House NT)
There used to be a Wildernesse at Knole, but it
is now a golf links with tame deer and a few
ancient oaks. The name has been given to a
nearby housing estate – a touch of planners'
irony perhaps. The park adjoins the town, and
five minutes' walk takes you in. Parking in the
town or at the house is expensive, but you can
enter the park from several points around its 6-
mile perimeter.

Woodland tends to be at the edges, but
parkland on this massive scale is in a category
of its own. It seems permanent, a vast broad
composition, using trees and grassland like
giant building blocks or simplified cardboard
cut-outs. But of course it has been growing
into this shape for three centuries; on closer
investigation the very mature character of the
'clumps' is revealed, each great beech or
chestnut practically a wood in itself with dead
limbs and even dead brothers lying about in
picturesque decay. Since there are fallow deer
there is little hope of natural regeneration.
There are some fenced-in stands of conifers.

You can walk where you like, when you like.

Andrew's Wood *502 615,* ♀ ♠, *1½m, easy,*
muddy, FC
Shoreham and Badgers Mount are villages
north of Sevenoaks, and Shoreham is of course
the better known. Andrew's Wood is ¼ mile
east of the roundabout junction of the A21 and
A224, so it can be reached by looking out for
this junction from London or Sevenoaks. It
can also be reached from Shoreham. It is a
decent-sized mixed plantation on the hilltop,
where pockets of clay in the chalk provide soils
suitable for oaks, Norway spruce and Norway
maple. Old yews and beeches and well-used
chestnut stools indicate the former character of
the wood, and there is a stand of close-set
young beech; all the trees are ready for
thinning.

All paths lead back to the parking place,
except for one cross-ride, and a level terrace

along the edge of a hillside, here facing east
across a smooth chalk valley. Beyond the next
hill lies little Shoreham, where Samuel
Palmer's church is, but not much of his
celebrated atmosphere. Here at the terrace
edge are dogwood, buckthorn, whitebeam,
yew, and birches hung with traveller's joy. A
footpath crosses the valley to another stand of
Forestry Commission trees, Shoreham Woods,
then downhill again to the village.

The car park at Andrew's Wood is much
used by dog walkers in the daytime and take-
away eaters in the evening – the dogs being
apparently much tidier. The wood is nicely
managed and productive, serene and wrapped
in its own sweet breath – not sour and
neglected. The self-important howl of traffic
beyond is almost muted.

Shoreham Woods, on the ridge nearer to
Shoreham and ½ mile across the fields from
Andrew's Wood, are quiet, and are controlled
by the Forestry Commission. This is a nearly
mature beechwood invaded by sycamore.

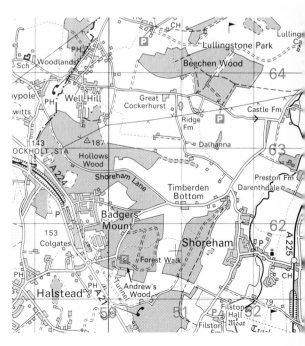

Beechen Wood *516 637*, ♀, *easy, LA*
Lullingstone Park, north of Shoreham, is
managed by Sevenoaks Borough Council, and
cleverly combines a large golf course with a
very interesting fragment of woodland. An
open car park, *516 637*, leads one into a belt of
overgrown chestnut coppice which, not very

attractive in itself, serves to shelter a
wilderness of the first order, municipal though
it may be. Towering beeches and hornbeams
are dwarfed only by the massive trunks of
earlier specimens lying on the ground, and
they are surrounded by thickets of their own
offspring. Gaps are full of dead hulks overrun

by brambles and willow herb, but with new trees growing spontaneously everywhere. Lovely! – and very good bird land, even though patrolled by a great variety of dogs every day.

Trosley Towers Country Park 644 613, ♀ (♠), 160 acres, many walks, some steep, LA

North-east of Sevenoaks, where the M20, A20(T) and M26 meet deafeningly under the escarpment cliff with the much quieter Pilgrims' Way or North Downs Way, you can turn off northwards on the A227 to Vigo Village where Trosley Towers Country Park, 160 acres, lies behind the village, clearly signposted. Trosley is really the local way of pronouncing Trottiscliffe. There is a woodland parking area and a choice of three waymarked walks which wind along this heavily wooded, steep escarpment. The Pilgrims' Way is here a name for the lane below; the North Downs Way

Long Distance Path passes above. As with all ancient routes there are several roughly parallel paths where beasts and men have avoided hazards such as mud and fallen trees.

This is a great place for natural shape and form, and a play of dark and light against an inspiring view of the Medway Valley. There is a whole gamut of woodland, from mature park plantation among old native trees through overgrown coppice and new-cut coppice, ragged thicket and shattered yew, to a rich chalk scrub with wayfaring trees, whitebeam, maple and privet. At the far end of the wood I found very old stools of hornbeam, ash, birch and sallow – the last producing enormous leaves. Obviously this wood has a very long history of woodland management.

You can follow a level, terraced path along the hillside, or descend by rough steps to the lower slope – any height you lose is regained at the expense of your calf muscles. The park is closed at sundown, but since the village roads

A hornbeam grove in Beechen Wood

Trottiscliffe church from Trosley Towers Country Park

run along the back of the woods you can find an entrance – there is nothing to stop you walking in. I met a horse bearing a lantern at each stirrup – a strange pilgrim in the dusk;

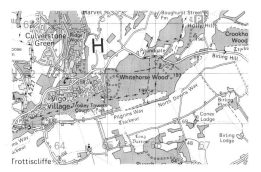

but, surely, not a new sight on this ancient ridge path.

Holly Hill, *670 629*, has a neat square of gravel to park in, guarded by a little cottage, and some humble sycamores and horse-chestnuts. The car park was made by a local gentleman, perhaps to discourage further exploration of the quiet lane. There *is* woodland, little more than a shelter-belt between fields. A great beech and some grown-up chestnut coppice show that it is a fragment of the large woodland of this downland. The walk here is breezy and light, and several children who arrived when I did seemed to find it promised sufficient adventure. Eastwards, down the steep Birling Hill, by

Crookhorn Wood, the lane tunnels through native trees to industrial Snodland on the Medway.

Oldbury Wood *576 558*, ♀ *(♣), 2m walks, NT*
North of Ightham Common on the A25, 4 miles east of Sevenoaks, there is a neat and capacious car park set among slender birch trees, deep in a hollow. It serves Oldbury Hill, a prehistoric earthwork cared for by the National Trust. This is perhaps the most beautiful of Sevenoaks' woodlands: old oak coppice with beech and birch, bilberry, bracken, alder, buckthorn, sallow and rowan; hardly any chestnut. The birches are grey with lichen and there are subtle tones of grey in all the colours; all are seen against the dark side of the valley. There are many fungi and a nice smell of decaying damp leaves.

Seal Chart, *566 557*, westwards, also has pleasant oak woodland with bracken; here the oaks are middle-aged standards. The common is open to all.

Dene Park *605 511*, ♀ *(♣), forest walk, FC*
This is part of the Forestry Commission's Shipbourne Forest, a dreary circuit of twenty-year-old spruces on paths of yellow Wealden slime, served by a dirty car park. Across the road is a fine old oakwood planted with young Norway spruce, Norway maple, red oak and Japanese larch. All the underwood is to be thinned to leave a stand of pure oak; I hope we shall be allowed to walk there.

Boxley Hill *775 590*, ♀ , ♣ *(yew), 3m of escarpment woods, part LA*
Box and yew are native on the very steep chalk scarp 2 miles north-east of Maidstone. The box seems to be a little thin on the ground but the yews are fine. The Pilgrims' Way here is a narrow metalled road along the foot of the Downs, and at the west end of this road there is a rough parking space for modern pilgrims. The path is very worn where it leads upwards, tunnelling beneath the ancient yews. The climb is worth the effort. In the spaces between the yews are old coppiced hazels, hawthorns

and whitebeams, richly diversified in form. Spindle trees, leaning away from the shade of the ever-vigorous yews, are overturned but continue to fruit in abundance. Native privet fills every gap. Dog's mercury covers the ground.

Towards the top, yew gives way to pedunculate oak, and there are many wild maples, unusually large, which in autumn cover the ridge paths with gold. Here the going is easy, in and out of the heavy, sheltering yews. In the perpetual dryness beneath them, large round mushrooms or blewits, brown with age, are marked with sinister double crosses. This fungus is at first a delicate brown-pink, deckled at the edges like an antique Doulton dish; many together are spread out like a dinner service.

Mote Park, in the eye of Maidstone itself, is large and old, and remarkable for some very large and unusual trees, among them the largest field maple probably in the world, 78 feet, and black walnut, 97 feet by 19 feet.

Mereworth Woods on the B2016 south of Wrotham Heath loom large on the map. Part is Forestry Commission and there are bridleways. The National Trust has a corner at the south, Gover Hill. The woods consist of miles and miles of chestnut coppice on the Weald, and conifers, but all with the old hedge banks. This is working woodland, good perhaps for horse riders. The countryside around is much more relaxed than in the downland, people not afraid of square corners on their roofs and

walls, and not so worried about trespassers –
though nut orchards of course have plenty of
barbed wire. There are plenty of trees even
without the elms, and a generally woodsy air
in villages and lanes; a faintly detectable blue
of wood smoke.

I had no idea there was so much chestnut in
Kent. These 4 square miles of woodland must
be the last hollow kernel of Andreadsweald,
which stretched from beyond Canterbury to
Winchester and was 30 miles deep; a forest so
dense, that the Romans, who named it SYLVA
ANDERIDA, made only two small roads across it,
preferring to sail round to LONDINIUM. If it was
the Romans who introduced the chestnut, as
some people believe, the seed has certainly
found fertile ground in the nineteen centuries
since they left.

Brentwood, 22 miles from St Paul's, is an old
town, once a small clearing in the Essex Forest
where pilgrims on their way to Canterbury
from East Anglia and the Midlands used to
stop. Essex County Council has rescued
considerable areas of parkland including old
woodland to form the green belt – or green
skirt – of what is now a large dormitory town.

Weald Country Park *574 946,* ♀, ♠ *, 428 acres, LA*

The park was bought for £27,500 in 1953.
Nineteenth-century conifer plantations felled
during the war were then already replanted.
The deer park to the south-east existed for 700
years before most of it was ploughed in 1948 to
try to cash in on a war-time ploughing subsidy,
rumoured, wrongly, to be due for removal. But
many beautiful ancient oak, hornbeam and
beech trees remain – some at least must be
almost as old as the park itself. The deer were
let loose by the Army during the war; fallow
deer descendants are now wild visitors to the
park. A belvedere, with a view of the dullest
part of the park, is close to the site of the
former house, which was demolished in 1950.
On the slopes are well-grown specimen
conifers and a group of particularly fine tall
hornbeams.

The woodland part of the park is to the
north, beyond an area known as the Forest,

which used to be fenced as a sort of domestic
wilderness. The woodlands were originally
agricultural fields, the tenants expelled or
bought out in the eighteenth century so that
the land could be enclosed into the park.
Planting is well documented and much can be
learned about how forestry trees grow. Native
vegetation creeps in at the edges. Alder is
luxurious by stream sides. The thinnings from
the woodland are sold, but the object now is
conservation, for public pleasure and
instruction. Partly by design, and partly by the
accident of the pleasantly varied shape of the
land, the woodland rides make some of the
prettiest walks to be found in south-east
England.

Thorndon Park lies to the south of
Brentwood. It is really two parks. The larger
northern section, with an extensive picnic area,
608 916, amongst very pretty birches and
picturesque old oaks, is reached by the B186,
turning off at Eagle Way, or by the A128,
turning down The Avenue. Close to a built-up
area, this park at weekends is full of dogs,
children, horses and lovers, but the old oaks
are worth anyone's time. Woodland beyond the
birch thicket is varied from oak with hornbeam
or chestnut to beech according to minute
changes in the texture, and no doubt acidity, of
the yellow mud and gravel which the trees
seem to love.

The venerable oaks of these Essex parks are
remnants of one of the most extensive and
long-established forests of England. Thorndon
Park North is not, however, a mediaeval deer
park but an old common, Childerditch; grazed,
and its trees pollarded, since perhaps men first
settled in the forest.

Thorndon Park South, *632 899,* is older
parkland with old pollard hornbeams. The hall
itself may be reached by a footpath from
Thorndon Park North. It is an impressive
great barracks of a place which is now being
converted into something useful.

Norsey Wood *692 957,* ♀, *165 acres, easy, wet, 1 hour, LA*

Although at first apparently solid sweet
chestnut in various stages of growth after

coppicing, this little wood also includes some old gravel pits with oak, hornbeam, and birch, and a system of wet valleys where the dominant tree is alder, with willows, and even some *Sphagnum* moss. Much of the oak is *Quercus petraea*. In the 1930s houses were built within the old area of the wood in the north-west and the south-west, obscuring a 'deerbank' (the wood was once, long ago, a deer park) which surrounded the whole, unchanged for four centuries. Rackham (1980) notes a wide (70 feet) bank of unknown origin across the whole width of the east end. Roman kilns have been found, and there are Bronze Age barrows; the former suggest coppice to fire the kilns, the latter, eight or so centuries earlier, are likely to have been on open ground.

Perhaps too much emphasis is placed upon the evidence of occupation before the Middle Ages; but the wood just might have been chestnut coppice ever since the Roman (?) introduction of the tree. References to Norsey Wood, then Nossesheye or Notesheye, go back to 1250. The 'notes' might have been hazel – nuts – it is a more familiar mediaeval tree, but now rare in the vicinity. The largest chestnut stools cannot be dated earlier than the eighteenth century, but pollen analysis, when it can be done, may provide the link.

Coppicing continues, at least in part of the wood, and the products are used on site in traditional ways. The nature trail is clearly marked by white engraved arrows on varnished posts, and takes one on a comprehensive tour of the whole range of woodland.

Near Basildon are **Langdon Hills Country Park West** and **East**, *680 865* and *697 860* respectively. These are instant parkland created out of surviving woodland and scrub. Two car parks, each with woodland, are accessible and signposted from the surrounding trunk roads and are linked by a very narrow lane and an extensive nature trail, which has two car parks of its own.

Hadleigh West Wood *804 879*, ♀, *several paths, LA*

An obscure notice-board and a rusty gate opposite Windsor Gardens mark the entrance to this wood. It is reputed to be very old and perhaps not even tamed or managed by the time of Domesday. But there are few signs of its age – some struggling wild service and the usual hornbeam stools and coppiced durmast oak – nor is there much sign that the wood is integrated into its urban surroundings. In fact the local people seem to avoid it. Very little coppicing is done. Bits of the edges are fenced into an adjacent field for cattle and horses to shelter. There is a great deal of chestnut and some aspen and, unusually, alder buckthorn, one tree 30 feet high. Several banks, apparently very old, lie across the width of the wood suggesting a once wider shape divided into east-west bands or strips. A deep stream flows west to east across the lower half and the only bridge is near the centre.

Much of the ground was covered by ripe chestnuts which were good to eat because I roasted some, but no one had gathered any, or even walked that way for many days.

Hadleigh Great Wood, $\frac{1}{2}$ mile to the east, was probably once joined to West Wood. It is now deeply penetrated by detached residences, yellow sodium lights and rusting metal. There is hornbeam with oak standards, and again durmast oak, *Quercus petraea*. This wood is very much used compared to West Wood, for riding and dog walking at least. It is dank and overgrown.

Hockley Wood *834 924*, ♀, *350 acres, public park*

The old village of Hockley is now as large as a town, but much quieter than the main-road-ringed Hadleigh and Thundersley. The wood is a hornbeam coppice for most of its area, with tall oak and birch at the north, and some chestnut. I found a standard wild service among the hornbeam stools and several groups of aspen. Little coppicing is done and the wood is dark with the floor mostly quite bare. There are several ways into the wood from practically every one of the residential roads which border to the north and east. Walking is easy but occasionally very muddy. In spite of the darkness and a certain sameness it is a cheerful place which makes one glad it has been preserved as a town park.

North Bucks with parts of Oxon, Herts and Beds Landranger sheets 152, 164, 165, 166

Near Oxford, and still on the Oxford Clay, is **Bernwood Forest**, *612 117*, the Forestry Commission's name for a plantation of softwoods which includes several old woods from **Waterperry** in the south to **Oakley** in the north.

These were ancient oakwoods, or ancient woods planted with oak, clear-felled in the last war. Native trees remain or are encouraged along rides, and the forest is described as a nature reserve because of its insect life. Birch, oak and wild service now flourish with a background of alien spruce. The rides are airy and well surfaced for walking – they also provide access for persons with nets and macro-lensed cameras to plunge into ditches. Will there still be space and suitable wet scrub for this activity when the forest grows to maturity?

The **University Parks** in Oxford, while hardly woodland, have pleasantly informal corners as well as containing many fine specimen trees, native and exotic – well-documented in a reasonably priced guide.

Beechwoods on the Chilterns in Oxfordshire, Bucks and Herts are rarely ever fenced and offer easy walking, since mature beech always completely shades out the shrub layer. The Chiltern scrubland in this section is especially rich in variety and of great ecological interest.

Ashridge Estate *973 130*, ♀ (♣ *phased out*), *4000 acres, many paths and waymarked trail, NT*
There are two large car parks, and others, and the B4506 runs through. Tring Railway Station is $1\frac{1}{2}$ miles to the west.

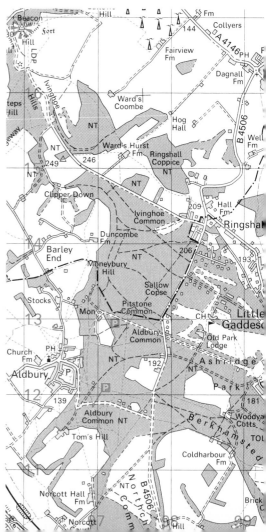

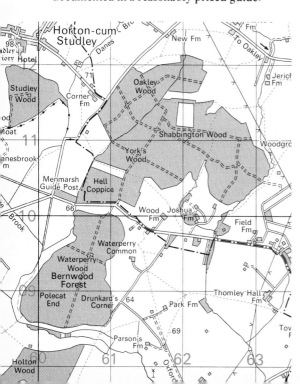

Ashridge may well have been an ash ridge long ago – ash trees to be found in the woods and as pioneers in the scrub – but the estate was famous for its beeches and oaks in the eighteenth century. Some old oaks remain on Aldbury Common, along with the lines of overgrown hawthorn hedges which are now used as private corridors by the herd of fallow deer. Muntjak and Chinese water deer are also established here. Great beeches are everywhere along the escarpment, as high woodland over typically bare leaf litter and in grotesque lopped forms on the old boundaries and lanes which criss-cross the estate.

At the least, this is a great beechwood with a view, traversed by an easy, dry bridleway which emerges onto the bare down towards Ivinghoe Beacon at the north. But it is also a

BELOW: a birch thicket at the margin of an oakwood on Berkhamsted Common, Ashridge

richly varied and large piece of woodland countryside which requires many days to reveal all its secrets: an old avenue of yews deep in the woods; a mature stand of sweet chestnut; a dense plantation of sycamore; heathland with bracken, birches, hollies and oaks; a group of tall aspens; a large bluebell wood, little frequented except by deer and birds; clay-filled hollows retaining water for much of the year and rich in mosses and rushes; many orchids and fungi for those who can seek them out. Over fifty species of bird actually breed in these woods.

Ashridge is well known and attracts its thousands on a fine summer weekend, but the woods are scarcely disturbed. Looking out from the high beechwood you are at the still centre of a web of lines of communication. You may glimpse the prehistoric Icknield Way, deeply hollowed where it follows a contour of the hillsides. Below, in a deep cutting which is itself a monument of nineteenth-century engineering, runs the main-line railway from Euston to the North; beside it the Grand Union Canal, fed by the great reservoirs which usually gleam in the distance near Tring. The

Box trees at Great Kimble

monument in the middle of Ashridge Estate is to the Duke of Bridgwater who built the first canal. You will see the chimneys of a modern industrial complex rooted in this chalky soil at Pitstone; the quarries are carefully restored to grass. The ancient wooden windmill (National Trust) and the charming, lonely Pitstone church are not disturbed, except by a light deposit of white dust.

Wendover Woods *890 090 and 890 100,* ♀ *(♣), 400 acres plus 4 forest trails, FC*
You may feel as I do a twinge of regret that 400-odd acres of beechwoods were clear-felled for these conifers, but it should not be allowed to spoil one's appreciation, for these ridges and steep valleys clothed in firs and spruces provide a scenery just as appropriate to Britain, if you stop and try to imagine it all before the Ice Age.

    Dancer's End, a nature reserve, *903 097,* 70 acres of typical Chiltern woodland, adjoins the north-east arm of Wendover Woods. Look for wood vetch, herb Parlo, Solomon's seal, orchids and the Chiltern gentian.

Coombe Hill *847 072, NT*
Ellesborough Warren, Great Kimble
and **Pulpit Hill** *828 048,* ♀*, 4m, easy or very difficult walking according to your divergences from the footpath, NRs*
This is a line of steep scarp slopes and ridge paths looking over the Aylesbury Vale, and traversing a great variety of scrubland backed by fine beechwoods. Starting from the south-west end, Pulpit Hill has a large area of dogwood, impressively pink even in mid-winter, fading off to scattered juniper bushes. Above Great Kimble is a steep meadow interestingly neglected and returning slowly to forest via dog rose, field maple and sycamore. Above this is a warren containing dogwood, buckthorn, spindle, privet and an apparently spontaneous small wood of English elm (a rare occurrence), now completely dead. Beyond, in a deep coombe with ungrassed chalk sides is a natural history gem: a box coppice gone wild – if it was not wild before it was coppiced. Several walnuts are also to be found and these have clearly regenerated naturally in the past, though no seedlings are now present and the

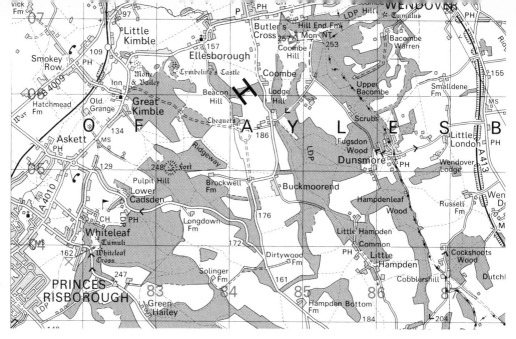

trees die comparatively young. Spindle trees survive the nibbling of rabbits. There are patches of dogwood completely overlaid with old man's beard. Amongst the box, which ranges from low scrub to quite mature but many-stemmed trees, are the stalks of *Daphne laureola*, the spurge laurel. There are other native trees, including a wych elm, long surviving the disease. But a group of Scots pines on the hilltop is so nicely placed that one suspects the perfecting touches of an Edwardian lady, perhaps from nearby Chequers. (You will be watched, probably, by a very quiet man amongst the beeches.)

Through a natural arch of box on the east side you pass to open grassland falling away to escarpment woodland where a probably Iron Age earthwork known as Cymbeline's Castle supports wayward beeches. A stile leads to Ellesborough. Coombe Hill, beyond, belongs to the National Trust and is also ecologically interesting. The other sites are under the control of the County Naturalists' Trust. Please do not take or trample any living plants.

Stockgrove County Park, Heath and Reach 920 295, ♀(♣), LA

This small woodland (600 yards long at the most) on sand with clay-with-flints started off with waymarked nature trails but is now riddled with paths – a little over-used I fear.

Oak, most of it old coppice and now a cheerful open-textured wood (some small-leaved lime), merges nicely with patches of pine on the sands. There are some old pines and English cherry by the lake, which is a square-sided tank, probably deep. Bakers Wood, which is fenced off to the south-east, is planted with hemlock and cypress, still young.

A coppice of small-leaved lime in all its splendour is down a muddy lane on the opposite side of the road – King's Wood. The land is private but bridleways are accessible and you can also walk from the north side. Somebody *drove* in with a load of waste paper.

Bucknell Wood 660 451, *about 450 acres, 2m or 1m, can be wet, FC*

This forestry plantation is to the north-west of Whittlewood Forest. The village of Silverstone is impossible to miss on the A43(T), and the road to the forest heads north to Abthorpe out of the village. With battery-hen production to the north and south, the wood may strike you as too rigidly productive in style, but the picnic place is open and attractive and the longer of the two walks takes in hardwoods as well as conifers. Once again, one must be grateful to the Forestry Commission for providing access to any woodland in an area of woods that are not easy to enter.

Great Wood *282 040, ♀, CP, about 500 acres, woodland trails mapped and waymarked, LA*
Closed at sunset and otherwise very well organized, this Country Park has much woodland lore to offer, with Bluebell Walk, The Beeches, Grimes Brook, Ash Grove, a coppice, a line of pollard hornbeams and a blackthorn copse. All is carefully conserved and observed. There is a charge for parking.

Bencroft Wood and **Wormley Wood**
326 065, 332 065, ♀, CC and WT
Bencroft Wood contains a short woodland trail and also provides access to Wormley Wood, a 340-acre recent acquisition of the Woodland Trust. Oak/hornbeam with a long history of coppicing, this is the largest woodland of its type still in its 'semi-natural' state and is designated a grade 1 Site of Special Scientific Interest for this reason alone.

The hornbeams of Wormley Wood are a sight to be seen. They will be found along a well-marked track. Part of the wood was coniferized in the late 1970s and the Trust will restore it to hardwoods.

The hornbeams of Wormley Wood, now in the care of the Woodland Trust

Galleyhill Wood *395 030, ♀, about 100 acres, less than 1m long, an easy path, probably GLC*
This remote-seeming corner of Essex woodland is an outlier of Epping Forest. From the eastern end of the short bypass at the

northern side of Waltham Abbey take the road to Upshire, turning left after ¼ mile to Aimes Green. You can walk northwards by a dark hornbeam coppice into a serene old wood which actually looks like a forest, with great spreading oaks; the twisted, rather under-nourished hornbeams here behaving like underwood. The path runs by the east margin of the wood and you can look out over the fields, eventually emerging into them, the forest seeming to run out of trees. A few oaks standing isolated in long grass invite you to sit and reflect. If you did not know it, you would never believe you were only 12 miles from the City of London.

Hatfield House *236 085, a stroll in the grounds of a great private house*
No one cannot want to see the house (1611) I guess, but once you have, the part of the garden open to visitors and the trees beyond it are something between a woodland garden and a small arboretum. What you can well believe is a real Jacobean pleached lime walk leads to a venerable chestnut leaning on sticks, and one or two false acacias, *Robinia pseudoacacia*, that must be as old as any in the country. These stand among fine, large oaks which guard the west of the house, with its curiously appealing squared-up and turreted architecture.

You can walk exactly southwards in a lime avenue (ordinary hybrid lime), then turn right into a plantation of tall specimen trees including a many-stemmed redwood and a gracious-looking beech. The park north of the house contains many ancient oaks scattered about in the traditional way of English parkland.

Rowney Warren Wood *123 404, ♠ ♀, 1½m, easy, FC*
The picnic place is nice, signposted RAF Chicksands on the A600, 2 miles north-west of Shefford. The forest walk or Robert Bloomfield Trail is a fairly simple affair – the wood is narrow and you can usually see the

light at one side or the other. Pines Austrian and Corsican, larch, Douglas fir, and oak, birch and beech grow on little hills and dales of sand which vary from a yellowish to dark reddish colour. There are lots of squirrels, grey of course, and a few beer cans. I met only one person and he was riding a bicycle.

Maulden Wood on the A6 just north of Clophill has a picnic place away from the foul lay-by where you have to park, *072 395*. I suppose it's all right inside: there is a school trail, and a forest walk of $1\frac{1}{2}$ miles, described by the Forestry Commission as pleasant – rather faint praise.

The edge of the forest, Galleyhill Wood

36	37	38
21	**22**	
18	19	

SOUTH-EAST ENGLAND

Essex and South Suffolk

Landranger sheets 167, 168, 169

Hatfield Forest *547 203*, ♀, *1000 acres,*
NT (CP)

This important forest (not to be confused with
Hatfield, Herts) is now indicated on the
Ordnance Survey map as a Country Park, but
it has been in the hands of the National Trust
since 1924. At that time it was, largely, saved
from the timber merchants by a far-sighted,
quick-thinking – and rich – man, E. N. Buxton.
Probably because since the Norman invasion it
has been a royal hunting demesne, with its own
special laws to protect the game, it has retained
its ancient character through many generations
of landowners. Notable amongst these were the
Houblons, who shared its manorial rights from
1729 onwards, and in 1854 bought out their
neighbours the Barringtons of Old Barrington
Hall. A Houblon made the lake, and another
enclosed the land and then made drains which
saved the forest from becoming a mire every
winter. One Laetitia Houblon had complained
of 'splashings in our forest', and perhaps it was
she who planted the horse-chestnuts, at least
one of which is remarkable for its unusual age
and grandeur.

Although it is at the edge of the Great Essex
Forest of old, this is not now the place to see
ancient oaks. There were many, but they were
felled in the early part of this century. Some

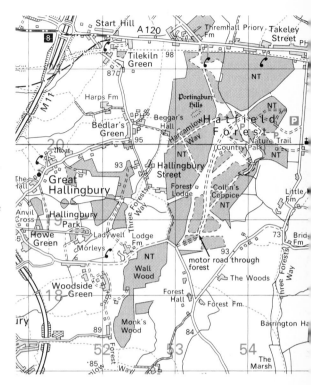

Hatfield Forest. A ride between hazel coppices.

very spectacular hybrid elms remained – with
great buttresses and heavy horizontal limbs –
but elm disease has killed them. The oldest
trees, and most notable, are the great pollarded
hornbeams scattered about the open chases.

Hatfield Forest is unlike other scheduled
Country Parks in that cars can park anywhere.
For those unable to leave their vehicle, there is
an area of old coppice and standards with all
the richness of old woodland, which can be
viewed from the metalled road. This 'safari'
approach does not disturb birds such as tree
creepers: walking does. Hanging lianas of
traveller's joy, *Clematis vitalba*, are a particular
feature of the coppices.

It is the coppices, now overgrown, which
constitute the chief value of Hatfield to the
student of woodland. Sadly, they are no longer
cut as they were for centuries, on an eighteen-
year rotation; for the first seven or so years of

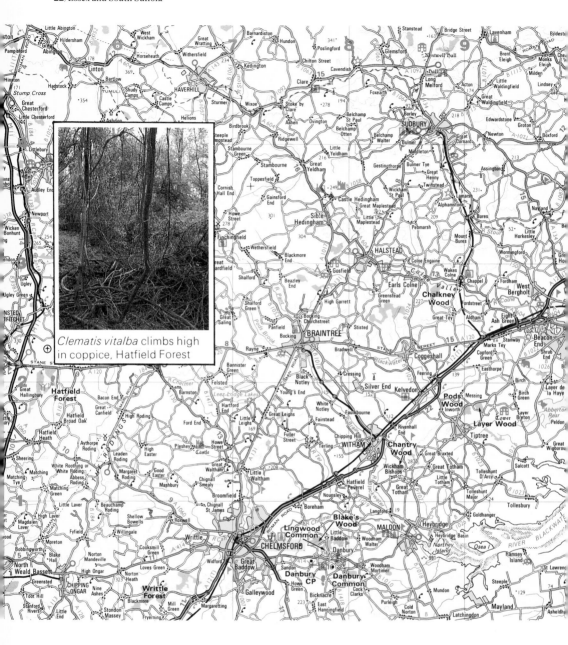

Clematis vitalba climbs high in coppice, Hatfield Forest

this period cattle were fenced out so that new shoots could become established – and along with them many wild flowers, including the oxlip for which the area is known. Beside grazing and pannage (pig food), commoners of the forest could take fuel and fencing material, so that the coppices would have always been tidy. Now, many of the woodland floors are permanently bare in the heavy shade.

Trees in the coppices are hazel, oak, wych elm and other elms, maple, birch and, darkest and dampest, hawthorn. The presence of large, old stools of wych elm and hornbeam within, for example, a hazel coppice says much for the

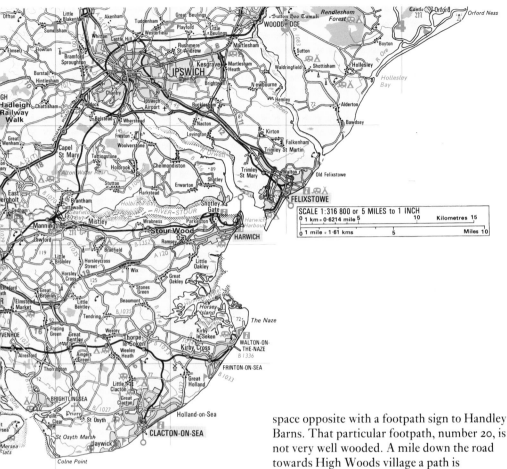

SCALE 1:316 800 or 5 MILES to 1 INCH

historical nature of the forest: such trees would be 'self-sown' centuries ago. All the coppices have names, often those of the men who spent their lifetimes in the woods: Emblem's, Hampton's, Collin's Coppice. Grassy rides, also named, run between the camts, and quiet visitors will certainly see fallow deer.

The soil is London clay over chalk but there is a sandy patch near the lake.

Writtle Forest is a vague area about 4 miles south-west of Chelmsford. I could find no formal access to woodland apart from many signposted footpaths in the area.

The Viper pub, *640 018*, has a small parking space opposite with a footpath sign to Handley Barns. That particular footpath, number 20, is not very well wooded. A mile down the road towards High Woods village a path is signposted into the woods south-west of the road, that is, on your left. This wood appears to have no name. It is oak, with chestnut, birch and hornbeam, and there is a steep bank and ditch in the middle. The wood is not perhaps special, but it is very quiet and easy to walk in. Turn left on emerging – which may be on to the farm road or the motor road to Mill Green. On the other side of the road is a birchwood surrounding Moore's Ditch. You may then meet a footpath returning to the Viper. You will walk 2 or 3 miles according to the route you take through the wood.

The footpaths are very well signposted in this area if they are not always clear on the ground, and most woodland paths appear to be open to serious walkers. But this is a forest only in name, like many another.

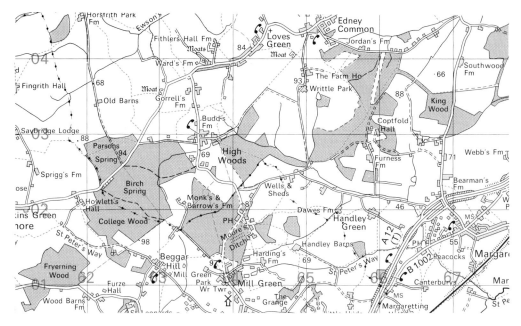

Danbury Country Park 770 048, ♀,
41 acres
This park has parking for 200 cars and is
visited by 60,000 people a year, and their dogs.
The picnic area would accommodate 5000, and
there are lakes for catching small fishes. A long
triangle of plantation surrounds some great,
sculptured trunks of oak, much, much older
than the rest of the wood; some are twisted and
scarred, seemingly eloquent in death. Others
still support leafy wandering limbs. All were
last pollarded in Good King Charles' time.
There are hornbeams and beeches too.

A notice-board complains of erosion caused
by many feet, and sensibly suggests we go
somewhere else next time. However, if you
want to see these histrionic wooden torsos, take
the Chelmsford road out of Danbury for ½ mile
and turn left into Wood Hill Road.

Danbury Common 782 045, ♀, *many
paths, NT*
It is just south of Danbury church and fans out
from the parking place in a pattern of open and
wooded land. In a way it is ordinary; patches
of gorse and birch with odd small oaks and
sallows, and in between bracken and grass, and
also some reedy stretches. But it is lovely, there

is no denying it. One can see why the National
Trust took it over, and why everyone wanted
to come and live here, and why it is criss-
crossed with so many little paths. There is
hornbeam coppice – that sounds so workmanlike, and yet it is a fairyland, even in a cold
drizzle. Old oaks grow on the boundary and
two-seeded hawthorn on the higher ground.

Lingwood Common 784 057, ♀, *steep
and muddy, NT*
On the other side of the Chelmsford road
(which is very busy), Lingwood is densely
wooded, and completely hemmed in by
suburban-style houses. It is dark and steep,
and there are more chestnuts and oaks than on
Danbury Common. There are the expected
hornbeams, some, on the well-marked boundary bank, reminiscent of Arthur Rackham's
fairyland illustrations. On the top of the hill
to the east side is a patch of oak coppice;
unusual in Essex. The open field which
occupies the south-western part is reverting
to scrub, and it would be a good idea if some of
the local riders grazed their horses here.

Blake's Wood, *775 068*, is also National
Trust property, 80 acres of hornbeam and

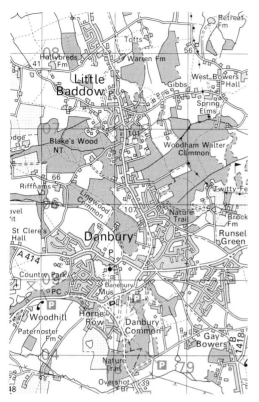

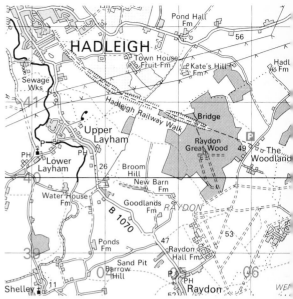

chestnut coppice near Little Baddow, 2 miles to the north-west of Danbury.

Wickham Bishops' **Chantry Wood**, *838 130*, is also an overgrown hornbeam coppice – very attractive but only partly open to walkers, who are probably mostly local. Old hornbeam coppices are almost collectors' items in south Essex, a sort of bygone woodland, useful for walking your dog in.

Hadleigh Railway Walk *055 405 (The Woodlands old station), ♀, 2m, easy walking*
Raydon Great Wood, $\frac{1}{2}$ mile south-east of Hadleigh, Suffolk, has no access apart from the Hadleigh Railway Walk. The wood is under private forestry, well guarded at the sides but penetrated by the old single-track railway which has been most imaginatively converted. You can cover the 2 miles of straight track from Hadleigh, through orchards and scrub to The Woodlands, Raydon, under your own

steam. Both the wood and the railway banks are rather overgrown, limiting the light for flowers, among which are orchids. The north side of the wood is fairly original oakwood, the south much planted.

Cotoneaster microphylla, a garden plant, grows at the western edge facing an old airfield.

Chalkney Wood *871 275*, ♀, *200 acres, 63 accessible, easy muddy routes, CC*
This is a mediaeval wood. Boundaries shown as well established on a map of 1598 remain today. The north-eastern two-thirds were coniferized in the 1950s, not so thoroughly as to destroy all evidence of the former tree population. Small-leaved lime in the south-western third is now coppiced, some remaining elegantly overgrown as a background to oak and ash standards.

A straight, wide path divides the wood, and a hollow-way identified as an early British road adopted by the Romans intersects this at a shallow angle. There are numerous ancient pits and hollows.

The complex of long-established woodland patterns here is worthy of detailed study, with Rackham (1980) as the infallible guide. He points to ash/hazel with maple on calcareous patches (at the south corner particularly); to

Part of the varied pattern of coppice and standards in Chalkney Wood

areas where chestnut is co-dominant with lime; to groups of aspen, more or less evenly scattered, and alder at the rather inaccessible northern side, by streams, but also in small amounts near the south on a plateau. He has analysed the original vegetation of the coniferized portion, and shows that the lime area interpenetrated with a hornbeam-dominated northern section. There was some elm in the small valleys, and a different elm, used to hedge the boundaries, has crept into the wood, but only shallowly. He does not mention some sallow, but he identifies two stools of wild service.

Some lime stools in the middle of the south-western – original – part are at least 5 feet across, rotten but still putting out shoots. Paths or tracks in the coppice wander in a serpentine way amongst the stools in what is described as a mediaeval system – partly replaced by straight rides. When the lime was cut recently, after a lapse of more than fifty years in the coppicing cycle, raspberry, dormant in the soil, suddenly became prolific. Bluebell dominates

the field layer, but there are also primroses, bracken and bramble: dog's mercury in the ash-maple-hazel areas.

The dark earth of the fields from here to Coggeshall has probably been under the plough for as long as the woods have been cut. This is a clean, shapely countryside with old, black wooden barns and well-kept, handsome houses. Hedges now are few, and the landscape is returning to a pattern suggesting the open fields of long ago.

Stour Wood, *190 315*, Wrabness, is an important acquisition of the Woodland Trust in a part of the country where woodland is very scarce. It is a chestnut coppice, but a more diverse distribution of trees is to be encouraged in the future – there are eighteen species of tree already, including the wild service tree, which alone indicates that this is ancient woodland. The Stour Estuary is just to the north and the wood is managed by the Royal Society for the Protection of Birds as part of an internationally important reserve.

Wales & the Marches

Start of the Watkin Path up to Snowdon

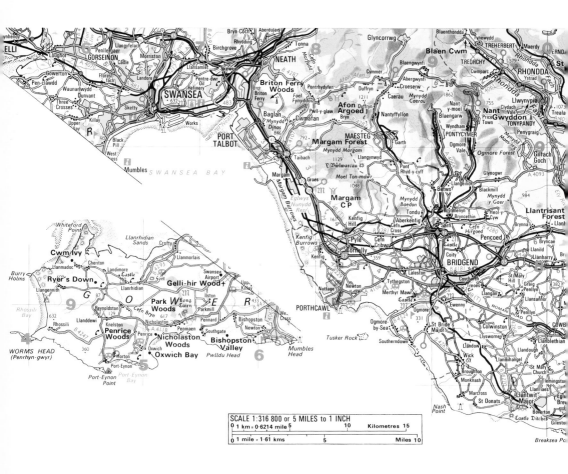

SCALE 1:316 800 or 5 MILES to 1 INCH

For English visitors two main routes
westwards tend to iron out the north-south
intricacies of this region, suspected to contain
little but chimneys, chapels and choirs. From
the upland route, the Head of the Valleys
Road, the A465(T), a descent into any one of
the valleys will reveal surprising riches, both
municipal and arboreal. The road reveals moorland and occasional stunning hillsides of tiny,
coloured houses and gigantic, purple pit tips.
On the southern route the excitement of the
Severn Bridge is soon forgotten on the
motorway, which looks like any other except for
the oddity of bilingual signs. I turned off
at junction 27 for Ebbw Vale.

Ebbw Forest: *Abercarn village 216 945,
Forest Drive,* **Cwmcarn** *220 932,* ♠,
various walks and picnic places, FC
The forest drive is clearly signed from the
valley road, the A467, but the entrance was
locked in October. This is a 7-mile drive with
promising picnic places and walks en route. In
Abercarn the road signed 'Llanfach' leads into
the forest.

After the smooth *longueurs* of the motorway
and the ordinariness of the industrial valley,
the terrific height and steepness of the forest is
exhilarating and even heavy rain could not
obscure the grandeur of the landscape. Take
the right fork, not signed, for the picnic place.

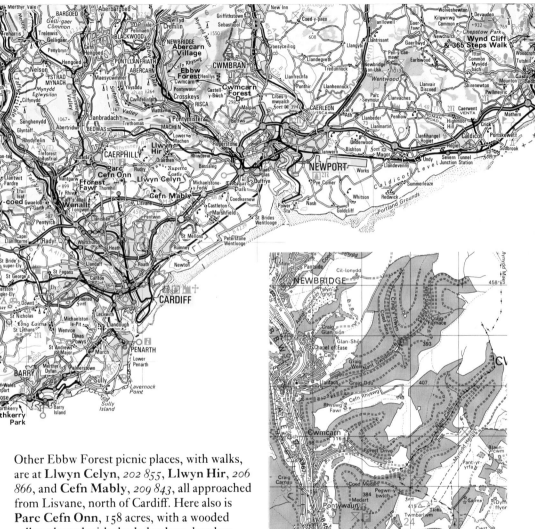

Other Ebbw Forest picnic places, with walks, are at **Llwyn Celyn**, *202 855*, **Llwyn Hir**, *206 866*, and **Cefn Mably**, *209 843*, all approached from Lisvane, north of Cardiff. Here also is **Parc Cefn Onn**, 158 acres, with a wooded valley planted with rhododendron, bamboo, cypress, *Berberis*, willow and water-lilies.

To the south of Cardiff, just west of Barry, is **Porthkerry** Country Park, *099 673*, with mature woodland of native trees on the limestone cliff top. Nearer to Caerphilly is the new Forestry Commission plantation of Coed Coesau Whips, with walks from *202 854*, the car park, and from the forest entrance, *200 866*.

Two miles east of Cowbridge is the Forestry Commission's Tair Onen Nursery, with an average 25 million seedlings in stock, and in the **Hensol Forest** north of this, two picnic places with walks, *038 764* and *033 768*. These are easily reached by turning south from junction 34 of the motorway. North of the M4, beyond Llantrisant, is a picnic place, *025 845*, among larches dating from 1922. **Llantrisant**

Forest is one of the earliest Forestry Commission plantations. Turn north from the A473 after Talbot Green, at the humped-back river bridge. Still north of the M4 is Tŷn-y-coed picnic place at *084 826* – a young plantation with old native trees retained.

Near Cardiff is the Fforest Fawr picnic place, *143 838*, in deciduous woodland with many pathways. Wenallt, *153 832*, a mile south-east, has nature trails run by Cardiff city, 140 acres of woodland and heath.

When in the 1930s many thousands of miners were out of work, reafforestation of the hillsides of Glamorgan, and even of the slag heaps, began, with large forests of spruce and pine planted by the Forestry Commission. Now the Commission's Coed Morgannwg (which includes Margam and Cymer), with Rhondda, covers about 40,000 acres of forest land.

Rhondda

North of Pontypridd are picnic places at *033 957* and *046 966* in the St Gwynno Forest. **Nant Gwyddon**, *987 945*, north of Tonypandy, has a walk of 1½ miles.

In the Rhondda, with **Treherbert** as the centre, are three forest walks. Blaencwm to the summit of Pen-pych is steep – park by the disused railway bridge, *923 990*. Two others start north from points on the A4061.

Margam Park Country Park, *814 851*, embraces eight centuries of privileged land-use from Cistercian abbey to nineteenth-century Tudor-Gothic castle. It is now patrolled by a battered single-decker bus, which carries park-and-ride visitors to the finest orangery in the world (a very fine building restored to contain both orange trees and public gatherings), stopping at the nicely converted centre and café. Modern sculpture was added to the landscaped deer park in 1983. Trees are mainly Scots pine in various shapes and sizes; specimen conifers and broadleaves, above rhododendron, are between the castle and orangery. There is a long walk to Afan Argoed, part of the 23 miles of the Coed Morgannwg Way.

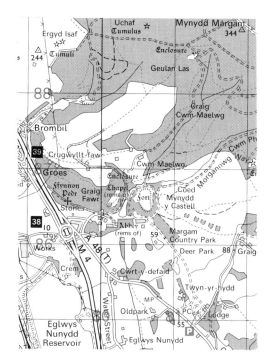

Afan Argoed *821 951*, ♀ ♣ , *7 forest walks, ½–5m, CP, (CC and FC)*
All the walks including the Michaelston Forest walk of 5 miles, and the Argoed walk in remnant oak woodland, 2 miles, start from the Centre.

Walks are all mapped in a single leaflet issued by West Glamorgan County Council, and all explore the 140 acres of the Country Park within the enormously larger context of the forested hills and high moorland.

Walks with sea views are on the oak-covered cliff above **Briton Ferry**, near Neath, *745 940*. The Neath Canal at Tonna is beautifully wooded.

The theme of Gower is moorland and coast, the latter intricate on the south and desolately marshy on the north. There is primary woodland only at Gelli-hir, but limestone cliffs and valleys are rich in vegetation.

Oxwich Bay *502 865*, ♀ , *3m including cliff-top path, NNR*
The woodland walk starts at the church on the

Forestry above Treherbet, Rhondda

cliffside, to your right as you enter the beach car park. The Nature Conservancy has a busy centre here.

Stick to the footpaths: with several thousand visitors here annually the wood could soon become degraded. Sycamore is also a threat, and has to be cleared. There are old field boundaries within the wood, as well as limestone quarries. The path emerges onto bracken, gorse and grassland, returning via the cliffs and then through an old hazel coppice to Oxwich village.

Nicholaston Woods, on the north side of the bay and inland from the Burrows, which are a National Trust property, meet the road at *503 882*. A footpath 'To Nicholaston Woods' from the road 1 mile west of Penmaen emerges onto the sands.

Penrice Woods: Millwood *488 883*, ♀ ♣, *350 acres, walks ¾m and 2m, FC*

Turn off the main road, the A4118, opposite a prominent converted granary on stilts, down a steep and narrow tunnel of a lane which ought to lead to a wonderland. The Forestry Commission's Coed Abertawe is not that, but the trees here are tall and vegetation generally at least lush where a picnic place has been made by the reconstructed mill pond. The longer walk through young spruces and beeches is dull, but it's a walk.

Park Woods, Parkmill *547 892*, ♀ ♣, *3m of roadways, FC*

Green Cwm is the official name of the valley, technically a dry limestone one, which extends and divides north and west from the pretty ford at the north-west corner of Parkmill village. Magnificent larches seem to reach the sky from the deep cwm over a mixture of native trees with much holly. A footpath from Gower Inn, Parkmill, to Ilston church is through private woodlands in Ilston Cwm.

Gelli-hir Wood *562 925*, ♀, *71 acres, fp, NNR*

Gelli-hir means long grove: the wood is narrow. Wet oak-birch woodland with alder leads to ash and wych elm with small-leaved lime: there are interesting pools; but most

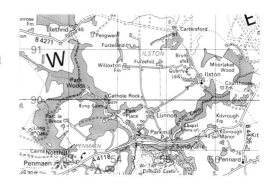

impressive was the sudden immersion in true ancient woodland. In the grass were yellow pimpernel and cow wheat. A former warden, the only other soul encountered, spoke of neglect, but I liked it like that.

Cwm Ivy *439 937*, ♀ ♣, *dunes, fps, NR*

Turn right at Llanmadoc church. The path leads to the dunes of Whiteford Sands over dreamy slacks where hawthorn, burnet rose and cloudberry are populated by thousands of grasshoppers. Above on the grey Hills Tor, Welsh Blacks cling like flies. A wood of Corsican pines lightly anchors the sands, while inland is an avenue of sturdy *Pinus radiata*, Monterey pine – past the warden's house; a good short walk on a wet day. You can continue to the open marsh, where marshmallows bloom in a shade of mauve, and return alongside Cwm Ivy Wood, a collection of noble ashes rising above larch and beech plantations.

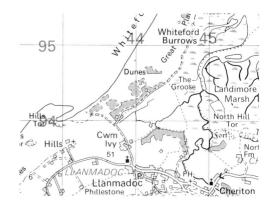

There are Forestry Commission sites near Blackpool Mill (a working mixed wood near the Eastern Cleddau), *064 145*, 4 miles west of Narberth. Blackpool Mill is an agricultural museum. The car park is at a viewpoint for the Pembrokeshire National Park. A waymarked walk of a mile or so can be extended to 5 miles.

In the Gwaun Valley, east of Fishguard, are two sites at *006 348* and *045 349*, with another picnic place at Pontfaen, in between. Near **Cenarth** are two woodlands: one has a Forestry Commission walk and picnic spot, *264 406*; nothing memorable except for the cleared and planted part of the wood (through the white gate) which has strangely retained the sense of a woodland place, though of course the spruce and larch will eventually suppress this. The indicated walk is a polite one, among broadleaved trees, in a tiny stream valley fenced for safety. The other wood, Tyddyn du, on the opposite side of Cenarth, cannot be recommended at present.

Pencelly Forest *134 396*, ♀ (♣), *162 acres, fps, NNR (and FC)*
This is almost certainly the most beautiful wood in Wales. Although I had a brief flash of

sunlight, as can be seen from the picture below, towards evening, my visit was in extremely stormy conditions and I did not see much of the lower part of the wood. Even so, the coppiced oak of the upper, drier part is close to perfection and of the greatest interest, well justifying a long journey to see it. There are some hazel and beech; ash and alder are dominant on lower ground. The wood is now sheltered from the west by Forestry

Patterns of forestry in Pencelly Forest

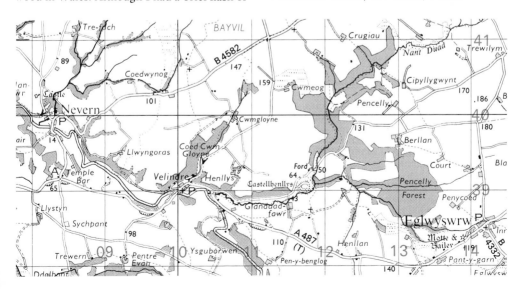

Commission larches, a belt of which is apparently to be left standing although clear felling is in progress. Bits of woodland by the lane are also richly beautiful.

The 'Forest' occupies a double valley north-west of Eglwyswrw on the A487(T) between Cardigan and Fishguard. The more romantic of two entrances forks from the main road $\frac{1}{5}$ mile east of Velindre (*after* the road to Moylgrove). There are several grassy, shaded lay-bys on this little road, which continues over a ford and nearly 2 miles to the oakwood, which is clearly marked as a nature reserve. The ford will be too deep for most cars after heavy rain. There is a footbridge. To enter from Eglwyswrw turn off the main road opposite the inn, go past the garage and left, right and left along the farm lanes. There is a space to park just inside the shelter of the larches; or perhaps you will avoid storm-force winds! The *Nature Reserves Handbook* mentions *Crataegus laevigata* and aspen, both very localized in West Wales. One hundred and twenty species of flowering plants and ferns are recorded, we are told.

Pembrey *402 005,* ✦ *, 519 acres, several trails, easy walking generally, CP*
Only a comparatively small part of the Pembrey Forest forms the seemingly endless dunescape of the Country Park. There is a Forestry Commission picnic place and a walk in the pines close to the housing estate of Pembrey, and you get an idea, as you cross the railway bridge, of what happens to old caravans when they die. But the road to the Country Park takes you smoothly to the many acres of parking space which are sheltered below the shoreline dunes. The shore is untouched by the hand of man, except for the planting of marram grass – actually sprayed on along with a coat of fixative. The openness and freedom of the place, its little dry hills and nicely grouped Corsican pines and sea buck-thorn, make you want to walk – and you can walk anywhere at any time; but there is a portentous undertone.

You soon notice that most of the hills have flat tops, straight sides and holes through the middle. They are old loading bays for high

explosives, which were manufactured here for 80 years. If the idea of making bombs does not quite fit in with your idea of nature walks, then I can only sympathize. The RAF drives the point home with noisy mock dogfights over Carmarthen Bay. Across the shallow sea the Gower lies grey, bordered by the more innocent dunes of Whiteford Burrows: but it is a longish drive round.

Vale of Neath, Lampeter and Llandeilo Landranger sheets 146, 159, 170

The Head of the Valleys Road descends to Swansea by the Vale of Neath. There is a Forestry Commission picnic place with three walks at **Glyn Castle**, *835 028*, overlooking the vale: turn off the A465(T) for Resolven, straight on at the war memorial and then bear left and uphill. The Melin Court Valley, Resolven, *825 017*, has a waterfall and oakwood, private but with a path from a car park on the B4434.

However, the vale, containing the trunk road, is rather a dismal corridor. The upper valleys of the Nedd and Mellte, with many waterfalls and limestone gorges, are within the Brecon Beacons National Park and in what the Forestry Commission calls Coed y Rhaiadr, 'wood (of) the waterfall'.

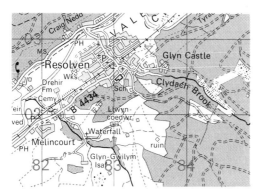

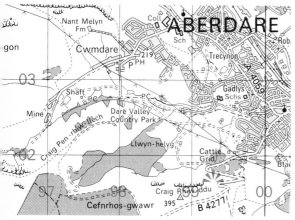

Parking places are 1 mile south of Ystradfellte at *928 125* on the Mellte, or at Pont Melin-fâch, grassy with good deciduous trees, *907 105*, for the River Neath. Continue north of Ystradfellte 2½ miles (for Heol Senni) for an open picnic place by Afon Llia, *927 164*.

The valley of the Mellte is beautiful and said to be neglected.

Dare Valley Country Park, 477 acres, is accessible on foot from Aberdare or by car via Cwmdare or Highland Place (B4277); the centre is at *982 027*. National Coal Board and British Rail lands have been reclaimed with the help of 20,000 trees from the Forestry Commission planted in 1973, the Year of the Tree. Moorland walks extend beyond the park.

Caio Forest Walk *679 405*, ♀ ♠, *2 walks, 1m each, FC*
The pretty picnic site is all that can be desired, near a bubbling stream. But where are the 'very attractive high-amenity plantations on land leased from the National Trust'? A few acres of red oaks was all I could find, and walking along the path to find the views of 'twelfth-century Caio Church' I found my way barred by a fence. Two other paths also met the same fence. After a dull climb to the top of the valley side – it is almost a wall – I found a scattering of the original oak and bilberry; only enough to make one sad. The forest road here levels out and is old enough to have heather along it – an amenity, I suppose, in its way. I descended between spruces in a fraction of the time it had taken to follow the graded forest road. I'm afraid it is all geared for production, and the red oaks are just a gesture. The other walk 'meanders along the streamside with remnants of old natural oak'. Remnants is right.

Lampeter: Pantmawr *576 494*, ♀ ♠, *picnic place and walk, FC*
The little forest is easily reached from Lampeter – it is about ¾ mile north of the town

centre. It is a mixed wood where one might have spent happy hours playing Red Indians. There are enough dark stands of hemlock and spruce to give an authentic sense of being off the map, and some tall bracken and scrub for stalking in. Older trees are both conifers and Angiosperms. As a visitor I slightly felt I was

trespassing. The wood is much walked in by local people – and long may it continue so.

Forest of Brechfa

This large forest south of Lampeter has several picnic places. There are views of very individual and intricate country with quiet

Oak gives way to spruce in the Caio Forest

roads and many old woodlands as well.
Forestry is very much integrated with the
landscape. There are miles of forest roads to
explore. Four picnic places give access to the
forest roads. Minor roads west from Llanllwnt
and north from Brechfa itself lead into the
forest. Only about 12 miles from Carmarthen,
this interesting countryside is little visited, and
I shall certainly go back there when I have no
schedule to make me hurry. Especially worth
exploring is the valley of the Cothi.

By Llandeilo, which looks unbelievably pretty
from across the river, is the ruined and
romantically sited Dynevor Castle. There is
also a new castle with its own private grounds,
but the Castle Woods, overlooking the Tywi,
are a nature reserve of 62 acres, reached by a
gateway in the town. Tall wych elms are now
being removed after Dutch elm disease has
done its worst; oak will be planted.

Gelli Aur or Golden Grove 590 190, ♀ ♣, *99 acres, walks being planned, CP*
The sadly empty grey school of Golden Grove
faces a little decorative well, with an
inscription in barely Latinate capitals: 'DRINK
AND BE THANKFUL'. Within the enormous park
– much more than 99 acres – is a great Regency

house, a fine ageing arboretum, a forest of
young spruces, a farm with a large herd of
Friesians. The mansion is now an agricultural
college, and the grounds are open only during
holidays. Out of season, I explored as much as
I could without disturbing anything larger
than a rather weary hedgehog, and without
actually seeing the house. Keeping to the
edges, one can stride out on a ridgeway path
from the south-west corner (above the map
reference) to enjoy a fine view and a quite
enormous group of *Quercus ilex*.

An important woodland reserve of the RSPB,
Gwenffrwd and **Dinas**, now totals 1723 acres.
The hill of Dinas is wooded with oak and
circuited by a nature trail. It is 12 miles north
of Landovery at *787 470*, near the Llyn
Brianne Reservoir. The larger woodland of
Gwenffrwd is protected, especially during the
breeding time. A limited number of permits
are available from The Lodge, Sandy, Beds
SG19 2oL. Kites are frequently seen in winter,
rarely in summer when they take to the moors.
Sessile oak and downy birch are the dominant
trees of the woods.

27	28	33
25	**26**	11
23		9

WALES & THE MARCHES
Brecon Beacons
Landranger sheets 160, 161

Nine thousand acres of Brecon are National Trust, including most of the mountains. Pen-y-Fan was given by the Chairman of the Eagle Star Insurance Company, Sir Brian Mountain; one wonders if his physical stature was as great as his generosity. North and west of Brecon are many woods in the valleys.

Nature Reserves near Brecon

Pwll-y-wrach, near Talgarth, *164 328*, is a small oak and ash wood with spindle and dogwood, a nature reserve of 20 acres, with a muddy track to a waterfall. You can park in the lane south-east of the hospital. **Nant Sere**, Cantref, *038 238*, is a stream with deciduous woods 3 miles south of Brecon.

There are large 'Danger Areas' north and west of Brecnock District: take OS sheet 160.

At **Ponde**, *110 365*, 6 miles north of Brecon, is a gorgeous gorse and birch common, with

ponies – a good stopping place with a view of the Black Mountains. Bracken and thorn trees take over the rising ground at a clearly defined natural boundary.

Moorland and enclosed pastures alternate about the 1800-acre **Brecon Forest**, called Brycheiniog by the Forestry Commission. There are picnic places at *058 378*, 7 miles north of Brecon on the minor road to

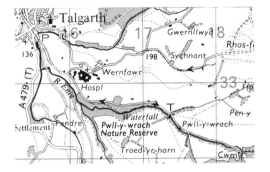

Gorse Common at Ponde with the Black Mountains beyond

Crickadarn – fine beeches and a good view southwards – and at Battle Hill, *012 347*, 1½ miles north of Battle (turn right at Battle End).

North of Merthyr Tydfil. Take the A470(T) for picnic sites and walks around Llwyn-on Reservoir, easy enough to find.

Below the reservoir and reached via the village of Cefn-coed-y-cymmer is the Forest Nature Reserve of Penmoelallt on the west bank of the Taf Fawr. The 17-acre wood on and below the limestone cliff is the home of

Sorbus leyana, known in this valley only. Extra specimens have been planted for study. The leaf rather resembles that of its close relation far away in the Isle of Arran. *Sorbus rupicola* grows large here, and there is a good range of lime-loving trees and shrubs.

Take the minor road north-east for Pontsticill at the interchange of the A470 and the A465. Three miles beyond the village the 'No Through Road' leads to Blaen Taf Fechan and Pont Cwm-y-Fechan. The Taf Fechan (*blaen* being merely a tip or leader) is fed from

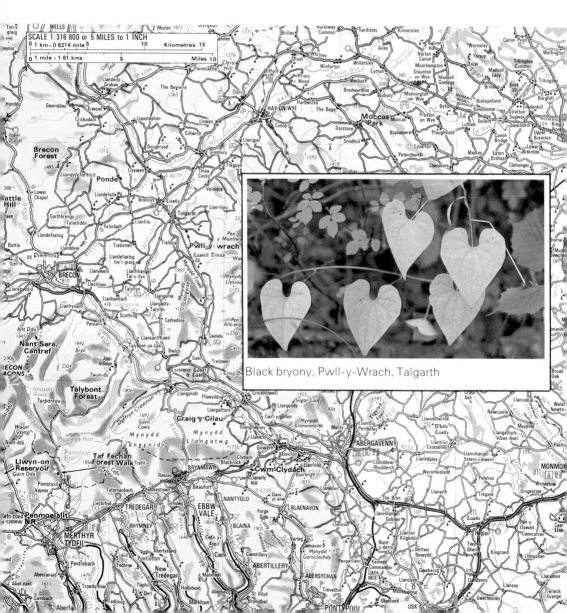

Black bryony, Pwll-y-Wrach, Talgarth

the mighty Pen-y-Fan, 2906 feet. Turn right at
'No Through Road', for, in ½ mile, Owls Grove
Picnic Place – streamside, with waterfalls and a
forest trail. These picnic sites and walks are
beyond Pentwyn Reservoir. Close to Pontsticill
is the Taf Fechan Forest Walk from *056 121.*

Craig y Cilau *186 168,♀ , 1m or more, very difficult, NNR*

Take the right fork upwards out of Llangattock
and park just beyond the cattle grid. The 'Rock
of the Retreat' is a limestone cliff: an awkward
scrambling sheep track below it and very rough
walking above. On the cliff grow native trees,
among them lime and whitebeams. Two of
these are found only in Brecon, one only at this
place. They are distinguished only with
difficulty from the common whitebeam, *Sorbus
aria*, which also grows here, and are reached
with even more difficulty.

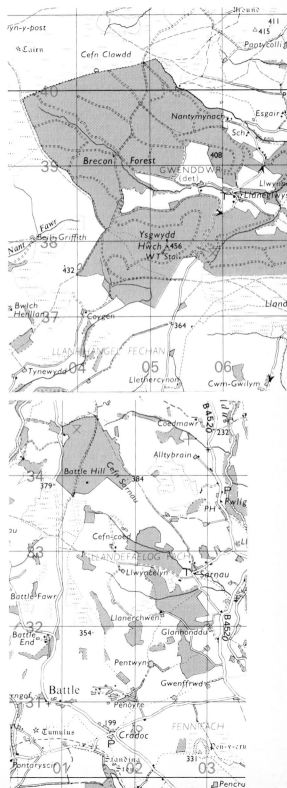

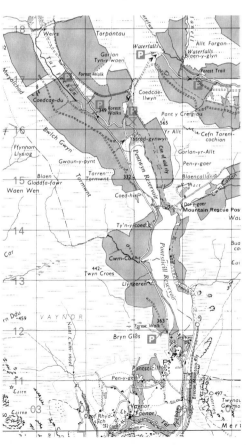

A waterfall on the Talybont trail

A beechwood of 57 acres, a National Nature Reserve, Cwm Clydach, *218 125*, lies close below the Head of the Valleys Road about a mile east of Brynmawr. Turn off at Clydach and head for Daren-felen. A leaflet from the NCC at Cardiff is highly informative.

Talybont Forest *064 170*, ♀ ♣ , *trail 1¾m (steep), or shorter alternatives, FC*
Talybont has a charming stretch of tree-lined canal. The Commission parking ground seems carved out of the spruces and larches; generous and monastic, it could contain a crowd. But here, in this grand mountain valley, one may experience solitude. The trail takes in some waterfalls and viewpoints. The spruces are the not-too-alien Norway species, and there are many native trees, even a sweet domestic plum by a ruined wall. Streams flush out of the tree-clad slopes, frothing like ale, and lichens gleam in the grey light of yet another rainstorm.

At **Moccas Park**, *355 425*, the Black Mountains to the south seem far away in the rich, sheltered valley of the Wye. Moccas is a deer park, a surviving wood pasture. 'Every one of Moccas' ancient trees is a unique and irreplaceable monument. Those "gnarled, low-browed, knock-kneed oaks" are living records of centuries of interaction between natural

growth and human work, and their like may not be seen again'. So writes Richard Mabey, quoting Francis Kilvert 100 years before him.

This ancient park does not provide a woodland walk, unless you write for a permit to the NCC at Hereford, or Attingham Park, Shrewsbury. A good deal can be seen from the road.

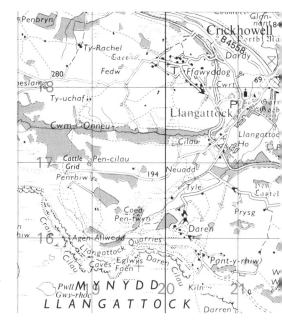

29	30
27	28

WALES & THE MARCHES
Mid Wales

| 24 | 25 | 26 |

Landranger sheets 135, 147

The Rheidol and Ystwyth Forests, owned by the Forestry Commission, provide a semicircle of picnic places and walks within 15 miles of Aberystwyth. Closest, to the north-east, is Plas Gogerddan, *633 838*, near an old estate with oaks and redwoods – and rhododendrons. Take the road for Penrhyn-coch from the A487(T) or the A4159. Through Penrhyn-coch the small road continues eastwards through the forest to Llyn Pendam, where there is another picnic place amongst the conifers, *708 839*. South of this quiet place is Bwlch Nantyarian Visitor Centre, at a viewpoint on the A44(T), with bookstall, slide show and disabled facilities, *717 814*.

Devil's Bridge, *742 770*, on the A4120, has no Forestry Commission connections and is heavily commercialized, but quiet enough out of season. It is the end of the line for the little Rheidol Railway with its sharply picked-out Victorian lettering, and a viewpoint for the curious patterns of local forestry on the wide valleyside. The Nature Conservancy's Coed Rheidol, an oakwood, is below. Two miles south-east on the B4574 the largest planted area of the Ystwyth Forest begins at The Arch, a Forestry Commission picnic place, *765 756*, with a trail, indicated by a dignified stone archway memorial to George III's Golden Jubilee, built by one Thomas Johnes, a pioneer of upland forestry in Wales. Johnes planted over a million trees, especially larch, before 1830, and also restored oakwoods depleted by mining furnaces. There is a viewpoint to look down Cwm Rheidol and to Pumlumon and Cadair Idris if it is clear. Two miles further south-east at Cwmystwyth begins the mountain road down Afon Elan, quiet and treeless for many miles above the gleaming meanders.

The Arch picnic place is in the Ystwyth Forest, which has two other picnic places south-east of Aberystwyth. One is Black Covert, *668 727*, near Trawsgoed (Crosswood) Bridge, off the B4340. Here the trail leads to a butterfly reserve. The other is further south

The Arch in the Ystwyth Forest

along the B road. Turn at a sharp bend onto a riverside road to Pont-rh-y-dygroes – about $\frac{1}{2}$ mile along is **Ty'nbedw**, *695 717*, with alders, and a walk which circulates in typical estate woodland, attractive and mature in a stream valley, then emerges into modern forestry just to emphasize the difference. Chanterelles under the spruces turned out to be quite tasteless, probably because of the very wet weather.

Hafren Forest *856 868*, ♣ , *walks 3–8m, mostly strenuous, FC*

Llanidloes is the nearest town, but Hafren is nowhere really, though a great forest and very beautiful. I suppose a few thousand oaks and alders had to be destroyed to make it, but probably less than for most. Here below Pumlumon Fawr (Plynlimon) some 8000 acres of very green trees maternally enclose the infant Severn or Hafren, no weakling, as, monitored by hydrologists using a variety of weird constructions, it gambols over the first 4 miles of its 200-mile journey.

The walk up the Severn, to its source if you wish, starts at a very pleasant stopping place with tables overlooking a meadow where Welsh ponies with Arabian connections pose daintily against the background of spruces. Old ash and sycamore trees survive from a former farmstead, difficult to imagine now. There are four other walks.

The forest road north-eastwards makes an impressive forest drive, emerging in moorland pasture just above the almost unnoticeable village of Staylittle. Continue a $\frac{1}{2}$ mile north up the B4518, and turn left for the shrunken corpse of Dylife, a mining town now conserved among heaps of grey spoil. Thousands of tons of lead a year left here at one time – by packhorse. Follow the mountain road, the old route to Machynlleth, which was the mediaeval Welsh capital, for a fantastic view of the hills, so uneven and varied as to be almost ugly, and shapes of Welsh forestry: great wedges, caps, belts and gussets.

Above Dderw *953 688*, ♀, *100 acres, fp, pf*
Dderw, usually *derw*, is Welsh for oak. Leave
Rhayader by the B4518, immediately turning
right onto the signed 'Mountain Road'. The
wood is 1 mile up the valley. There is space to
park near the cattle grid. The road continues to
the Elan Valley.

Gwastedyn Hill *976 677*, ♀ ⚘, $1\frac{1}{2}m, fp,$
very steep
The woods overhang the main road and the
Wye, and though it is possible to stop by the
roadside and start climbing, the footpath gives
a more gradual approach and good views. Park
near the lane which branches off left from the
A470 going south $\frac{1}{4}$ mile out of Rhayader. The
footpath is signed. It goes through three fields,
and by an ancient hollow-way, with hollies and
ashes, up to the bracken moor and then into
the top of the oakwood.

Tywi and **Irfon Forests**
North and north-west of Llanwrtyd-Wells the
Forestry Commission has a whole string of
picnic places along the Irfon and the riverside
road to Abergwesyn, notably at Crug, by the
waterside, 4 miles from Llanwrtyd-Wells, and
others downstream. At a bridge over the Irfon
stream, *836 556*, is the entrance to the Craig
Irfon Reserve, 20 acres. **Nant Irfon** is the
name of a much larger reserve 340 acres, which
includes high oakwood with rowan, hazel and
ash. This is a National Nature Reserve: a
permit is required from the Regional Officer,
NCC, Plas Gogerddan, Aberystwyth, Dyfed
SY23 3EB.

In the very large central part of the Tywi
Forest above Llyn Brianne a picnic place at
Fannog, *815 500*, is the only one to offer a
forest walk – to a viewpoint over the lake:
viewpoints also at Clochdu and Cwm Bys
nearby.

Oaks at Dderw, Rhayader

29	30	39
27	**28**	33
25	26	11

WALES & THE MARCHES
Radnor Forest and the Borders
Landranger sheets 147, 148

Coed Sarnau and Abbeycwmhir
042 705, (♀) ♠, picnic place, FC
This is an amazing landscape of hills, pointed or rounded, all with funny hats provided by the Forestry Commission. There are long drives through or beside the trees, and forest roads are open, visitors being scarce. Close to, the spruce forests are lacking in charm, but the wider vista is always compelling; and even wrecked undergrowth scattered with old fuel cans takes on a certain melancholy character.

There is another picnic place, *085 612*, with more varied woodland at the **Shaky Bridge** on the Ithon, 1½ miles east of Llandrindod Wells. Turn off by the famous automobile palace.

Radnor Forest *205 638 (parking for NR)*
♠ ♨, *forest road, FC*
From Kinnerton, *244 633*, take the small road north-west towards the trees; turn left after ½ mile and continue up the gentle gradient of the forest road, ignoring a left and right fork and passing a stile on the left. After 2 miles you emerge into newly planted ground. A road

ABOVE: Abbeycwmhir Hall BELOW: Looking east from the summit plateau of the Radnor Forest.

turns left towards a radio mast. Park by the locked gate. The nature reserve's south-west corner is $\frac{1}{2}$ mile along the fence, not marked.

As a woodland walk this belongs to the space age, but the view is slightly more than hemispherical and the hills look primaeval, which of course they are. In poor visibility this is hardly worth the drive, merely to exchange the Forestry Commission's Sitka/willow herb/coltsfoot for the nature reserve's equally monotonous heather moor. Note, however,

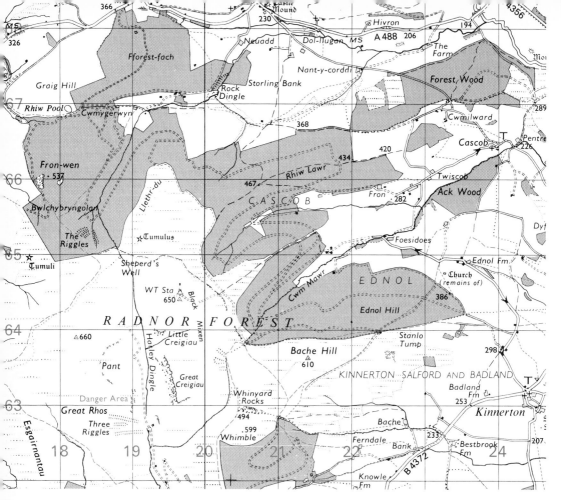

that inside the fence of the radio mast are many
lowland weeds soon there may be a birch or
sallow seedling. The height is 2080 feet.

Bradnor Hill, *282 584,* is 340 acres of
National Trust common, but there is a golf
course on the top. The steep west side of the
hill is half occupied by a slab of the Forestry
Commission's Radnor Forest.

A more interesting National Trust hill, part
of 1385 acres attached to **Croft Castle,**
455 655 (avenues of chestnut, oak and beech),
contains Bircher Common, appropriately
capped by Oaker Coppice. Croft Castle has an
arboretum with a great avenue of chestnuts.

In between is the handsome country of the
Arrow and the Lugg, nearly every hill dark
with trees and anciently fortified. The faces of
Pembridge's half-timbered houses, under their
paint, speak of the forest.

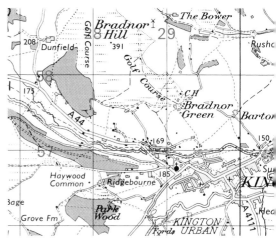

31	32
29	30
27	28

WALES & THE MARCHES
South and Mid Gwynedd
Landranger sheets 115, 123, 124

**Cwm Cadian (Valley of St Cadfan),
Dyfi Forest** *751 052,* ♣ ♀, *2m or less,
forest trail, FC*
This is an award-winning forest trail, with
good trees, good marker posts, a good car park
and a leaflet which makes intelligent use of two
colours. The car park is planted around with
alders, a grand fir, beeches, cotoneasters,
laburnum, a tulip tree and some cypresses.
The walk is largely on the hillside above the
cwm, with a detour to a small waterfall.
Numbered posts are placed as guides, and
numbers 6–10 are on a level forest road which
forms a high terrace and a viewing platform for
a display of perfect trees. These include
unusual masses of Lawson cypress grown as a
forest tree, with very well-formed, tall Sitka
spruces in the foreground (south-east of post
6). The path rises through tall, dark Douglas
firs into an equally dark beech plantation about
forty years old – the trees were planted under
oak coppice, some sad stumps of which remain.
This is a severe loss of original character
considering that the beeches are not
impressive. One can climb beyond the forest
road to the brow of the hill, admiring the
cypresses, which form a wall of foliage on the
outside of the planted group, unlike other
conifers. Here on the mossy, gorsy bank is an
old open beechwood, a truly poetic piece of
landscape and a very unusual one in Wales.
Larch and spruce are planted in the midst of its
perfection, and its days are numbered.

Taking the road to Aberllefenni there is
another car park beyond the interesting village
of Corris at *770 093,* and a waymarked trail.

The **Nant Gwernol** walk (2 miles) starts
from the station of this name on the Talyllyn
Railway, *682 066.*

Native oakwoods remain in the pretty, upland
country above Talsarnau and west of
Trawsfynydd, at Coed Lletywalter (Woodland
Trust, 94 acres, *600 275*), 3 miles south of
Harlech, and at Coed Maentwrog. Lletywalter
was scheduled as a National Nature Reserve

Beech, and a woodland floor, Cwm Cadian.

but funds were not available and the Woodland
Trust saved the day.

Above Talsarnau *629 372,* ♀, *roads
(notably at 626 364) and fps, private land
within Snowdonia NP*
Take the steep, uphill road out of the village
opposite the Ship Aground and Williams's
Garage; either fork takes you to the same place,
then you are on your own. You will find many
marked footpaths, and, at the map reference,
the nicest place to stop that you could imagine,

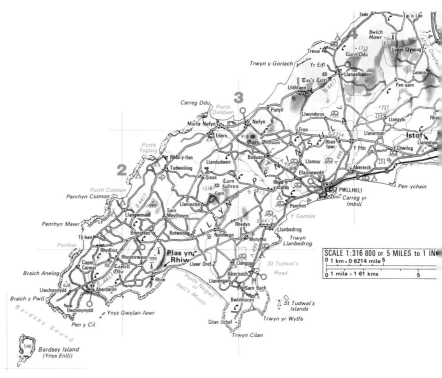

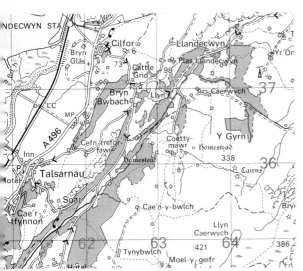

by a small lake. Lichen on stones and trees is a joy in itself, and sessile oaks, mostly quite small, are in every sort of shape. Northwards the little hills become even prettier, but are sadly polluted by pylons.

Coed Maentwrog *665 413,* ♀, *2m nature trails and paths, 169 acres, NR, NT*
The wood is spread irregularly along the steep north side of the Vale of Ffestiniog, the river meandering below. Maentwrog is a small place, hidden amongst trees. The vale is dominated by a grandish hotel, but there is a pleasant pub, with good food, in the narrow street where the A496 heads south. The Ffestiniog Railway runs above the wood and a nature trail starts from Tan-y-bwlch Station (35 minutes from Porthmadog) or from a car park, *651 416,* at Llyn Mair close by. The reference given is convenient for the middle of the wood, but parking is extremely limited on the roadside.

This is officially described as a 'relict valley oakwood'. There are many fine, large oaks as well as rowans and birches. There is too much bracken in places, and not as much natural regeneration as one would have hoped; but this is a good woodland walk by any standard. The little trains hoot beguilingly, and echoes confuse the ear. There are also supposed to be

nuthatches, pied flycatchers, redstarts and warblers, none of which I saw, as usual.

Between Dolgellau and the Lake of Trawsfynydd is the Coed-y-Brenin of the Forestry Commission, with a Visitors' Centre at Maesgwm, *715 276*. This was closed when I approached and I'm sorry to say that I did not try the forest walk from the picnic place at the old Pont Dôl-gefeiliau, nor the one from the Ty'n-y-groes car park 3 miles south, nor did I, to my shame, examine the Forestry Commission arboretum at Glasdir, 1 mile east of Ty'n-y-groes. Instead I drove up the eastern

163

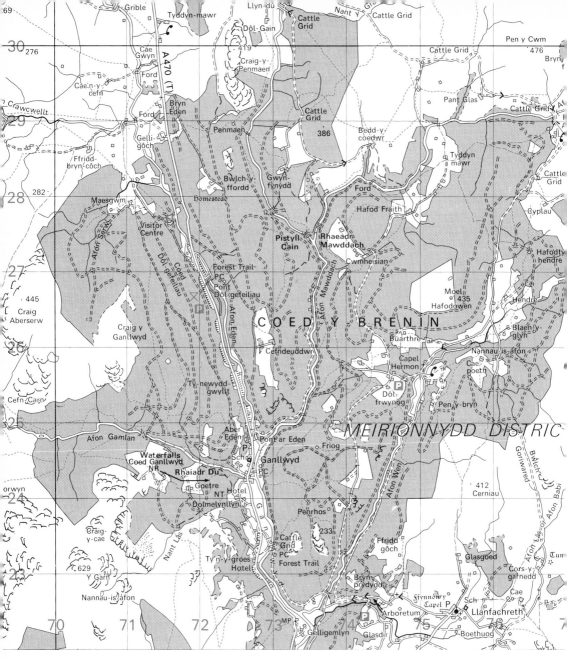

side of the wide Trawsfynydd Vale, obsessed with the mountain views and the ever-changing light. I drove, or was blown, into a peaty hole and had to be hauled out by a kindly giant called T. D. Jones. The twin towers of the power station gleamed at the end of this extraordinary avenue of hills like a distant castle in a Turner watercolour, and all around the hills the widely scattered, dark plantations of Coed-y-Brenin fitted snugly into the view. The Forestry Commission maintains 50 miles of footpaths here, and it was ungrateful of me not to set foot on any of them. Oaks remain beside a mile or two of the very smooth A470(T) in the Afon Eden, and especially at Coed Ganllwyd, *723 243*, a National Nature Reserve of 59 acres.

Aberglaslyn *597 462,* ♀, *1½m of riverside (easy),* NT *(517 acres)*

Here is the first view of Snowdon, or its head of clouds and its southern rampart, Yr Aran. Beautiful trees of somewhat mixed origin lean over the crashing white waters of the Glas. The path follows the track of an ancient railway, through its dripping, short tunnels and on to Beddgelert. You can shorten the walk by crossing the old railway bridge, now a footbridge, and returning by the road. The rather bare bank which rises very steeply 600 feet or so above is gradually being invaded by rhododendron, so the effect is distantly Tibetan. *Rhododendron ponticum* is not of course Tibetan, but the idea is there. It didn't look very nice, but if it helps to prevent erosion we can't complain. Perhaps one day the hillside will be clothed in oaks – the natural succession from rhododendron scrub, if any, is as yet uncharted so far as I know.

To continue into the mountains, turn to Section 31.

The Lleyn Peninsula

On the Lleyn Peninsula the Forestry Commission has the Istof picnic place at Llanystumdwy, *468 386,* with a short walk in varied woodland, including old beeches, and, 1 mile north of Llithfaen at *354 444,* a short walk with good views from this north coastal hilltop near Yr Eifl.

Plas yn rhiw Estate is 416 acres about a National Trust restoration of an ancient manor which became derelict in the nineteenth century; wild country with some trees down to the shore in places, but access on foot only. The map reference is *237 282* for the manor house.

Aberglaslyn, the walk

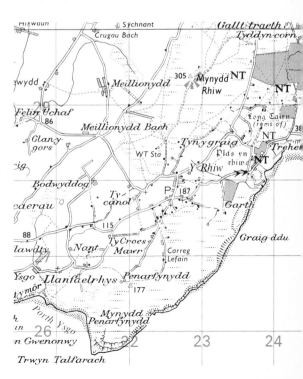

31	32	45
29	**30**	39
27	28	33

WALES & THE MARCHES
The Central Borders
Landranger sheets 125, 126

Powis Castle *215 064*, ♀ ♠, *parkland, 1m of driveway only, NT*
Just in Wales, the pink, stone castle is worth seeing on any account, and is surrounded by fine trees. In the gardens (open seasonally) are large silver firs and sequoias, and *Populus lasiocarpa*, a Chinese tree with very large leaves and pretty chains of fruits. At any time of the year you can walk across the park by the main drive and admire well-shaped old oaks and tall, very tall, Douglas firs – over 180 feet.

Leighton Hall, *242 046*, is the home of the Leyland cypress, the gardener's friend, which emerged from the chance crossing of two Western American trees, the Monterey and Nootka cypresses, in about 1888. Though the

Cypress and stonework at Leighton Hall

hybrid has grown taller elsewhere, it is nice to see it here, in an architectural setting that, to say the least, emphasizes its purity of form. One can walk through the grounds at weekends – less than $\frac{1}{2}$ mile. The house is now a college. (*Cupressocyparis leylandii* is over 100 ft in Devon.)

Earl's Hill, Pontesbury *407 057*, ♀, *105 acres, 2m, ps, NR*
Earl's Hill rises to a craggy 1047 feet, an outcrop of some ancient volcanic rock. In the scree on the south-east side a thicket of ash makes a startling effect. There are sessile oaks and some large-leaved lime. Old thorns on the grassy northern slope lead to the reserve centre, housed in an old barn – a hillside of larches beyond. Pontesford Hill belongs to the Forestry Commission and is coniferized, but bordered by large sycamores, old yews and some nice firs.

Turn off the A488 at Alexander and Duncan's Garage. You are supposed to park here, but you may find a niche where the footpath is signposted 'To the Barn and the Reserve', if you follow the single track road.

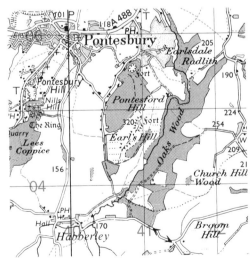

Ceiriog Forest

Picnic places at *174 382* and *165 384* are in the forest proper. The Forestry Commission's Nantyr Walks are a series of easy waymarked walks, and the World's End Walk, under the cliffs of Eglwyseg Mountain, $1\frac{1}{4}$ miles, is laid out by the North Wales Naturalists' Trust, *243 477*. This mountain is a limestone cliff, in the chain which extends from the Great Orme.

Yews at Overton, near the Dee, were once one of the Seven Wonders of Wales, in what used to be Flint.

31 32
29 30
Snowdonia and Anglesey

Landranger sheets 114, 115, 116, 124

Snowdon

From Beddgelert you have the choice of two passes, west or east of Snowdon. The mountain produces an annual rainfall measured in feet (over 13 feet), and since most of this comes from the west you may be influenced by the weather in your choice of route. The right-hand pass, Nantgwynant, leads to the head of the Llanberis Pass, and Llanberis is the popular Snowdon playground, with railway connection to the peak itself,

daily weather report gives the cloud ceiling as well as other, perhaps more predictable, factors. A gap in the wall leads to a short, stiff climb through the richly lichened trees, or you can follow the Watkin Path as far as the waterfall and the adjacent Coed-yr-allt, also oak.

several nature trails and a Country Park, **Padarn**, of 320 acres, *584 606*. This manages to live alongside a massive hydroelectric scheme and includes the largest slate quarry in the world (which ceased operation twenty years ago), as well as the surviving native oakwood, Coed Dinorwic, which is a local nature reserve.

Nantgwynant: an oak walk *628 506*, ♀, *very steep, length optional, fp, NNR*

Real walkers take the Watkin Path, striding up by waterfalls and the ruins of the incredibly gloomy South Snowdon Quarry to the summit ridges, here to look down to lonely Glaslyn – *glas* meaning green, silver or blue, a versatile word such as English cannot aspire to. All was grey when I visited this south-east cwm, but small oakwoods above the pass are extremely rich and beautiful, though grazed and therefore unlikely to perpetuate themselves. On the opposite side of the road are the extensive plantations and green fields of Plas Gwynant. The parking place is a large roadside one with decent facilities. Cross the bridge where a

Beddgelert Forest *574 508*, ♀ ♣, *various walks, campsite, wayfaring course, FC*

The car park and picnic place given above is at Pont Cae'r-gors (Glan y Gors) where start 'extensive systems of walks leading to viewpoints of Snowdon and Moel Hebog'. With all this wonderful mountain scenery about one does not want to plunge amongst the musky spruces, but the walks are there, and with fine silver firs to start you off.

The large campsite 1½ miles south is extremely nicely situated, with 300 pitches in varying degrees of seclusion amongst attractive birches, oaks and alders; open all year with reduced facilities in the winter.

Betws, where Telford's Waterloo Bridge takes his A5 over the River Conwy, waits to sustain

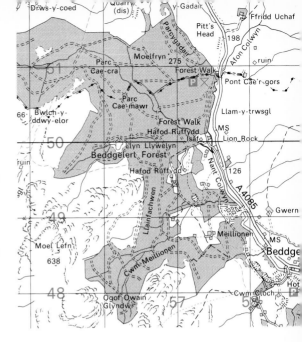

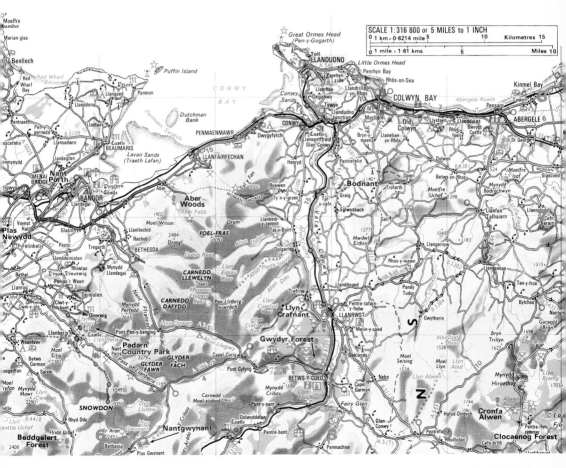

169

Afon Machno from the A5 at the north-eastern gateway to the National Park

the traveller, even on Sundays, and to lure him into the forest. It is difficult to imagine Betws-y-Coed before 1920, when certainly it was wooded, and the hotels put up a few gaitered and flap-hatted walkers to the Swallow Falls (on the unpronounceable Llugwy) and famous climbers practised on Snowdon and Tryfan while planning to bag Everest or Annapurna.

Betws means an oratory or a chapel, *y-Coed*, in the woods, but *capel*, as at Capel Curig nearby, is a chapel, and it is perhaps the rushing waters that sing here. It is a tourist centre, but an umbilical centre too for the mountains, forests and rivers, and you feel the pressure of their immensity around you – or perhaps it is just the mildness and dampness of the sheltered air.

The Information Centre has pocket folders, containing, in all, twelve walks leaflets.

This is the **Gwydyr Forest** (20,000 acres, including 7000 acres of grazing and farming land). The story of its planting with every sort of forestry tree on sometimes the most difficult of ground, the fighting of fires by the railwayside, and the constant battle to keep out the sheep, is told in unselfconscious detail in the very moderately priced *History of the Gwydyr Forest* by Donald Shaw of the Forestry Commission (booklet no 28).

Local walks start from the car park at Pont-

y-Pair, and for starters make for this. The B5106, the alternative route to Llanrwst, leaves the A5(T) by the bridge, Pont-y-Pair. Turn left *immediately* for the car park, *792 568*, and for the minor road, which bumps around a triangle of land with Trefriw at the apex, and the Ugly House (Ty-hyll, *756 576*, an unmistakable landmark on the A5) at the west. This uneven plateau with its associated valleys, and Llyn Crafnant on its north-west side, is varied and ruggedly pretty, closely woven with trails, walks and forest roads. Artists' Wood, tall beeches done by Cox and others, is on the

Male fern, Crafnant

south side of the A5 with a disabled trail starting opposite the Miners' Bridge, a footbridge at *780 569* just along the road from Pont-y-Pair, while the minor road itself runs into the plateau along the Llugwy Valley on the opposite side, through immense Douglas firs. Almost as tall above the Ugly House are hemlocks on a boulder-strewn hillside; a glimpse of a giants' countryside.

A forestry exhibition is at the Visitor Centre and Forest Office near Llanwrst (**Gwydyr Uchaf**, *790 612*), and from here Lady Mary's Walk runs up by degrees to give good views of the Conwy Valley and, in autumn, a splendid array of woodland fungi. Some of the viewpoints are now obscured by new trees; old beeches remain, but the walk is somewhat dark and sad. Lady Mary was presumably of the distinguished Wynn family whose estate forms the basis of the Forestry Commission lands.

Llyn Crafnant *757 621*, ♀ ♣, *3m or much less, easy, FC*

The lake is separated from, and to the north-west of, the main part of the Gwydyr Forest by the road system, which joins the valley at Capel Curig to the south-west or the next valley to the south-east, containing Llyn Geirionydd. Take an uphill road out of Trefriw, leaving the cemetery on your right. The road is lined with woodland oaks and there are various places to stop, but the walk begins from a fine car park just below the lake, and there is a map displayed. The walk around the lake uses the tarmac road, a farm track, a footpath and the forest road through Douglas fir, Japanese larch and spruce, planted about 1937.

Alternatively, the forest road going east from the car park then turns to follow the lakeside road, climbing about 250 feet before turning away to cross to Llyn Geirionydd. After a boring slog, it does give you a fine view of the picturesque crags of the head of the valley, where are remains of native oakwood.

Don't miss, at the first turning of this forest road, crossing the stile to a ruined lead mine, where a stupendous cave shelters, dripping a bit, the gold lichened stonework of what must have been cattle stalls or stabling, now occupied by magnificent ferns. The male fern

may be the commonest (after the common brake) but in this dark and sheltered place, with the extraordinary coloured walls, its beauty is absolute. Was the world once all like this, dark, still and damp, when these precursors of the trees evolved? The stillness is almost horrific.

Out in the wind the careful stonework of the mines above the green valley survives amongst the screes of spoil colonized by birches. There is no sign of mechanization in this lonely work-place. Note that the scree is dangerous and in any case should not be disturbed.

The famous gardens of **Bodnant**, 97 acres, National Trust, *803 721*, are on the east side of Afon Conwy 6 miles downstream.

The National Trust owns woodland at Llechwedd, near Harlech, and at Llyn Mair. The Maentwrog and Ganllwyd woods are leased to the NCC. South of Betws the National Trust has 25,820 acres of hills and valleys, mostly west of Ysbyty Ifan village and above the high Llyn Conwy and Tryfan, roads B4406 and 4407. The Trust also owns the mountains Carnedd Dafid, Tryfan, the north slopes of the Glyders and the north-west slopes of Carnedd Llewelyn: 15,800 acres altogether.

Nant Porth *567 720*, ♀, *19 acres, fp, NR*

This small ashwood on a limestone cliff is about a mile from the centre of Bangor and is in sight of the Menai Bridge. Turn off the A5(T) by a tyre service garage, next to Normal College, and drive around the sports field – Normal hockey girls may be seen. There is a car park at the end of the lane. *Sorbus porigentiformis* grows here, not as remarkably different from its very near relation *Sorbus aria* as its awful name might lead you to expect, but beautiful in leaf and in berry.

Aber Woods (Coed Ydd Aber) *664 719*, ♀ ♣, *trail, 1½m or 3m, leaflet, NR*

The trail is fairly basic stuff, but the valley has a great number of Iron Age and Bronze Age remains, where evidence has been found of birch woodland up to about 2000 feet. The longer trail includes a hut circle, cairns and hill fort, and part of the Forestry Commission's 350 acres of spruce and larch. The plantation

Alders in Aber Woods

borders onto the nature reserve woodland and interpenetrates with original oakwood. The Forestry Commission might have left these fragments of oakwood alone, allowing regeneration behind their sheep fence; but no, they have planted larches in between. If they thought that old oaks are just sentimental why did they bother to plant a row of seven *Populus trichocarpa* on the reserve boundary? What sort of sentiment is that? At least the conifers make a neutral background. On the mountainside above, an arm of the conifer plantation reaches to a giddy height. This we can and must admire.

The chief interest here for me is a fine alder swamp. The Welsh for alder grove, *gwern*, also means a meadow; a revealing synonym. Alder coppices were common once in the north Welsh valleys, the trees sold to itinerant makers of clog blanks and sweeping-brush

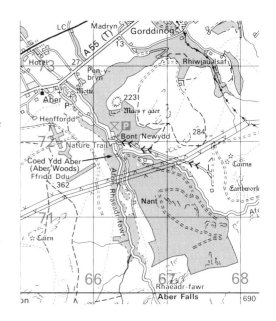

heads. The clogs were finished, and worn, in Lancashire. Alder wood is light and water-resistant, and might still have its uses, but the trees do tend to occupy valuable meadowland, while the much less resistant softwoods can be grown on soil that is no use for anything else.

This little wood of maturing coppice trees has a distinct atmosphere, and it is a valuable piece of conservation. However, it is grazed by sheep, and I would plead for their exclusion, for obvious reasons, from at least part of it.

The nature trail leaflet draws our attention to the rich lichens of the trees, indicating unpolluted air – and so the air should be, only 2 miles from the sea. But we should be grateful that Irish industry is not developed enough to produce the acid rain that our own industry sends – on the prevailing wind – to Scandinavia.

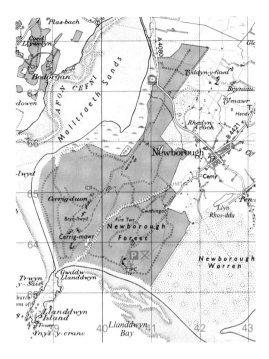

Cronfa Alwen *949 539,* ✦, *Visitors' Centre and forest walk, FC; Clocaenog Forest*
The large clean-lined Alwen Reservoir fills the valley, where lie submerged the non-too-fertile fields of a farm whose buildings are now restored as an exhibition room and a shelter. The walk of 1 mile is marked out.

There are 1800 acres of trees spread each side of 4 miles of the road northwards, and an even larger reservoir on the right hand side, Brenig. The vistas of bluish verdure are inspiring, even when it is raining.

ANGLESEY

Newborough Forest *406 635,* ✦, *1800 acres, forest roads, trail, FC*
Two miles beyond the village, signposted 'To the beach', is a splendid large car park which must be the Forestry Commission's best. It is elegantly formed of pools of tarmac amongst the pine-clad dunes, where slacks known as winter lakes will not support trees. Newborough Warren is the best known of Anglesey's several dunelands, permanently shifting and with marram grass as the dominant vegetation. A whole village, Rhosyr, is supposed to be buried in the sand; one old house has been uncovered and forms a feature

of the short trail. Green meadow grass grows where once was a floor of beaten clay.

The foresters have planted many incidental bushes and trees, as if determined to create a garden of trees, rather than replace the monotony of the warren with the monotony of the Corsican pine. I found a horse-chestnut which will one day suppress the pretty and local variety of round-leaved wintergreen which was shining in the grass like a constellation of sad stars in the endless dark corridors of pine. Sallows, which grow here naturally, are supplemented by osiers and poplars from the nursery garden. Creeping willow is a native weed in the grassland.

By the road can be seen the richer green of *Pinus radiata*, which grows quickly but not always straight. Lodgepole pine is also used further inland, near a much less formal parking place, *412 672,* on the road to Aberffraw. Here the view outwards is only of saltmarsh and sea, while the sun sets over Wicklow and Kilkenny to the slow chiming of bells, the fluting of organs and the crooning of tenors. Fish-and-chips down the road at Malltraeth – sounds Irish!

Clocaenog Forest, East

The silence of the spruces is absolute, the tiny road deserted, the land uneven, untidy as the sky. Large, grey-floored clearings in the forest disclose distant blue mountain ranges, and small Welsh trees flourish by a wandering stream. Old walls are vividly patterned with lichens, black and white over the grey. The forest is not quite continuous – it is broken in places by green farms full of fat sheep. The silence is broken too, sometimes, by a noise of diesels, for the landscape, despite its purity, is that of a highly mechanized timber-production industry, spread over 10,000 acres. It is spread

out in time too, for the trees impose a very slow rhythm, and there are miles of twilight here where nothing perceptible happens for twenty years at a time. The forest floor is deep, piled with millions of leaves measuring two centimetres by two millimetres, each marked with ten lines of tiny dots – stomata – perfectly geometrical but, like finger prints, never matching any other. These are the leaves of Sitka spruces and the trees were planted here, of course, but they grow as their ancestors must have grown two million years ago above these ancient rocks, gregarious and containing darkness. There are quantities of the squashy, cylindrical cones, each one bearing who knows how many useless seeds, and grey, dead twigs, rather bony-looking. Many shining, clean fungi nose their way from the dampness below,

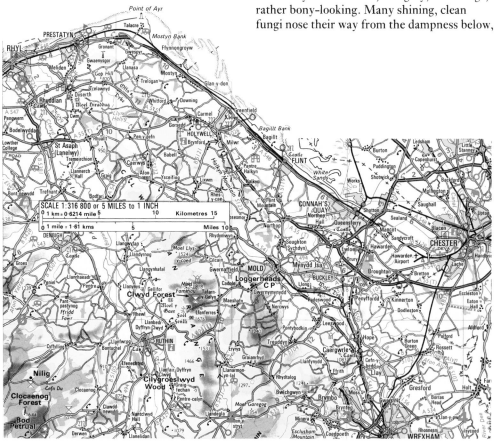

Amanita muscaria, Clocaenog Forest

among them the fiery red, white-spotted, globes of the hallucinogenic fly agaric, *Amanita muscaria* – strange fruit for grey, chapel-going North Wales.

Forestry roads of gravel weave a complex pattern amongst these remote highways, and all are open to the walker, or even the driver,

daring the Forestry Commission's wrath.

On the road to Cyffylliog, is a picnic place by a little bridge, Nilig, *017 549.*

Cilygroeslwyd Wood *126 553,* ♀, *10 acres, NR*

This is a patch of ashwood with the odd yew and some hazel on carboniferous limestone, not much of a walk but a valuable nature reserve. Take the Corwen or Bala road, the A494(T), south from Ruthin, and turn left at the sign 'Llanfair DC'. There is parking space over the little bridge (and a good view of the hills). The wood lies 250 yards beyond a wooden stile in the iron fence along the main road.

Clwyd Forest *173 612,* (♀) ✦, *1500 acres, trails, fairly steep, FC*

East of Ruthin the beautiful sequence of hills running north and south has a focus for walkers at Moel Fammau, 1772 feet. The car

Clocaenog Forest

Helleborus foetidus, Cilygroeslwyd, October

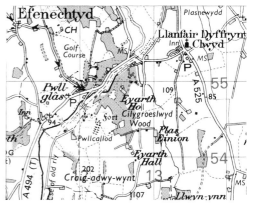

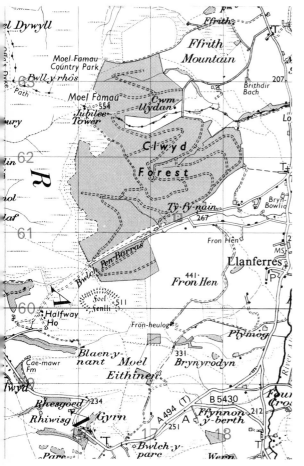

park is shaped like a railway siding, and has electric cables running over it. It serves the Country Park of Moel Fammau (2375 acres of heath and mountain top). It boasts a grandiose lavatory block with perspex domes where I spent an agonized hour persuading a blue tit to fly out of the door.

Trees planted by the road are larches, chestnut and, a bit surprising, laburnum. It should be pointed out that laburnum seeds can be fatal in quite small quantities, and while no doubt the effect of the granite loos surrounded by brilliant yellow blossom in early summer is impressive, the whole adds up to an ecological nonsense, with hazards for birds and children. But straight forest roads and dark bands of forest trees subtly emphasize the curves of this glacial valley, and the foresters have left even straighter rowans, which grew up amongst the larches. I examined a boulder, an erratic of some sort of conglomerate, which the glacier had left at the bottom of its lake. In the intervening 10,000 years some moss had grown on its reticulated surface and, shaped like a miniature of the hills around it, it caused me to reflect that even Forestry Commissions come and go, and the apparently indestructible plastic bags stuck in the gorse, the granite loo, the electricity cables and the gregarious multicoloured cars – and you and I – are all very temporary.

Loggerheads, *198 627,* a mile east, is a Country Park and a Site of Special Scientific Interest, on limestone, which outcrops in impressive cliffs on the next line of hills.

Central England

Alder buckthorn in New Fallings Coppice

Queenswood CP, *Dinmore Hill*

506 515, ♀ ♣, 170 acres, easy walking, LA

The A49 from Hereford to Leominster curves up the hill of Old Red Sandstone. The wood really did belong to the Queen, until the eighteenth century. All the fine oaks and beeches were cut down in World War I and the land left as wilderness. The Council for the Preservation of Rural England saved it from being gradually built upon, and it was bought by the County with the proceeds of a memorial fund to King George V's Silver Jubilee; it was then dedicated to the public 'for all time'.

Half is forestry, oak and other native trees, and is a nature reserve. The centre plateau contains a beautifully planned arboretum of 400 varieties of tree – probably over 200 species. All are grouped and arranged as open woodland, with blocks of conifers and stands of native oak intervening. Infant *Sequoiadendron* and others, planted out, seem to suggest a plan in the grand manner to be realized in the next century. Then, floating up from Hereford by hovercraft, you will see Queenswood crowned with a ring of the largest trees in the world.

On the A44, 2 miles east of Bromyard, is the large **Brockhampton** estate of the National Trust, with woodland walks: *693 543.*

Wenlock Edge

The Edge is characteristically wooded, there not being much else to do with it, but most of the woodland is a very steep, narrow strip of thicket. Whatever troubled the wood in Housman's time has resulted in a number of car parks in a place where there is not room for them, and an even greater number of large, ugly concrete litter bins. The National Trust part begins where the cement works finish, on the B4371 a mile or two south-west of Much Wenlock, and there are ways into the escarpment wood. Avoiding all this, you can drive on to Rushbury and take the road past the church and over the hill into Hope Dale; there is space to park in a muddy lane which leads promisingly off westwards, at the map reference given below: it is signposted Bridleway. This is north of Upper Millichope.

A Hope Dale Walk *518 898, ♀ ♣,*

2½ hours, very muddy (clay), fps

The bridleway is churned by farm tractors but the voices of sheep in the upland air will charm you, and the light beckons beyond a wooded hill, a lesser Edge. The way leads through very straight poplars, contrasting with crooked old oaks – some are durmast oaks. Then at the gate, Sitka spruce forestry on the right, you can follow the lane to the farm, which is lovely, all patches of corrugated iron, with an open paddock full of geese and ducks, and, in March, expectant ewes loudly demanding more to eat. A hollow lane leads uphill beyond the farm; you will then see a small gate into the wood at the top of the pasture. The view of Wales is terrific. The wood, once a coppice, no doubt to supply fuel to the farm, is now quite neglected, with dog's mercury in the deeply engraved path. With some difficulty you can reach the plateau, which has a most impressive group of old Scots pines and larches.

Turning back, the ridge passes around a healthy stand of Corsican pine, which makes a plain, dark frame for the pretty hills beyond. When you reach the larchwood beyond the

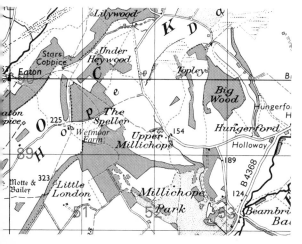

Prunus incisa in April, Queenswood

iron railings of Millichope Park, turn downhill, sharp left, to return to the farm. An old birchwood offers another contrast with the geometry of modern forestry. Leaving the farm on your left, a gate leads into the pasture with its picturesque durmast oaks, one of which has a yew growing out of its top, and back to the poplar patch.

A Severn Valley Walk *718 970*, ♀, *about 2m, easy*

Go north out of Bridgnorth on the B4373 for ½ mile, then turn right at the first opportunity, down Stanley Lane. A small area of tarmac marks a parking place for fishermen, and here you can strike off by a well-trodden bridleway through a larchwood, to join a dirt road on the track of an old railway. The steep terraces and the riverside are wooded, but more interesting for their shapes than for their trees. The area is rich in wild flowers.

A lovely white suspension bridge at the now converted railway station of Linley was built in 1909 and carries a cast-iron inscription by which Mr Foster, presumably of Apley Park, across the water, allowed no one but his estate

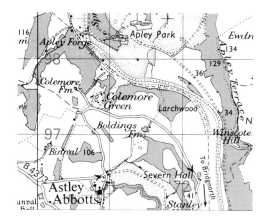

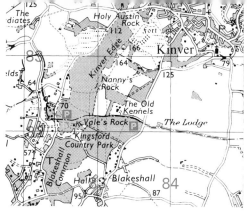

workers to use the bridge without permisssion.

Long-distance walkers can continue to Coalport and to Iron-Bridge, but to regain your car retreat to a farm track which leaves the valley by a cottage, passing an ancient, gnarled alder, to Colemore Farm and the road.

Highgate Common CP 836 901, ♀ ♣, 350 acres, easy, many paths, LA

This is a Black Country common on black sand with dark stands of pine and a splendid wide sweep of heather and birch, all strangely tinged with the colour of the soil. Even the silver birches have a distinctly darkling gleam as if drawn in Indian ink.

The common was the subject of intricate legal arguments over ownership: the Lord of the Manor claiming it was his freehold; the Forestry Commission acquiring a lease to plant the usual pole crop, and the County Council opposing this, then buying the land for us.

Kinver Edge 837 836, ♀ ♣, 400 acres, ridge walk, easy but a stiff climb, NT
Kingsford CP 823 823, ♀ ♣, trails, including a disabled trail, CC

The better of the two areas I think is to the north: here, there are many parking places. The Country Park has all the amenities – and 160 acres of forestry conifers if you want to shut out the world. But the Edge is something else; an experience of superb birchwoods

sweeping up to the cliff, where oaks and thorns cling, with gorse to catch you if you fall. The wide path on the top gives views of what looks like most of the Midlands, smooth green fields and farms intervening. At the Kinver end, over the town, is Holy Austin Rock, site of the last troglodyte dwelling in Britain, vacated only in the fifties.

Wyre Forest 762 779, ♀ ♣, at least 6000 acres, 2 picnic sites with various forest walks, FC

Wyre was originally home to the Weogorena Tribe. The Romans named Worcester VVIOGORNA CEASTRE and Wyre stuck for the forest area, then almost the whole county including part of Shropshire as well. Later, the Crown held some rights, and the locals tried to contain the deer with a 4-mile fence. Tall trees were cut to make charcoal for the iron industry. Coppicing and itinerant charcoal burning continued well into this century, and most of the forest woods are either commons or named coppices. Bewdley's Town Coppice is at least 300 acres. Industry, demanding a renewable source of fuel, preserved the coppices, which also supplied the valuable oak bark for tanning. Not only for harness and clothing, leather was essential for bellows, even more so when coke began to fire the furnaces in the nineteenth century. It was left to the Forestry Commission to destroy most of this centuries-old heritage of woodland.

The major portion of the forest is now contained between the B4194 and A4117 running west from Bewdley. The Forestry Commission maintains two parking areas with picnic places and shortish walks. The map reference above is for the quieter place,

Hawkbatch, on the B4194. It is a lovely spot and gives access to the Severn Valley side and **Seckley Wood**, *765 786*, home of some ancient beeches. At the main car park, *751 742*, on the A road, the longest of three walks from the Visitors' Centre takes you right into the forest over Dowles Brook. Knowles Coppice and Fred Dale, together 72 acres, are nature reserves in the valley, served by footpaths along the brook. Coppices have grown up into oak forest. Knowles Mill by the brook is National Trust property with an old orchard. Somewhere in the forest grew the famous, lonely Whitty Pear, recorded as *Sorbus pyriformis* in the seventeenth century, the only wild individual of the species in Britain (the tree is native as far north as Brittany). That old tree was vandalized in the nineteenth century but its seedlings were used to replace it. Now a neat label identifies the 'sorb tree' – it is *Sorbus domestica*, and all the mystery is gone, along with the oaks removed by the Forestry Commission.

Walking into the forest from the west, say at Sturt Common, *725 774*, can give some idea of the older countryside where farms, forest and heath interpenetrate. Half a square mile of the Longdon and Withybed woods north of Dowles Brook are protected by covenant to the National Trust, and we may hope that all the forest is not lost to the Douglas fir and the pines, though the view from rising ground to the west seems to say otherwise. The best walk is probably along the Dowles Brook, left from the B4194, one mile north-west of Bewdley.

Worcester has an oakwood, **Nunnery Wood**, *875 545*, of 55 acres, only a mile from the city centre on the A422 behind County Hall and owned by the County Council, containing ash and wild service, with helleborine, cow wheat, tormentil and hairy rush.

Only 12 miles south-west of the centre of Birmingham the **Clent Hills** have a Country Park, *927 799*. The common of 166 acres and Walton Hill Common, 86 acres, were purchased by the county from the Lord of the Manor, Lord Cobham. Lords of Manors own little but the soil of a common, and have many responsibilities. The County Council wanted

Whitty pear leaves

Lord Cobham to continue his lordship of the Manor, against his inclination. A Royal Commission had to sit. Eventually, 362 acres were given to the National Trust, and, with many local authorities assisting, Lord Cobham was allowed to retire.

Shrawley Wood, on the Severn at *805 663*, is described as an oakwood containing the greatest remaining concentration of the native large-leaved lime.

Shrawley church is about a mile south of the wood. It is very pretty, pink and lopsided, and flanked by two fine large trees: a hornbeam and a sweet chestnut.

Chaddesley Woods, *914 736*, oak and conifer, attempt to show that conservation and commercial forestry are compatible: a National Nature Reserve too, with ancient woodland.

Waseley Hills Country Park, *979 768*, contains **Sedgbourne Coppice**, and scrub.

Pepper Wood, *940 750*, 134 acres just 5 miles north-west of Bromsgrove, is a valuable acquisition of the Woodland Trust, particularly as it is so close to the great conurbation. It is a wet, overgrown coppice-with-standards.

Piper's Hill Common, *957 648*, astride the B4091 north of Hanbury, is wooded and carefully controlled by the Lord of the Manor. It is a Site of Special Scientific Interest.

Himley Plantation, Wombourne, *870 914*, was saved for us by the Woodland Trust and is part of an old estate. Rhododendron is present, with mature oak, beech and pine. A disused railway managed as a Country Park penetrates the wood.

Birmingham and Warwickshire

Landranger sheets 139, 140, 150

The Forest of Arden

Rosalind: Well, this is the Forest of Arden!
Touchstone: Ay, now I am in Arden, the more fool I! When I was at home I was in a better place . . .

As You Like It

Rugged, shapely oaks remain, though not in the forest glades of Shakespeare's time. Charcoal burning for industry reduced the forest to coppice; then, as coke and coal became the main fuels, farming took over all the land to supply the ever-growing population. Great elms there were – it was the

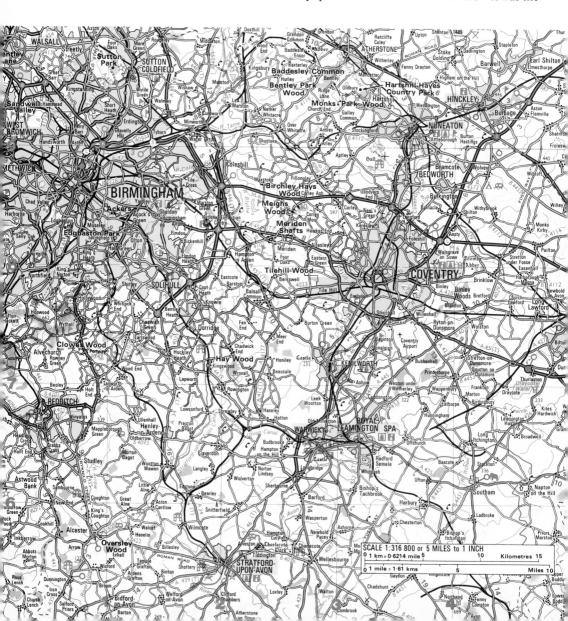

'Warwickshire weed' – but all are now dead. Still the oaks persist, but not in the woods.

Oversley Wood, Alcester *112 570, ♀ ♠, 1½m around, FC*
There is supposed to be a trail, but the marks are lost. A right of way leads into the wood from Primrose Hill, Oversley Green – you have to park in the village. A stout border of blackthorn has been cleared, but you have to hop over barbed wire to get on to the forest road. There is maple, birch, hazel, cherry, rowan, sallow, holly and even a bit of oak in places, but you look out of the wood to older oaks. Inside are solid blocks of Corsican pine, hemlock, larch: but the foresters have left wide margins, birch-dominated at present. The intention was to replace the hardwoods eventually, or so said H. L. Edlin of the Forestry Commission in 1958.

The proper entrance is at the north-east corner from the A422 (Alcester to Stratford). Here you have to park in a lay-by. Do visit the wood if you can, to help convince the foresters that there is some public interest in this rather isolated piece of the Forest of Arden.

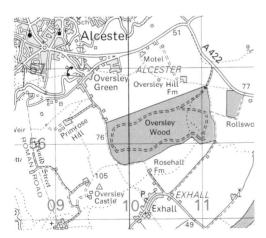

Hay Wood *207 706, ♀ ♠, picnic place, FC*
Hard to find unless you know it, here is a woodland corner with beautifully rural surroundings. The foresters have left only a small corner to walk in, and even here have planted hemlocks amongst the native trees. Some oak-ash-holly character survives. You

can walk down the quiet lane to Baddesley Clinton old church.

The National Trust Packwood House, timber framed, *171 722*, has, besides a famous set-piece of topiary, 113 acres of park and woodland, and is well signposted 2 miles west of Hay Wood. But there is no right of way through the park when the garden is closed during the winter. A 'Leisure Drive', through wooded lanes, is a substitute for a walk, perhaps.

Meriden Shafts, *near Eaves Green,* Meighs Wood and Birchley Hays Wood, *near Hollyberry End: all around 257 835, all FC*
These coniferized corpses of old woods are non-starters for walking in, but there is a wide grassy verge to park on at the map reference, and we have marked the footpaths, hoping that you will do the exploring. Meriden Shafts is actually closed, the Forestry Commission having let the sporting rights, but this need not be permanent.

Hartshill Hayes Country Park, *316 947*, has woodland and adjoins Forestry Commission plantations where facilities are being developed. Monk's Park Wood and Bentley Park Wood, the largest woods in the section, are private, but there are footpaths from Birchley Heath, Ridge Lane (south from the B4116) and at Bentley Common: consult the OS map, sheet 140. Baddesley Common, *277 978*, has the remains of an oak coppice,

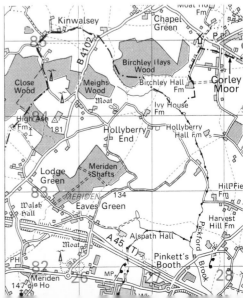

Baddesley Common, an attractive fragment in a tired landscape

next to a coal-mine – a pleasant place to stop if you are slogging up the A5: north-west of Atherstone, turn left at the Black Swan, Grendon.

Near Coventry is **Tilehill Wood**, a slightly sad survival between new housing and new factories and schools, but with some good oaks, hollies and chestnut coppice. The only place to park is on the east side, in the streets, *283 790*.

Clowes Wood and New Fallings Coppice *098 738*, ♀, *150 acres, LA*

Between Birmingham and Redditch, at Tanworth-in-Arden, is Clowes Wood, a nature reserve of 77 acres, oak and beech woodland. Wood Lane, *102 743*, is one point of access, by many footpaths through New Fallings Coppice; or from Earlswood Lakes Station, across a field. Wood Lane is signposted from

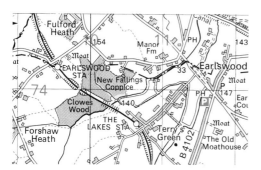

the north-west; to find it from the B4102 turn down at the Reservoir pub, then left *beyond* the lake. New Fallings Coppice is no longer a coppice in appearance: it has been 'promoted' to an oakwood. Alder buckthorn and aspen in Clowes Wood (beyond the stream to the south), suggest antiquity; these trees are never planted. Clowes Wood is very varied and will repay patient exploration. The woodland continues across the railway.

The reservoir, half of it used for sailing, is a popular recreation place. There is a walk under willows along the south-east side.

There are dozens of small woods in Warwickshire, and according to statistics they contain 8000 acres of oak. Please explore, and claim your right to your woodlands. Join the County Naturalists' Trust, WARNACT. Tilehill Wood and Clowes Wood are two of close on thirty sites which the West Midlands County Council has designated as nature reserves in or very near the urban areas of Birmingham and Coventry. Twenty sites are currently being worked on with the help of British Trust for Conservation volunteers.

Among old-established reserves are **Edgbaston Park**, with a bird lake and famous botanical garden, and **Sutton Park**, *103 963*, large and popular but with some unfrequented woodland.

Northamptonshire

Landranger sheets 141, 152

Rockingham Forest

Rockingham Forest is still recognizable by a scattering of green patches on the map to the west of Oundle on the Nene and bounded by the Welland to the north-west. Place-names like Melton Mowbray and Stilton, with Laxton and Caldecott in the forest area, put one in mind of hunters leaping over hedges, and good solid food; woodland reduced to copses, coverts and apple orchards. The Forestry Commission is very much in control and occupies pieces of land not up to the standard of profitable arable farming. Occasional oaks look as if they were not up to timber standards, but confer a forest character hard to reconcile with the dull fields and hedges.

A great monument of a beech tree remains at the approach to the Forestry Commission's picnic place in Wakerley Great Wood. Perhaps it was the last of the Fox Trees – awarded to keepers in Rockingham Forest for prowess in killing foxes.

Wakerley Great Wood *963 986, (♀) ♦,*
100 acres, easy walks, forest trail or toughish hikes, FC
Fine larches surround a capacious parking place and vistas of oaks and pines open out beyond. There are also unofficial grassy picnic spots along the by-road through the forest.

This is a cheerful-looking forest with much more to it than the regulation forest trail. On

Ancient beech in Wakerley Great Wood

the opposite side of the A43 is Fineshade Top Lodge, the Forest Office, with Caravan Club site. Here an old railway cutting plunges into the trees to the south-west, offering another sort of walk, and Westhay Wood, a good square mile of Commission forest, is also open to walkers.

Short Wood, *020 912*, by permit from the NTNC, is described as a remnant of the forest and is famous for bluebells: 62 acres. **King's Wood**, *864 874*, also contains old oaks of the Rockingham Forest in over 100 acres. It is a nature reserve in Corby. **Lings Wood**, *803 640*, is in Northampton, a 56-acre nature reserve.

At **Thrapston Gravel Pits** on the Nene you can walk by fine white willows, sallow scrub on shores not yet woodland: *995 796*.

Eyebrook Reservoir *853 964, (♀)♣,*
1½m (3m there and back), cinder road,
WA
The south-east side of the water is planted with conifers and willows at the water's edge; a peaceful place. Walkers are expected to behave and not be burdened with dogs or children.

Salcey Forest *794 515, ♀♣, 1300 acres,*
2m forest trail, often muddy or wet, FC
The M1 skirts the forest but is not too audible, being in a cutting. Approach by the B526 from Newport Pagnell, or from Northampton turn off the A508 at Wootton, and then through the village of Quinton. The nearest M1 exit is junction 15. Numerous unofficial parking places on the east–west road through the forest are provided by the concrete platforms remaining from wartime RAF occupation.

A mile of oaks is a refreshing sight on the road through the forest. The oak plantation is a Site of Special Scientific Interest. The picnic place is civilized and the forest trail, which takes in an ancient landmark oak, won the Countryside Award in 1970, presented by Prince Philip. Salcey means willowy (Salicaceae), and the trail crosses some very wet ground where a considerable *salicetum* might well have flourished. Now only a few sallows remain, sycamore having taken hold in the rides where, apparently an odd choice, the foresters have planted many English cherries and sweet chestnuts. There is a stand of giant fir, *Abies grandis* – this tree, happily, is being used increasingly in forestry. There is also *A. alba*, the common silver fir, now not very common. A 200-acre lawn in the middle of the forest is preserved, adding enormously to the potential habitat.

Perhaps one is always influenced by the weather: this was a brilliant, misty, autumn morning which would have flattered the dullest surroundings; however, I think the forest walk would be very interesting and pretty even on a dull day. There are half a dozen ancient oaks left standing in various parts of the forest.

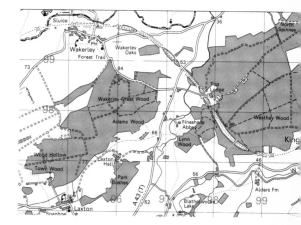

Coprinus disseminatus, fairy toadstools –
Salcey Forest

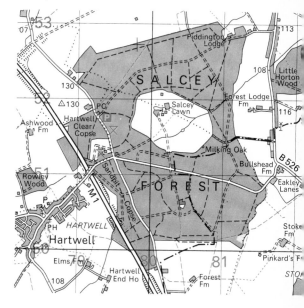

41|42|43
35|**36**|37
20|21|22

CENTRAL ENGLAND
Cambridgeshire
Landranger sheets 141, 142, 153, 154

Hayley Wood *295 537, ♀, 150 acres,*
muddy, CNT
Turn off the A14 (Stane Street) at Longstowe,
9 miles north of Royston. At Longstowe are
several fine elm trees – in flower in 1983 –
though others are lost. The survival of these
few is surprising considering that Wimpole
Park, nearby, lost all its famous 2 miles of elms.

The way to the wood is signalled by a water
tower and two white posts: you have to park at
the roadside. A permit is needed from the
Cambridge Naturalists' Trust to enter the
wood, but much can be seen and learnt from
the perimeter track, a public footpath.
Coppicing is carefully controlled in the wood
which is famous for its rich ground flora,
particularly oxlips. Hayley is a classic ash-
maple-hazel wood and has been much studied.
As a walk, the footpath to Hayley, turning
round the wood and then on to the disused
railway to return, is a matter of taste. There
was a thunderstorm when I explored: the
breathless minutes before the storm, when
birds began to seek the shelter of the trees,
I would not have missed; the next half hour
I could have done without.

Gamlingay Wood *239 539, ♀ ♣, about*
160 acres, very muddy, pf
Take the B1040 north out of Gamlingay: the

Earth star fungus on decaying ash stool,
Gamlingay

wood is visible on your right, but the only way
in is by a field track nearly opposite a gate of
Waresley Park.

Parts of this old wood have been coniferized,
but without obliterating the many stools of ash,
oak and, here and there, maple. Patches of
birch are on sand (deposited by wind over the
Boulder Clay). Ash is now the commonest tree
apart from the spruce and pine. There are a
group or two of aspen, some hazel, some
sallow. The floor is carpeted with dog's
mercury, a very good green in early spring, and
there is wood sorrel. A prominent bank in the
more impenetrable northern part is covered
with bluebells, as are several other drier
patches, and the paths are full of primroses.
Stout and weirdly shaped oaks remain on a low
bank surrounding the whole wood.

Knapwell: Overhall Grove *337 633, ♀,*
43 acres, fp, NR
Mediaeval Knapwell was a large, busy place,
its streets and gardens lined with pollard elms
which have miraculously survived as 'old
dodders' in the bumpy fields. The Manor,
ruined long ago, lies immersed in woodland,
mostly of elm, which has spread from the
Victorian-planted Grove, among ash, oak and
maple. The cellars are occupied by badgers.

Many but not all of the elms – it is the
smooth-leaved elm – are dead, and the extra
light in the wood will benefit the spring flowers
for which the place is well known. A path
wanders roughly parallel to the village street,
muddy at the south end where it emerges at a
style near a small pump house, at *334 624.*

There are woodland corners, and many
beautiful specimen trees and shrubs, in
Cambridge Botanical Gardens. Enter by
Bateman Street, off Trumpington Road, less
than a mile from King's College, to get the
useful map leaflet. The gardens are closed on
winter Sundays except to key-holders. There
are pines, some rare, honey-locust, golden rain
and cucumber trees, tree of heaven.

Wandlebury Ring *493 533*, ♀ (♠), *¾m or 1¼m, easy, Cambridge Preservation Trust*
Wandlebury is signposted on the A1307 (A604) 3 miles south of Cambridge. The Ring is the 1000-foot-diameter rampart and ditch of an Iron Age Fort, close to the Gog Magog Hills.

Much planting has been done recently on the Ring, with a wide range of species to add to the existing pattern of box, yew, holly and beech. The ditch is full of elderberry: it was probably used to dump rubbish in former times and the chalky soil remains rich in nitrates. There is a great deal of ivy. Wild flowers were resplendent even in mid March:

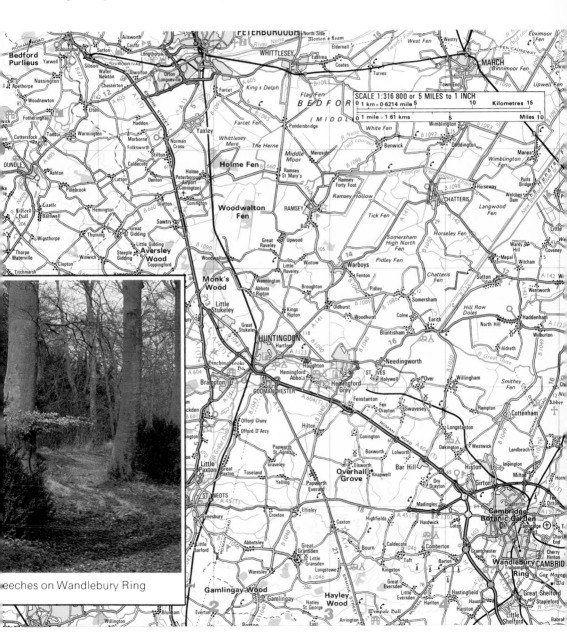

Beeches on Wandlebury Ring

stinking hellebore and the naturalized winter aconite spreading beneath beeches; snowdrops in drifts; daffodils, not wild, in rather self-conscious clumps.

There is a wide south-sloping meadow for picnics, a pond with ducks tame enough to amuse anyone, and a shop (open Easter to October) with a booklet that probably tells you all about the archaeology of the Gog Magog Hills and a Roman road, now grassed over, that passes ½ mile to the east. The stable clock is beautiful and the car park is nice.

Aversley Wood *165 818, ♀, 152 acres, allow 2 hours, very muddy, WT*
The wood is now entirely owned by the Woodland Trust and access from Sawtry (by Manor House Farm) is feasible: the gate is in the middle of the south-east side.

Oak-ash woodland appears to have been the original vegetation on higher land in these parts, a somewhat featureless area of clay resembling rich cake and obviously very productive of food crops. But hills and clearings seem to have been synonymous in Saxon times, and Aversley ('Aefic's Lea') sounds like a clearing (near Sawtry, a 'salt-landing place' on the edge of the Fens). The presence of a large elm community in the middle of the south-west half also implies early clearing and habitation: the elms, now dead and in process of being cleared, were tall but grown up from old coppice stools, some of

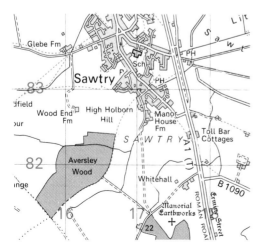

which have stout shoots and flowers in this year (1983). The tree is a wych elm hybrid. Elms dead at the north-east corner seem close in character (no leaves now available) but obviously did not coppice so freely: they probably invaded from the field hedge.

There are good wild service trees, woodland hawthorn (*Crataegus laevigata*), and blackthorn as well as hazel, ash being slightly more common than its co-dominant oak, *Quercus robur*. Bluebells are everywhere, and there are many birds.

Holme Fen *215 884, ♀, 640 acres, permit required for any thorough exploration, NNR*
Off the B660 which leaves the A1 eastwards, 2 miles north of Sawtry a typical fenland (dead straight) by-road leads into the wood by Middle Covert and Jackson's Covert. Here you can take a footpath into the wood to see the finest birch trees in lowland England. The trees have spread from areas planted in 1870 for game cover. They are certainly beautiful.

Both Holme Fen and **Woodwalton Fen**, *234 849*, are subjects of elaborate scientific studies and one can understand the Nature Conservancy Council not encouraging casual picnicking, dog walking etc. Woodwalton is the only British home of a certain rare butterfly; also the history of the place is known since the Ice Age through fossil pollen preserved in its peat. Holme Fen was drained for agriculture, which later became impossible because of peat shrinkage (measurable at Holme Fen Post). Nature returned in the elegant form of *Betula pubescens*, with many grasses and rushes, birds and insects.

Bedford Purlieus *052 991, ♀ ♣, many tracks, varying lengths, FC*
The Forestry Commission manages the intriguingly named Bedford Purlieus, 3 miles east of Wakerley. The map reference is approximately the best place to park, where a sandy lane leads to a piece of wasteland (and further if not too wet). The edges of the wood contain many concrete platforms and sinister-looking pits, the sort of thing the military are so good at making and so bad at removing. A purlieu is simply a piece of private land next to

Holme Fen birches

a forest – often only partly released from forest laws: a sort of forest suburb. The Bedford Purlieus holds the record for the number of vascular plant species it contains – approaching 400 – and has been described as a patchwork of woodland types. I visited it at the wrong season, but there was certainly a fine display of mosses. Coppices at the south contain stools of sycamore and there is a great deal of birch, planted, much of it falling about in confusion: the occasional stands of conifers are much less neglected looking. A patch of lime coppice, *Tilia cordata*, is in the northern part beyond the conifers. Also coppiced generally are oak, hazel, wych elm and ash, with scattered maple: some chestnut at the north and even a few horse-chestnuts.

The wood was studied by Peterkin and Welch in 1975 and their publication *Bedford Purlieus: Its History, Ecology and Management* is available from the Institute of Terrestrial Ecology, 68 Hills Road, Cambridge, at a very reasonable cost.

CENTRAL ENGLAND

North-West Suffolk

Landranger sheets 143, 144, 155

Thetford Forest. A desert of sand made into a forest of poles.

Thetford Forest

Thetford is the second largest forest in England, and almost all planted within the past sixty years – first with Scots pine, now with the higher-yielding Corsican pine. There are over 70 square miles of trees and nothing but trees, except for a total of 10 square miles of farmlands. This great natural machine projects into the air every day 555 tons of wet pine wood; more in summer, less in winter. A corresponding drier tonnage is delivered each day for sawing, for pitprops, woodwool, chipboard, pulp, fencing, telegraph poles and fuel, in that order of importance. The figures will nearly double by 1990. For every 200 tons of coal mined, the Forestry Commission tells us, 1 ton of pinewood props is used – an annual 23,000 cubic metres of peeled logs from Thetford Forest alone.

The plantation occupies about a fifth of the area of Breckland. This is the name of a very large sandy heath over flint and limestone, where the Scots pine was once a native, scattered tree – perhaps even a forest – destroyed by fires, or resulting from the clearings of early man. The prehistoric flint mines at Grimes Graves are in the middle of the present forest. The remaining Breckland heaths are converted to farmlands (where you can see the dust blowing in dry weather), or are occupied by the Army. Some original fragments are maintained (fences to keep the rabbits *in*) at Weeting Heath and Santon Warren.

It was the alien rabbit which in the seventeenth century finally removed much of the long over-grazed Breckland vegetation (heather, a few grasses, sand sedge and common reed). The few patches of pine which had held the whole thing together could not regenerate, their seedlings either too dry or eaten. As early as 1668 the village of Santon Downham was nearly buried in a catastrophic sandstorm. The region which had supported the earliest settlements of man in Britain became one of the least populated – the 'British Desert'. There may be a moral in that.

To **Santon Downham**, nowadays cool and leafy, you must go for Forestry Commission information: and it must be said that the Commission has done everything possible to

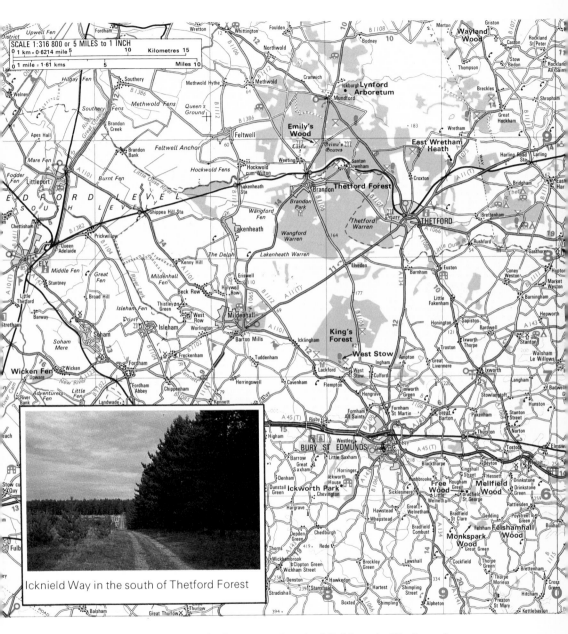

Icknield Way in the south of Thetford Forest

welcome and entertain the visitor to the forest. The approach roads from the Thetford to Brandon road are magnificently shaded by broadleaved trees and there are very many, typically not-quite-secluded, parking areas on grass. At Santon are a small but good post office and stores, WCs and hot water, the old church of St Mary the Virgin, a pleasant open picnic site and an easy forest trail. Also a railway, a river, and, of course, the Forest Office, with leaflets, books and a small exhibition.

There are nine other picnic sites in the forest, most with marked walks and trails. If you despise laid-out walks you are free to explore all the Forestry Commission rides, but where the Commission only leases the land you are meant to stick to public rights of way. Be prepared for monotony, but that sort of monotony *may* be what you want! There is a long-distance walk of 23 miles marked with red posts from West Stow to High Ash through varied country and including Grimes Graves and the arboretum at Lynford (see below). No guide is published for this walk apart from the somewhat simplistic Guide Map for the forest.

Harling Drove was originally 14 miles of Stone Age track, later a drove road for cattle, and part is now a sandy public road through the woods from (west) 1 mile north of Brandon to (east) near Longmere. The Pilgrims' Walk, via St Helen's Well, roughly follows the Little Ouse.

Emily's Wood *795 895*, ♀, *easy paths, FC*
This is a square mile of native hardwoods acquired as part of a lot by the Forestry Commission. The dominant pedunculate oak flourishes here with every characteristic burr and epicormic shoot, and a wealth of very healthy-looking galls on bud and leaf.

There is a group of large beeches at the west side of the wood and the main path is marked by lines of young beech. Prolific ash shoots in less than their usually demanded light also suggest the Forestry Commission's hand improving on nature; but we should not complain. Healthy wych elms were still found in 1982, and you can see some fascinating fungi of dead ash and oak.

The wood is indicated by a picnic site 2 miles out of Brandon on the A1065 to Swaffham. The roadside is lined with Norway

The names refer to single trees or small groups. Old Pines (Scots pine) etc are indicated by patches of shade. Not all the specimens named may have survived and there may be specimens not named but the relation of one group to another is roughly as indicated here.

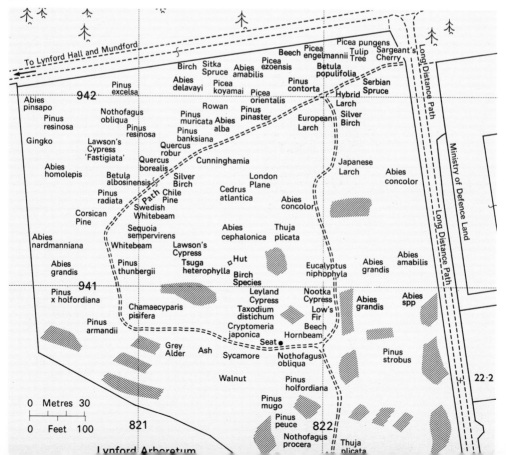

Lynford Arboretum

Spruces and cypresses in Lynford Arboretum

maples – and much evidence of temporary settlement by *Homo sapiens*. But don't let this put you off; Emily's Wood is lovely, and you may have it all to yourself on a fine afternoon in spring or autumn.

Lynford Arboretum *822 942*, ♀ ♠, *FC*

The arboretum is an example of a good small conifer collection. There are some hardwoods, none particularly rare, the main value of Lynford being the comparatively young specimen conifers – as against the decayed and overgrown atmosphere of many Victorian plantations.

You do not have to walk more than about 200 paces to find a particular group. Many large and shapely Scots pines are the original and oldest trees planted here. There are picnic benches in the open land towards the lake.

The forest continues north beyond Ickburgh (High Ash), where there are camping sites, and there is a large patch south-west of Swaffham; picnic site on the A1122 with attached walks. Outlying plantations to the east have picnic sites, with walks, on the A1075 (Hockham Forest) and off the A1066 (Bridgham Lane).

West Stow *815 705*, ♠ *(♀)*, *long and short walks*, *FC* and **Icknield Way**

The Forest Office for the southern part of Thetford Forest is at the north of this pretty village, beyond the secluded detached residences of Bury St Edmunds' commuters. The long-distance walk begins here and penetrates the **King's Forest**, as does Icknield Way from Lackford Bridge. Here a wide ride, the Way is leafy at first, then in solid Corsican pine, but the ride is bordered by nurse trees of birch and beech and some old sweet chestnut. Clumps of broom and Coca Cola cans break the monotony, jet planes break the silence.

There is easy parking at Rampart Field, *788 715*, on the A1101 (Suffolk County Council) for the Icknield Way, or a little further along the West Stow road, *802 713*, where an Anglo-Saxon village is being reconstructed.

Returning to West Stow itself there is a shortish (two hours?) trail with yellow posts which proceeds prettily through plots of various ages of pine after a dramatic start in the deep twilight of a stand of Douglas fir.

Mellfield Wood *925 605*, has a footpath

right of way through the middle running east to west, which continues through **Free Wood** to Bradfield St George. However, new houses at Bradfield St George have made the footpath awkward to locate. I parked on the Beyton to Felsham road. The footpath notice had been removed with the hedge, I was told, but the entrance to the wood can be seen at a slight angle in its outline. The farmer was removing more hedge (leaving a finely shaped oak by the ditch) and I am not sure that any crossing will

be available – be prepared to jump. Alternative routes will be clear from the map, and you can plan a round walk. The north end of Mellfield Wood is coppice of long standing, hazel and elm, and some cutting is being done. An old stone road, half buried, crosses here, and the ground flora could be interesting in the next few years. All sorts of management seem to have been tried in the wood – some conifers – and there is a fine stand of hybrid poplars near Free Wood Farm, which itself has the air of belonging to another century, not because of any architectural feature but just by its ambience. Please do not try to invade by car.

Bradfield Woods *935 581*, ♀, *160 acres, NNR*

Felshamhall Wood, which is on the road from Bradfield St George to Gedding, is of great interest. With part of the adjoining **Monkspark Wood** it is scheduled in the highest category of National Nature Reserves. Oliver Rackham, in his *Ancient Woodland*, 1980, describes these woods as a microcosm of the ancient woods of England. Coppicing here is recorded as 'before 1252' and there is an unbroken record of management up to the present. Monkspark Wood was not coppiced: it was a deer park.

The reserve is a working wood yielding most woodland products and retaining its 'social links'. Particular sizes of underwood are used by a factory that makes rakes, scythe-sticks and articles of turnery. The woods yield poles and stakes and thatching wood of various kinds, and supply the neighbourhood with fuel. Even the twigs are not wasted, for the ashes of bonfires are collected and sold to potters for use in glazes.

Plant communities are complex and they interpenetrate over very varied soils: acidity varies from pH 3.1 to 7.4 (from highly acid to calcareous), almost the maximum possible in Britain. A calcareous patch is on the Gedding side behind the cottage, and the most acid areas are in the centre and beyond the Fish (shaped) Pond in Monkspark Wood near its new boundary at the south-west.

Access is restricted: you need a permit from the NCC in Huntingdon (0480 56191).

Wicken Fen *562 705*, ♀☘, *700 acres, usually wet in places, NT*

The National Trust's oldest property, dating from 1899, this is a remnant of the now dry Great Fen of East Anglia. Wicken remains as an oasis of wetland where once all was wet, except for a few 'islands' – so called traditionally. Water is pumped up from the surrounding land into the fen: the Wicken windmill, built to drain the land, now works to keep it wet, aided at times by a diesel pump.

The fen is an example of undrained fenland – calcareous peat over clay – virtually unparalleled in all of Europe. With all its individual plant life and history, the fen is the habitat of, it is claimed, 300 flowering plants, 5000 insect species including 700 moths and butterflies (the British subspecies of swallowtail butterfly has been reintroduced here), 200 spiders, six known nowhere else, and many birds including the bittern, shoveler, smew and goosander. In the woodland are species of woodpecker, and in the fen redpoll, reed-warbler, sedge-warbler and many other small birds.

Some 'droves' (wide pathways) are very ancient, maybe even Roman. The whole Fenland was farmed by the Romans until the final rise in sea-level, about the fourth century, made habitation difficult.

Birches, grey poplars, alders and, probably, elms are not native vegetation but date from planting at the turn of the century by the then private owners. Guelder rose, a native shrub, grows by the flooded, lily-filled Brickpits. Its bark was formerly used to relieve the cramps suffered by workers in the wetlands.

Wayland Wood *925 995*, ♀, *permit required, CNT*

This is reputedly the 'Babes in the Wood' woodland, but it belongs to the Norwich Naturalists' Trust. (Apply to 72 The Close, Norwich, for a permit.) It is a secretive place, not to be disturbed by noisy parties, dogs, or, particularly, babes. In a coppice clearing, ash trunks gleam around large bushes of lesser burdock almost of tree proportions. It is an ash/oak wood mainly, with hazel, and, if you can find it, bird cherry.

East Suffolk and part of Norfolk

Holly stool of landscape proportions in Butley Thicks

Blo Norton Wood *027 788*, ♀, *CNT*

An oakwood with sweet chestnut, birch and
some conifers, and a lot of stinkhorns in
autumn, it provides 10 minutes' easy walking
on the bridleway at the western end; elsewhere
adopt a crouching pose. There is woodland
also at Redgrave nearby and at Bruisyard
(coniferized) and Heveningham. The last is the
interesting old park, with ancient thorns and
others, of a great house.

Dunwich Forest, *462 713*, is a large, easy-

going pine plantation, with Walberswick
Marshes and nature reserve to the east and
north. This is a holiday coast: take things as
you find them. A Forestry Commission picnic
place is $\frac{3}{4}$ mile from Dunwich village. There
are many sandy footpaths and nature trails:
Dunwich Common on the Sandlings is
heathland, but there is woodland attached to
the RSPB reserves of Minsmere and North
Warren – north of Aldeburgh.

Rendlesham Forest ♣, *easy walks, FC*

This is a vast forest, inland from Aldeburgh
and Orford. Picnic places, particularly at
Sandgalls, *380 560* (on the Iken road from
Tunstall), are by no means all 'honeypots' to
keep the swarms of ignorant townspeople out
of trouble. The car park at Butley Corner, *354
502*, Orford road from Woodbridge, offers,
wisely without any mention, an anchorage for
those who would embark on the best and the
worst woodland walk in Britain, in Butley

Thicks. Best because the oak and holly wood
have remained strangely undisturbed for
centuries; worst because walking in anything
like an erect posture is impossible. It is private,
but well known to naturalists. A little-used
bridleway goes by the west side of the Thicks
and into the park.

Staverton Park and **Butley Thicks**
formed a deer forest in the thirteenth century

197

and they have reputedly not been touched since. Many deer parks were grazed to semi-deserts, so something must have gone wrong – or right. Some people believe these woods to be a fragment of original English forest. This cannot be so, since most of the trees in the Thicks have been coppiced at some time, and any sort of clearing alters the woodland ecology. The enormous size of some holly stools – 4 or 5 feet across – certainly suggests ages of 300 years or more, and this is, of course, almost unknown for a holly. All the oaks are extremely picturesque and there are ancient coppiced rowans and ashes as well.

Tunstall Common, *378 548*, is a fine open place, remarkably free of rubbish and notices about rubbish. The colours are of heather, sand, bracken-gold or green, and gorse; and beyond, the fine orange-pink and blue of Scots pines, not too geometrically laid out, but with trunks as straight as rulers. There is another open heath at Blaxhall, to the north. You can walk anywhere. As one learns to expect in the 'quiet' places of eastern England, there are frequent roars and whistles from the latest and most lethal jet planes.

32	45	46
30	**39**	40
28	33	34

CENTRAL ENGLAND
Stafford and Shrewsbury
Landranger sheets 126, 127

Attingham Park, Shrewsbury *542 093, ♀, 3826 acres, 1m walk, NT*

The map reference is for the main gate on the A5(T) near the bridge at Atcham. The house is open in summer months, but the park has the virtue of being always open. It was designed by Repton, but this need not inhibit one's appreciation of its wide spaces and well-marked groups of trees.

The classical façade of pale grey stone is beautifully balanced by the group of oaks and chestnuts at its side. The effect transcends mere classicism and looks other-worldly and poetical on a sunny, misty morning; and, I dare say, in most other lights. Cedars behind the building are silhouetted against the unexpected hump of The Wrekin to the east – and one notices that young cedars are well grown, ready to replace the old. Dramatic shadows cloak the rear entrance under its cupola – there is a miniature forest of butcher's broom under the beeches – and the driveway seems to enter an entirely different world from ours. It is a very convincing sort of stage set, and makes one shiver for an instant in the breath of a distant era. What more can one ask of a National Trust property?

There is a walk of 1 mile signposted behind the stable block, which leads into the trees.

The Wrekin *634 093, ♀ ♣, 1½ hours easy walking but steep, MoD*

Only the most conspicuous of the series of outcrops of ancient limestone which distinguishes this part of the country, The Wrekin, 1300 feet high, accommodates a sessile oak coppice, a beechwood, and a rifle range on its north-west side, above a birchwood containing more than its fair share of rubbish. The south side is largely covered by larchwood.

Turning off the M54 at junction 7 towards The Wrekin, it is best then to turn right – signposted Uppington – where appears at once a rough parking place under the birches. Climbing straight up through the coppice brings you to an easy, broad path, lined with beech, leading to the summit and a fine view.

Cannock Chase (west) *982 175 (Chase Road Corner car park), ♀ ♣, 2700 acres CP, 6000 acres FC*

Entering the area from Cannock you may be reassured by a series of very clear signs to a 'Visitor Centre'. Take no notice, they simply lead you to Rugeley through miles of forestry. You will not then be surprised to be informed, in Forestry Commission pokerwork, that the conifers yield 33 tons a day.

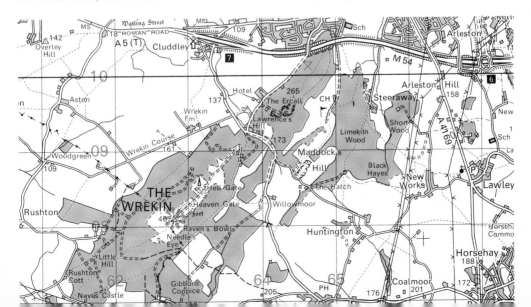

Cedars in Attingham Park, The Wrekin beyond

To the north of Pye Green (the southern limit of the Chase, marked by a Post Office tower) are car parks at Brindley Bottom, *993 153*, Flints Field, *995 156*, and Whitehouse, *995 162*. These are all in the Corsican pine belt, but there are open spaces: there is nothing much to choose between the car parks.

Going north from Pye Green but forking left, past the Post Office tower, takes you towards the Country Park area of much more open birch heath broken by stands of pine. Quite without identification except for a 15 mph limit, the Chase Road turns off right at *966 184*, leading to several car parks and a

Cannock Chase. Birches near Chase Road

viewpoint before descending to Brocton at the
north of the Chase. A through footpath, the
Staffordshire Way, runs south to north parallel
to, and east of, the Chase Road. The path
follows the Sherbrook Valley and leads on to
Shugborough Park (National Trust, 900 acres
with neo-Georgian monuments), or, if you
turn off left or north-west, spills out into the
uneven acres of Milford Common – an
attractive destination.

Scattered woods, totalling a considerable
acreage, between Market Drayton and Stoke-
on-Trent are all in Forestry Commission
hands. There is a picnic place at Harley
Thorns, in **Swynnerton Old Park**, *838 396*.
Downs Banks, near Barlaston, is a moorland
National Trust site of 166 acres: *902 370*. **Hem
Heath Wood**, Trentham, *885 410*, is a
woodland nature reserve of 20 acres leased
from the National Coal Board. Many woods
also are in the hands of the Staffordshire NCT.

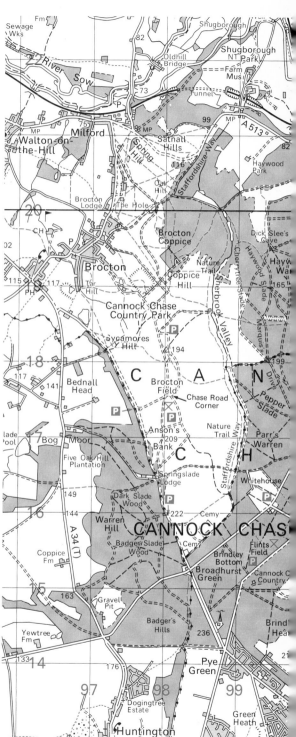

45	46	47
39	**40**	41
33	34	35

CENTRAL ENGLAND
Trent and Churnet
Landranger sheets 128, 129

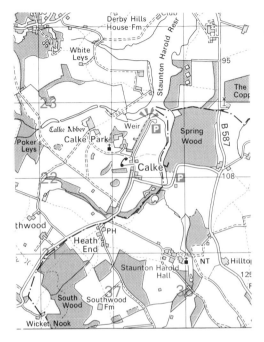

Calke and **Staunton Harold Reservoir**
379 220, ♀ ♣, parking place
The reservoir is a place for views, and there is a viewpoint car park, *376 227*, beyond the village of Calke, where you can succumb to the effects, whatever they are, of gazing at a sheet of water. A very nice car park at the map reference is on a wooded hillside shaded by vivid yellow hybrid poplars. The ridge above leads by a semi-official footpath to Staunton Harold Hall, National Trust, with a nice mixture of trees and grass above the shapely valley. To the east, Breedon on the Hill continues the theme of Charnwood Forest, here charmingly formalized by a church set on a scrub-patterned hill, great cooling towers beyond.

Elvaston Castle *412 332, ♀ ♣, 200 acres, CP*
Elvaston was one of the first Country Parks. The castle is just a big house, with an ancient corner. The gardens and grounds are in the grand manner with old, well-kept topiary, very geometrical. Look west of the chapel for a group of Irish yews, birches, pencil cedars and other larger conifers: all beautifully organized and good of their kind. There is a short walk laid out in the trees flanking the Grand Avenue – which looks south, the lawn delicately ramped to hide the road. The park is always open and can be entered on foot at Elvaston, Borrowash or the Golden Gates on the A6.

Ulverscroft, Copt Oak *488 125, ♀, 120 acres, 1½ hour walk, NR*
Described as the richest valley in Charnwood Forest, with woodland the breeding site of the wood warbler, this is a varied, mostly scrubland nature reserve which well deserves the name. The entrance is in the wood about a mile down Whitcroft's Lane, off the B591 ¼ mile south of Copt Oak. Apart from the scrub, which is heavy with bracken but contains quite mature birch and rowan (including the oldest rowan I have seen), there are small beech plantations enclosed by walls

Woodland walk in Ulverscroft Nature Reserve. This is fine, mature, secondary woodland.

of the angular, hard-looking pre-Cambrian stone: walls and beeches alike are mostly an acrid green. Pedunculate oaks, planted in the woods, have spread to the scrub. There are patches of heather, gorse and bramble full of flies, wasps and butterflies. A pond, almost unbelievably rich in insect life, smells awful.

Cannock Chase (east) *039 153 (viewpoint, car park and picnic place)*, ♀ ♣, *CC, FC*

The large area of Cannock Chase, one of the largest accessible tracts of wooded country in England, is on this side Foresty Commission managed, but the viewpoint given is cared for

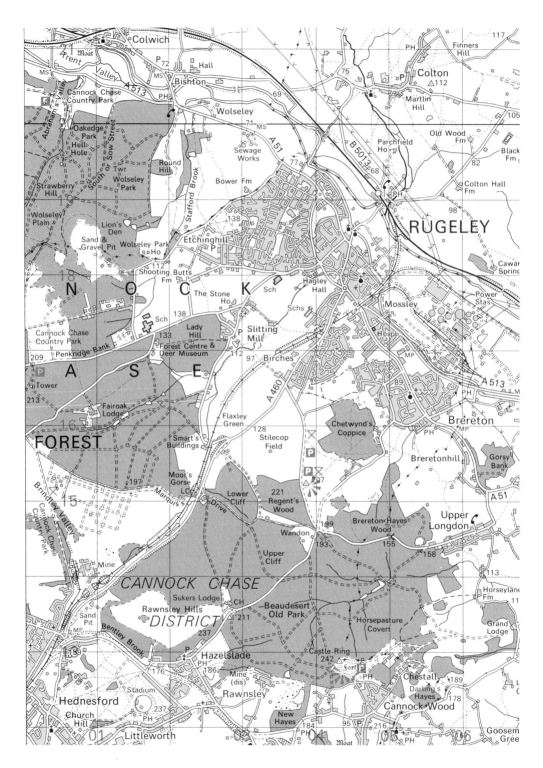

From the viewpoint at *039 153*, Cannock Chase (east)

by Staffordshire County Council. It is an old gravel-pit hill looking over forestry and industry and in any but the dullest light is most appealing. Take the Hazelslade road from the A51 in Brereton, and turn sharp right as soon as you reach the trees.

The Forestry Commission's Forest Centre, *018 171*, is educational in purpose and displays statistics amongst the pines. There are trails. For older woodland go south of our viewpoint above. Woods are open, but you need a map.

A Forestry Commission car park called Penkridge offers a 3-mile walk with red markers; as this is close to yet another of those Army firing ranges, follow the markers.

Churnet Valley
In the north-west of the section the River Dove is the boundary of Staffordshire. The River Churnet joins the Dove below Alton Towers, and above this landmark is heavily wooded, especially near Oakamoor, the Forestry Commission being mostly in charge. A National Trust woodland, **Hawksmoor**

Wood, *033 440*, with a separate patch to the north-west by Wood House Farm, occupies the north-east-facing valley side, opposite a conspicuous, loudly humming factory. The wood is dull, but of course is a valuable bird sanctuary, if birds don't mind humming noises. Old trees, oaks, beeches, rowans, are at the margins. The obvious entry point, a triangle of old quarry land, is neglected and rubbishy.

This is a large wood, 307 acres, at present of more importance as a natural refuge than as a place to walk.

The RSPB has a large reserve in the **Coombes Valley**, upstream: *009 534* – old estate woodland with thick rhododendron in places, as well as pasture and heathland. The reserve is not open on Mondays, Wednesdays and Fridays (and no weekdays in autumn), and is closed in January, February and March. There is an entrance fee and you should report to the Information Centre.

Charnwood Forest

Leicestershire has been short of woodlands since before Domesday and there has been some doubt as to how the people obtained any wood at all: there must have been a fairly extensive Leicester forest. Perhaps part of Rutland Forest also supplied the very necessary wood. The Leicester Forest, anyway, was sold by Charles I for £7000. North-west towards Ashby-de-la-Zouch, a hilly area with outcrops, or islands, of ancient sandstone, and some of the most ancient and hardest rocks and slates, became known as Charnwood Forest. It was the waste of manors of Whitwick, Groby, Shepshed and Barrow, and by the end of the eighteenth century it had become little more than heath and bracken; extensively quarried, it was a forest of stones, not trees. It was enclosed under an Act of Parliament in 1808 by various owners, who planted some trees.

Swithland Wood *537 117*, ♀, *with Bradgate Park 1238 acres, many paths, CP*
Swithland Wood is I believe ancient. The oaks are sessile and some old stubs, the remains of coppice trees, clearly predate the Inclosure period. The land has been much disturbed by quarrying and birch has spread; but, while many of the oaks may have been planted, the whole has grown up into a very fine woodland.

Swithland's slate is well known. Probably the quarrying interest ensured the survival of the coppice. The wood was preserved for the nation in 1931 by the Leicester Rotarians, who perhaps remembered boyhood expeditions and by then owned nice houses in the district: an enlightened gesture all the same.

Bradgate Park, *523 116*, just south of the wood, is easy to find in the middle of Newtown Linford – picturesque oaks in the park, and deer.

The **Outwoods,** *515 159*, are oak and conifer woodlands in a nature reserve of the ridge above the Soar Valley.

The nature reserve of Ulverscroft, 120 acres, is just off the map to the west, at *488 125*. See Section 40. The Leicester and Rutland Trust for Nature Conservation controls at least four important woodlands, including the large (300 acres) Pickworth Great Wood, but you need permits to visit these.

Forestry Commission sites just off the A1 to the east offer riches unexpected on this uneventful stretch of road.

Morkery Wood *955 193*, *(♀)* ♣, *600 acres, 1 short walk and forest rides, FC*
100 miles from London is this great army of conifers, spruce and pine, with a fringe of oak and beech and the inevitable ash, the hedgerow tree of the district. Turn off the A1 for Castle Bytham. The 'farm' marked on the map to the south is in fact an HM prison, and the road through the forest is thus a dead-end and an extension of the parking area. It is enlivened by a mysterious stone carved with a horse and a lot of orchid and yellow vetch. The picnic place offers both shade and (an old quarry) a place in the sun. There is a short track which, the Forestry Commission claims, follows old deer trails.

Clipsham Yew Avenue *980 170*, *a short walk, FC*
A yew avenue is not exactly a woodland walk but this remarkable, large-scale topiary is worth seeing on any account. The yews are 200 years old. The car park, quiet and secluded, has a more rapidly run-up backdrop of Lawson cypress. This is a lovely place. The bit of Kesteven Forest beyond the yew avenue is a young assemblage of smart spruces and vigorous pines, and the rides or firebreaks are dreamy corridors of grasses, marsh orchids and small native trees framing the large skies. There are oaks, ashes, maples and even wild service trees along an informal pathway which leaves the parking place, follows the northern margin and turns left and left again along the rides, returning to the yew avenue about midway down its length.

A mile south-east is **Holywell Wood**, private, and the quietest place in England – even the rabbits go on eating as you approach them. Only tentatively coniferized, this is a wood of oak, ash, hazel, maple, birch, aspen, elder, hawthorn, guelder rose, dog rose and wayfaring tree, roughly in that order. There is a right-of-way through from the farm at *986 156* continuing through the adjoining **Pickworth Great Wood** to the village of Pickworth. The right-of-way gives no right to deviate from it; please do not go this way unless you intend to be perfectly quiet and please do not take a dog.

Clipsham yew

Twyford Woods 946 238, (♀)✚,

700 acres, ½m walk plus miles of concrete runway, FC
Preserving the blunt triangle of the wartime airfield on which it was planted, the wood is largely of youngish, regimented conifers as you might expect, but the walk meanders first through a rich variety of native trees as well as plunging into small darknesses of silver fir and hemlock. Ragged robin, comfrey and guelder rose grow by the spruces. Fallow deer browse in the remains of the RAF's bomb store. On the runways the spruces stretch away in enormous vistas: a good place to jog.

Ragged robin, Twyford Woods

Ropsley Rise Wood 972 347, ♀ ✚,

150 acres, ½m trail, FC
Badgers, foxes and long-eared owls may be seen, says the Forestry Commission. It is a pleasant, open wood flanked by a ditch full of sallows and a variety of rushes, with horsetail and some orchids of the *Dactyloryhiza* genus, common marsh orchid, here pale mauve. The walk progresses through scented red cedars, *Thuja plicata*, to attractive young firs, *Abies grandis*, all planted amongst ash and oak, with native undergrowth.

Belvoir: Terrace Hills Woods 797 321,

♀ (✚), *1½m of the Jubilee Way, easy and dry*
The map reference takes you to a minor road where the Jubilee Way walk crosses and there

is a triangle of grass for parking. The Terrace Hills along the walk have really fine sycamores and horse-chestnuts, and rhododendron as a quite welcome understorey in place of the fearsome nettles which flourish here.

The castle has a nature trail, but you have to pay to get in, and since the place always has junketing of one sort or another going on (jousting for instance), nature seems a secondary consideration.

North of Grantham another great park, **Belton**, *929 395*, on the A607, also has nature trails (lakeside) among any number of other activities: again there is a fairly steep charge to drive in. Typically the trees of the parkland are large and well formed.

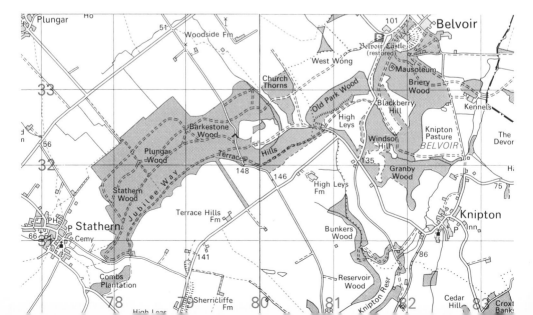

South-West Lincolnshire and the Soke Landranger sheets 131, 142

Southey Wood *109 025, (♀) ♣, 3 way-marked walks, ½–1½m, FC*
The picnic and parking place is pleasant and clean and surrounded by tall Corsican pines and equally tall birches, and oaks. The woodlands are a series of compartments put together like Scrabble cards, mostly newly planted with various conifers.

Helpston *122 056*
This is John Clare's countryside. He was born and died (at seventy-one in 1875) in Helpston, the 'peasant poet' who, apart from a period in a lunatic asylum, lived here. He described the English countryside as no other poet has. His life spanned the decline of the old country of large heaths, grazed over, with picturesque small woods and streams. He ranted at the Inclosures. Now there is little he would recognize: his birthplace whitewashed, the heath devoted to crops, conifers, gravel-digging and rubbish disposal, in that order. Worst of all, his village, the centre of his universe in a network of heathland pathways and rural lanes, is now merely a collection of houses and a church at a crossroads.

There *is* a stone monument in Helpston, apparently designed by the local pastrycook, and it carries the following verse, as if Clare had written his own epitaph:

> The bard his glory ne'er receives,
> Where summer's common flowers are
>   seen.
> But winter finds it when she leaves
> The laurel only green
> And time from that eternal tree
> Shall weave a wreath to honour thee.

White campions, elder and dog rose in the hedges are his best memorial.

A mile down Heath Road is a large grassy parking place which has a few native trees and has been planted with more, including whitebeam, a tree which local authorities always seem to have a lot of. Another mile further south brings you to a common, *123 024*, called, for some reason, **Castor**

Hanglands (Castor is the next village), which has been a National Nature Reserve since 1945. There has been time for a wilderness to develop around the grassland where rare butterflies breed. There are large hawthorns, very twisted, and biggish blackthorns amongst the ash and oak. You are not encouraged to enter. I don't think Clare would have recognized this either. The common he knew would be a fine, open place – though with secret corners.

Bourne Wood *077 201, ♀ ♣, 700 acres, easy rides and paths, FC*
The small-leaved lime was supposed to be here, but I could not find it in this part of the woods. There are, however, fine young Huntingdon elms near the parking place (which is large and open) and other elms within. Good-quality ash and larch are being taken out, Corsican pine put in, but there are plenty of native trees left and some *Populus × euramericana*. This is a nice, workmanlike wood, noisy with saws and smelling of larch logs; but I could not explore miles of woodland.

Callan's Lane Wood, Kirkby Underwood *060 270, ♀ ♣, 300 acres, 3 forest walks, FC*
There is a picnic place but cars have to stay outside. The wood is a spruce and Douglas fir

Dog rose in Bourne Wood

plantation with some Lawson cypress, western hemlock and noble fir amongst native trees. The full-length walk is a longish trail, but you are rewarded with small-leaved lime, aspen, and a bit of beechwood with, in June, three sorts of orchid. The lime is an old coppice and two large stools had been cut recently. The

surrounding fields appear now and then, the corn like a sea beating against the walls of the wood. Ash is dominant if you ignore conifers.

Woods are rare about Sleaford and apparently unknown around Boston. Trees are not absent however, and indeed are often impressive, though the map suggests a desert.

Thetford Forest (Section 37) extends to a large but comparatively young series of plantations west and south-west of Swaffham and there is a Forestry Commission picnic site on the A1122 – **Swaffham Heath**, *775 098*. This is the name only of what was once a very large heathland. A network of small sandy roads at the south-west side provides unofficial access to the pinewoods, which are especially attractive where there is a no-man's land of heath and grass between fields and forest. Wind-blown, distorted Scots pines along the roads remind us of the pre-afforestation scenery.

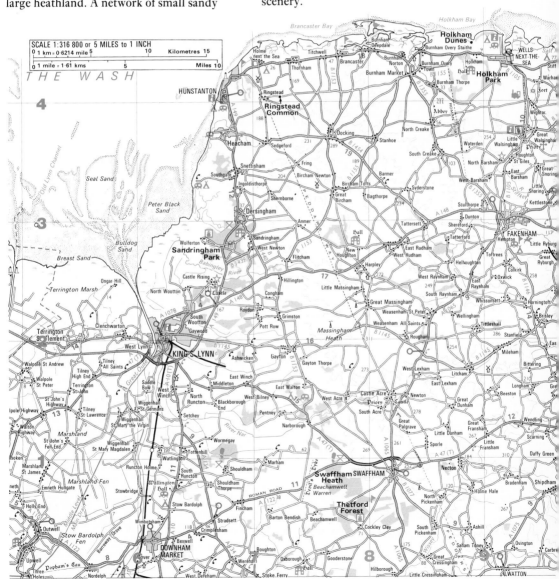

Sandringham, and a nearly cloudless afternoon

Sandringham Park *695 286*. Visited by millions and not short on tourist amenities, Sandringham is still effectively a nature reserve. A little ungratefully, I must report that the many very nice car parks seem to be taking over the space. For a really easy short walk, the Scottish Belt, planted, perhaps as a bit of Balmoral, can be recommended. Dogs, naturally, are not discouraged, and children can have a whale of a time in the bracken or take the nature trail seriously.

Ringstead Common *727 405*, ♀ ♣
Inland from Hunstanton is the superbly brown and grey-patterned village of Ringstead. Take the narrow road to Burnham Market and stop at the first cross track for the Ringstead Charity Lands, where walkers are welcomed by a discreet notice. A mile of narrow but rather amazing woodland on the ridge to the north is planted like a wild arboretum, and crossed and recrossed by mown green paths.

Holkam is beyond the Burnhams near Wells-next-the-Sea; it may attract you into its Park, *892 435*, on weekdays or, as it is closed at the

weekends, you may choose to walk along the path of a Roman road for 2 miles beside a monumental brick-and-flint wall enclosing the estate. Start from the Burnham Thorpe to Wighton road at *862 400*. The woodland is of mature beech bordered by *ilex*; invaded by sycamore where not so mature. On reaching the coast road you can turn right and at the police notice saying 'No Parking' continue to the sea coast. Here the sand dunes are wooded with Corsican pine for 2 miles to the silted entrance of Wells Harbour. This is a most untypical British wood, but refreshing.

No less than 9763 acres of, mostly, mud on the coast are a National Nature Reserve.

North-East Norfolk

Sheringham – West Runton – Cromer.
The steep Norfolk Heights above Cromer are
well wooded and **Felbrigg Great Wood**, *204
403*, is an old oakwood. West Runton has a 70-
acre section under National Trust care.
Roman Camp, *186 413*, here is the name of
the highest point in Norfolk, which of course is
not saying much (329 feet). There is a pleasant,
informal parking place near a caravan site
(which is not intrusive and has a useful café),
at **Beacon Hill**, *185 415*. The woods are
superficially pretty but a little dusty and

frayed, being too much frequented. Walking is
directionless because of the many paths, but
the very steep hillside guides our steps.

Holt Country Park *083 370*, ♀ ♠ , *various
routes mapped on site, CP*

Holt is inland: a boom town but nice. Just
outside the town on the Norwich road, the
B1149, the Country Park is signposted from
the new bypass. This is an old estate with
curious sculptures; although there is much
coniferous woodland there remain many gaps
for a lush native vegetation to creep in. It is
especially attractive towards the Hempstead
road. Beyond this road there is a belt of mature

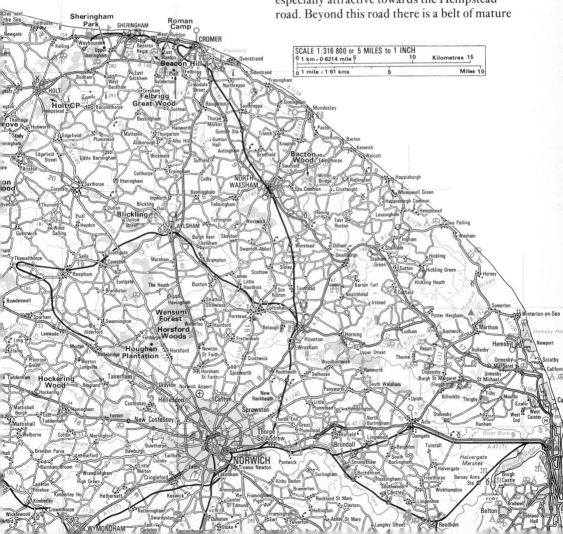

pine some 2 miles long with softly overgrown rides; a lonely place.

Swanton Novers, further inland, is an ordinary small village under a great mass of tall trees. Swanton Great Wood, *020 315*, is a nature reserve where small-leaved lime is abundant, and it is remarkable for many ancient coppice stools, one measuring 27 feet across. There are 50 acres of coppiced oak, and patches where sessile oak and lime share the

The path by Bullfer Grove

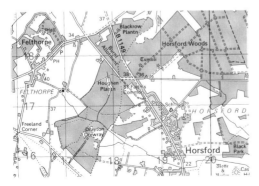

ground, along with native bird cherry, *Prunus padus*, unusually far south.

Bullfer Grove *017 359*, ♀ ♦ , *8 acres, NT* North of Gunthorpe off the A148, this small wood makes a very short walk. The wood surrounds an old quarry. Its chief attraction appears to be its edges, particularly along the lovely deep, oak-lined lane.

Blickling Hall, *178 286*, one of the very finest National Trust properties, is in a well-wooded valley and the parkland is always open.

North of Norwich are the scattered pieces of what the Forestry Commission calls **Wensum Forest**; perhaps the pieces will one day join together. Nearest the sea is **Bacton Wood,** *317 312*, locally known as Witton Wood; once it was Witton Heath, with ancient oaks. Here are now no less than thirty different forestry trees. The Forestry Commission has exploited a varied sandy soil to combine timber growing with deliberately attractive planting.

A leaflet guide is available from the Forestry Commission at Santon Downham.

About the large patches of green on the map approximately 5 miles north of Norwich there is less to be said. As far as I can see the best walks are in the deciduous **Houghen Plantation,** *187 172*, and through **Horsford Woods** – conifers in straight lines, but you *can* step out. Private property development has spoiled the old unities of land and villages and laced the woodlands with eyesores and fences.

South of Norwich, and not easy to find, at *172 004* is the **Hethel Thorn**, or Witch of Hethel, a nature reserve consisting of one tree. It may have been planted in the reign of King John, but it is more likely that it just grew there. There is no record of anyone planting any tree at that period of history (AD 1200). Before it was made into a nature reserve someone unkindly cut it down, so it is only the witch's sucker shoots that you see now.

At the western edge of the Wensum Forest complex, near East Dereham on the A47(T) is Hockering. Turn off north, 1 mile, for **Hockering Wood,** *072 150*, 200 acres, an ancient stronghold of the small-leaved lime.

North Cheshire and the Wirral Landranger sheets 108, 109, 117, 118

Cheshire has three per cent of its land under woodland, only half the national average, and the woods are hard to see as you drive over the wide, softly undulating plain which is filled with heavy, rather small trees – oaks and sycamores – and smells of cow dung and nettles. Clay overlies a sheet of rust-coloured limestone through which sandstone outcrops dramatically, particularly at the Delamere Forest, or what remains of it.

Delamere Forest *556 704 (Delamere Railway Station)*, *(♀)* ♠, *2m by 1m. Forest walks and trail, FC*

There are 2000 acres of trees here, half of all Cheshire's Scots pines (800 acres) and nearly all her Corsican pines (600 acres). That leaves 600 acres to be made up mainly of larch, spruce, oak and birch. On the ground, the pines seem very much to dominate, with narrow strips of pretty oak-birch woodland along the two roads which cross the forest (meeting at Hatchmere). The Sandstone Trail, 14 miles long, passes through the forest. The pinewoods are full of the sour smells of fox and bracken and the monotony is broken only by an occasional bog full of rushes, or an elder tree seeming exotically perfumed here, or a great clearing splendidly sprouting millions of foxgloves. But the path lives up to its name of Sandstone, and you could pad along in silence

for two hours through the trees.

There are four Forestry Commission walks, some linking up with the trail, and three picnic areas, two with WCs (actually Portaloos). The road running west from Hatchmere (where water-lilies spread and caravans cluster) is the prettier, but has parking bays all the way along, ready, one feels, for the thoughtless crowds on bank holidays. Rather wider margins of hardwoods would have seemed a bit less cynically production-minded. There is a pleasant grassy picnic place just beyond the forest, at Woodside, *523 707*: clean grass with willows augmented by planting.

Little Budworth Common *583 663*, ♀, *200 acres, CP*

This is a large birch common of loose sand covered by dull ling – and a few spots of purple heather. Oak, however, seems to be spreading.

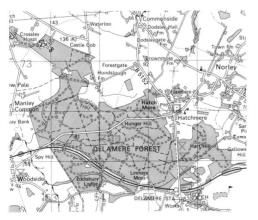

Seedling oak in the heather, Little Budworth

Parking places are unpretentious. Motor racing occurs at Oulton Park, adjacent. The **Marbury Country Park**, *649 763*, 190 acres, and more secluded, would be a better choice for a day out.

One of the first Country Parks was that of the Wirral. It is linear, following an old railway from Hooton to West Kirby, through thick and thin, suburb, farm and town, emerging onto the sea-wall at *273 790*, north of Neston, to confront an amazing 'sea' of grass and rushes. This trail is only occasionally wooded.

Thurstaston Common and Irby Common *244 846*, ♀ ♣ *(Scots pines), about 200 acres, many paths, NT*

The Wirral proves unexpectedly bony here, with exquisite stratification of the sandstone revealed where the A540 cuts through the hill near the car park. Thurstaston Common is mainly heather, but has a fringe of beautiful birch-pine woodland, the pines to the east widely spaced, tall and uncluttered. A wooded pathway leads from the south-east corner (at the end of Sandy Lane – there is space to park) up to the much smaller Irby Common, a birchwood. Here gorse is dying and oak coming up with lovely hair grass.

Peckforton *540 575 (access point)*, ♀, *steepish fp, pf*

South of Beeston Castle, which is on another of those sandstone knobs, is a 3-mile escarpment covered thickly with oakwoods. These are private, but the Sandstone Way runs along the west side, and there is a feeder path across the hill, through the oaks. On the minor road from Beeston to Peckforton look for the massive Victorian Baronial lodge gates; at the left, where you can scarcely see it if you are not looking for it, is a footpath sign.

Ness Gardens *305 756*, ♀ ♣, *¾m round, Liverpool University*

Small but stunningly well looked after, the gardens have benefited from well-established patches of shelter-belt woodland to the south-west and the north-east, and there are many young and mature trees of interest as well.

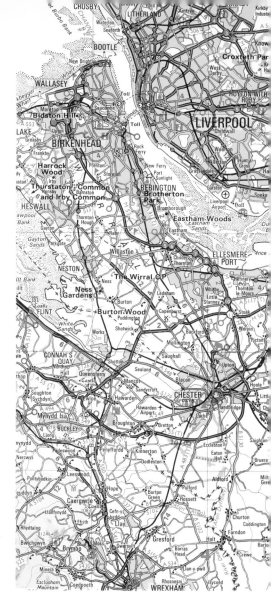

There are well-contrasted groups of Lawson cypress cultivars, a pinewood 200 yards long, good blue spruce, Delavaye's fir, Italian alder, a fine heather garden, a 'spinney' of spaced-out beeches, a magnificent rock garden with a rich pattern of small and dwarf conifers contrasted with a tall yew hedge. The wide Dee Estuary is glimpsed beyond. There are a herb garden with Braille labels, a reading room and a Visitors' Centre.

At **Burton**, a handsome village 1 mile to the south, is a small (20-acre) wood, of old oak augmented with tall pines, belonging to the

National Trust. There *is* space to park at the north-east side of the wood, *315 747*, but the road should not be attempted with an ordinary car (though it may now be repaired).

On the Mersey side of the Wirral, **Eastham Woods**, *363 820*, is a 27-acre Country Park. Between Eastham village and Bebington is the Dibbin Brook, with rather occluded ancient woodland in a local nature reserve, **Brotherton Park**. The National Trust has a 10-acre piece, **Harrock Wood**, *263 846*. Across the water, only 3½ miles from the Liver Building, is Liverpool's **Croxteth Park**, now

Country Park, 500 acres, *399 943*: hall, old orchard and walled garden, parkland and woodland, even forestry.

Styal *835 830 Northern Woods and Mill, 840 821 Southern Woods,* ♀ ♠, *252 acres, riverside walks, NT, CP*
Only 8 miles from Piccadilly, Manchester, as the magpie flies (they are now more common and visible than crows) are impressive tall beeches, larches, and one *Sequoiadendron* left over from a group which must have got too tall for comfort. These are in the Northern

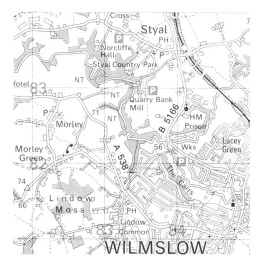

The path to Tegg's Nose summit, lined with heather

Wood: picturesque, but eroded by too many feet – and the River Bollin smells. Worse, the noise of jet take-off from Manchester Airport is quite killing.

Further upstream the Southern Woods are quieter, occasionally weird, still smelly, and full of policeman's helmet (Himalayan balsam). Beech and pine level out to willow and, of all things, hornbeam, towards the meadows and Wilmslow. I like to think the hornbeams – one is a reasonably old coppice tree – were planted to provide teeth for the cogs of the mill around which this plantation is orientated. The mill, 1784, and the village which grew around it under the enterprise and care of one mill owner are all a National Trust property of 252 acres.

Alderley Edge *860 773,* ♀ ♣ *(Scots pines), 200 acres, many paths, wheelchair route, NT*
Poor old Alderley Edge, famous as a beauty-spot to many Mancunians long before 1947 when it came to the National Trust: dug into by miners from the Stone Age to the nineteenth century, then privately owned and loved, planted with pines and beeches (over natural birch and oak); and now with erosion and litter problems. The view through a delicate lattice of beech boughs to a wide countryside heavy with trees, cows and nice detached houses, is still attractive: Black Hill and Shining Tor to the east. There is a large

parking place near The Wizard (pub, now a restaurant, National Trust). A wheelchair path circumnavigates the woodlands, which can still be enchanting, like a lovely melody on a scratchy old record. So many people have

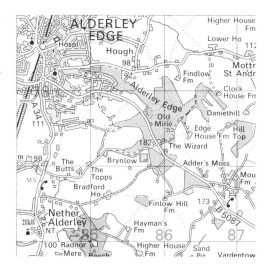

w, with a view to the Macclesfied Forest (rain)

loved this place: one American even donated a brass plate to mark the site of a beacon fire. A footpath from the Alderley road (at the west end) is signposted in native cast iron: 'To the Edge'.

Macclesfield Forest *975 722 (village),* ♀, *100 acres, roads through, W A*
The lovely smooth green mantle on the hills south-east of Macclesfield is perhaps best viewed with its reflection in the still waters of Ridgegate Reservoir above Langley, or from **Tegg's Nose Country Park**, *950 723*.

Tegg's Nose summit is on the Gritstone Trail long-distance path. The Forest Chapel is the next stop. The old hilltop quarry is not the worst place to spend a wet Monday morning, and should be exciting on a fine day, with its bird's-eye view of the surrounding hill pastures, reservoir, roads, the great forest and the skyline of tors. The quarry workings are covered attractively by heather and sallows, and are scattered with preserved relics of the stone-workers. Gritstone, we are told, is easy to work when first quarried. Glass-covered panels explain the geology and its exploitation, in a gritstone shelter, with gritstone blocks cemented to the ground outside. It looks fairly hard stuff – and touchingly familiar to one whose childhood was 4 feet closer to similar drains, kerbs and setts. These silent blocks of stone and half-dismembered machines in the rain are a strange memorial perhaps to the generation of craftsmanship and sweat; but better than an empty hole in the hill, however prettily overgrown. Quarrying ceased in 1955.

Lyme Park (*965 844* for the Country Park, or walk in at any of several points around the 1300 acres) is one of the greatest houses – Palladian façade but looking rather as if transported from central Liverpool. The park is high, up to 1220 feet, and 9 miles round.

And so to the clouds. Congleton has a Cloud, *903 636*, National Trust, and there are others.

49	50	51
45	**46**	47
39	40	41

CENTRAL ENGLAND
The Peak District
Landranger sheets 110, 119

The Peak District is an upland, not a woodland area, and only dimly remembers being a forest. The woods are in the deeply cut valleys or on moorland reclaimed for forestry. The farmland of the southern or 'White' Peak is too rich to be wasted on mere trees, but much remains green, with white drystone walls protecting the rich wayside flora of the Mountain Limestone. The National Park is ringed by great conurbations: beauty-spots are under pressure.

The Roaches *005 621, ♠ ♣, 2m, fps*
Hen Cloud, with gritstone feathers raised to the winds, the Roaches, and the Five Clouds below them – five chicks really – are strangely shaped and weathered outcrops overlooking the Cheshire Plain. You can walk over the top of the Roaches and then back through mostly dying larchwoods below, keeping an eye out for wallabies, resident since evacuated in the Second World War to a nearby zoo. Dead larches are extravagantly beautiful, grey skeletons.

Goyt Woodlands *013 757, ♀ ♠,*
1½m trail, 3m long wooded valley, FC
These woods on the west side of the Fernilee and Errwood Reservoirs are reached by turning off the A5002 north of Buxton at the signpost to Goyt Valley. The narrow road, which turns south along the reservoir and then climbs out along the moors to the Cat and Fiddle Pass (A54) is now one-way and is closed to traffic on Sundays and bank holidays. The map reference is for the disabled car park by the water. There are several parking places in the woodland along the road. If you want to park in shade you have to take your choice before reaching the attractive but exposed quarry car park, *012 732,* at the upper end.

Large, impressive larches, Scottish-looking pines and big beeches are mingled with the native oaks, rowans and birches above the stony River Goyt: smooth moorlands beyond are planted with the Commission's pines, at well above what appears to be the natural tree-line. A wide, easy path follows the stream as the trees become fewer: but at a final picnic place at Derbyshire Bridge, *018 716,* well onto the moors, a large wych elm, perfectly healthy, shows just what trees can do. The Goyt Valley, with its reservoirs, is sometimes gloomy, always impressive with beautiful woodlands.

Dove Dale *north from 147 509, ♀ , 854 acres, NT ; several adjoining properties, woods and valleys, easy riverside walk, 2–8m (very steep valley sides), nature trail from Ilam CP*
The valley is heavily wooded but far too

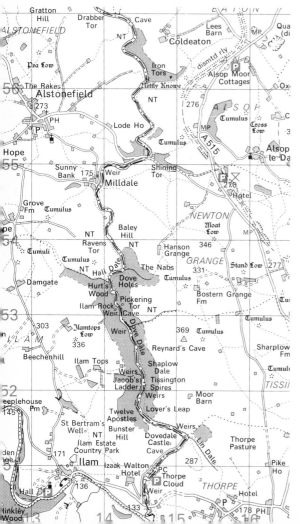

famous: claustrophobic, hot and busy in summer, at least as far up as Milldale. The Country Park at Ilam is gracious but I thought the Manifold looked dirty and the Dove at Milldale not much better. Avoiding the crowds on a hot July Monday (what could it be like on a Sunday?), I tramped across the Ilam Tops between little woods of sycamore to look down the valley. The view of Tissington Spires and Thorpe Cloud was impressive. A footpath from Air Cottage at the Tops descends through the woods, which are heavily invaded by sycamore from the upland shelter-belts.

Ash proved to be the native dominant tree.

Castern Wood, *121 538*, is a 55-acre nature reserve in the Manifold Valley, with a great diversity of trees and shrubs.

Besides Dove Dale and the Manifold Valley there are, near Bakewell, Miller's Dale and Ravensdale, Deep Dale and Monsal Dale, and, recommended as an alternative, **Lathkill Dale**, 3 miles, wooded, east and down from *175 655* to Over Haddon, *205 665*, where one can park. Part of the dale is a National Nature Reserve; with **Monk's Dale** to the north-west,

In the Goyt Valley

141 725, a total of 650 acres. Monk's Dale has an unspoilt range of habitat from woodland, scrub and grass to marsh and bare rock. Cheedale, *124 736*, has a 60-acre reserve of the Derbyshire Naturalists' Trust. A permit is needed for this and other woodlands of the Trust, including the large Miller's Dale woodlands below them. **Taddington Dale**, *165 708*, has 60 acres of National Trust woodland, but it also has the A6(T).

Darley Forest *293 655*, (♀) ♣, *1200 acres, roads and rides, FC*
Come here if you can, there's plenty of room.

The air is intoxicating, the dew in the morning sunlight like blue and yellow crystals – believe it or not. The rows and rows of pines are saturnine; birches and rowans line the roads, where the drystone walls, set well back, give plenty of room for cars to stop. Buttercups and clover line the verges with patches of bedstraw, milkwort and tormentil. It doesn't matter where you walk, and there is no nonsense about picnic places. While I ate my breakfast I talked to a man old enough to be my father, who walked 4 or 5 miles in the forest every morning on a cup of tea. He said he wasn't very well, and was thinking of writing a book instead.

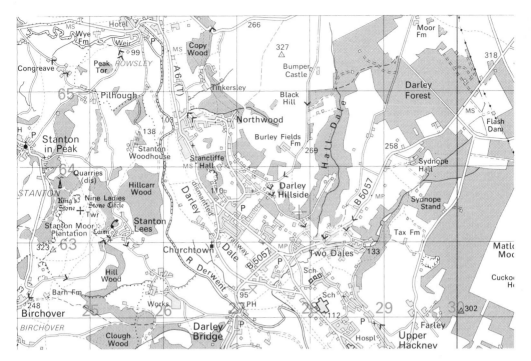

Nine Ladies, Stanton Moor *253 630*, ♀, *2m, fps, NT*

The Nine Ladies above Darley Dale are the stones of a not very impressive henge, looking more like well-worn teeth than ladies and surrounded by a protective wall which must surely damp any vibrations for those sensitive to such things. Henges, at first wood henges, were I believe a diagrammatic representation of the ancestral woodland home, built on land cleared for grazing. This is just a theory of mine – but why should the people bury wood charcoal under the main stones unless it was the sacred earth of the woodland? The woodland here is of birch, partly old coppice and partly burned. I don't know whether the National Trust knows its birchwood is being burned. The remains of this birch coppice high on the moors are interesting, I don't know quite why. There are many old quarries with rowan and birch spreading, one quarry working.

At **Matlock Bath**, *290 585*, there are trees to walk in, actually advertised as Lovers' Walks, and you have only to cross the valley road for a bag of chips.

Cromford Moor and Black Rock *291 557*, (♀) ♣, *waymarked walks, FC, CC*

These black rocks south of Matlock are of Millstone Grit, only black by contrast with the limestone of the 'White Peak' – both are visible here. Elsewhere, black basalt 'toad stones' surface above the limestone. The picnic place is in a moderately built-up area and opposite a busy quarry which is noisy on weekdays. On fine Sundays the very capacious car park, on several terraces of the hillside, is full of people sunbathing on the banks while the children climb the rocks.

The High Peak Trail, sensibly waymarked with numbered posts, passes here (post number 6) before descending to the Derwent.

In the large, ragged-outlined plantation east and south of the rocks are the Forestry Commission's 300 acres of vigorous young Scots pines, with some Corsican pine at the edges and pretty Western hemlocks by the trail. The rides, full of native plants, are parallel to the path at the cliff edge. The atmosphere is wild and remote, for the plantation covers a shallow bowl on the hilltop, strangely out of contact with the surroundings.

Chatsworth Park Woods 271 685, ♀ (♠), 3½m plus return or as you choose, pf

Parking at the house is reasonable, but you may be too early, or wish to avoid the crush on a fine holiday. The map reference is for Beeley Hilltop Farm where you can pick up a yellow-arrowed footpath northwards to Robin Hood. The estate woodlands are of mature beech with infillings of pine and infiltrations of sycamore; some old yews near the house. Rhododendron is much in evidence. There are several more or less parallel routes signalled by lilac or white arrows, the lower paths being walkways with grotesque features as designed in the late eighteenth century. The spectacular plumbing arrangements – aqueducts of rustic stonework – of the Chatsworth landscape can be viewed, with longer views (in good weather, thrilling ones) over the house, park and moors.

On a busy day you will be overtaken by parties of old-age pensioners attired for hiking and moving fast: to them the park is just an incident, just a change of scenery. Walking is a very popular hobby in Derbyshire, almost a way of life. If you are a moderate walker like me and the day is fine, take food and allow a whole day for this picturesque place.

Longshaw 266 799, ♀ ♠, 1000 acres plus, network of paths, NT, CF

The parking ground given is among trees and you can walk north-westwards by the Sheffield Plantation. Much of this has been fenced off as newly planted, but it is now quite well grown and the fence could be removed. The mixture of pine and hardwoods will need thinning before it can be walked in, but the final result should be effective. A pleasant though rather thin wood of mature pine survives on grazing lands and marsh to the north. Grindleford Station will bring you from Manchester by train: you only have to cross the road.

The whole of the east bank of the Derwent southwards to Froggatt is wooded and belongs to the Trust as does the moorland edge above. To the north-west the Trust's land extends south of the A625 to within a mile of Hathersage.

In Derwentdale, to the north of the section close to Huddersfield, Sheffield and Glossop, are large Forestry Commission plantations around the great Derwent and Ladybower Reservoirs, with many parking and picnic places. The Forestry Commission lists the **Lady Clough Forest Walk** from a lay-by on the A57 at *110 915*, and recommends stout footwear.

Ladybower Wood, Bamford, *205 867*, (track east of Ladybower pub 1 mile on the A57) is a nature reserve, 40 acres of native trees. **Ogston Carr** and plantations, *372 596*, also on the gritstone, form an 80-acre reserve.

The roads eastwards to Edwinstowe and Sherwood Forest are the A617 and the A6075.

Along the Derwent towards Belper the deep valley is clothed in trees: on the west bank are **Shining Cliff Woods**, National Trust leased to the Forestry Commission. These shine only in places and are difficult to get into from the valley, but National Trust ownership does at least ensure that no more houses will be built in the woodland. A broad arm extends westwards on the hilltop where, at *322 525*, you can just about park and then walk into the woods, here under young conifers; whitebeams along Jackass Lane.

CENTRAL ENGLAND
Sherwood Forest, Newark and
Gainsborough Landranger sheets 112, 120, 121

Sherwood Forest

Sherwood has been described as a purely literary forest, and it is true that the 25 or so square miles of Scots and Corsican pines between Nottingham and Worksop are largely reconstituted from the chases, parks, coverts and warrens of the Dukeries. The dukes and earls, however, did not neglect to plant trees as well as mining coal: the demands of the First and Second World Wars finally demolished the forest, which is on sandy ground where regeneration is not automatic. Heath with scattered birch is the result of clearing the oaks, at least for a century or so as the oaks gradually creep back into the maturing birch thickets. Mining has probably very much lowered the water table.

All is not lost however. Robin still lives, powerfully preserved by the Robin Hood Society, Mansfield, and in numerous Ladybird books and others sold at the Visitors' Centre, and in the propped-up limbs of the great Major Oak, visited by 200,000 people a year, piously believed to be his favourite tree. And 450 acres here are claimed to be the oldest piece of ancient oak forest in western Europe.

An ancient coppiced oak in Sherwood Forest

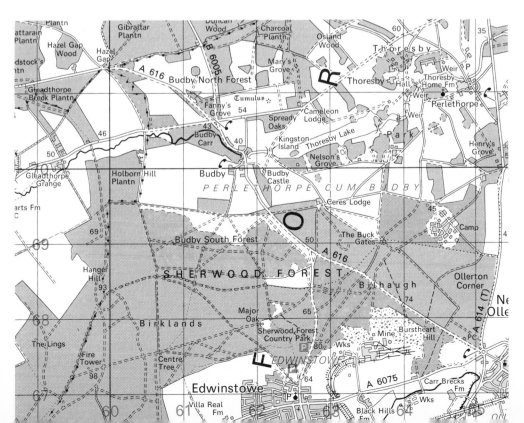

Sherwood Forest CP, Edwinstowe
627 677, ♀, 500 acres, 5 walks as below, CC
There are a wheelchair path, 1 mile to the
Major Oak, a blind trail with handrail, ¾ mile,
and 3 other walks, the longest 4½ miles. All
start from the Visitors' Centre at Edwinstowe.

Go straight for the Centre, in spite of the

'tasteful' script lettering, actually very vulgar,
and the often-repeated 'portrait' of Robin
Hood. Collect the leaflet and get away. The
longest walk is marked yellow and is arranged
by the Rotary Club of Sherwood Forest to take
in a large, grassy heath used for Army training,
which area the Rotary believes, I think rightly,

to be typical of the original Sherwood Forest. I did this walk and whilst in the process was able to sample the other walks, bridleways and footpaths which join and cross. I also sampled the forest ride through the pines. I feel I saw enough large, dead oaks and scrubby birches to last me a long time, and I honestly think that if you don't want to walk far you can see everything worth seeing by combining shorter routes. Separate and quite short is the trail for the blind, with a tapping- or hand-rail on the right all the way, and with patches of gravel to indicate features. The 'features' are pathetically limited, culminating in an opportunity to compare oak, yew and birch bark in the cool of a tiny yew wood. I tested the whole thing: bird song was magnificent, for the rest I felt very glad to have the sight of my eyes. I couldn't even smell the bracken.

Regeneration of the oak is quite vigorous, especially in areas which have been rabbit-fenced. Several of the large old trees are sessile or hybrid, but all the young trees I looked at were pedunculate. Stag-headed old trees have almost certainly suffered from a reduction in their water supply too rapid for adaptation; obviously, or this is their way of adapting.

Fanny's Grove, *612 709*, has a cruelly shadeless car park but the grove of well-grown oaks is a splendid sight – and a very short walk, though not a quiet one.

Clumber Park *645 773 (main entrance)*, ♀ ♣, *4000 acres, drives, walks, bicycle rides, nature trail, NT*
The house is gone, but the Capability Brown lake remains. Eighteenth-century planting is now past its prime, and the National Trust is replanting. The 2-mile double avenue of common lime is nearly 200 years old and probably passed its best about 180 years ago – it is now an aphid-riddled tunnel, but nice to drive through. Heathy ground at each side can be driven on to, with forestry conifers beyond. There are odd corners of interest, like an alder coppice just beyond the south end of the avenue, where you cross a bridge.

Hannaw Park Wood, *590 773*, is a 14-acre remnant of Sherwood Forest, with yew, a Woodland Trust property local to Worksop.

Treswell Wood, *761 799*, is an ancient coppice, 119 acres, on clay. A permit and booklet can be got from Mrs E. G. Gilbert, West Croft, Welham, Retford, for 50p.

Stapleford Wood, Newark *859 563*, ♣, *1100 acres, forest rides, FC*
The Forestry Commission, in its crusade to bring happiness to countless dogs, homeless lovers and some itinerant woodland investigators, has really excelled itself in the parking place to this otherwise functional forest. The road through the wood is lined with rhododendron – impressive when in bloom, but not, I imagine, bringing much joy to the foresters who find it almost impossible to remove. There are no organized walks, but miles and miles of straight rides.

Laughton Forest: Tuetoes Hills
845 014, ♀, *2000 acres plus, short waymarked walk, FC*
Inland sand dunes are the 'hills' of Tuetoes, and others among the fertile fields of the Trent alluvial plain: not very noticeable hills, and distinctly dune-shaped. The great wastes of the commons of the tiny villages of Scotter and Laughton now bear a mighty harvest of pines where you could get quite lost – there are nearly 4 square miles of solid trees. The beautiful picnic place is at the northern corner near Susworth, with reassuring glimpses of the flat, arable fields on three sides of a tall stand of pines, where the foresters have even induced some grass to grow. There is a rather tame little walk here, but obviously you can strike out into the depths to the south and east if you take careful note of your route.

On the western margins there is a considerable variety of trees, with poplars and willows. A mile away the cold Trent flows between its lines of cottages like a wide, silent street that no one can cross – there are no ferries now. Instead of the 3-minute crossing you have an hour or so in a bus to get from the east to your neighbour in the west. You can just hear the dull shriek of the M180 to the north, otherwise all is very very quiet: visually relaxing too. I found it rather difficult to drag myself away.

Woodhall Spa : Kirkby Moor and **Moor Farm** ♀ ♠ ♨, *3½ miles or less, NR*
Ostler's Plantation *215 630*, ♠, *300 acres, several routes, FC*

The two woods are on each side of the road to Kirkby on Bain which leaves the Horncastle road in the suburbs of Woodhall Spa. The Forestry Commission plantation is a massive block, or several blocks, of Scots pine which fit

in neatly with the local battery-hen industry.

The small Forestry Commission parking place can be used as the base for a very interesting exploration of oak coppice and birch heath in the nature reserve on the opposite side of the road. There is coppiced rowan too. Birch is cut back to encourage the grass, which is a lovely pink in June. With a wet meadow absolutely full of rushes, cotton-

grass and marsh orchid, and drier heath yellow with trefoil, one cannot regret the loss of a few trees. Intermediate stages are retained as well, and the reserve is well looked after. Do not be put off by the small blanket of pine which has been put over the oaks by the road.

At **Martin Moor** a parking place in a pretty birchwood, *217 647*, is on a section of the Viking Way – the Spa Trail – a cinder track on a disused railway with scrub. It would give most Vikings claustrophobia. A few trees have been planted at the start of the trail: rowans (which are appropriate) and whitebeams (which are not).

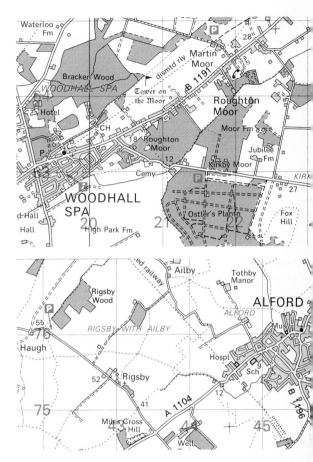

Snipe Dales, Winceby *320 683*, ♀ ⚘, *2m, dry but uneven, LNR*
This beautifully shaped valley is a nature reserve of the Lincolnshire and South Humberside Trust and is a model of its kind. No apologies for including a non-wooded area.

Other woodlands, such as Dole Wood and Hoplands Wood, in Lincolnshire, can be visited by permit from the Lincolnshire and South Humberside Trust.

Rigsby Wood, Haugh *421 761*, ♀, *37 acres, easy, marked circuit, NR*
Small, but rare, is this ancient ash-oak wood in the lonely fields at the escarpment edge. The reserve is carefully managed and labelled – as one has learnt to expect from the Lincolnshire and South Humberside Trust – and the path is mown: essential this. Much work is being done cutting overgrown ash, and removing dead elm, pine, rabbit wire, etc. It is beautiful too.

Gunby Park, *467 669*, National Trust, nearby, is only open on Thursdays. If you feel like a breath of fresh air and can face traversing Skegness, the dunes at **Gibraltar Point**, *556 582*, have scrub of native sea buckthorn – now a National Nature Reserve of 100 acres.

Lindsey is not heavily wooded – it never has been since Domesday, but The Wolds certainly have their charm not least because minor roads are practically deserted. The wide, well-kept verges – most are drove roads and are even called droves in places – have bright green grass glistening with wild flowers, and the wayside trees are large and well formed.

Chamber's Plantation, Wragby
148 739, ♀ ♣, *2½m, FC (Bardney Forest)*
This is a special Forestry Commission wood which is managed as a Forest Nature Reserve as well as to produce timber. The show-piece, **Hatton Wood**, *163 748*, is a mature oak-lime-ash wood. It may be the only wood of its kind under proper management, although other woods around do contain oak and lime. Some of the limes are cut, others are standards. The path is well marked and mown and there is no advantage in deviating. There are lots of birds. Jet planes, no doubt loaded with twice their weight of people-frying devices, exercised at tree-top level, frightening the author.

Willingham Woods, Market Rasen
139 885, ♣, *1m and 3m walks, FC*
A large picnic place on the main road has space

The path though Hatton Wood: oak and lime

for ball games and a pull-in for lorries. There
are some ponds. This a large forest of pines,
strong on geometry. Much quieter is a nature
reserve at **Linwood Warren** to the south,
opposite the golf course: some oak–birch
woodland (with lily of the valley) around an
open heath, *133 877*. You can also walk along
the margins of the Forestry Commission's
spruce woods which adjoin. Some of the
spruce, as well as some of the pine, is spreading
onto the heath grassland, which surely should
not be allowed. The grass is a beautiful pink in
June, but I could find no flowers, only leaves,
of the lily of the valley. It is said to be
decreasing everywhere. Other wild flowers
were abundant. I did not find the round-leaved
sundew, probably because I kept to the
footpath, as directed by the *Nature Reserves
Handbook*, 1982. According to the *Guide to
Britain's Nature Reserves*, 1984, I should not
even have been there without a permit.

I did stray into the small birch and oak
woodland. Here I did not see, nor did I expect
to see, the badger, red squirrel, or the water
shrew. If you do wait long enough to see any
wild life you will be bitten to death by the
gnats or mosquitoes which breed in the
woodland ditches.

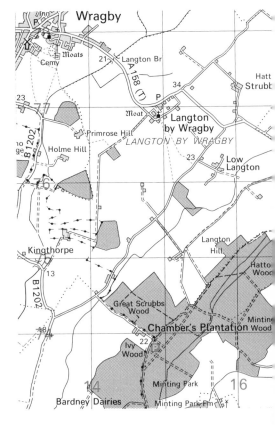

The North of England

Solemn evening at Cragside

Formby Point *275 083, (♀) ♣, 472 acres, many paths, NT*
The pines here were first planted in the early part of this century, in the hope that the dunes would become stable enough to allow a promenade to be built. But the coastal sands happily remained wild, only 10 miles from the centre of Liverpool, until acquired by the National Trust.

The dunes are amazingly high, and Scots pines, with a few Corsican and some maritime, cover about two-thirds of the acreage; wooded land to the south and north is also accessible – as far north as Ainsdale Hills. The Ainsdale woods, in a National Nature Reserve of 1200

acres, may be explored by defined footpaths.

Slacks in the dunes containing fresh water in the winter are the breeding ground of the natterjack toad, extremely rare, and there is a section of mature pinewood reserved for the red squirrel, here an imported strain but separated from the competition of the grey squirrel in an 'island' habitat: even built-up areas have their uses.

Poplars, birches, willows and even alders are naturally added to the more settled parts, and I found some oak and many sycamore seedlings under the pines; the humus composed only of sand and pine needles. The sea may come quite close over the wide sands, but a lady I spoke to would not let her dog swim, as she said the sea was polluted.

Further towards Southport the dunes carry a distinctive scrub of creeping willow and sea buckthorn over hundreds of acres, and golf courses are planted with white willow. Southport's **Botanical Garden**, *366 186*, has

excellent specimen trees in a limited space; *Metasequoias*, an old thorn with large leaves, *Sorbus intermedia* and *torminalis*, a mulberry. The flowerbeds are pure Victoriana, perfect and fiercely coloured, like glass paperweights.

The Plantations, Wigan *592 078*, ♀, *350 acres, various routes and paths, CP*
The woods are bounded on the west by the River Douglas. A stream which feeds the river has banks and bed of a vivid orange mud from deposits of iron, and in former days the river varied in colour from day to day as the dye-

works changed its tanks. Roughly parallel to the river is a branch railway, now dismantled, over which the driveway to Haigh Hall crosses by a wide Victorian iron bridge planted with rhododendron, presumably to mask the ugly sight of a railway from the eyes of the carriage-folk. Between the railway and the next, parallel, interruption, the Leeds & Liverpool canal, are fine, mature beeches; a Victorian plantation which suffers here and there from the Victorian enthusiasm for *Rhododendron ponticum*, an unsuitable and unremovable understorey. The ground is clear, of course, under older beeches.

Iron and coal built the estate (of the Earl of Crawford and Balcarres); the people of Wigan were given the freedom of half of it for fifty years – it was probably old common land anyway. Now they have all of it.

Lever Park, Rivington *635 128*, ♀ ✦, *400 acres, roads and rides, LA*
Rivington Pike is a well-known landmark to the east of the Lancashire Plain – it indicates the first moorlands. On the hillside above the large Rivington Reservoir the Lever Estate was given or given back to the people by Lord Leverhulme and has been popular for years. It is a little untidy and eroded, but has many avenues of mature trees, particularly oaks.

Beacon Fell *564 426*, ✦, *270 acres, rough fps and rides, CP*
The Fell is an isolated massive hump, up to 1050 feet, covered with Sitka spruce and with a one-way road all the way round at about 800 feet. There are parking places, some large, every few yards. The Information Centre and emergency telephone are ½ mile south-east of

Spruces on Beacon Fell

the woods at *578 422*. Three hundred thousand people visit here annually, negotiating a maze of small roads – well signposted, at least from Broughton, north of Preston.

Near Preston is Squire Anderton's Wood, with a woodland trail: *560 337*.

Hodder Bridges *704 393 and 698 412,* ♀ ♣, *2m of fp by the river*

The path from the lower bridge is on the Lancashire bank, over fields at first, the stony riverbed cut into shallow steps of the rock strata. You continue by the back drive of a château-like building described on the map as a ruin but now very much restored. There are spruce woods beyond, then the route settles down to a riverside walk over the roots of oaks, sycamores, wych elms and alders: perhaps better in winter when you can see more.

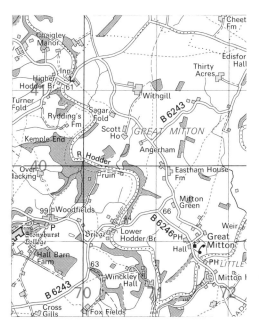

Spring Wood *742 363, ½ hour walk, LA*

One mile east of Whalley, across the A671, is a decent picnic place in a little wood which could provide a welcome break on a Lancashire journey. Though bathed in road noise it has a charm of its own. It contains the expected sycamores, but they are formidable ones;

beech and oak, with birch at the rocky top corner. An alder survives and some larches have been inserted. The birches are greenish rather than silver and the beech trunks seem carved out of the dark rock.

Great Harwood, south of Whalley, has a nature trail at *745 339*; 9½ acres with woodland. At Roddlesworth, *665 215*, off the A675, is a trail in wet woodland controlled by the Water Authority: many ferns, and, they say, kingfishers.

Witton Country Park, an old estate of 130 acres, is near Blackburn: *663 276*. Chorley has its Astley Park, *574 143*.

Ashton-under-Lyne, well inside the Manchester industrial conurbation, has 16 acres of country belonging to the National Trust: Medlock Vale, including Daisy Nook, *922 008*, part of a Country Park of 50 acres.

Rochdale, north of this, provides its citizens with three nature trails: Alkrington Woods, *864 053*, oak, birch and beeches by the river; Healey Dell, 102 acres at *883 159*; and Hopwood Clough, *878 079*, about 2 miles long.

But you are in a magnificent old industrial landscape – why look for pretty woods? For the real country, head for Burnley and cross to Downham, by Pendle Hill.

Planted beech and invading sycamore, Spring Wood

South and West Yorkshire

Landranger sheets 104, 110

Cannon Hall, Cawthorne *273 080*
Deffer Wood *267 086, (♀) ♠, 200 acres,*
fps, FC

Barnsley is not badly provided with
countryside of a mixed moorland-industrial
character which, while not perhaps conforming
to south-east English ideas of country (any
more than the idiom of local speech conforms),
nonetheless is full of excitement and interest
for those who have eyes to see: abandoned
farms, broken walls of flat stones, all sorts of
old pits full of rubbish, crudely rigged-up gates
and fences; and marvellous views broken by
chimneys and towers. All has been exploited at
random and is beyond repair from a
conservation point of view, except perhaps by

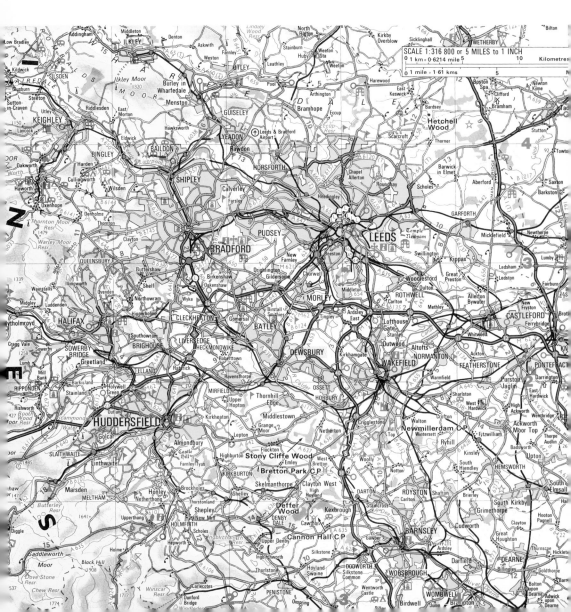

forestry, yet it can be loved for its richness of texture and pattern.

Down by Denby Dale the country softens, and large patches of woodland have the quality of water in the desert. Cawthorne, surrounded by the old residences of those who turned the muck into brass, is now a conservation area, and nearby Cannon Hall, solid, rectangular, is a museum at the centre of a well-used Country Park of 24 acres. The parkland is grand, with beeches, oaks, pines and cedars.

The shrubbery of Cannon Hall is worth seeing; beautifully kept flowerbeds and lawns, nice trees and bushes and charming relics of local church architecture incorporated. (Churches tended to be rebuilt in the period of nineteenth-century prosperity.) The specimen trees are not perhaps remarkable, but even an ordinary *Robinia* gladdens the eye here.

North-west from the car park you can find your way through the rhododendrons and beside mellow, green walls to the Forestry Commission's Deffer Wood, across the road. You can easily park by the roadside if you want to avoid the car park. The woods are pleasantly uneven, oak and birch planted with assorted stands of conifers in the experimental Victorian manner: try anything. A footpath crosses the road into the wood, north of the (inhabited) folly marked on the map. Return by a yew walk and south of the folly by the road. Here a row of quite large elms has been removed, every stump sending out a bush of suckers. Perhaps in 200 years there will be a row of large Dutch(?) elms again.

Bretton Park *290 131,*♀(♣)*, 94 acres, LA*
Bretton Park, north of Cannon Hall and near the M1, is a Country Park of 94 acres which adjoins a nature reserve surrounding an artificial lake dating from about 1800. Several pleasantly printed leaflets are available at the car park; one of them gives details of three walks. There is mixed woodland and the surrounding farmland is open to the walker. The warden was appealing for 3-foot-high deciduous trees to maintain the stock: phone Bretton 550.

A mile or so north along the A637, parallel to the M1, turn left at a fantastic monument in

West Bretton, to the Yorkshire Sculpture Park and Bretton Hall, which is a College of Higher Education specializing in the arts. Terraces, sunken gardens, stables and open woodland are used to display new sculpture along with some remaining, and looking much more at home, from the Hall's heyday. Elizabeth Frink's monumental heads were quite wonderful on a formal terrace, while her freer figures on the lawns seemed a bit silly.

Sculpture happenings with smoke and fire, assisted by the Arts Council, had left some charred stumps. Geodesic domes for shelter and vigorously designed bollards for car control seemed somehow more sculptural than the sculptures. How a sculptor competes with natural forms is a question I for one would not like to answer with hammer and chisel.

Further north, the parking place at *275 159* on the B6117, is **Stony Cliffe Wood**, a nature reserve of 100 acres; an oakwood area adjoining Stocksmoor Common, which is a heath of 30 acres near the road. Another Country Park is at **Newmillerdam**, *331 157* – lake and

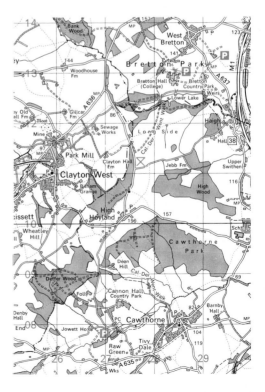

Hetchell Wood: beech sapling and dog's mercury

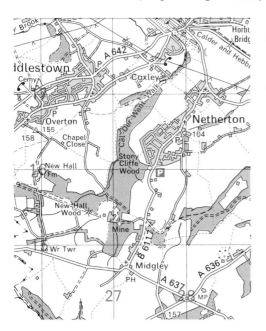

Bradford and Leeds and contiguous conurbations occupy the northern part of the section. There is a nature reserve of 29 acres, **Hetchell Wood**, noted for its insect fauna, *380 422*, near the village of Thorner, north-east of Leeds. Nearby are other attractive woodlands, some open, some private.

This was in fact the last wood I visited in my single-handed survey of British woodland. The November day was dark and damp, and I certainly didn't see any insects. I noted with muted pleasure that the tall beeches were surrounded by saplings, the reddish leaves characteristically held long after the parents were naked. Dog's mercury below was still a good green. It will be all right, this bit of limy woodland, 10 miles from the middle of Leeds. I took my last photograph on the last frame of my last reel of Kodachrome 25 at $\frac{1}{4}$ second, performed a natural function, and left for the south. (I can't help it if The End is in the middle.)

The A65 north-west of Leeds via Ilkley leads to Bolton Abbey and Wharfedale (in Section 57) with Grass Wood beyond (56).

woodlands, 239 acres with fifty honorary wardens(!) – north-east beyond Woolley Edge, which has parking places. (Might be a good place for some fringe sculptures.) More impressive visually than anything else in the area is the Darton Colliery, busy extracting the fossil remains of much earlier woodlands, where nobody walked.

Yorkshire, Ouse-Land and Scunthorpe Landranger sheets 105, 111, 112

Broughton Woods *955 100,* ♀ ♣ *, many paths and forest roads, pf*

On the Lincolnshire ridge where Ermine Street (here pronounced 'Er Mine) runs, are old estate beechwoods shielding the inhabitants of Broughton and Brigg from the nasty smoke of Scunthorpe. The beeches are now relics amongst rectangular stands of spruce and larch regularly harvested by clear felling, which gives a pattern of cross-sections along what are still 4 miles of woods, though the M180 has sliced off the tail at Scawby.

Skipwith and **Riccall** *653 374 and 669 377,* ♀ *, paths, roads and tarmac, NR (600 acres) and common land*

Skipwith Common is a wonderful open space with shelter-belts of birch where young oaks breed. Lots of good places to park are off the narrow road which leads north from the A163, about a mile west of North Duffield. The shelter-belt birches merge gradually into the mostly wet heath woodland of the nature reserve, with good alder buckthorn on the south edge of the reserve. The reserve proper

has spaces to park as indicated above, and waymarked paths through sallows on old RAF concrete. Off the path it is usually wet. There are many small meres, very busy with birds: 90 species breed. The habitat is described as varied, but this is relative: the effect was remarkably homogeneous – silver birches, white clouds, and little flocks of ducks in the wind.

Skipwith and Riccall Nature Reserve: birches and wet heath

Three miles west of Selby the Forestry Commission's **Bishop Wood**, 850 acres, occupies an ancient site and is organized to be a wildlife sanctuary entirely open to the public, as well as, of course, producing some timber.

Two car parks are as on the map, at *551 346* and *561 334*. A forest guide booklet, modestly priced, gives general information and a map, scale 1 inch to 350 yards. Walks and trails are detailed on site.

South of York, **Askham Bog**, *573 479*, 105 acres, is a nature reserve to be reckoned with, mostly now covered by trees and shrubs. There is a book about the natural history of the Bog: *A Wood in Ascam*, by Fitter and Smith.

Allerthorpe Common *755 480*, ♣, *150 acres, woodland walk, FC*

The wood has been converted into a poky spruce plantation with a small parking and picnic place. I would rather picnic practically anywhere else around here.

Doncaster: Sandall Beat Wood

609 037, ♀, *200 acres, fp, LA*
Featureless but pleasant, beyond the racecourse, this is a good oak and birch wood with little sign of ancientness. There are many well-trodden footpaths. There is, or was, a Roman road along the eastern margin, but the feature that here holds the attention is a great, slimy pyramid of a slag heap (known elsewhere as a pit tip) with grey drainage channels around it. Along the Roman road is nothing more ancient than rosebay willow–herb (known here

as the pit orchid). The wood is bisected by several tracks of railway to a coal-mine, with a footbridge over – a beguiling feature.

Sandala appears in the Domesday Book, Yorkshire entry for 'sandy', and beat may refer to a 'walk' or a boundary, or perhaps to the extreme flatness of the place.

Melton Wood *516 033*, ♀ ♣, *260 acres, easy roads and paths, car park, FC*

It is a cheerful, square sort of wood, busy with walkers and riders at weekends, with a good

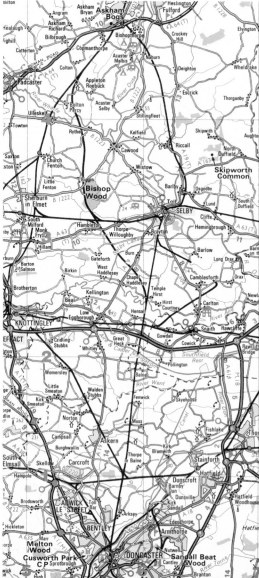

variety of trees. Beeches were being thinned to make the brick-like, 2-foot blocks which are used for heavy-duty pit propping. The blocks stacked about the rides looked remarkably strange, like Aztec architecture.

There is a small Country Park at **Cusworth Park**, *548 038*, 2 miles east of Melton Wood, the Georgian house now a museum. Of several Forestry Commission plantations around Doncaster, forming the Don Forest, the largest is north-west of Bawtry. It is not accessible – yet.

Melton Wood: beech blocks

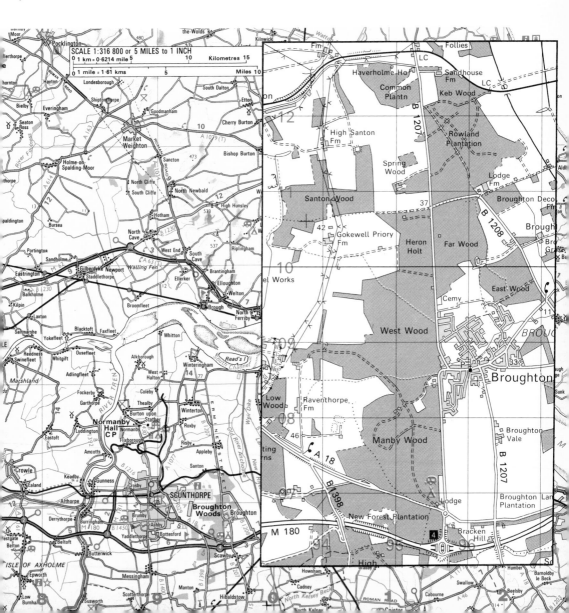

No one need be afraid that the island is too small to contain TT races, electric trams, day trippers to Douglas, fairies and cats without tails. There is space, and there is peace. The number of visitors in fact has slumped since the peak of half a million a year in the 1930s. The government has been able to think in terms of improving conservation.

Manx scenery ranges from bleak, but not too enormous, moorlands, mostly government-owned and quite free of restrictions, to sand dunes in the north and fine cliffs in the south. The island is a block of slate, 227 square miles, with granite peaks and corners of sandstone in the west, limestone in the south. A series of miniature woodlands is contained in the National Glens where streams drain the central massif through deep-cut valleys.

Forestry plantations on the moors are nicely irregular in outline and varied in texture, in keeping with the relatively intimate nature of the country. Larch is much used.

Molly Quirk's Glen, *405 787*, is 5 acres of woodland. Bibaloe Walks adjoins. (Bus.)
Groudle Glen, *415 786*, 2½ miles from

Douglas, is deep and rocky with beech above, larch and pine below. (Tram.)
Laxey Glen Gardens, *432 843*, is 7 miles from Douglas – exotic trees, wooded banks, boating pool, café and the Laxey Wheel of 1854 (made in Wigan). (Bus or tram.)
Port Soderick Glen, *342 728*, 4 miles south of Douglas, is sheltered, with a stream, amusements and shops at the shore end. (Bus.)

Ballure Walk, *457 936*, is on the outskirts of Ramsey near the beach and the second highest Manx mountain, North Barrule. **Ballaglass Glen**, Cornaa, *465 897*, has a waterfall and woods, a stone circle and a nature trail of the

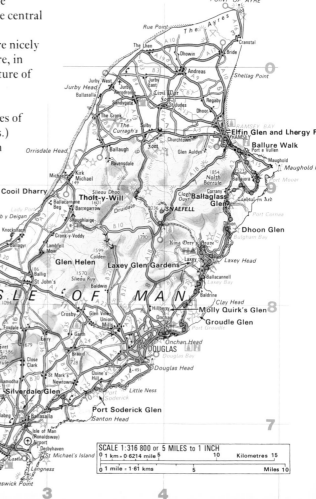

SCALE 1:316 800 or 5 MILES to 1 INCH

0 1 km = 0.6214 mile   5   10   Kilometres 15

0 1 mile = 1.61 kms   5   Miles 10

Manx Conservation Society. (Tram.)
Dhoon Glen, *456 867*, 5 miles from Ramsey,
has 44 acres of wood and a majestic waterfall.
Path ⅗ mile, steep, to the sea. (Tram.)
Elfin Glen and Lhergy Frissel, are in Ramsey.

Tholt-y-Will, *378 890*, is 28 acres in the
mountains under Snaefell. A forestry
plantation adjoins and there are picnic places
and viewpoints on the A14 down Sulby Glen.

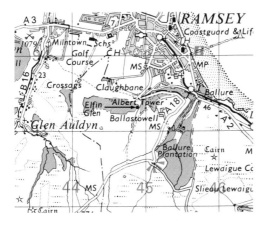

Cooil Dharry trees

Glen Helen, *295 844*, is a large wooded glen
with Victorian conifers, oaks and beeches. Path
¾ mile to Rhenass Waterfall. A children's
playground and other facilities are in the Glen.

Bishopscourt Glen, **Glen Wyllin** and **Glen
Mooar** (with Spooyt Vane – 'white sprout')
are all close to Kirk Michael on the A3 and
reached by the Peel-Ramsey bus. **Cooil
Dharry**, *314 902*, opposite Glen Wyllin and
just south of Kirk Michael is a 15-acre
woodland reserve of the Manx NCT. Mixed
deciduous trees include beeches, maples and
wych elm, prettily clustered about the stream
in something like native woodland.
Glen Maye, *235 797*, is 3 miles south of Peel,
with walkways by a waterfall in woodland
which contains Spanish chestnut. The path
continues down to a nice beach. From the road
above, northwards, you can see the mountains
of Northern Ireland and the Mull of Galloway.

Colby Glen, *232 708*, and **Silverdale Glen**,
275 710, are lesser attractions; the first has
spring flowers, the second a children's playground. The Silverdale countryside belongs
to the Manx National Trust, most of whose
properties are in the south and west: Bradda
Head, Spanish Head and Calf of Man, all
barren lands, but lovely. There is a deep-sea
aquarium on the front at Port Erin, and there
was, when I was little, an ancient mariner with
a cormorant trained to catch his fish.

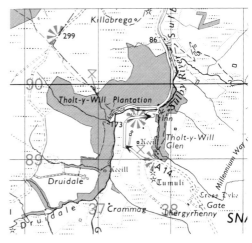

Silverdale and South Lakeland

SILVERDALE

People live here: hay is made, cattle and sheep are looked after, and stone is quarried. All these activities continue in peace in a landscape as charming and as intimate as any in Britain, soft yet craggy. Arnside Knott and Waterslack Woods are National Trust lands, and the Trust holds covenants over 50 acres of woods west of Arnside. The most important limestone pavement in the area, with scrub, is in the middle of a wood at *480 772*, a National Nature Reserve of 170 acres, called Gait Barrows.

Eaves and **Waterslack Woods** *471 760*, ♀ ♣ *(yew and Scots pine)*, *100 acres*, NT Paths easy but limestone can be dangerous.

After Lancashire's Swelterdales, Flydales and Nettledales, Silverdale is refreshing. By the National Trust car park that Lancashire tree, the sycamore, which was dark green and full of shadows and spiders in the dales, has here much lighter green leaves, flapping delightfully in the wind from the sea. The tree-weed has little chance of advancing far into Eaves Wood – there's far too much going on there already, well established long before the sycamore came to Britain.

Take the right-hand path, less than 100 yards from the gate, and keep on turning right except where a path exits obviously at Waterslack Farm. The eastern flank of the wooded hill is much more interesting than the west. A line of small-leaved limes, old coppice

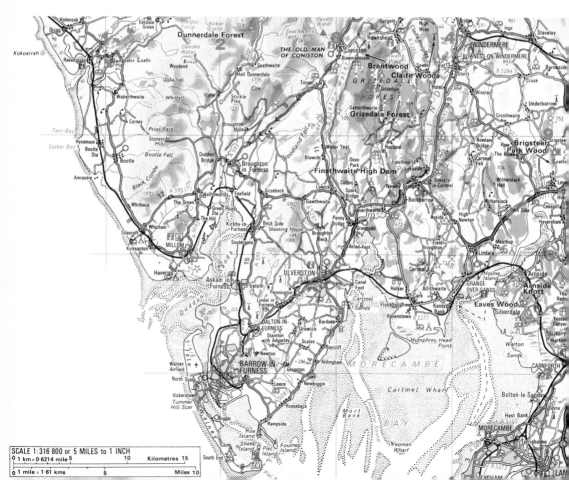

SCALE 1:316 800 or 5 MILES to 1 INCH
0 1 km = 0·6214 mile 5   10   Kilometres 15
0 1 mile = 1·61 kms   5   Miles 10

trees of a wood-bank, may indicate a former dominance – one grotesque stool must be the oldest tree hereabout, although one or two sessile oaks are large. A series of limestone terraces, typically eroded into clints and grikes, contain yew, ash, hazel and wych elm, and there are pines, privet, hawthorn, rowan, holly – and one whitebeam looking suspiciously as if planted to complete a textbook flora; or perhaps it is *Sorbus lancastriensis.*

With the inevitability of the best native woodlands, Eaves Wood is garden-like. Stretches of limestone platform, beautifully patterned by the natural fissures, have the roots of trees married into them as if with affection, yews creep over the stones as well as growing straight up, and there are nice ferns, hart's tongue and spleenwort, and various cranesbills. Privet is common, and there is much hazel coppice, still cut to preserve the light. Pines obviously were planted some time ago, probably to complete the effect of a natural garden, and this in places they do, their roots particularly well integrated with the rocks, and low branches wandering picturesquely near the ground.

To the north is a fine meadow with shining cranesbill, lady's bedstraw and dropwort, and a view of Arnside Knott, with an outrageous camping site intervening. Beech is common on the west of the hill, including a planted circle of fine, straight, silver-barked trees. Everywhere old walls, floors and boulders are white, shapely and soft with mosses.

There is a nature trail with numbered 'stations': the booklet is available at Silverdale village shops. For **Arnside Knott**, *456 774*, a booklet is in the Arnside shops.

A very small nature reserve, Beach Wood, *452 782*, includes in $1\frac{1}{4}$ acres an amazing variety of plants, not all indigenous, but including many ferns. At Arnside the woods go down to the shore. Unfortunately the sea seems not to come up to the shore very often. Across the sands the Cumbrian hills beckon.

THE SOUTH LAKES

The valleys of the two large southern lakes, Coniston and Windermere, must always have been densely wooded: they favour trees, being sheltered, moist and too steep for cultivation. The inhabitants have not neglected to improve on nature with beech, spruce, larch, Irish yew, *Sequoiadendron* and even *Calocedrus decurrens.* The Forestry Commission has added large conifer forests on higher ground formerly grazed to semi-desert. These plantations decorate most of the skyline here and descend to the water near Coniston. The whole area is riddled with woodland walks, public footpaths and forest trails.

I must select, and have largely avoided tracts of conifer plantation and sought after easy walks among native trees. There is no lack of information if you want to scale the heights; the excellent works of A. Wainwright are available at all Lakeland bookshops. Only 3 of the 56 gruelling hikes in his *The Outlying Fells of Lakeland . . . for Old Age Pensioners and Others* are in woodland. They range from 2 miles to $11\frac{1}{4}$ miles. His route to the limestone crag of Whitbarrow is partly in woodland and partly in a nature reserve; he describes it as 'beautiful every step of the way': 8 miles. It is only 1 mile from Witherslack Hall, *437 860*, to Lord's Seat on Whitbarrow, though the path ascends 600 feet. Out of respect for this fine craftsman/walker, we reproduce below, by permission, his drawing of part of the Whitbarrow Scar. Whitbarrow, a 250-acre nature reserve, is also known as Hervey

Reserve. There are a few ash trees on the clints, rooted, I suppose you would say, in the grikes. (*Grike* does not appear in dictionaries.)

A more heavily wooded limestone pavement is by Hutton Roof, called Lancelot Clark Storth: Pickles Wood adjoins. This nature reserve is of 143 acres at about *546 776* (on our map). A good range of lime-loving trees and shrubs may be found here, including some juniper; but note that sycamore cares not where it grows.

Brigsteer Park Wood *488 876*, ♀ ♠ *(yews)*, *150 acres, ¾m bridleway, NT*

With oaks and birches over the quiet minor road, several shady places to stop, and mossy limestone walls, this looks like a strip of National Trust wallpaper woodland. It is more: ancient yews surrounded by old coppiced ash stools; lilies of the valley and butterfly orchid. Perhaps the yew and ash were the original vegetation, the oaks planted for usefulness, birch creeping into clearings.

Finsthwaite High Dam *368 883*, ♠, *1m, easy but steep, LA*

A broad path leads up from the decent parking place, through oaks, to the lovely tarns planted with larches, where ducks and geese live in peace, except on fine sunny days when people dive in. Marsh cinquefoil, with purple-red stars, grows by the lower dam, and there are

Claife Woods, Windermere: Douglas fir and beech

white water-lilies in the upper tarn.

For a woodland road to Hawkshead from Newby Bridge, go by Dale Park to pretty Esthwaite Water. There are several pleasant stopping places, with footpaths and bridleways to right and left. It is worth climbing through fine oaks, up to the spruces where bogs in hollows are full of rushes, myrtle, asphodel and heaths. The midges can be ticklish.

Claife Woods, Windermere *385 995* (*Red Nab*), ♀ ♠, *750 acres, easy or tough according to direction, NT*

The National Trust guide describes this as the least spoilt part of Windermere's shores. It is, certainly, a long time since it *was* spoilt by conversion to beech, larch and Douglas fir. The trees are now impressive, even solemn. There are a few oaks and alders near the water. There is no access by car, but this was the noisiest wood I had ever been in, with water skiing, and tasteless demonstrations by the RAF. What are the spoilt bits like I wonder . . . but this was a fine Saturday in July. There was a good deal of non-biodegradable material on the shore, 1 mile of which is wooded from Belle Grange south. 'Water birds may be seen', says the 1984 *Guide to Britain's Nature Reserves.*

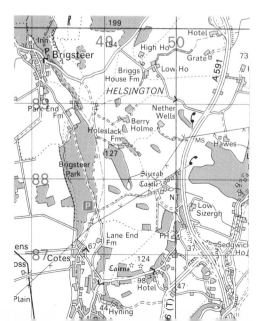

Bog asphodel, Dale Park, Grizedale

Grizedale Forest *336 945*, ♀ ♣ ,
6000 acres, walks and nature trails, FC
Much fine oak and some parkland trees remain
around this very civilized Visitors' Centre. The
Forestry Commission runs a shop, with
groceries.

I'm afraid I didn't do any of the walks, but
I certainly felt the Forestry Commission was
falling over backwards to welcome visitors'
interest in trees and wildlife, and to provide
access.

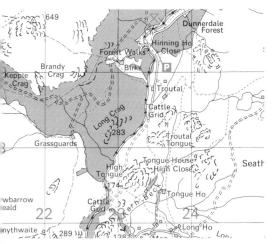

Brantwood *313 958*, ♀ , *nature trails, not
on Saturdays, pf*
I expected the grounds of Ruskin's house to be
full of exotic trees, if only to make the place
look more like the Switzerland he so admired,
but I was quite wrong. The woodland is pure
sessile oak with birches, simple and dignified.
Ruskin at Brantwood was a lonely, sad figure,
and there is a simple footpath only, through
what was probably an oak coppice with an
alder slade. The view across the water is
entirely satisfactory: he knew about views.

Working south from Brantwood there are
several National Trust woods preserving the
local vegetation. There are also several parking
places. Climbing 800 feet takes you through
6-foot bracken, old birches, fine, straight oaks,
ash, yew, thorn and more bracken, the slope
being definitely 1:3.

Dunnerdale Forest *234 994*, *(♀)* ♣ ,
1500 acres, 4 walks, FC
The Duddon, looking sweet and pure, wanders
between marsh spotted orchid, sweetgale, bog
asphodel, shrubby sallows. Here is a beautiful,
small, oak-birch wood with a grassed-over
track winding between the rocks: this is what
the original woodland of Dunnerdale was like.
Cow wheat grows vigorously. The lichened
stems of the sessile oaks are well formed, fine
timber that nobody wants: at least, I hope they
don't. Near the picnic place the Commission
has planted some Norway maples and some
cherries. I don't suppose it matters, but surely
Dunnerdale can do without 'amenity' trees?

62	60
54	55
53	56

THE NORTH OF ENGLAND
The Cumbrian Lakes
Landranger sheets 89, 90

Irton Pike *120 012*, ♀, *1 hour minimum, moderate, FC*

For a really invigorating view over Wast Water to Great Gable and outwards to Seascale and Windscale this is a very short and easy climb up a forest road shaded by spruces. Emerging onto Irton Fell is dramatic. This is a marvellous place to be on a fine morning.

Irton Road Station on the minuscule Ravenglass and Eskdale Steam Railway (regular service in summer) is handy for Eskdale Green and a walk arranged by the Forestry Commission – called Giggle Valley Walk; ¾ mile of larch and beech.

Greengate Wood, Santon Bridge
114 024, ♀, *600 acres, NT*

There are several National Trust woods about

Nether Wasdale: this is the finest. Sessile oak is well spaced over grass, or rather grass and honeysuckle which here spreads as a field layer. There is a large larch in the middle, which is rather odd, but also a lovely bog. Cow wheat, with the absence of invading vegetation, does suggest long occupation by the oaks. But there are no ancient trees as such.

Wilkinson's Wood *107 047*, ♀ ♣ ✿, *13 acres, no path, NT*

Disturbingly, I found this to be a wood almost without trees. A great part has been planted with larch, and I find this unacceptable. It would have been better to leave it alone.

High Birk How and **Lords Wood** by Wasdale Hall, *145 045*, at the foot of the lake are also National Trust, leased to the YHA. At Wasdale Head is a small wood called **Fence Wood**, *183 065*: obviously if it hadn't been fenced it wouldn't be there: or perhaps it was used, and preserved, to make fences. But the truth is stranger: the fields of Wasdale Head were enclosed as early as the sixteenth century. The road ends here.

Bowness Knott *109 154*, ♣, *forest walks, FC*

Straight lines are a feature of the fells around Ennerdale, edging the forestry plantations – a landscaping sin, but it must be admitted that the old drystone walls often go straight. Too studied a harmonious effect could look worse. In contrast are many rows of wind-distorted, grown-up hawthorn hedges which are a feature of the hill-farming country by the lakes. These quaint pigmy avenues, while now useless as hedges, do provide shade and shelter and frame the views.

Good use is made of larches bordering the edges of plantations at Bowness Knott, a large, attractive and well-appointed car park and picnic place. Ennerdale is the only one of the large lakes which does not have a motor road alongside, and the aspect is both green and peaceful. The popular Smithy Beck Trail starts

along the forest road – there are two sections, taking one or two hours. The Smithy was a mediaeval iron bloomery using charcoal from the native forest. The industry supported several settlements and, for as long as the soil of the cleared forest remained fertile, there were many farms.

A 9-mile walk also starts here and provides 'many majestic views'. Most of us will be satisfied with one view from the lakeside, which truly is majestic.

Holme Wood *122 224,* ♀ *(♠), 150 acres, fp, lakeside, NT*

The car park, grassy and with a good view of Loweswater, is a mile from the wood. The top of the roadside wall is covered with wonderful greenish patterns of the map lichen,

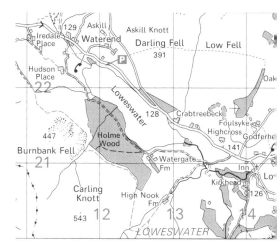

Scales Wood

Rhizocarpon geographicum, and the walk is also enlivened by meadowsweet, campion, small tortoiseshells and cows, just like a colour plate in a Shell Guide. There are water-lilies and reeds in the lake. The wood is of good oak trees, with ash, elm, and alder by the water, but again there is larch planted. Why is the National Trust so keen on larch? I suppose with 200 properties to care for, it needs lots of timber. I wish they would grow it elsewhere.

Scales Wood *175 170 (Buttermere village)* ♀, *100 acres, NR and NT*
The streams from which spout Sour Milk Gill and Scale Force cut their beds in the fells before the glaciers cut this classic U-shaped valley. Perhaps the trees of Scales have been there since the last Ice Age. It is certainly a very appealing wood, much the most original that I have found in the Lake District. On heavy boulder scree covered with moss are dead and living birches sprawling amongst the rocks, while the oaks grow nearly straight, and down to the boggy foot of the slope. This wood gives every appearance of being undisturbed for a very long time, and this is not surprising considering the steepness and roughness of the ground. It is not really a wood to walk in at all, but one to clamber through, as careful not to disturb anything as not to break your own limbs. These mossy boulders can be very dangerous – and it is a $\frac{1}{2}$-mile limp across the lake delta to Buttermere village. There are paths above and below the wood. Sometimes described as a birchwood, Scales is really an oakwood with a lot of birch as well as rowan and sallow. A straight boundary at about the foot of Buttermere divides it from the coniferized Burtness Wood, where Forestry has reached out its calculating grasp, and taken a slice out of the perfect landscape.

Crummock Water is the artists' lake; it gleams like steel below the variegated peaks to the west, or looks engagingly inky from the fellside. The poets' lake is Derwent Water, and the road between is steep up to Newlands Hause, a National Trust viewpoint over 2000 acres of Trust bracken in the awesome cavity down which flows the Sail Beck, back to Long Howe. Hause is from *hals*, a neck or ridge,

which is true enough; but the Sail, from *sealh* (Old English), sallow, is no longer a willowed beck. Above Keskadale Beck, which flows east, are the **Ard Crags**, *207 194*. This is the site of a high-level oakwood of about 30 acres, set at an angle of 45 degrees. Astonishingly at this height and angle it is a small coppice. This little wood is a remnant of many thousands of acres, converted to arable or pasture, then becoming poor rough pasture or, in better soil, useless bracken. Apart from the many essential uses of small timber the bark was stripped for tanning leather. A local industry was the making of oak swills – woven baskets which were used for carrying practically everything from fish through babies to coal. They are still made in Furness.

Squirrel eating breakfast, Brandelhow

Brandelhow Park *249 200*, ♀ *(♠)*, *80 acres, easy fp, NT*
You can stop your car in the shade here and feed the red squirrels – mine had Weetabix – then wander down easy gradients to the lake shore, which is clean. There is a pretty view of Derwent Water and its wooded islands – two are National Trust lands, but not the nearest, St Herbert's. There, an eccentric owner once built himself a prehistoric stone circle, and other follies. The woods of Brandelhow are oak, larchified but nice, with springy moss underfoot and plenty of flowers.

On the east side of the lake are many parking places – a lido effect – but turning up to Watendlath (Old Norse for something) brings you to the beautiful birchwood and oakwood of **Ashness**, *270 195*, as well as to Lodore

The view from Brandelhow across Derwent Water

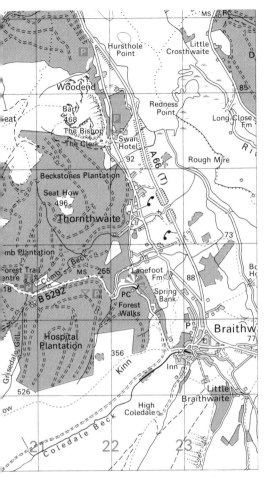

Cascade. Beyond the tarn (where you can park) you have to walk to investigate scattered birches and oaks of the fellside and see Blea Tarn.

Thornthwaite Forest *210 245, 4000 acres at least, many trails, FC*

Bassenthwaite is the King of the Lakes, throned between Skiddaw and Grisedale Pike and with a a spreading cloak of dark spruce and fir. Unfortunately he also has the A66(T), at his side – a good smooth artery, but no asset to the immediate environment. Turn off at Braithwaite for the Forestry Commission's well-maintained car parks and as many as ten graded forest walks (including those of Dodd Wood on the opposite side and reached via the A591). The Whinlatter Visitors' Centre is a haven of peace after the holiday lakesides and roads, and is negotiable by wheelchair.

The coniferous character of these mighty woodlands is complete: you really could be anywhere hilly in the north temperate zone. The effect is severe – no friendly native sycamores creeping in here, although there is a sycamore plantation, as well as an oak plantation, at Nobel Knott, the picnic place which overlooks the lake. Douglas fir, larch and spruce, particularly spruce, are the main trees, but hemlock and silver fir are used as well.

To complete the circuit: Thirlmere is afforested on either shore and has several places to park, and forest trails, at *308 156* and *315 167* (Helvellyn Gill). The great Ullswater has one important oakwood, **Glencoyne**, *385 185* (National Trust, 189 acres), while **Brothers Water**, *404 125*, has more woods than water. If you are tired of woods, Haweswater and Blea Water, each side of High Street, 2400 feet, have none.

Haweswater, a bastard between Mardale and the Manchester Corporation, has no decent stopping places (to avoid pollution), but the **Naddle Forest**, *500 155*, which climbs its south-east shore above the road is ancient oakwood on ground almost too steep to see it properly. The trees in the valley bottom are domesticated native – clothed in mossy stockings and rough-kneed with lichen.

253

THE NORTH OF ENGLAND
Eden

54 | 60
55 | 59
53 | 56 | 57

Landranger sheet 91

Lowther Castle has a 'wildlife adventure park' open until October and the road runs through the park, as do various footpaths. You are clearly informed where not to go. The castle is Gothic, and surrounded by fine parkland and woodlands down to the River Lowther.

The Lowther estates have large forests on the far side of the M6: Melkinthorpe Wood and **Whinfell Forest** – perhaps a whinberry fell before being planted. The forest is shapely but dull – and practical within. Still, there are mossy drystone walls and other reminders of the old countryside, and one is always conscious of the Pennine massif to the east. There are two walking routes from *585 267* on the road north from Cliburn.

Flakebridge Wood, Appleby

SCALE 1:316 800 or 5 MILES to 1 INCH
0 1 km = 0·6214 mile   5   10   Kilometres 15
0 1 mile = 1·61 kms   5   Miles 1

Appleby: Dufton Gill Wood *687 250*, ♀, *25 acres, WT*

Most of the wood has been cleared and replanted, but the Gill is interesting and can be followed south-east to Greenhow. The bed of the stream is of the deep-brown sandstone of which the handsome Dufton village is built. A branch of the Pennine Way leads up to High Cup Nick, 4 miles away, if you have the energy.

Flakebridge Wood can be seen from the Dufton road at *687 237* – a beautiful bit of oak and birch, which soon gives way to conifers. A well-known local walk is from Well House, *698 203*, north out of Appleby and across a Roman road, and then north-east to the wood and left along its edge to an old bobbin mill – birch was the wood for bobbins, now collectors' items – and back down by the mill lane.

Hoff Lunn *657 169*, ♀ ♣, *400 acres, fp, pf*

Haughr Lundre is, I believe, the Old Norse for hill copse, and it is a heathy birch coppice which has been largely put under spruce. You can park near the farm, called, less felicitously, Mount Pleasant (and which has a caravan field). Through a gate nearly opposite the farm the path follows the forest road, which is very rough, into the middle of the spruces. It is not an elegant or an interesting walk, until you reach a glade where the original vegetation remains. Here, insulated from all the world by the acres of spruce, is a completely silent place – perhaps to picnic on the hummocks of hair grass beneath the birches. There is, too, a considerable amount of pretty birchwood at the west border of the wood.

Kirkby Stephen: Smardale Gill Woods *741 082*, ♀, *3m of old railway, NR*

From the A685 south-west out of Kirkby Stephen near its junction with the A683 to Sedbergh, follow signposts to Smardale. The low bridge of the old railway before Smardale Hall (Farm) has steps up to the nature reserve. The walk is good along the line itself, but the woodland ½ mile along is only penetrable by enthusiasts: old hazel coppice with ash and birch, some oak, many old hawthorns and (the guide says) small-leaved lime, aspen and

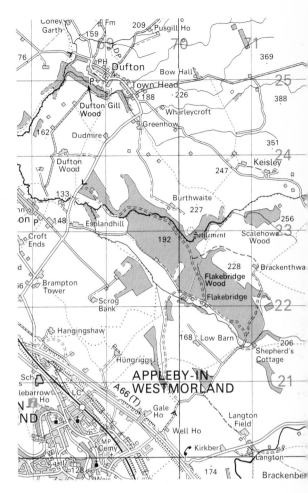

spindle. These last three I did not see, but it was rather dark and wet. Melancholy thistle and broadleaved helleborine were fine and other orchids were many but rather faded in late July. There are 50 breeding bird species also, says the guide: I saw a thrush and a blackbird and some wagtails. Kirkby Stephen has wooded walks up and down the river.

Upper Teesdale National Nature Reserve is very large, 6500 acres, and includes High Force, *882 283*. The complex geology supports many rare plants, including the non-woodland dwarf birch, *Betula nana*, in its only English home, where it has survived since the last ice retreated about 10,000 years ago.

54	55	59
53	**56**	57
	49	50

THE NORTH OF ENGLAND
The Forest of Bowland and North-West Yorkshire
Landranger sheets 97, 98, 102,

Bowland is traditionally a treeless, or woodless, forest, but it now contains a large plantation on Calder Moor above Dunsop Bridge, and, at its eastern side, the great Gisburn Forest, by the Stocks Reservoir. This is called by the Forestry Commission Bowland Forest. The 14-mile pass from Lancaster to Dunsop Bridge is the Trough of Bowland.

Trough of Bowland: Tower Lodge
600 539–610 539, ♀ ♠ (Scots pines), 1½m of road and streamside, pf
The Trough is justly famous and is not without trees – and at Langden Brook, hot dogs. Here a signed walk to Langden Castle begins promisingly enough in an avenue of trees but it is a moorland valley walk. People

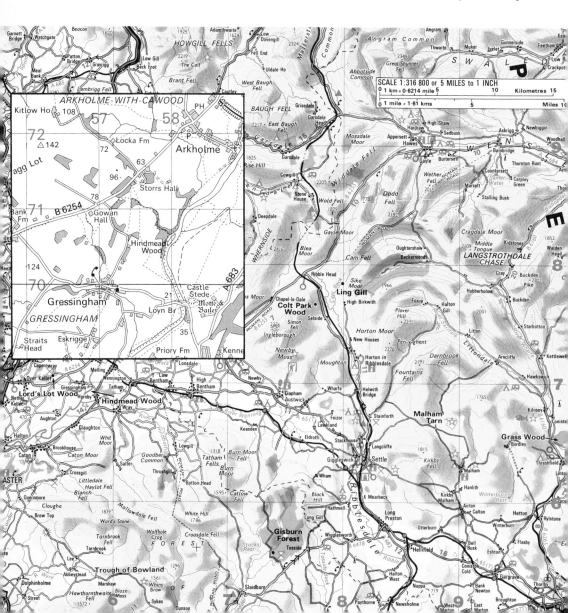

still 'do the Trough' on foot, more by car.

At a natural stopping place it was a lordly inspiration, about 1900, to plant clumps of beeches and pines. Not quite a wood, it is certainly a lovely place, only spoilt by the people who stop to admire it and leave little bundles of white paper all over the ground to show their appreciation.

Gisburn Forest *745 551, ♀ (♣), 3000 acres, forest rides and roads, FC*
The picnic place, Cocklet Hill, at the map reference, leaves nothing to be desired, at least by me. Some people like to sit at a table to eat their sandwiches, and there is a scrap of old oakwood dedicated to that function. As I left it was full of a large Indian family who looked marvellously colourful in the shade. As for walking, you might feel like a flea exploring a rug, but there is a path on the north side of Bottoms Beck to some waterfalls, and a bit of space to park here – just past the Causeway, where the great banks of pine and spruce look their most impressive. If it is hot, you will find it difficult to park in the shade, your butter will melt and your milk go sour. But it can't be like that very often. The Forestry Commission has left a narrow band of picturesque oak, ash and elder along a part of the road.

Hindmead Wood, Lune Valley *581 697, ♀, ¾m, easy, fp*
The footpath, to Arkholme, is marked near the elegant old Loyn Bridge which takes the road from Hornby to Gressingham. The wood is just a few beeches, oaks, sycamores, alders, and, not least, elms, on the steep pasture where the Lune has cut into the hillside. The alders are fine trees and there are bluebells and, later, forget-me-nots and delicately formed wood speedwell, with small balsam covering the floor in places.

Grass Wood, Grassington *982 655, ♀ ♣, 55 acres, NR within larger FC wood*
Here, in what is technically an ashwood on mountain limestone, you may find a great variety of plants and smaller trees such as are rarely found in northern England. Whitebeam, not common, is very visible growing out of the

In the Trough of Bowland

rock face, and there is a lot of very attractive burnet rose. Lily of the valley leaves are strewn among the fissures of the rocks and there is buckthorn and much guelder rose in pockets of deeper soil. Privet grows to almost tree proportions. Ash springs up everywhere and is threatened in places by maturing sycamores. Rock rose and bloody cranesbill grow, and herb Robert. A common flower in the late summer is the devil's bit scabious.

Within the Yorkshire Dales National Park, **Colt Park Wood**, *779 774*, is a National Nature Reserve of 21 acres, a strip of now rare, high (1100 ft) ashwood on the limestone of Ingleborough: by permit only. **Ling Gill**, *803 785*, is a ravine birch and ashwood with a rich limestone flora beneath, also by permit only. **Malham Tarn** has a Field Centre of the Field Studies Council, surrounded by oakwood, on its north bank. From Malham village, *900 625*, through Malham Cove to the Tarn and to Gardale Scar is National Trust land, over 3000 acres.

In Wensleydale, south-east of Bainbridge, the National Trust owns 288 acres of **Scar Top**, *959 892*, with a view of the whole dale.

Wharfedale and the Vale of York

The Strid

Bolton Abbey: *riverside 077 552* and **Strid Woodlands** *059 563* ♀ *(♣), various walks, easy but steep, pf (Chatsworth Estate)*

Bolton Abbey is not just a pretty place, but an industry. The nearest village down the Wharfe, Addingham, which sounds as if in Surrey, is black and narrow. It has a sophisticated furniture and antique trade, a pottery (Helyg), producing fine craft stoneware, a lacemakers' shop (Seba) and good local produce. (This is the only book on woodlands which tells you where to buy a crochet hook.)

The very large riverside parking field with a view of the Abbey and some symbolic sheep is relatively expensive. The tracery of the ruined windows glittered inimitably against a misty sun; the set piece all cushioned in rich oaks.

A mile and a half upstream is the capacious parking place for the Strid, less expensive, with a nature trail, also chargeable, but no one tried. 'Geological interest' is the term (on the notice describing half-a-dozen walks) for the beautifully water-sculptured, brown rocks of the stream, where it narrows to the width of the daring Strid. The trail starts in a grove of

258

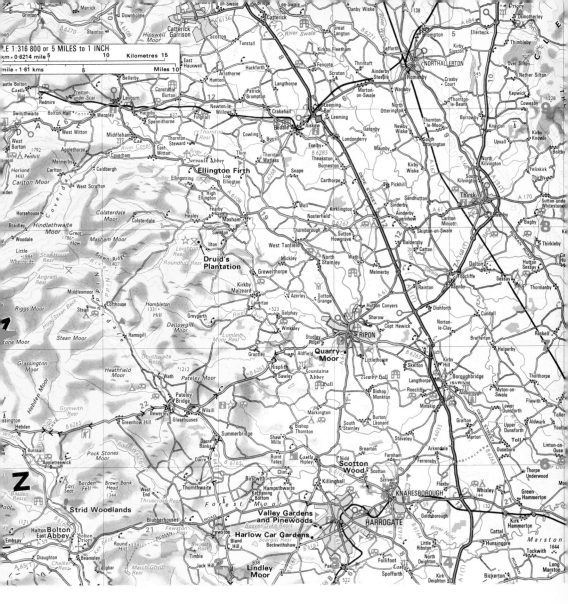

yews, and there is a legend that the monkish builders of the Abbey lived under the native yews when they arrived from the south.

In the steep valley everything chimes in; tawny Yorkshire fog grass, reddening rowan and the twisted oak leaning over the brown river and rocks: it is probably just as pretty at any season. There are nice beeches at the Strid itself. (See the map on page 260.)

Harlow Car Gardens, Harrogate, *283 539* (Northern Horticultural Society), is about 60 acres, more than half of which is woodland:

birchwood, oakwood, young arboretum with streamside garden, swamp cypress and woolly willow, and a good collection of trees chosen for what bark, flowers or foliage can do for gardeners. The woodlands contain a classical portico from the demolished Spa Rooms.

Across Crag Lane the **Valley Gardens and Pinewoods** bravely offer a nature trail with a good cross-section of native trees in a narrow space between sprawling legs of suburbia.

The Dales National Park
Nidderdale, Wensleydale and their tributary

Birk Gill Wood

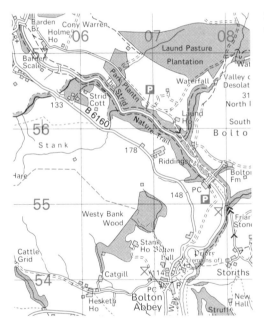

my help; although I did look at **North Wood** on Grimes Gill, *155 786*, and **Birk Gill Wood**, *140 815*. The first is out of reach, but its serene beauty may be admired from the road bridge: it is on Water Authority land. The second, on the Swinton Estate, is attractive and of great interest. A level, grassy stopping place by the Gill is inviting, though unfortunately the footpath is fenced off half a mile upstream and walking is thus limited. In that half mile the oaks are as natural and beautiful as you may hope to find, with a white drystone wall completing the pattern of lichens on the bark.

Jervaulx, the Abbey and Park beside the Ure meandering in lower Wensleydale, gives its name to a Forestry Commission complex which reaches up to the Stang in our Section 59 and down to Masham, with nothing much in between. There is a roadside picnic place on the A6108 at Ellington Firth, *193 843*, and one at Druid's Plantation, by a curious, ugly rock 'reconstruction' on a hilltop. A short walk here is waymarked and gives a good view back to Leighton Reservoir and Masham Moor.

On the east border of our section the North York Moors project woodland at Over Silton and at Mount Grace Priory. The National Trust owns 257 acres from Osmotherley to Whorlton, the Cleveland Way through the middle heading for the open moors.

dales lead in to the Yorkshire Dales National Park, our third largest. James Fisher waxes lyrical in the taut columns of his *Nature Lovers' Atlas*: 'A mosaic of limestone crags, gorges, sweeping moorland gouged by the Ice Ages ice, hidden woodlands; loved alike by farmers, adventurous potholers, tender artists and dedicated naturalists . . . .The scenery is consistently moving.' I am afraid you will have to seek out those hidden woodlands without

Dalby Forest *856 873 (Low Dalby Visitor Centre),* ♀, *forest drive and many walks, FC* South of Fylingdales High Moor the map is complicated by many dales, holes, ghylls, riggs (ridges), the dales often dividing at grains (groyns). Numerous nabs (knobs) and knoddles project from the riggs, and knowles (knolls) and toppings stick up at any level where harder Jurassic Sandstone stands among softer Jurassic Limestone, for what geological reason I cannot discover – islands in the warm Jurassic Sea? Scars (scarps, from the Norse *skarv* for a line of rocks) reveal a geology too complicated for me. Many trods (Norse *tra*, tread), causeys (causeways) and sprunts (some

sort of steep road) survive from early occupation by man. At Star Carr (old Norse *kjarr*, marshy woodland) near Flixton, south of Scarborough, was found a tool made from an elk antler, 10,000 years old. Star Carr, now inland, was then a coastal settlement, but is evidence of very early occupation. The hills were covered in woodland of oak, alder, birch, hazel, elm and pine, and clearing did not begin until some 5000 years ago in the New Stone Age. Excavations of New Stone Age burial mounds reveal the remains of forests below and of infertile podzol above (*podzol*, Russian for ash, describes the grey, leached soil of heathland and spruce forests). The Stone Age

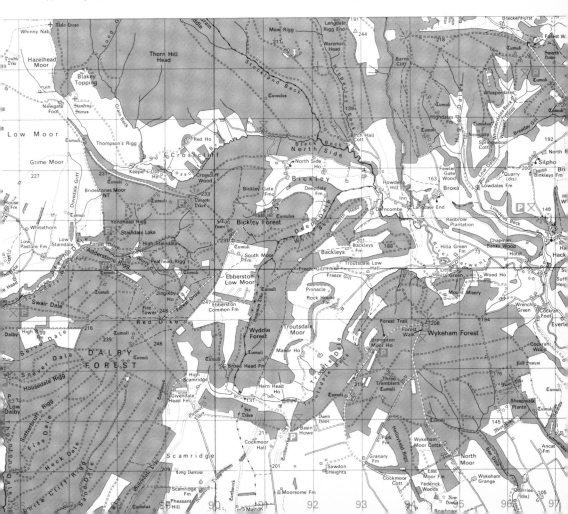

settlers would move on, once the humus-rich forest soil was exhausted, and moorland would ensue as beasts were grazed over the old sites.

The Forest of Pickering was a royal hunting ground, ceded by Henry III to his son Crouchback and thence to the Duchy of Lancaster. The deer had all gone by the seventeenth century, while sheep farming, long established by the monks of Rievaulx and other monasteries to the west, gradually took over the moorland. There were large rabbit warrens, where the rabbits were trapped by driving or luring them into brick-lined pits: a ghastly pie, but better than going hungry.

Nearly all this information comes from the Forestry Commission guide, *North Yorkshire Forests.*

By 1920 the Forestry Commission began to return the Dalby Moors to woodland. At first conifers were grown with difficulty on the tops, until in 1943 a giant plough was designed and built in Kirkby Moorside. Existing scrub and woodland was used to nurse up some plantations, and was then removed. Now the forest, still only supplying a fraction of Yorkshire's pit props, lies over the riggs like an unevenly woven overcoat, contrasted with the prettily tree-vested, sheltered dales.

Bridestones Moor *880 904,* ♀ ♣, *(and rocks) 1½ hours, easy FC, NT, NR (500 acres)*

Thornton Dale, the attractive village 2 miles east of Pickering, is the gateway to the Dalby Forest. To reach what must be the nucleus, and certainly is a good introduction to the

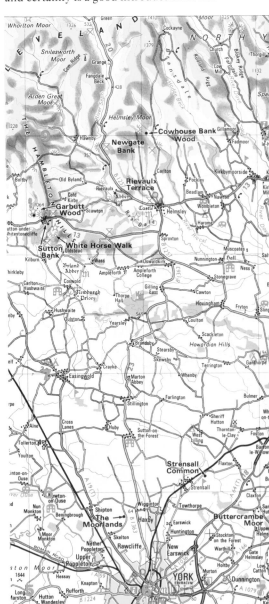

The Bridestones

terrain, Bridestones Moor, you have to pay the toll for the Forestry Commission's forest drive. What you do if you have no 50-pence pieces I leave to your imagination. Three miles from the information point at Low Dalby, via Snever Dale, Seive Dale and Swair Dale, you arrive at Stain Dale Lake picnic area, one of the nicer parking places on the route. A notice-board map clarifies the route to the Bridestones, which are prominent nabs, Jurassic vol-au-vents of perhaps 200 tons apiece made by the great Pastry Cook 150 million years ago, by what process I know not, nor do any of the reference books enlighten

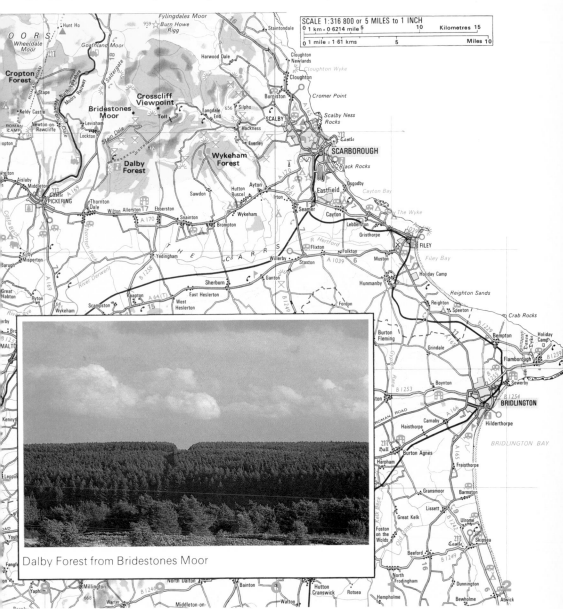

Dalby Forest from Bridestones Moor

me: 'passage beds', according to the *Nature Reserves Handbook*. Upland heath surrounds the stones, but the distant views are of forest ridges, while birch spreads over the bracken and heather. Sessile oakwood has remained in parts of Stain Dale and great plantations there of Douglas firs are already clear-felled.

Crosscliff Viewpoint *894 915*
This can be a 3-mile 'exciting' walk according to the leaflet, but it doesn't say where you start. (This leaflet is about the worst Forestry Commission production I have come across, very crude and vague in four awful colours and exorbitantly priced.) In fact you can drive to within ten minutes' walk of the viewpoint by a loop of the Forest Drive. It is worth visiting and there is an information board drawing to explain the scenery, which includes Blakey Topping, Fylingdales radar station and a prehistoric site on the ridge, with deciduous woodland and pastures below you.

There are eight other walks starting from different points on the Forest Drive. The 'forest drive' through Broxa Forest – miles of spruces, larches and pines – joins a straight, minor road through the trees, parallel to the A171; places to park and access to Whisperdale.

The Forge Valley Woods, near West Ayton, are a 90-acre National Nature Reserve.

At Wykeham, the next village towards Pickering, you can enter the **Wykeham Forest**, 3000-odd acres with three easy forest trails giving views over Trouts Dale, *933 885*.

Cropton Forest Drive and Walks
817 911 to 797 943, ⚲, *FC*
The drive from Levisham Station up through 5 miles of forest to Mauley Cross, north of Stape, is not now a toll road – a notice indicates 'permitted use'. The picnic place 1 mile north of the start, at Raindale Mill, is on a superb, wide grassy bank and there is a short easy walk across Raindale Beck. There is another stopping place, with a view, near the uncomfortably named Raper's Farm, and a walk to Needle Point begins 3½ miles along the forest drive, nearly at its highest point. Here the spruces are tall and the dark floor is

scattered, in September, with gleaming, golden fungi presumed to be members of the chanterelle family. At the Mauley Cross – a touchingly featureless, brown monolith – an Interpretive Trail is listed by the Forestry Commission, but I'm afraid I missed it in the drizzle. Larches border the road north and south of Stape.

At Keldy Castle are tasteful Forestry Commission 'cabins' to let: a very quiet holiday village deep in the forest. Equally quiet is the picnic spot by the Keldy Bridge, *777 908*. Richly growing oak and birch fill the valley.

The North York Moors National Park Committee maintains a nature reserve in Farndale, *666 974*, 1500 acres, for the daffodils.

Sutton Bank *516 831*, ⚲ ✿, *display, walks, viewpoints, NPA*
Between Thirsk and Helmsley and at the top of the cliff is the Park Information Centre, manned during business hours and nicely designed in a patch of birch heath. Very good sunsets can be watched from here: while I was doing just that my tape recorder was stolen from my car: be warned!

Garbutt Wood, *505 835*, is a 60-acre nature

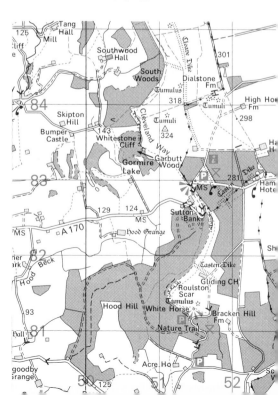

Bilsdale from Newgate Bank

reserve above and around the pretty Lake Gormire immediately north-west of the car park: woodland is largely scrubby with birch the dominant tree of the area. Heath continues on the surprisingly level top of the very steep, high, Whitestone Cliff, of sandstone, which rises to a thousand feet. There is a continuous path along the cliff edge, part of the Cleveland Way, and fragments of the ancient Cleve Dyke run parallel, north of Sutton Bank, while southwards is a wide green drove road, now probably obscured by conifers. South of the Sutton Bank Centre are three other parking places at the White Horse of Kilburn (Victorian, turf-cut, 300 feet long). A nature trail leaflet and a White Horse Walk leaflet are available at the centre, if it is open. Follow the road marked Yorkshire Gliding Club, east of Sutton Bank for a Forestry Commission White Horse Walk, *514 813*, including some coniferous woodland.

Newgate Bank *564 890*, ♀, *viewpoint, FC*
The B1257, Malton to Stokesley, is a favourite road of mine, now becoming rather busy with tankers and heavy lorries. Three miles north of Helmsley the Forestry Commission has arranged a splendid large car park using the conifers as walls to back up a viewpoint looking wide over Bilsdale. The breadth and clarity of the whole are in decided contrast with the claustrophobic Rievaulx Valley. The forest roads, north-east over Rievaulx Moor to East Moors and downhill to **Cowhouse Bank Wood**, connect with the Forestry Commission car park at *612 888*: a walk of 4½ miles. Take Landranger sheet 100 and a compass.

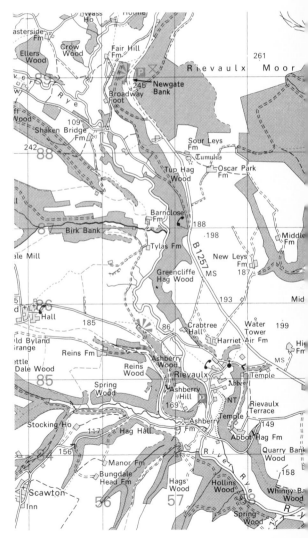

Teesside and Wear

Landranger sheets 88, 92, 93, 94

Clay Bank *573 035 viewpoint and 579 039, open moors, walks indefinite, FC*
Looking north is fine, but the view is much excelled by a similar position 300 feet higher, reached by the expenditure of a little energy. The Lyke Wake Walk meets the Cleveland Way here and staggers between boulders, heavily eroded, before setting off eastwards for the treeless rigours of Farndale Moor and Rosedale Moor. West of the road the long-distance path looks over woodland and sometimes enters it. The second car park is downhill amongst the trees.

Another Forestry Commission car park is above Great Ayton, *592 110*, **Gribdale Gate**, on the Cleveland Way about ¾ mile from Captain Cook's monument, which challenges another, older landmark; the nipple-shaped Roseberry Topping. The hills here enclose the peaceful bowl of the Ingleby Beck.

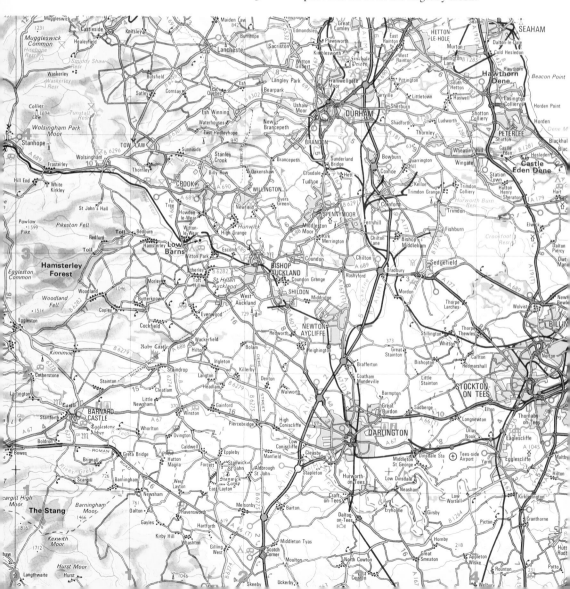

North-north-west, now enmeshed in Middlesbrough's outskirts, **Ormesby Hall**, *530 168*, remains lovely – preserved by the National Trust, with graceful perimeter woods. Great elms are gone from the park.

Within the North Yorkshire Moors National Park, near Whitby, is **Little Beck Wood**, a nature reserve of 32 acres; oak, ash, hazel and alder, *880 050*. In **Roxby Woods**, *755 168*, inland from Staithes, the road is on a ridge within a tree-filled valley.

There is little else to satisfy Teesside tree-lovers until, westwards, south and north of Barnard Castle, are two great lungs of forestry.

The Stang *023 075*, ♀, *1500 acres, 1m walk, FC*
The switchback road from Barnard Castle eventually climbs to a little car park at 1600 feet, through picturesque groupings of various

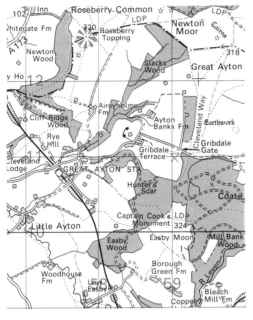

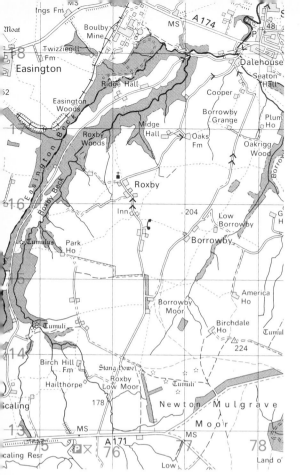

evergreens which contrast with cleared and replanted areas and even larger areas of blanket bog. There is said to be a good view, but visibility was reduced when I visited. A lovely wild place – but bitterly cold in the mist.

Hamsterley Forest *093 314*, ♀ ♣, *4800 acres, forest drive and walks, FC*
Aim for Bedburn from Hamsterley village. There was no toll point and the drive appeared to be open. It is in a rather dark valley, but has its moments. A bit more elbow room for native trees in the valley would be more cheering – it was planted with conifers as well as beeches long before the Forestry Commission took over.

Witton-le-Wear has a nature reserve at **Low Barns**, *161 316*, 84 acres: a mature alderwood. **Hawthorn Dene**, *433 456*, is a nature reserve of 165 acres which includes woods with snowdrops, hawthorn scrub, and badgers.

Castle Eden Dene, *410 387*, is a 300-acre mixed woodland valley or ravine, on limestone and clay, with a network of paths. There is a fine larch plantation: alder and bird cherry by the burn. The nature reserve is run by Peterlee town council.

The Stang

Kielder Forest and Tyneside

Landranger sheets 80, 81, 87

The Border Forest Park

One hundred and fifty-eight thousand acres or 245 square miles of once bleak and empty moorlands, where hardly a tree was to be seen half a century ago, are now Britain's largest forest. Even H. L. Edlin of the Forestry Commission, writing in 1958, admitted that there was 'a certain sameness about our Border spruce forests'. You have been at the Forest Centre at Kielder Castle only ten minutes before you are told that the forest is beautiful. It is a strange beauty; the visitor is more likely to react immediately to the immensity of the forest. On a clear day it really does look quite stupendous, as ridge after ridge of the hills reveals the dark, dense cover of even-aged conifers.

All the Border hills were once naturally forested with oak, alder, birch and pine, but centuries of grazing by deer, cattle and sheep, while the trees were gradually removed, reduced the land to grass – which first grew well in the woodland humus, then, gradually, exposed to the direct action of the weather, began to form peat. Eventually even the Cheviot sheep could not find sufficient to bite on and the moorlands, wild and remote, became a desert. Planting was begun at Smales in 1923, with Sitka and Norway spruce. At first each acre had 1750 turves cut by hand and a seedling planted in each inverted square, but from about 1940 various large-calibre ploughs were being used. By 1950 thinnings were already being extracted at the rate of 3 tons per acre. About 1500 men are now employed in the Border forests. They and their families live in gleaming villages which would make the best-kept southern village look quite a mess. The forest *is* beautiful, but it is almost the man-made beauty of a new, very efficient, machine.

Bakethin Reservoir, Kielder Forest

The English part of the Border Forest Park consists of the Wark, Redesdale and Kielder Forests, covering 125,000 acres (including 45,000 acres of peaty hilltops and grazing). The area is rich in ancient historical remains.

Kielder Forest: Kielder Castle *633 935,* ♣, *Visitors' Centre, FC*

The centre is reached via the North Tyne Valley road and the new forest road from Bellingham, or by the B6357 to Scotland, turning off at Saughtree. Kielder Castle is comfortably occupied by the Forestry Commission and is not generally open to the public. The Visitors' Centre has various amenities and wheelchairs can be accommodated. It is a pity that the Commission could not manage a few trees to shade the parking ground.

Forest walks of 1½ miles, 2 miles or 5 miles start from here. A Forest Drive is in effect a toll road east to Blakehopeburnhaugh on the A68 – there are several picnic places on the way with short waymarked walks. Around Kielder Reservoir are several more.

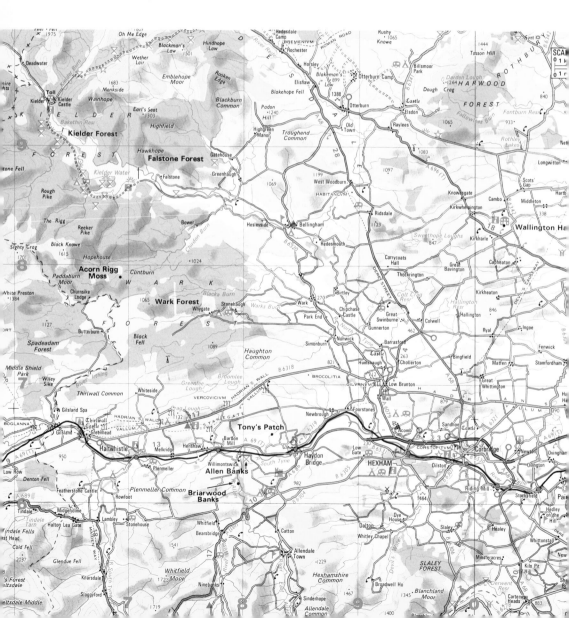

Wark Forest has a campsite at Stonehaugh and a picnic place, Warksburn, *790 762*, among tall spruces. There are three waymarked walks.

Falstone Forest, joining Kielder, Redesdale and Wark, has a picnic place at Sidwood, *777 890*, by Tarset Burn.

Allen Banks *797 643*, ♀ ♠, *riverside walks, NT, NR*
South of the Roman wall in pretty Allendale the National Trust has 193 acres; parking in the old kitchen garden of Ridley Hall, and

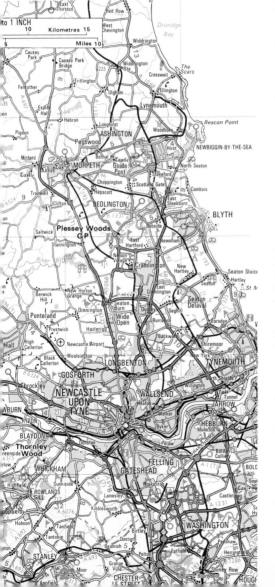

riverside woods for about 2 miles.

Briarwood Banks is a 29-acre nature reserve on the west bank of the Kingswood Burn, *796 622*. This is claimed to be the best fragment of ancient woodland in the Allen Valley.

Tony's Patch *820 654*, ♀ , *4 acres, NR*
Anthony Clissold led three expeditions to Iceland in search of whooper swans before drowning at the early age of 37 in a local reservoir. This tiny but wild wood is his memorial: healthy elms, with a wide range of other native trees, oak dominant, but only just, and a rich field layer by the Honeycrook Burn. Permit required.

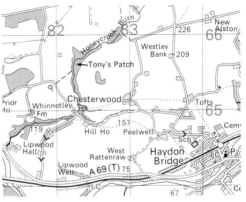

Plessey Woods, *240 799*, is a 60-acre Country Park, with fishing as well as woodland, near Bedlington. Gateshead has a nature reserve of 48 acres at **Thornley Wood**, *185 612*.

An ash-tree drive
Nearly 20 miles of ashes line the rolling road from Walwick, north of Hexham, along the A6079 and B6342 to Rothbury.

Before this, **Wallington Hall** (National Trust), *028 845*, is a really beautiful house and park; the woods are always open. Round about are no less than 12,970 acres of Trust lands, including Cambro village.

Nearer to Rothbury, a picnic place, *037 996*, is signposted '2 miles west', and this is a popular Forestry Commission stopping place close to the hills of Simonside.

North Northumberland
and Coquet Valley Landranger sheets 80, 81

Cragside, Rothbury *067 032 (entrance off B6341)* (♀)♠, *CP, drive, walks, NT*
The house was designed mainly by Norman Shaw, and finished in the 1890s for Sir William Armstrong, inventor and armaments king. It was the first house in the world to be lit by electricity from water power (and is probably the only one to have a hydraulic spit in the kitchen). You would be wise to park by the house and walk along the drive for there is little in store for you, except rhododendron. The seven parking places which constitute the Country Park element here are all attractive enough, especially the one called Crozier on a bare rock platform with heather in the cracks – but the walks are merely jungle tracks through the heavily overgrown *Rhododendron ponticum* varied by *Gaultheria shallon* (the first plant described by David Douglas in America).

There are some very impressive large firs and Douglas firs by the lower lake, but you can hardly step back to see them. The upper lakes supplying the hydroelectric system are quiet places for birds, including heron, with moorland beyond, young pine and larch and, a final irony, pylons.

Holystone Burn *942 020* and **Holystone North Wood** *945 028,* ♀*, 93 acres, NR*
West out of Rothbury through Thropton and Sharperton are more roadside ash trees, here glittering against the yellow morning and evening skies which seem to be characteristic of the cold beauty of this nearly perfect countryside surrounded by smooth, bluish hills. At Holystone is a well, associated first with St Ninian and now with the National Trust. A little further west is a Forestry Commission car park among spruces, grassy and fungusy; and indicated on a notice-board map are the old oaks of Holystone North Wood. The sessile oaks, over 38 acres, are varied in habit, some straight, some old

Oak and bracken in Holystone North Wood

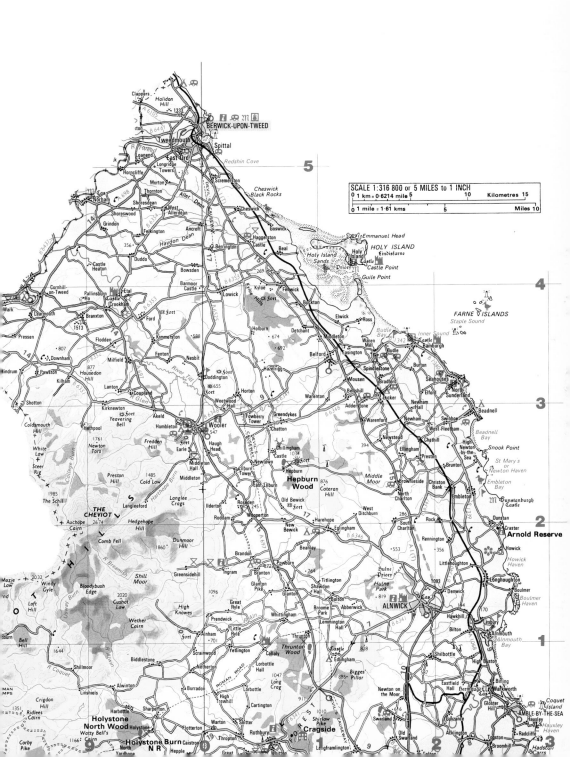

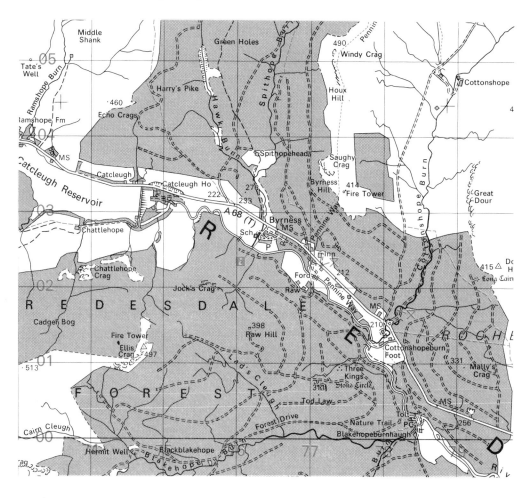

coppice trees, some obviously once exposed. Now they are sheltered by the spruces and one misses the sense of being enclosed in a native wood: only at the top is an open patch where the oak trees stop and heather, with a patch or two of birch, takes over. There are also rowans. In winter you may be glad of the shelter of the conifers.

Drive up the Ministry of Defence private road, or walk to where a forest road forks off about a mile from Holystone. Downhill from here is the Holystone Burn Nature Reserve with native trees which include juniper and oak, with bog myrtle. The Army range is beyond the reserve.

Hepburn Wood, *075 245*, near Chillingham Park (with its famous herd) south-east of

Wooler, has a picnic place and waymarked walks.

The **Northumberland National Park** is largely of moorland and is shared with the Ministry of Defence, who often have a lot of red flags flying. Maps are placed at suitable access or non-access points, but seek guidance from the Information Centre at Rothbury, where Forestry Commission leaflets for walks are available.

Redesdale Forest (offices at Byrness) has three picnic places on or near the A68, and trout fishing on a mile of the River Rede.

The **Arnold Reserve** at Craster is an old whinstone quarry with 3 acres of trees and shrubs: *255 197*.

Scotland

Loch Eck, Argyll Forest Park

Galloway and South Strathclyde

Landranger sheets 69, 70, 71, 77, 78, 83

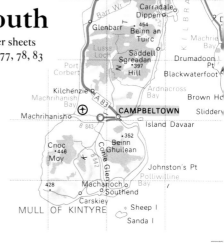

Forest of Ae *982 912, ♀, about 30 sq m, forest walks, FC*

Ae is just an ordinary Scottish forest, one of many, but it is half as big as the New Forest. Nothing much happens there, except that spruces grow, and burns rush from the hills into the Water of Ae. By the water is a level, grassy place for picnicking, surrounded by some of the spruces – tall Norway spruce about forty years old. The two walks are easy, and reveal little more than does the drive in, about $1\frac{1}{2}$ miles up the river from Ae village. (Stop at the Forest Office here for a leaflet.) There is a longer Green Hills Trail. Pony trekking can be arranged, as at many Scottish centres.

Tynron Juniper Wood *828 927, ♀ (♣), 15 acres, NNR*

Driving from Thornhill to Moniaive (pronounced Moanyive) on the A702 – do not turn off for Tynron village – the wood is on a hillside above the road, where a stream runs parallel on the other side.

The wood looks a little tame from the road, perhaps – almost like a cemetery. But beware; this wood is not for walking in. A path leads around the top of the wood from the by-road which turns off uphill. There are picturesque ash and cherry trees as well, and broom on the slope with gorse below. Juniper berries take two years to ripen from green to their lovely grey-bloomed blue. The name of gin, a Dutch invention, comes from that of the berries formerly supplying the flavour, now achieved chemically. Only here at Tynron can you appreciate the beautiful striated bark of the trees. The timber is hard and fragrant.

The strip of land between the road and the wood looks a mess, and it is a pity that the farmer cannot either give it up or be a bit less careless with barbed wire and other equipment.

Follow the road to Auchenbrack by Shinnel Water for bird cherry, white in June. The Forestry Commission has provided picnic places in the **Mabie Forest**, *950 711*, with old

sawmill shelter and four forest walks, and at **Dalbeattie Forest**, *836 600*, with walks on granite quarry tracks.

Galloway Forest Park

Loch Ken is known for oak and alder woods. There are many stopping places on the western lochside, along the A762, and here is the eastern border of the Galloway Forest Park, 240 square miles of forests, moors, mountains and lochs, and the Raiders' Road.

Forest Drive: Raiders' Road *654 720 (Loch Ken) to 546 752 (Clatteringshaws), ♀ (♣), 12m, FC*

The drive is really good value, especially at the south-east end where spruce is being extracted leaving fantastic great heaps of roots, and foxgloves. The Stroan Loch is beautiful. There are walks waymarked from here. Stands of trees are named, so that you can read as you flash by at a maximum 20 mph.

Clatteringshaws *552 765*

The name is so resounding that the 1900s' brutalist architecture of the dam comes as a shock. However, the view, over the great stony-margined lake, of the Rhinns of Kells and the Merrick (when visible), is unimpeded. The National Trust for Scotland looks after a boulder on which Robert the Bruce leaned in 1307, now nicely surrounded by Scots pines instead of dead Englishmen, and the Forestry Commission has a deer museum: neat, clean, informative, deserted and warm. Down the

road is the Deer Range with a viewpoint and a hide for hire.

Towards Newton Stewart on the A712 is a wild goat park and Murray's Monument. Murray was a shepherd's son who became a professor – you get a monument for that? **Talnotry** is a class B campsite, and there is a forest trail, *487 716*, of rough walking for 4 miles over uneven but interesting country. The leaflet, said to be essential, comes from the camp shop or other Commission offices.

Kirroughtree Forest, which includes the

Cow wheat in the Wood of Cree

campsite mentioned above, also has a forest garden walk, $\frac{1}{2}$ mile, which includes sixty tree species. The picnic site, *451 646*, is a little exposed but pleasant, by a village that is quiet in the way only a Scottish village can be. The neat, grey school now functions as an 'education centre'. The Forestry Commission provides a forest schoolroom with, amongst other things, a useful collection of rock samples.

Wood of Cree *382 708*, ♀ ♣, *200 acres approx, fp and forest road, RSPB*
Numerous streams pour down the steep, oak-covered banks, forming dark pools where rowans hopefully spread their delicate branches. The oaks, sessile of course, make a continuous pattern constantly varied by their wayward coppiced trunks, over a ground flora which itself varies from bilberry to cow wheat to grass or even honeysuckle, with patches of bluebell. There are very occasional birches. Such a large area of ancient oak coppice is a rarity anywhere and it should be highly valued.

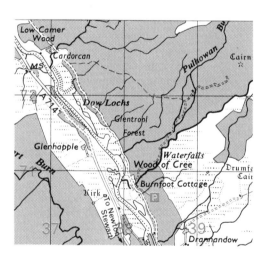

Loch Trool *416 803 (Bruce Memorial)*, *399 789 (Caldons Wood)*, ♀ *(♣)*, *FC*
Interest in the region centres on the Glentrool Forest; and the loch itself, narrow, serpentine and, one imagines, mysteriously deep under the slope of Merrick (2764 feet), is to me in a class of its own, always still and dark.

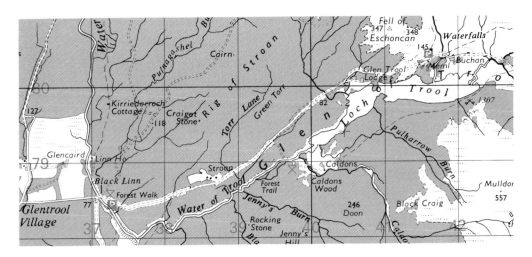

The Bruce Memorial at Loch Trool is decently below the skyline and is a good viewpoint. A trail all round the loch starts at the Caldons Wood campsite, entailing a rather embarrassing circuit of people's tents before starting a $4\frac{1}{2}$ mile tramp partly through oakwood remnants of the ancient forest. These are also evident on the short walk to the Martyr's Tomb, where the six martyrs were 'surprised in this house by Colnel Douglas, Lieutnant Livingston and Cornet James Douglas and by them most impiously and cruely murthured for their adherence to Scotland's reformation . . .', 1685.

Another trail goes back along the glen already traversed by road, and there is a stiff walk up the Merrick from the Bruce Stone – for experienced hill walkers.

It was late, and I had only time to pay my respects to the martyrs before the midges made life impossible. There are three ways of dealing with Highland midges, and these do not include ultrasonic devices or insect repellents. One is to keep moving, a hard discipline after a long day; two is to make a very smoky fire and sit in the smoke; three, and most effective, is to get indoors and to stay there.

North of the Merrick and approached by Straiton there are two forest walks: a hill walk and the Stinchar Falls Walk from Stinchar Bridge car park, *396 956*. There are picnic places at Tairlaw Toll, 5 miles south of

Straiton, and Changue, near Barr on the B734. Fishing is the main preoccupation here; details from the Forestry Commission, Straiton.

Culzean Castle *246 100*, ♀ ♠, *560 acres, easy walks, NTS, CP*
The z is silent. There is a fairly heavy charge to take your car in, justified by the amenities available, and the restoration of the Robert Adam farm building as the Park Centre, not to mention the upkeep of the superlatively fine castle and its gardens. Walkers may enter at various points: north of Maidens on the coast, at Morriston off the A719 and at Kennels Mount, *242 097*. An old railway track which skirts the policies runs from Maidens north-east to Dunure, and is a right-of-way for walkers.

Two pleasant, partly shaded picnic places present themselves as you drive into the main castle car park. You can take your car on, to the Deer Park (herd on view) and Walled Garden or to the Swan Pond, a mile from the centre. The Happy Valley Wood, roughly south of the Walled Garden and east of the Swan Pond, is the home of some remarkable conifers, but fine silvery beeches are perhaps the most attractive woodland feature in spite of the exotics.

Lambdoughty Glen, Straiton *392 052*, ♀ ♠, *22 acres, $\frac{3}{4}$ hour walk, pf*
The modest joys of Lady Hunter Blair's walk have been available to all since 1840, a gesture

of the 3rd Baronet of Blairquhan in memory of his wife. There are two linns, one with a Leyland cypress, and the other named after the poet Rossetti, who, staying nearby, came and contemplated suicide by drowning – too many bannocks perhaps. Sitka spruce is planted in the glen, and the leaflet, price two pence, on sale at the minute car park, reminds us that Britain spends more than £3000 million a year importing timber.

A desert intervenes between Upper Nithsdale, where, on the heights, people are content to live in concrete huts and keep bulls, and Clydesdale. But even the Upper Nith has moments of beauty. The desert was broken for me by the beautiful valley of the Crawick Water traversed by the B740. The town of Douglas is well wooded and in fine country, but the Forestry Commission's Douglas Forest has no apparent access, only a connection with the nature reserve below.

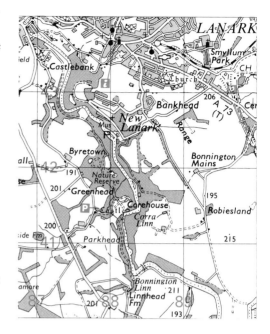

Lanark: Falls of the Clyde
878 415 (west bank), 881 423 (New Lanark), ♀ ♣, 2m of fps on each bank, pf, NR, FC
Glimpses of authentic oak and alder boscage can be got through the invading sycamores and inevitable spruces. There are great trees by the ruined Corra Castle, and water shoots forward with enormous force and sound, native trees projecting themselves into the mist.

The nature reserve has a total of 127 acres on both banks, and woodland is being converted to broadleaves. There are supposed to be kingfishers and otters, but the whole affair is a bit too close to Lanark for comfort, not that I've got anything against Lanark. A power station in concrete, cathedral style, is just below Corra, and is organized to divert the water that it needs from the falls, sometimes all of it.

Island of Arran
Arran Forest has two Forestry Commission picnic sites; off the A841, 2 miles south of Brodick, *017 343*, and off the Ross road, *012 297*, ½ mile from Lamlash Bay. The National Trust for Scotland has Brodick Castle, its garden, Country Park and woodland walk, and Goat Fell, 603 acres; 40,000 visitors a year.

Kintyre: Carradale Forest
Carradale Forest's information point is at *803 382*.

Scottish bluebells by the Falls of the Clyde

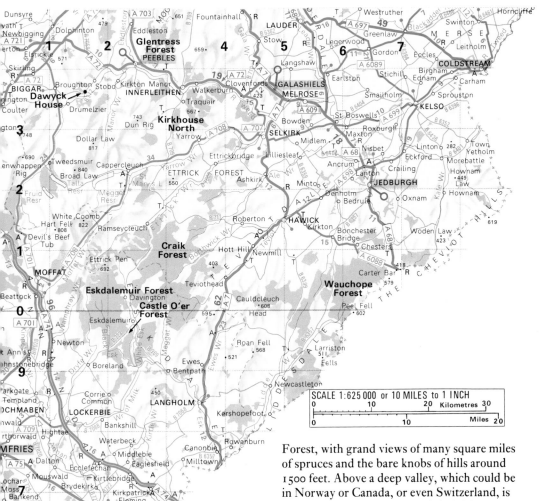

SCOTLAND
The Border Forests

Landranger sheets 72, 73, 79, 80

Forest, with grand views of many square miles
of spruces and the bare knobs of hills around
1500 feet. Above a deep valley, which could be
in Norway or Canada, or even Switzerland, is
the pine-shaded picnic site of Piet's Nest, a
high, quiet place, not much frequented and
with no irritating facilities.

Wauchope Forest *586 052 (Piet's Nest),*
♣, picnic place, FC

Driving northwards from Kielder village soon
brings you to the Scottish border, marked by a
plain notice and an improved Scottish road
surface (a pretentious heraldic sign for England
if you are coming south). A right turn on to the
B6357 takes you climbing to the Wauchope

Craik Forest *349 082 (Craik village),* ♣,
forest walks, 1½ and 3m, FC

The B711 west from busy Hawick has
wonderful views over Teviotdale. Craik, a
forest village, is signposted on a No Through
Road, 8 miles of it, along Borthwick Water, in
a rich, lovely valley with many ancient
settlements. The parking place is in the tiny

Wauchope Forest from near Piet's Nest

By Peebles the **Cardrona Forest**, Forestry Commission, offers a walk from a quiet parking place, and at Kailzie is an open-air restaurant, surely a brave venture: the view across the trees is really beautiful on a fine evening. Here the Forestry Commission's **Glentress Forest** parking place is a bit public, *285 399*, and threatened by a large tank within 20 feet of which no naked flames are to be used: but there is a picnic place up in the woods on one of the four trails, which include a short walk 'for the less energetic'. Towards Galashiels is the Forestry Commission's Ashiestiel Bridge walk. There is a viewpoint at The Nest, *433 354*, above the Tweed, with a painting in oils and pokerwork to help identify landmarks.

Dawyck Arboretum *163 353*, ♀ ♣, *Royal Botanic Garden, Edinburgh*
The Dawyck beech is a fastigiate form very like the Lombardy poplar, but nicer. There is a beech walk here too, the woods of surpassing beauty with silver firs and pines as well. Choose a fine day and go by Policy Bank, with large, perfect examples of such rare beauties as Armand's pine *Tsuga mertensiana, Picea breweriana* and *jezoensis, Calocedrus decurrens, Chaemaecyparis nootkatensis* 'Pendula', *Abies veitchii, homolepis, magnifica, mariesii*; and lesser, but there, *delaveyi* and *concolor*, one with the lovely silver spine along the shoot, the other with wide-spaced, lax and slightly clammy bright green leaves.

Above to the south-west are large Douglas firs, and on a sweep of lawn by the chapel very large Sitka spruce and strangely naked-trunked *Picea orientalis*. Here a Douglas fir is unusually spreading and clumsy, and enormously thick in the trunk.

The house, vague but decent in style, with its good lawns surrounded by crumbling, grey urns, contrasted with a field of mown hay beyond, and surrounded by these magnificent trees, looked the essence of peace and security in the late-afternoon sun. Useless, of course, to be sentimental about old unities, old continuities. But it was more than sentiment that made this tree garden, and it was not done in a lifetime.

The house remains private and is not open.

village with a picnic place beyond and walks in the forest – to Wolfcleuchhead Waterfall, 3 miles total, or a short circuit; or, if you feel like it, 8 miles due south to Eskdalemuir. **Eskdalemuir Forest** is large and abuts onto Castle O'er Forest, which has a picnic place near the Black Esk River, off the B723, not marked on the 1975 OS 1:50,000 map.

The B711 passes by Alemoor Loch and alongside a broad arm of the Craik Forest, where the young trees share the uplands with herds of sheep and cattle, and all is quiet and dignified.

If you go by St Mary's Loch (A708) then north by the B709 you come to a charming picnic place, *315 317*, planted with grey alders, and provided for the public by the **Kirkhouse North Estate**, in memory of John Parker, MP, a great tree man. You are invited to walk and not to leave litter. It is not clear exactly where you walk – much has been clear-felled – but the footpath goes through a pretty birchwood before disappearing. Climb to the forest road to explore further. A few feet of elevation here brings a richly rewarding view. As for litter, you'd hardly believe that people would throw things into this lovely stream.

64 65 South Argyll and Loch Lomond

ARGYLL FOREST PARK

Britain's first Forest Park was established in 1935, ten years before any English National Park, and covers 100 square miles, with 165 miles of forest roads open to walkers. Older stands of spruce, sea lochs and great mountains are its features, but there are also notable arboreta and gardens within the Forest Park.

Ardgartan Forest

The north of the Argyll Forest Park has its centre at Ardgartan, *275 030*, with a Forestry Commission campsite (class A) and fairly tough walking, waymarked in colours, from 3 to 12 miles. Shorter walks can of course be worked out. There is a Forestry Commission guide to the Forest Park. A small arboretum is at Lochgoilhead, near the Forest Office.

Benmore Forest *192 886 (Finart Bay, Ardentinny), 2 walks, fairly stiff, FC*

The forest around Kilmun Hill and the shores of Loch Long is picturesque, being largely of old-established Norway spruce and in a magnificent setting. The picnic place given is on the sandy beach of Loch Long. The walk from Ardentinny to Carrick Castle, 5 miles north, starts here. A walk, Black Gates to Puck's Glen, starts near the parking ground, *144 845*, for Benmore Arboretum.

The road, the A815, runs for 10 miles along the east shore of Loch Eck and gives access to a wide range of woodland. The forestry is productive, but mixed, and native trees flourish by the waterside. The glen, running north to south, and sheltered by 2000-foot mountainsides, is a world apart, with its own weather, usually wet, always mild – and unforgettable when the sun does come out.

There is a Forestry Commission picnic place at the side of Loch Eck. This, and Glen Finart, are part of the Commission's Benmore Forest, which is itself part of the Argyll Forest Park. A guidebook is available for the 165 miles of forest roads which are open to walkers.

Benmore (Younger Botanical Gardens) *144 854,* ♀ ♣*, 56 acres arboretum, 2 suggested walks, Royal Botanic Garden, Edinburgh*

The Younger Botanical Gardens surround Benmore House, now a hostel, and fittingly commemorate the gesture of H. G. Younger in presenting the great Benmore estate to the nation. His predecessor, James Duncan, planted 6,488,000 trees in this valley, creating a forest of 1622 acres.

As you enter the gardens (open daily from April to October) you cross the swift River Eachaig and are at once between two lines of giant *Sequoiadendron*, raising their saps to 130 feet or more – a disturbing opposition of watery forces to those sensitive to such things. But the trees, like the many other tall conifers here, are dwarfed by the cloud-topped mountains. By the house are some large and particularly opulent *Araucaria*. The warm, moist atmosphere of this region suits all the firs, and there is a Chinese Fir Garden at the extreme south-west of the arboretum. Here you will find the only mature specimens in the country of Delavay's fir, and beautiful they are, with thick, low-sweeping branches flashing streaks of white as you move. Only varieties of this tree are known elsewhere in Britain.

Besides the invariably well-grown conifers, there are old and young broadleaved trees, *Nothofagus* among them, a small and a large katsura, and several very healthy Hupeh rowans, a favourite here. There are 250 species of rhododendron, for most of which you have to climb the hillside above the house. This is the longer of two walks recommended in the booklet, which has pleasant photographs and a useless map.

Kilmun Arboretum *165 822,* ♀ ♣*, 200 acres, 3 suggested walks, FC*

Kilmun Arboretum is free and open all the year round. The approximately rectangular plots date from about 1930 and 1950, hung precipitously over the Holy Loch at what feels like 45 degrees or more to the horizontal. The climb is hard but worth every puff of it, if only for the view which is not spoilt – but perhaps it ought to be – by the American submarine supply ships in the loch.

Two groups of *Eucalyptus* plots can be reached easily from the forest road which runs at a gentle gradient from the south-east (church) entrance. The forest plots as a whole contain the widest selection of eucalyptus to be seen in Britain. Most of the trees are about thirty years old.

Nearly all Kilmun's specimens are in plots

of about $\frac{1}{4}$ acre, which means that one is usually looking at a wood of a single species. It is worthwhile to climb right to the top, where at 1000 feet the ground begins to level out and an open patch of Sitka spruce reveals an unexpected poetry in this overworked species.

There are paperbark birches (looking a bit damp and grey), lovely, shiny barked, young, grey alders (in the south-east) and red oaks and southern beeches (north-west). There are plots of monkey puzzles and dawn redwoods.

Kilmun, though designed for pure forestry

purposes, is full of a sort of wildness and has an invigorating aura. You will be tired at the end of a day there, but you can hardly fail to love the place. And if you have a few acres, or yards, of Scotland to plant with trees, Kilmun can provide excellent guidance.

Crarae *990 976, ♀ ♣, pathways and 'circular pathways', 800 yds to 1m, open daily, pf*
Crarae Woodland Garden has been built up over eighty years; so quickly do great trees grow here that only one original survives, a

Thuja plicata, western red cedar, 106 feet high, near the Crarae Burn below the house (Crarae Lodge). There are dozens of notable trees of which I will single out *Nothofagus dombeyi* and *Eucalyptus coccifera*, Honda and tiger tail spruces, Korean pine, Macedonian pine. There are attractive and vigorous birch plantations and many incidental beauties; hybrid poplars and 'exotic' maples among them. You can, of course, ignore the species altogether and enjoy a beautifully shaped garden, with a footbridge over the miniature gorge of the burn and many pleasant places to stop.

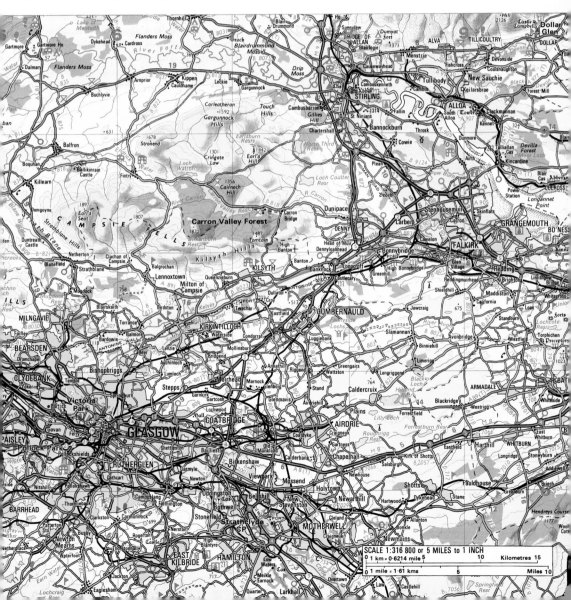

Betula pendula, Loch Awe

On the east side of Loch Awe the little road, the B840, reveals many attractive native trees heavily decorated with lichens: wych elm, alder, cherry, birch and sallow, with, rather surprisingly, chestnut as well as sycamore. There are National Nature Reserve oakwoods beyond in Glen Nant, and, steep, at Glasdrum.

For the more adventuresome the A83 continues south-west to the Forests of Kilmichael, Knapdale, Carradale and Arran: Knapdale Forest walks information from the Forest/ District Office, Whitegates, Lochgilphead. At Taynish, *725 830*, on the west bank of Loch Sween, is one of the largest remaining Scottish oakwoods in a National Nature Reserve of 800 acres.

Loch Lomond
All things come to an end, and a great glacier which flowed and scraped its way from Ben Lomond southwards eventually melted when it had made a trough large enough to contain 93,000 million cu ft of water. How many frosty winters and slightly less frosty summers it took

to do this I cannot compute, but it left us the largest lake in Britain, then open to the sea. After the melting of the ice, the land, relieved of its load, rose sufficiently to separate the loch from the sea. It is now a few feet above sea-level and contains a fish, the powan, once marine, that adapted to life in freshwater here and in Loch Eck, and nowhere else.

The wide southern shores of Loch Lomond are sandy, gravelly or stony with the remains of the sea-shore and the terminal moraine, while the upper, northern part, deeply excavated as far as 600 feet, has steep sides of pre-Cambrian rock. The natural vegetation of all the shores is a rich woodland of alder, birch and oak, with oak dominant, and with rowan and hazel up to 500 feet above the water – and further on the banks of streams. The woods contain and support a rich and varied bird population.

The oaks were used and neglected, cut for charcoal and fuel and then grazed by cattle and goats – the surest way to get rid of woodland – until the middle of the eighteenth century, when the demand for oak bark for tannin increased. Remaining oaks – 1800 acres in the

Oakwood, Loch Lomond

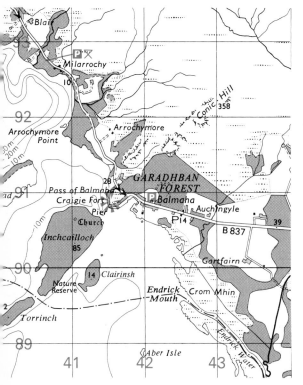

lost their soil and support the trunks well above the pebbles – an extraordinary effect as of mangroves which achieve the same effect in reverse by sending down roots from floating stations. A few yards inland, oakwoods, with their history of coppicing, are full of character.

Walks are laid out, one by 'ancient routes of iron smelters, slate quarriers, foresters and crofters, passing through the ruined township of Wester Sallochy and another to Sunny Bay by the bonny banks of the Loch'.

A lochside ring walk, very short, enables one to review the scenery from a car park, *405 927*, 1½ miles north of Balmaha.

From Balmaha you can visit the nature-reserve island of Inchcailloch. Here is a nature trail of 2½ miles, said to be one of the finest woodland walks in Scotland. 624 acres of Loch Lomond including five wooded islands and the marshy shore by Endrick Water are a National Nature Reserve. The islands are said to contain the best of Scotland's oakwoods – that is, least grazed and with the richest flora. Two small islands, Bucinch, which is wooded and with yews, and Ceardach, are the property of the National Trust for Scotland.

The Country Park of Balloch Castle at the south end of the loch, *395 830*, has a nature trail, shelters for wet-day picnics and fine grounds with views of Ben Lomond.

In Glasgow there are no less than ten nature trails – for information telephone Glasgow 221 7371/2. Victoria Park, *538 675*, Scotstoun (Dunbarton Road, A814), fortified on two sides against the fast traffic, has the strangest woodland walk of all: a fossil forest in a Victorian shelter. It is well worth seeing, particularly as the park has beautiful trees.

Pollock Park, *555 625*, is now famous for containing the Burrel Collection of very expensive bric-à-brac in a well-designed 'woodland museum'.

Country Parks at Muirshiel, *319 628*, in the remote Calder Valley and Gleniffer Braes, *450 608*, south-west of Paisley have woodland, and the great Strathclyde Country Park of 1601 acres, the third largest in Britain, has everything, with the M74 through the middle. At Lochwinnoch, *354 585*, is a large RSPB

Buchanan Woods particularly – were coppiced. Most of the woods, however, were replanted, using broom, pine and larch as nurses for oak, sometimes with beech, ash and sycamore. Latterly, the Forestry Commission has acquired the Buchanan Forest, which includes much of East Lomondside. Ben Lomond is now owned by the National Trust for Scotland.

From Balmaha, *421 909*, to Rowardennan Lodge, *359 993*, where there is a Forestry Commission campsite (class A), footpaths go on for many miles north along the shore and east as far as Loch Ard.

The little motor road, which sometimes cuts through rock and slate, is in great contrast with its snarling, overloaded counterpart on the west bank. There are four main parking places.

Buchanan Woods *380 958 (Sallochy)*, ♀, 1¼m and ¾m, FC

The shores of Loch Lomond in summer usually expose the roots of alders which have

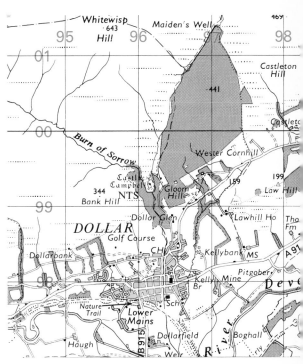

Dollar Glen

reserve, with some woodland, on the west bank of Aird Meadow.

North-east towards Stirling is the **Carron Valley Forest**. Forestry Commission picnic places are at Spittal Bridge – a winner this, on a river island breached by stepping stones, with safe paddling, *723 839*, at the eastern end

of the reservoir; and at Sir John De Graham's Castle (who ever heard of anyone called Sir John De Graham?) just east of Gartcarron.

Dollar Glen *965 986*, ♀, *1½m, steep, NTS* 'Dolour' it must be surely, where the Burn of Sorrow, flowing interminably, has cut deep into the rocks. Castle Campbell glooms above, while fairly well-to-do bungalows on Gloom Hill gaze across at Bank Hill. There is a nice oakwood on the Gloom side. The younger residents here have fought back, and installed a prize-winning outdoor gymnasium in the town field at the foot of the glen. Here the footpath up to the castle begins, with a warning to the unfit that the climb is steep. It isn't *too* bad, and, with well-maintained steps, walkways and footbridges, there is no rock scrambling to do.

It is scattered with empty sweet packets, but the glen is filled with the richest of foliage, and the rocks hung with ferns and moss. The walk is so intricately laid out between the rocks and even under them as to be almost a caricature of the Grotesque. Dollar Glen is the countryside equivalent of the ghost train at the fair.

SCOTLAND
Lothian, Dunbar and Duns

Landranger sheets 58, 65, 66, 67

The Royal Botanic Garden in Edinburgh, *244 754*, is worth anyone's time. A gallery of modern art is at the top of the round hill, which is swathed in trees like an embroidered crinoline. I noted some really good oriental white birches and, working upwards, good exotic oaks, ashes and a sculpture I thought at first was some sort of civil-engineering installation or a squash court. At the top are *Sorbus* among others, very clean barked for the middle of a city, with a Marino Marini sculpture like an untutu'd Degas dancer, going a bit grey. In the gardens below are interesting

crabs, many quite edible, and hawthorns, amongst them *Crateagus crus-gallii*, the cockspur thorn. There is a surprising sweep of heathers and conifers, miniature ones giving an illusion of perspective against the taller versions – surely a clever use of these over-used garden dwarfs. A fine luminous weeping willow is by the lake, and there is more to see beyond – walled gardens and glasshouses.

Within 9 miles of the centre of Edinburgh is a trio of Country Parks showing a leaning towards golf and water sports but still worthwhile attempts to make trees accessible to all.

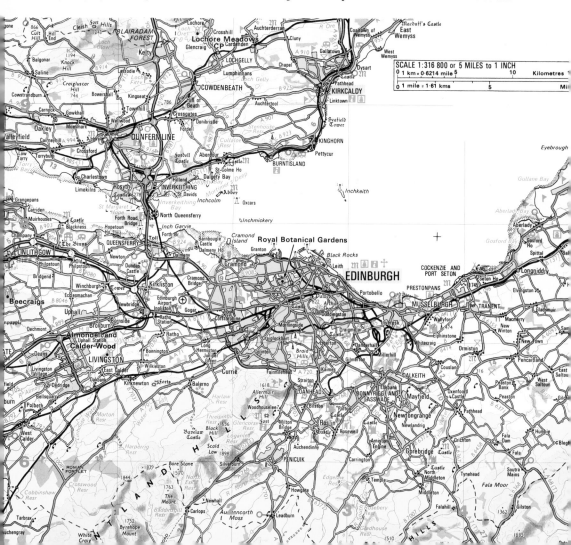

In West Lothian are **Beecraigs** *008 743*, *793 acres*, old forestry land and the reservoir a bird sanctuary. **Almondale** and **Calder Wood**, *076 677*, or *091 698*, *222 acres*, riverside woodlands. These Country Parks are well signposted from main roads and are always accessible to walkers.

In Mid Lothian is **Vogrie** *576 633*, *257 acres* of parkland. Vogrie is a new Country Park with oldish estate perimeter woods and very old policy trees, obviously loved as much for their eccentricities as their excellences. The walled garden, now a nursery and garden centre, has a fantastically well-built wall, and not much of the rest comes up to it, but there are a gorgeous unmown patch of grass – with the familiar lowland cocktail of meadowsweet and willow herb – and a grotto-like copse of cherry laurel. Coppiced limes are apparently hybrid but without the usual faults of twiggyness and aphids.

John Muir CP, Dunbar *652 788 and 626 810*, ♣, *1668 acres (200 acres woodland), pathless sands, LA*
John Muir was a native of Dunbar who migra-

ted to California aged eleven years. He was one of those far-sighted enough to create one of the first American National Parks, Yosemite, in the same year, 1890, as the National Park of the Giant Forest and the General Grant National Park, now all part of the Sequoia National Park.

This wide beach with its view of the Bass Rock is a good memorial. There are no giant sequoias, but you could not expect them in the sand. The pines are a low-profile group, rides streaked with ragwort and vistas stopped by sea buckthorn: fascinating, and a welcome retreat from the sun when I visited. But you will be drawn naturally to the wide shore: pink

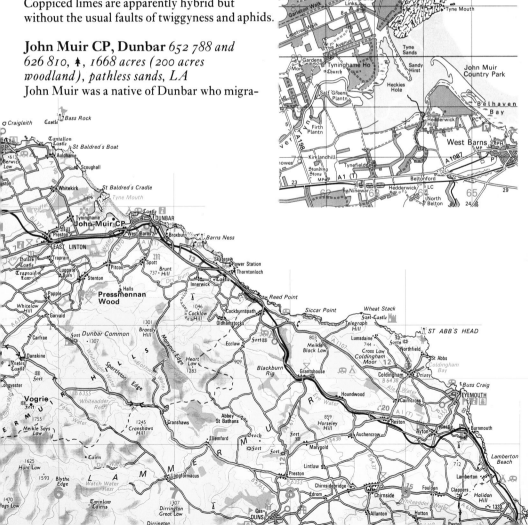

Pressmennan Wood

sand, whitish green grass and miniature forests of sea spurge, leaves as if made of soapy plastic. Maram spikes inscribe circles in the sand. Sea campion, an unlikely heliotrope, adds to a dazzling colour scheme against a sea of inky blue-black.

The large parking place (given first above) is shadeless and has the best designed WCs in Britain, a sawn-off broch shape perfectly suited to the dunes. Scots architecture rarely indulges in half-hearted compromise. The north-east compartment of the park, with more mature pines on the shore, is approached by long, shady lines of Tyninghame Estate trees, via the A198 to North Berwick.

Pressmennan Wood, Stenton *621 726,*
♀ ♣, *200 acres, 2m walk, FC*
This north-facing slope has wide views reached after a longish slog through a lot of Norway spruce. Oaks near the cark park are supported by guylines, their companion softwoods having been extracted, leaving them unable to cope with the strong winds. Towards the top of the walk a few oaks remain amongst

pines. Descending, never quite to the lake, the path enters dark *Thuja* and *Tsuga* amongst birch and ash, and there are some large beeches and oaks, about 160 years old.

Stenton village is handsome with red tiles, all about is quiet and lovely except for the Forestry Commission car park, which is quiet and dirty. Elms, wych and hybrid, are magnificent by roadsides.

Over the Lammermuir Hills to Whiteadder

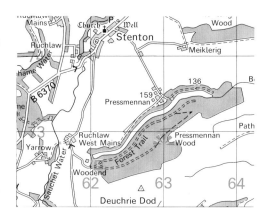

Hen Poo, Duns

gives you the same view as from the wood, even broader, with purple heather in the foreground instead of pole conifers. Bees here are transhumed for the heather, transported while they sleep at night by white-clad young ladies in veils. It's true, because I saw it happen! Whiteadder Water is a last home of native oaks, elms and alders, but most spectacular just below the reservoir, with flat pasture full of multicoloured cattle and dark, forested hills beyond.

Duns Castle *783 543, ♀, 3 walks, 2–3m, NR (SWT)*

The town of Duns is supposed to have an oakwood. I could only find the policy woods of the castle, open as a nature reserve, with the lake, agreeably called Hen Poo (Scots for Swan Lake?) and several shady walks. Duns Law, easily accessible from the town, is an ancient fort, 650 feet, patrolled by cows which use the stumps of once massive oaks as rubbing posts. A patch of pines obscures the view of the castle, which is private and much the most impressive thing in the landscape – positively

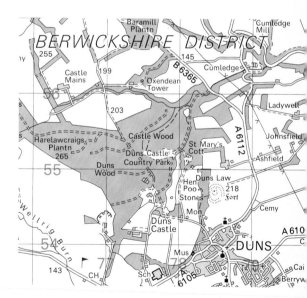

elephantine. You can enter the estate woods also by a sort of back door from the B6355 at *785 561* (dogs not allowed). Here you do not have to march down carriage drives before reaching the trees.

293

68	69
66	67
64	65

SCOTLAND
Central Highlands and North Argyll
Landranger sheets 40, 41, 42, 48, 49, 51, 57

Black Wood of Rannoch *573 565*, ✚,
walks 1 to 5m, forest roads 3m, FC
The Forestry Commission took over the Black
Wood of Rannoch in 1947, after 8000 trees had
been removed during World War II – these
were only available because, scheduled for
clear felling in 1918, the wood had been saved
by the ending of World War I. There was an
earlier period of Government ownership in the
eighteenth century when the commissioners of
forfeited Jacobite estates managed the
woodlands carefully, even removing competing
birch and alder. Apart from these two periods
of decency, the wood was ill-treated and
exploited, only its relative inaccessibility, and
the small size of the population it served,
preventing its destruction. Floating the timber
down the Tummel and the Tay does not *look*
as if it could have been easy, and many pines
were stolen – some were even 'washed up' on
the shores of Holland; a nice variant of the
back-of-a-lorry story.

Black Wood of Rannoch

Birches accompany the pines, increasing in frequency at the edges. Regeneration, on extraordinarily uneven bog, bilberry and heather, is obviously fine. Several varieties of the native pine are easily picked out: columnar and rounded crowns appear side by side, and there are many other variations of form, the reasons unknown. Great pines about *573 565* are heavily buttressed, and there is also variation in the bark pattern between 'plated' and 'flaky', with old trees very ruggedly ridged rather like Monterey pines. Juniper is fairly common. It is the variety of form, the curious grouping and the vigour of growth at all stages which give this wood its character – and make it a valuable source of information on genetic and other variations. (See map on page 296.)

At Loch Tummel there is the Queen's View (and it is a gorgeous loch, among high hills), and then the Forestry Commission's Tummel Forest walks, with slightly less regal views, but with native woodland on limestone rocks. The wetlands between the large lochs are fascinating.

North of Pitlochry the woods of Blair Atholl are famous. They were planted with hardwood trees by the Dukes of Atholl in the eighteenth and nineteenth centuries. The Pass of Killicrankie contains a woodland nature reserve of 55 acres and there is a much larger RSPB reserve here, with restricted access.

Callander Craig 636 093, ↟, 1¼m, steep, FC and LA

Above the town to the north is Callander Craig, a ridge rising some 650 feet above the town in a matter of yards. You can drive half way up, to a parking ground arranged for the Bracklinn Falls (footpath eastwards) and the Forestry Commission's Callander Craig Walk.

Queen Elizabeth Forest Park

The park occupies an area roughly 15 miles by 15, south-west of Callander and bounded by the eastern shore of Loch Lomond. Aberfoyle is the effective centre of of the area and the

Forestry Commission's David Marshall Lodge, 520 014, is uphill and north of Aberfoyle. The road from here, lurching and arching northwards to Loch Achray, is the twisting stem to which most of the visitors' plums are attached. There are several viewpoints, official and unofficial, along the way, not least at the David Marshall Lodge where a landmark-finding plate was presented by the Automobile Association. Inside the Lodge are a pleasant café, a quite superb map and an information desk.

At the top of the stem, branching left, is The Trossachs, world famous, but simply an obsolete Gaelic word for a cross-pass. Here a formidable symmetry of granite welcomes visitors to a large car park, not costly, and an array of facilities designed to extract a certain amount of cash. The best value is certainly the charming steamboat which leaves at 11 o'clock in the morning for a voyage on Loch Katrine, calling at Stronachlachar at about 11.40.

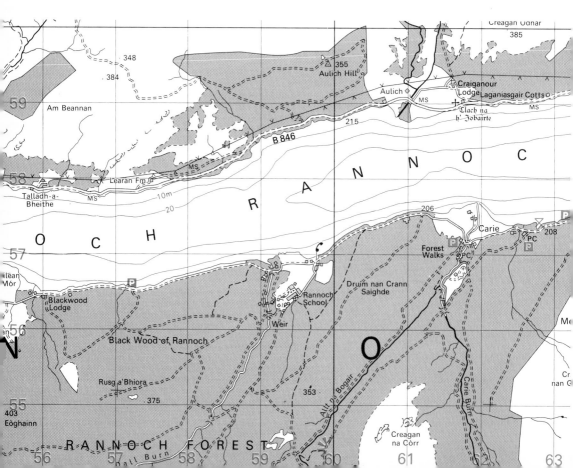

The Achray Forest, each side of the Duke's Pass, is thoroughly planted with spruces and looks quite magnificent from any angle. The foreground is often comparatively empty – bracken and heather studded with native birches, and a perfect foil to the richly shaped and wooded hills.

There are fourteen different woodland walks as well as a wayfaring course, and 70 miles of waymarked long walks through the forest, with coloured chevrons: several are orientated to east Loch Lomond side in our Section 64.

The Trossachs tree may be said to be rooted in the mysterious, roadless, Flanders Moss. The Lake of Menteith with the island Priory of Inchmahome has a nature reserve of 110 acres. On Flanders Moss the tall birches were once burnt with the heather so that invaders from the south (from the Roman army onwards) could not advance in concealment.

Strathyre Forest, by Loch Lubnaig, north-west of Callander, has a nature trail at *560 168* and a walk to the Falls of Leny at *595 090*. The Information Centre is in Strathyre village. Facilities in this forest include tougher walks.

FORT WILLIAM

South of Fort William, there is a useful picnic place at Corrychurrachan, *045 662*; turn off the A82(T) 1½ miles north of the Corran Ferry. Or, after the excitement of Glencoe, turn right in Glencoe village for Kinlochleven. There are several stopping places around the lake, with small streams and an abundance of rowan. North-bound traffic uses the bridge at Ballachulish; if you do not want the detour around Loch Leven you can instead turn right at Inchree, 1 mile north of Onich, for a picnic place and a short walk to the waterfall.

The ferry at Corran provides a short-cut to Glen Tarbet and Sunart, and to Mull, and quite incidentally has preserved the A861 along the south shore of Loch Eil in a condition of amazing grace. Fort William is a patch of irritant to be got through by travellers to the Western Highlands, and one forgets that

Queen Elizabeth Forest Park, Loch Ard Forest

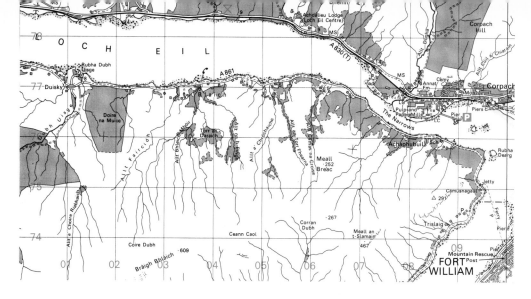

its setting is so spectacular – under Ben Nevis – yet on the shores of a sea loch.

A861, Loch Eil *965 787 to 095 765*, ♀, *6m of lochside road*

Loch Eil is gently tidal, and the mossy oaks which line her southern shores have the true character of the rural Highlands, untouched by twentieth-century engineering and chemistry. There are patches of extremely rich vegetation and dozens of places to stop and enjoy the views across the water. Traffic is purely local.

MORVERN, SUNART, MULL

The reason for the journey westward is a lochside oakwood.

Loch Arienas Oakwood *672 523*, ♀, *150 acres, NR*

The wood is part of the large Rahoy Hills nature reserve of 4325 acres. Recommended access is by Acharn, *701 505*, about a mile south-east of the wood, where you can park in the patchy shade of fine oak trees. A good track leads up to the Black Glen (Gleann Dubh) north-eastwards where, also, there are small native oakwoods. The quickest way to the lochside wood is to take the minor road signed to Kinloch, parking by the turn-off to Durinemast Cottage. There is a sort of path above the cottage. Remarkably wind-cut at the edges, the trees within are normal durmast oaks (though the leaves have rather short stalks

Loch Eil

and are slightly eared), and with the oaks grow rowan, wych elm and ash.

On the mountainside south of Loch Arienas the tall spruces of the Fiunary Forest are planted like corn through which giant swathes are cut as the trees are harvested.

Other oakwoods rather closer to Fort

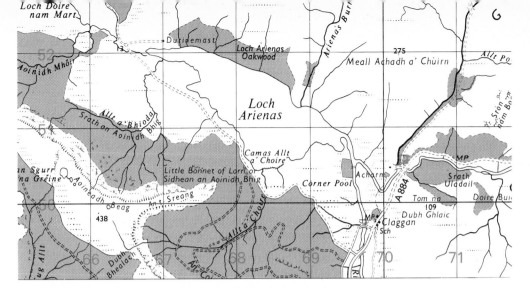

Loch Arienas Oakwood

William are at Strontian (A861): turn north to Ariundle, then signposted, *831 638*. A nature trail leads through the woods to old lead mines. There is a woodland car park also west of Strontian, at *745 620*, with a walk on the cliff above Loch Sunart.

At Lochaline I looked rather longingly at the ferry to Mull as it steamed in the silver Sound, but, behind schedule, I had to stay on the mainland. On the island I must leave you in the hands of the Forestry Commission with, by Tobermory, the Ardmore Forest Walk, *485 557*, reached by the Glengorm Castle road, ½ mile west of the town. South-east of Craignure, *721 369*, is a cliff path to Torosay Castle.

68	69
66	**67**
64	65

SCOTLAND
Tayside and Deeside

Landranger sheets 43, 44, 45, 53, 54, 58, 59

Tentsmuir Forest *500 242*
Comparatively easily reached from Edinburgh, the enormous, flat Tentsmuir pine forest on the sands north of St Andrews has a Forestry Commission picnic place on Kinshaldy Beach.

Edensmuir, Ladybank *292 095*, ⚲,
2 short walks, FC
East of the Lomond Hills, this is a really lovely pine plantation, balanced between the extremes of hill and beach. In mature open woodland the children can be adventurous, while remaining visible. It is hard to say just why this pinewood on flat land is so attractive: age perhaps contributes most.

Kinnoull Hill Woods and **Deuchny Wood** *135 235 and 145 236*, ♀ ⚲
The Kinnoull Nature Reserve on the Rhine-style crags above the Tay at Perth is nicely appointed and easily accessible. A well-worn path leads steeply into birch and oakwood. The trail connects with the Forestry Commission's Deuchny Wood and Kinfauns Jubilee Walk, which cheats a bit by following the contours for a mile or so out of the woods: but the view

is marvellous. Well signposted off Dundee Road, Perth, is Branklyn, a world famous National Trust for Scotland garden of 2 acres.

Scone Palace *114 266*, ♀ ⚲ (⚘),
Arboretum, 40 acres, pf
The palace is visited by thousands eager to see the gold of the Scottish kings, but you can choose the arboretum, which has an original Douglas fir from seed sent home by the explorer to his father, who was head gardener here. A most impressive assemblage of silver firs, *Sequoiadendron* and Sitka spruce were planted in a simple grid in 1860, around some earlier specimens.

Dunkeld
By the half-ruined cathedral stand the mothers of all Scottish larches, so it is said, very tall and elegant on the lawn beside the river. Some, 130 feet high, were planted in 1750. Here, on the estate of the Dukes of Atholl, emerged the hybrid between this European larch and the Japanese, called the Dunkeld larch, which has proved more productive and disease-resistant in Britain than its parents.

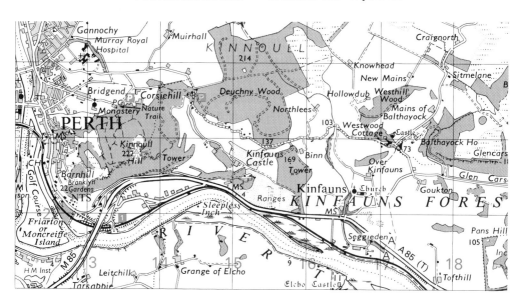

The Dukes of Atholl were leaders in the late eighteenth century in planting over 10,000 acres of previously unproductive moorland, much of it with larch.

From Dunkeld north-west to Pitlochry, the Atholl area contains twelve sites of natural-history interest, but in summer it also contains a lot of people.

Hermitage Woods *012 423*, 🌲
(off A9[T]), 1½m, riverside, NTS

The 8th Duke intended this tree garden, first planted in the eighteenth century, to come to the Trust, of which he was the first president. All the specimen trees are gone and *Pseudotsuga menziesii* is the present dominant. The centrepiece is the Black Linn, fantastically marbled with foam from the churning falls, and well worth a trip through the sweet wrappers. The Forestry Commission trail can be joined here.

Loch of Lowes, *041 435*, is a nature reserve with long woodland walks around the loch, and on the ridge of Craig Wood, once coppice:

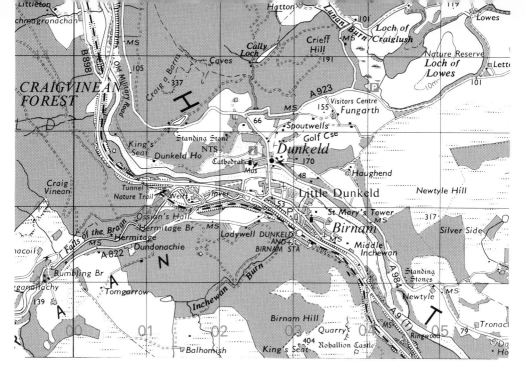

probably a better choice than the Hermitage.

Eastwards, **Glamis Castle**, blushing and demure amongst her policy *Pseudotsugas*, has magnificent trees all around. The castle is approachable any afternoon in summer except on Saturdays. Out of hours the road, the A928, is quieter than any Surrey lane.

Montreathmont Forest *557 531*, ♣, *3000 acres, no walks, FC*

The name Montreath emphasizes a similarity with the centre of Ireland. The vast and romantic-looking forest, mainly of pine, inhabits what must have been a frightening expanse of wet heathland. If it is peace and quiet you seek, come here. Nothing grows on the forest floor except three or four species of fern, some mosses and a grey, inedible-looking *Boletus*. The scenery changes imperceptibly from the deep dusk of Sitka to the less deep dusk of Norway spruce, brightening slightly in the Scots pine. A road runs through the middle for 2 miles, straight as a spruce. Here an oak tree is a major incident.

Braemar: Morrone Birkwood *143 911*, ♀, *560 acres, NNR*

Every glen has its birches, not so much in Scotland the 'Lady of the Woods' as a gaggle of village girls, all shapes and sizes. But at Braemar, on the slopes of Morrone, 2819 feet, is a gathering of really lovely birches, in most lights making a delicate pattern of greys on the uneven ground. These woods are of pure, downy birch with juniper, rich in lichens, biophytes and ferns. You are expected to keep to the footpaths. There is a viewpoint at Tomintoul.

Linn of Dee to Linn of Quoich *065 898*, ♣, *5–6m, pf*

There are fine stands of spruce as well as pine in the Dee glen, but the remains of the Forest of Mar are in the glens of Derry and Quoich (as well as in the royal estate of Ballochbuie) and it needs some determination to reach them. A relatively easy walk up to Glen Lui and then north-east across to Glen Quoich can give one a fair cross-section of the vegetation. This is a walk of 5 or 6 miles however. Topographically it is fairly simple since you are only going up one glen, crossing a short stretch of moor and then coming down the next glen.

For two centuries there has been a heavy red deer population and consequently little regeneration. Timber was extracted from the whole of the Forest of Mar in the eighteenth century, but the difficulty of transport has

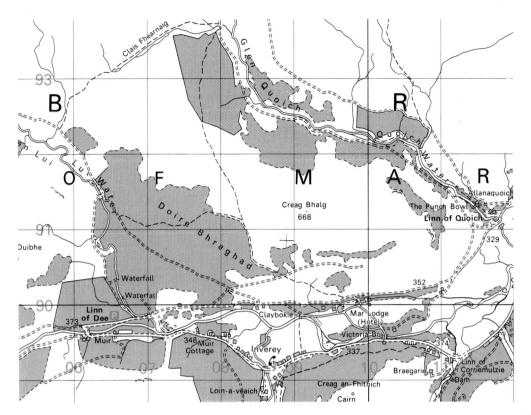

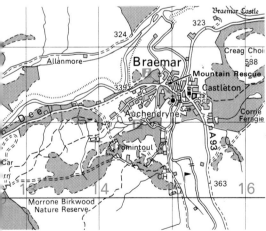

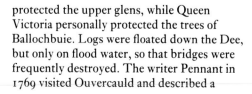

Scots pine, Balmoral, Mar Forest

protected the upper glens, while Queen Victoria personally protected the trees of Ballochbuie. Logs were floated down the Dee, but only on flood water, so that bridges were frequently destroyed. The writer Pennant in 1769 visited Ouvercauld and described a 'magnificent forest of pines many miles in extent'. The sawmill regularly produced planks 10 feet long, 11 inches wide and 3 inches thick. These were sold for two shillings each, which does not sound much – but it was more than a labourer's weekly wage.

Tree regeneration, Muir of Dinnet

Muir of Dinnet *431 997 (Burn o'Vat)*, ♀ ♣ ♨, *3600 acres, NNR*

This magnificent stretch of country includes lochs at Davan and Kinord, and according to the legend on the notice-board map 'land formed by glacial meltwater including kettle lochs, dry channels, unique pot holes (the Vat) and a complex of sand and gravel deposits'. The heather and bearberry moor, shows a strong tendency to return to forest, with birch and pine spreading rapidly and offering 'a challenge to conservation'. I hope that challenge will be met by supineness, so that a natural forest may be formed. Older woodland is at New Kinord.

This is a nature reserve which is sure to repay study and while not of primary woodland is, as it were, pregnant with woodland. There is a great variety and richness of habitat with large numbers of insect species and seventy-six breeding bird species.

The beautiful Dinnet oakwood, *464 980*, is south of the town. It is a National Nature Reserve of 30 acres containing both sessile and pedunculate oaks and their hybrid.

Glen Tanar contains a fine native Scots pine wood with juniper, rowan, aspen and birch – a National Nature Reserve. There is a Visitors' Centre at Braeloine.

Crathes Castle *734 968*, ♀ ♣, *600 acres, NTS*

Not at all remote, wild or forbidding, this is an astonishingly rich and tree-saturated place. In summer it could be described as visitor-saturated too. I found many unusual trees. The lawns, gardens and ancient hedges by the castle are impressive and very carefully and exploitively planted. Even an old quarry at the edge of the estate contains pretty birches and bird cherries.

The whole of Middle Deeside, with seventeen sites of special interest to naturalists, is both a nature reserve and an established tourist attraction – the two are still compatible in Scotland. Oakwoods at Craigendarroch and Aboyne, at Dinnet and Drum, are of varied interest – old coppices at Craigendarroch. Pines are spreading over the moors of the Glen Tanar estate and in parts of the Ballochbuie Forest, which have been fenced. Birch is the dominant tree, but bird cherries of both species reveal themselves in early summer.

Loch Maree

Loch Maree, with its surrounding shining mountains, is, in a sense, indestructible. Yet already the process of destruction-by-visitor has begun. The road, which used to be a Highland road, a single track of tarmacadam carefully picking its way from rock to rock, is now typically a well-engineered and finely surfaced one with neat, white curbs: destruction of wildness by framing the scene. Kinlochewe is virtually nothing but a tourist town. The Beinn Eighe National Nature Reserve, containing the natural stand of pines in Coille na Glas-leitire, has a Visitors' Centre and is somehow thus reduced to a museum exhibit. Once you are out of the way of these necessary facilities, nature reasserts herself.

But before all this, the hydroelectric wires pioneered their own route across what is now the nature reserve, and there they remain. You can avoid them, but I am quite certain they should have been buried long ago.

Coille na Glas-leitire *002 650*, ♣ *(Scots pines), nature trails, short, medium or long, NNR*

The Beinn Eighe National Nature Reserve is the oldest in Britain, 10,500 acres established

in 1951. The woods cover about 500 acres and the nature trails start from the parking place at the reference above. You pass the Visitors' Centre on your way from Kinlochewe. The rounded, dignified shapes of the pines, surprisingly green and soft looking, are scattered, here close, there sparse, up the sides of the 'Combe of the Steep Hillside'. Avoid late summer evenings – midges are fierce.

Slattadale Forest *888 723*, ♣ *(Norway spruce), 1000 acres, 3 forest walks, FC*

There is an island in this most beautiful of lochs: on that island a lochan, and in the lochan an islet. On the islet once grew a great pine. Surely the centre of the world! Not surprisingly the fairies gathered here. The island, Subhainn, with its neighbour islands, now seems to float with a cargo of trees.

The Forestry Commission is cutting down its spruces, and a strong smell of diesel oil rises from the settlement by the shore. The walks are: 5 miles to Poolewe, 1 mile in the trees, and a short path to see the falls named after Queen Victoria.

Inverewe Gardens, Poolewe *864 819*, ⚲ ♣, *NTS*

Over a century ago Osgood MacKenzie found only one tree, a dwarf willow, on his peaty headland. He made a deer and rabbit fence and planted a thick belt of Scots pine and Corsican pine, then hedges of *Rhododendron ponticum* which sheltered native trees, and larch and Douglas fir. Silver firs, *Tsuga*, *Thuja*, *Cupressus* and *Chamaecyparis* followed, and even *Sequoiadendron* where there was sufficient depth for the roots. Soil was brought in by the creel, seaweed used for fertilizer. Now there are tall woodlands for walks and shelter.

There are nearly 2000 acres of land at Inverewe, although most of the action is in a tenth of this. Nearly 100,000 visitors a year pay approximately a pound a head. The Trust runs an international-standard campsite nearby, bookable (Poolewe 249).

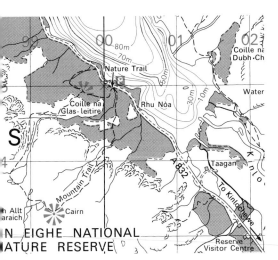

Rassal Ashwood

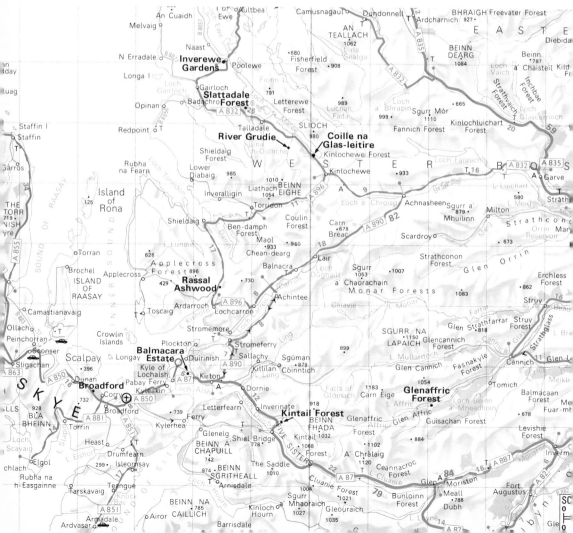

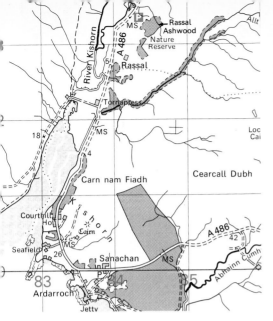

Rassal Ashwood *843 433*, ♀, *200 acres, NNR*

On a lumpy limestone platform covered by bright green moss are the lovely white and green trunks of the most northerly ashwood in Britain. There are also sallows and hazels which, fallen or riven by storms, put up their own strong coppice shoots. Part is fenced, and the richness of grass and herbs has to be seen to be believed, with moorland desert all around. Wild strawberries at this latitude? See for yourself, but go carefully, both to protect the woodland and your own ankles.

These are 200 acres of truth amongst millions under the rule of the Highland sheep. Of course, there are not many limestone outcrops. Nevertheless, the vegetation of the Highlands could be fantastically rich compared to what it is.

Kintail Forest, 12,800 acres, without many trees, is National Trust land, with a centre at Morvich, *961 211*, in the crook of the road by the algae-rich Loch Duich. The A87(T) is now short-circuited, avoiding Morvich.

Skye

From Kyle the ferry leaves every few minutes for Kyleakin and Skye. No one seriously goes to Skye for woodland walks, which might seem irrelevant in this remarkable place, at least until one has admired its astonishing mountains and learnt something of its crofting history. See Francis Thompson's *The Highlands and Islands*, 1974, for a good, biased summary.

In Sleat is Armadale Castle, *638 049*, ancient home of the Lords of the Isles and the Clan Donald. At Armadale there is a nature trail and the policy trees are in effect an arboretum.

In the north-west of the island is Dunvegan Castle, *246 491*. The castle policies east of the castle, planted in the late eighteenth century, are open to walkers – an environment in extreme contrast with most of the island's landscape. In between these two oases the Forestry Commission has a picnic place at *425 260* in the Glen Brittle Forest: views of the Cuillin Hills. Walks start from points on the A850 south of Portree and the A855, 7 miles north of Portree. Another walk is from a small

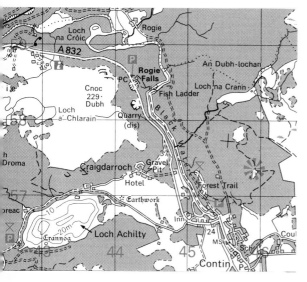

the road, the A832, as it rises from Loch Garve, north-west of Inverness, into the richly forested Glen of the Black Water. By Contin is a large picnic place deep in the larchwoods: a trail and a short walk lead into birchwoods. There is a system of paths around the Rogie Falls, *443 586*. A picnic place at the little Loch Achilty, *426 564*, is also in birchwoods.

Ardross Forest
Visible from viewpoints official and unofficial on the 'short-cut' road, the A836, from the A9(T) at Evanton to Bonar Bridge, are thousands of acres of steep mountainside scored with the massive trenches through the peat which make it possible to plant trees. This is great landscape design on the scale of landscape engineering. No one can fail to be impressed, provided the weather allows one to see it at all.

Black Isle
The Information Centre at Muir of Ord, Ross and Cromarty Region, provides a booklet, *Walks on the Black Isle*, which lists nineteen walks. This peninsula looked attractive and sunny, escaping the mountain weather.

Nairn
A detour through Ardersier from the A96 onto the B9092 will bring you to a drive-in pine forest, *805 550*; very attractive though surrounded by industrial and danger areas. It could be a useful place to stop, with wide grassy verges full of wild flowers.

Turn to Section 69 for the Culbin Forest.

Glen Affric
The more attractive route to Glen Affric is by Beauly to Cannich – there is a picnic spot at *469 427* – or you can follow the side of Loch Ness from Inverness as far as Drumnadrochit. From Cannich there is only one road.

Very beautiful birch woodland fills the glen by the road, above and below the Dog Falls, where there is a popular parking place at *286 284* and a forest walk through birch and pine.

The woodlands by Loch Affric and Loch Beinn a' Mheadhoin are important native pinewoods. This was a timber-producing area

car park at *625 249*, 1½ miles west of Broadford (or about 8 miles from Kyleakin). Ferries are seven days a week from Kyle.

Inverness
Five miles east is Culloden Muir, site of the battle in 1746. A road was built over the 54-foot-long grave of the Mackintosh clan in 1835, but in 1881 the 10th Laird of Culloden built a fine cairn and marked the graves. He had preserved the farmhouse of Old Leanach, heather thatched. The battle, when a thousand weary, hungry Highlanders were destroyed in one hour, marked the end of the Jacobite rebellion – and hastened the 'destruction of a social and economic order' to use the words of the *National Trust for Scotland Guide*. The Trust took over in 1944. What has all this to do with woodland walks? Well, the **Culloden Forest** covers most of the battlefield. There is a trail called the Forestry Commission Battlefield Trail, *718 456*.

The Forestry Commission also has, 1½ miles north-east of Inverness, near Smithton, a *jogging track* in Douglas fir woodland, with seven exercise stations!

Torrachilty Wood *452 574*, ♣, *4 forest walks, FC*
There are beautiful Lawson cypresses along

Glen Affric

flourishing in the eighteenth century, logs being floated down the Rivers Cannich, Glass and Beauly, with a large sawmill at Kilmorack Falls on the Beauly. Then sheep, fire and deer preservation further reduced the forest by limiting natural regeneration.

There were some young trees among the more sheltered heather (ling) when the Forestry Commission took over in 1951. But the foresters found it necessary to fence in the native forest and kill all the deer they could, irrespective of age or sex. They have planted pines from native seed in a 'natural' manner. I think they overdid it. As you approach from the final car park at the head of Loch Beinn a' Mheadhoin you are confronted by a neat notice announcing 'The Native Pines of Glen Affric'.

Glenaffric Forest

From the last car park, *201 234*, at the head of Loch Beinn a' Mheadhoin is a very short circuit round a section of old pinewood. To explore the forest, cross the bridge, whence you will reach a fork in the forest road and the notice mentioned above.

Going left takes you along the shore of Loch Beinn a' Mheadhoin and is not particularly enlightening. The loch was raised 20 feet by the Scottish hydroelectric authority and it may be this which gives it a Mediterranean look. A

complete circuit of Loch Affric involves a 10-mile hike – not too much for the beauty of the place, but you need all day. Glen Affric and Loch Beinn a' Mheadhoin are very beautiful and should not be missed. Indeed, to see the pines before they are overtaken by the Forestry Commission's panic planting, go soon. Most of the old trees are of rounded habit, with bark pattern plated rather than scaly.

Speyside: Aviemore

Stylish and modern, Aviemore is an international skiing and leisure centre. It has its own nature reserve, at Craigellachie, *882 124*, but for the Glen More Forest Park, cross the Spey and drive about 6 miles to the east side of Loch Morlich. Just by the large campsite is the Information Centre where a leaflet about the forest trails is supposed to be always available. There are now car parks by the sandy shores of Loch Morlich, a beautiful lake 1000 feet above sea-level with trees and mountains all around.

The Cairngorms National Nature Reserve is the largest in Britain, 64,220 acres (Visitors' Centre near Loch Morlich, *978 098*). The reserve is a mountain area. Only 4000 acres are forested, but part of this is the small Rothiemurchus Forest, well known as a remnant of the original Caledonian pine forest.

Glen More Forest Park 977 098, ♀ ♣
(pine and birch), 4000 acres, paths, FC
The immediate area of the campsite is
thoroughly explored by footpaths. Take the
Pinewood Trail, 1¼ miles, for a glimpse of the
old forest.

My walk took all day and was calculated to
explore the whole range of vegetation. I
followed convenient paths southwards and
then westwards, around Loch Morlich but in
the trees. Taking routes which tended uphill I
reached the tree-line near the small summit of
Castle Hill. The whole Spey Valley can be seen
from here, with its distinctive pattern of light
and dark green; birch and pine. I then struck
across the moor in a generally south-easterly
direction to meet a mountain footpath at 965
055. The trail home was easy walking with
tremendous views of the forest all the way.

I passed through differing stages of pine,
birch and juniper woodland which it was
difficult to believe had not been arranged by
some landscaping genius, so beautifully

composed they are. Capercaille flitted
lumpishly out of my way. Above the tree-line I
did not find the dwarf form of juniper, but that
is not to say that it is not there somewhere.
Isolated pines survive in the enormous open
spaces of moorland. A red deer rested without
cover on a steep bank, then moved away lazily,
as if offended by my gaze. At several points on
the moor were the old roots of pines revealed
by water courses, while the ravine of a snow-
fed river (with an unpronounceable name)
again looked like the work of man, here as if
blasted by explosives: a great sweep of rocks
and gravel, brought down by flood water.

The classic walk is right round the
Cairngorms from Rothiemurchus by Glen
Feshie to Braemar; this is a two-day trek. An
old drove road goes 37 miles from Abernethy
to Braemar.

Ryvoan, *998 104*, is a nature reserve of 300
acres, a Caledonian pine forest remnant with
birch and willow. Follow the Forestry
Commission track past Glenmore Lodge.

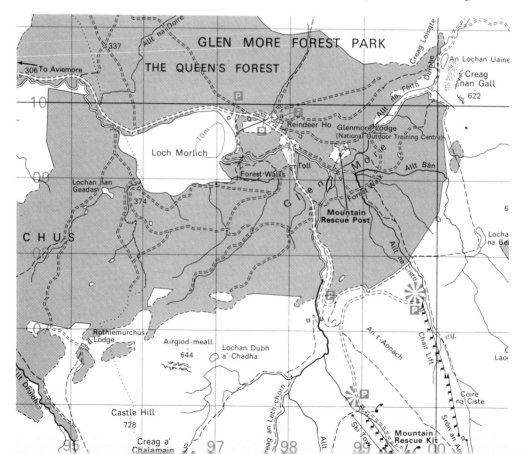

Kirkhill Forest *853 044*, ♀ ♣, *1000 acres, FC*

In the pretty, hummocky countryside of Countesswells is a patchwork of small conifer woods with several easy walks. The reference given is for the most westerly. This area is very close to Aberdeen's suburbs, between the two main roads west from the city – A944 and A93. A strip of beechwood remaining here and there adds greatly to the character of the woods. Kirkhill Forest proper is to the north.

Within easy reach of Aberdeen (about 15 miles) is a group of large forests called, from north to south, Benachie, Banchory and Mearns, all containing Forestry Commission walks, picnic areas and special facilities for the disabled. Map references for these are:
Benachie Forest: Don View Visitor Centre *672 193* and Maiden Castle *692 243*
Banchory Forest *633 944* ⎱ Section 67 map
Mearns Forest *696 801* ⎰

Drum Castle *796 005*, ♀ ♣, *411 acres, NTS*

The great square tower dates from the late thirteenth century. There is an arboretum and a woodland walk in the grounds, which are always open. There is supposed to be an Old Forest of Drum which is of birch, oak and Scots pines, but it has been entirely under-planted with alien shrubs. Nevertheless, it is valuable woodland with many walks and many natural history features. Information from the ranger at Crathes Castle (Section 67).

Craigievar Castle *567 097*, ♀ ♣, *30 acres, NTS*

The pink, pepper-pot shape of the story-book castle is rather dwarfed by the regulation *Sequoiadendron* and other trees planted in the early Victorian period, and this is a shame. Such a building, surely, should dominate the scenery, which here is hilly and strongly patterned. The woodland walk is mainly through perimeter beeches and horse-chestnuts with some oaks and hollies. The parking place is beautifully organized and well kept, as are all the grounds. There is an avenue of beeches.

The **Forest of Deer**, on the coastal plain near Peterhead, has Forestry Commission walks and facilities at White Cow Wood, *957 514*.

Roseisle

Mill Cotts Estate *236 562, ♀ ♠ , 350 acres, easy fps, LA*

Amongst a string of distilleries off the A941 below Elgin, this hillside woodland and lake has three parking places and a picnic area and is generally charming and picturesque, besides being a valuable nature reserve.

Speymouth Forest *349 586, ♠, forest walks, FC*

The forest is enormous, but this picnic area and large car park are on a busy road. There is a walk over a disused railway viaduct at *350 642*: woodland only in respect of the low scrub of sallows and osiers – but there cannot be many viaduct walks. Spey Bay is a very quiet place and the view of the river refreshing. Up-river the mountains are a nice Scottish blue.

Near Elgin is the coastal pinewood of **Roseisle**, with the beach beyond and parking and picnic place in the trees at *105 655*. Corsican pines give shelter and the sands are beautiful.

Culbin Forest *015 620 (Wellside), 7500 acres, 2 picnic places, FC*

The parking place is beyond the farm, just inside the forest. There is another parking place at Cloddymoss, *981 600*.

The sheer mass of this forest of pines on the sands, its comparative maturity – it dates from 1921 – and its remoteness, all make it great. It is not monotonous. The dunes vary a good deal in height, although most of the sands are flat, and time has allowed natural vegetation to build up. Birches, even oaks in places, and a scattering of cow wheat, suggest these were not

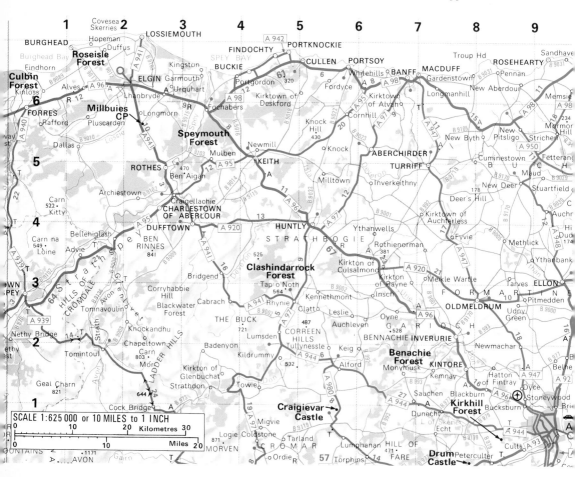

Sea aster, Culbin

virgin sands. A rich accretion of lichens is on every trunk and twig of the Scots pines, over moss that in summer is bright orange: the pattern is unforgettable.

Interesting though it all is, one cannot resist the pull of the shore. What happens at the edge? To find the shore from the Wellside car park, continue in the direction from which you entered for $\frac{1}{3}$ mile, then follow the forest road as it turns left. After about $\frac{1}{3}$ mile (passing a group of lodgepole pines on your right) turn right. You are now heading for the shore. It is not, usually, sea, but an expanse of wet sand.

What happens where the trees stop? Grasses begin, patterned with rings of sea asters.

The Darnaway Forest, to the south, is private, but has waymarked paths and a Visitors' Centre at Tearie Farm, *989 569.*

Shin Forest
The Drumliah Walk, *603 929,* $1\frac{3}{4}$m
This walk begins from a crude lay-by in larchwoods 1 mile north of Bonar Bridge on the A836.
The Shin Falls Walk, *576 993,* $1\frac{1}{2}$m
The walk is on each side of the river. There are good facilities, with a café 'open seven days a week' with loud music and moderately priced salmon sandwiches.
Carbisdale Castle Walk, *575 955,* $2\frac{1}{4}$m
Turn off the A9 at Ardgay on to the Culrain road -- before Bonar Bridge, so not immediately accessible from Lairg. The walk starts in the castle grounds, through varied woodland to a small loch.

A fourth walk is in the next section.

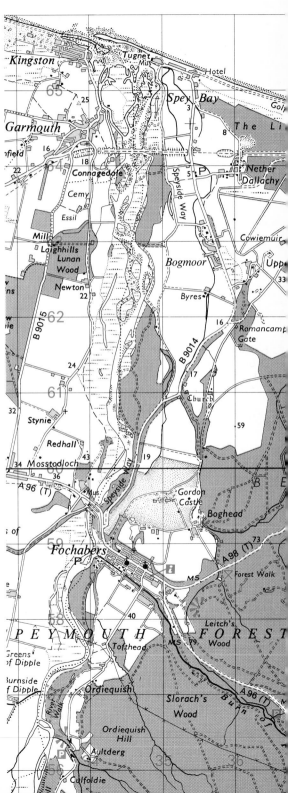

There are, of course, woods on the western side of the region and by the coastal lochs are three important nature reserves. Inverpolly (NNR, 42 square miles) adjoins Ben More Coigach, *080 070* (RSNC and SWT, 22 square miles). These are at 'the heart of one of the two 200 square miles of Britain . . . where no man sleeps', wrote James Fisher in 1966. There are relict woodlands around and on the islands of the lochs. A smaller reserve is Inchnadamph, *250 215* (NNR, 3200 acres). 'A limestone oasis'. Apply to local officers for guidance.

Passing through the Kyle of Sutherland into

the Shin Forest you enter a semi-Arctic region where birch is the dominant native tree. The luxuriant vegetation of the Achany Glen and Strath Oykel disappears, and the low hills are bare except for frequent stretches of Forestry Commission afforestation, cast around like clothes of green, and looking warm. Great clammy buttocks of mountains rise above lochs where a scattering of birches and one or two alders are the usual complement of trees. The birches climb the steep lochsides and cling in the burn sides, hardly ever forming woodlands.

It was not always so. Large pines are

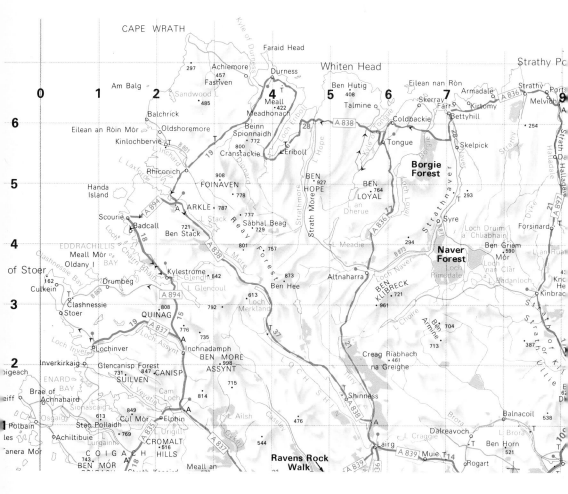

preserved as black logs in the peat. The most northerly group of native pine now surviving is at Glen Einig. A little further south in the Amat Forest near Croick, the surveyor Robertson in the eighteenth century wrote of pines with 30- or 40-foot-long uninterrupted trunks, $8\frac{1}{2}$ feet in circumference: a stump of a tree 3 feet 9 inches in diameter.

Ravens Rock Walk, *500 010*, *$1\frac{1}{2}$m*

The walk is quite splendid: larches are poised on precipices over the gorge of a small river, where everything green has its own way. The predominant tree is the Douglas fir.

There are fine groves of alder and good-looking oaks among the birches of Strath Oykel: forestry in Glen Oykel.

Naver Forest, Syre *691 428*, ♠ ✿ *(ruins)*, *$1\frac{1}{2}$m, FC*

The car park is reached by a stretch of forest road from the tiny village of Syre. The woods of spruce and pine are planted around the site of a deserted village which has been thoroughly researched and provided with well-written and illustrated information panels set in stone cairns. The site is described as a bright green island among the moors. One query raised by the thoughtful writers of the text is about the high fertility (still) of the soil. Did the villagers apply phosphates? they ask. Well, in a way I suppose they must have done. Why did they not expand their very limited crop-growing land? I think that the answer to the second question is that they were too tired, after wresting all their needs from this wind-swept (and snowed-on) hillside, and probably severely undernourished, if the diet described here is correct (porridge and more porridge). The poor people kept beef cattle, but rarely ate meat, the beef being taken on the hoof to the markets in the south. They used everything they could lay hands on to manure 'lazy beds' still visible by the various coloured grasses on the site: they had no woodland, at least not

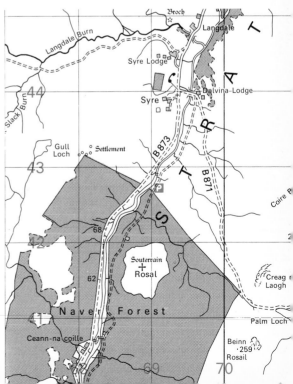

Borgie Forest and Ben Loyal

close at hand: the peat provided hard timber
(bog pine, rare enough to be handed down for
generations), fuel, building blocks, and roofing
and insulation. Stones indicate the base walls.

The cattle were kept in the houses in winter,
and in times of famine were bled, the blood
added to the gruel. In the summer the cattle
ate the moor grass. Sheep were delicate, with
fine wool, and were put to bed at night.

A more hardy breed of sheep that would stay
on the moors all year was developed in the
early nineteenth century. The value of the land
rose from tuppence per acre with people and
cattle to two shillings per acre with sheep and
no people. So the people were evicted by their
landlords, who by this time were either English
or, if Scots, had got English habits. If the
people would not go, their houses were
destroyed and the roof trees burnt, these last
being apparently the property of the landlord.
At Rosal there is no evidence of burning and it
is assumed that the villagers left when they
were told to. All this is explained in much more
detail on the site.

Borgie Forest *665 586*, ♠, *4000 acres,
2 short walks, FC*

As you approach the shore of the Stormy Sea,
the knuckles of rock begin to show through the
thin flesh of peat and there are frequent
lochans above sea-level. The great forest
around the River Borgie is not quite the most
northerly one; that of Strathy to the east is
slightly further out. There are firs here that
predate the Forestry Commission, at least one
being a really beautiful *Abies procera* var.
glauca – and more have been planted near the
forest road; spruce is within. The shortest
walks are not a way of seeing the forest: I drove
for a mile or so but there was little more to see.
From the hills above one gets an impression of
some variety in the forest, but from within
little appears except acres of spruce. I am not
complaining; the coastal views are stunning.

A large, sandy beach – in Tongue Bay
(Gaelic *Tunga*) with a good view of the Rabbit
Islands – was deserted except for two people at
4.00 pm on a fine Sunday in August. High
above Tongue I watched a strangely shaped
half mile of sand being gently licked away by
the waves of that cold sea.

Index